MAKING EMPIRE

MAKING EMPIRE

IRELAND, IMPERIALISM, AND THE EARLY MODERN WORLD

JANE OHLMEYER

OXFORD
UNIVERSITY PRESS

OXFORD
UNIVERSITY PRESS

Great Clarendon Street, Oxford, OX2 6DP,
United Kingdom

Oxford University Press is a department of the University of Oxford.
It furthers the University's objective of excellence in research, scholarship,
and education by publishing worldwide. Oxford is a registered trade mark of
Oxford University Press in the UK and in certain other countries

Published in the United States of America by Oxford University Press
198 Madison Avenue, New York, NY 10016, United States of America

British Library Cataloguing in Publication Data
Data available

Library of Congress Control Number: 2023934561

ISBN 978–0–19–286768–1

DOI: 10.1093/oso/9780192867681.001.0001

Printed by Integrated Books International, United States of America

Dedicated to the memories of
Aidan Clarke
Lindy Guinness, Lady Dufferin
Margaret MacCurtain
Hamish Scott

Preface: Definitions

Empire and imperial frameworks, policies, practices, and cultures have shaped the history of the world for the last two millennia. It is nation states that are the 'blip on the historical horizon' even if states, societies, and monarchies had long existed within empires.[1] This book re-examines empire as process—and Ireland's role in it—through the lens of early modernity. It covers the two hundred years between the mid-sixteenth century and the mid-eighteenth century that equate roughly to the timespan of the 'First English Empire' in the early modern period (*c.*1550–*c.*1770s).

And, it is an English, rather than British, empire. After 1707 and the political union between England and Scotland, the Scots participated as equals (at least on paper) in colonial activity. However, as John MacKenzie has argued, this did not make the empire 'British'.[2] That said, colonial initiatives in Ireland, the Atlantic, and Asia did involve peoples from all four nations that comprised the Stuart multiple monarchy. The First English Empire was, as Ken MacMillan notes, 'ideologically principled' with a 'broadly consistent (if generally un-intrusive) system of imperial governance'.[3] It was also a global empire intent on economic exploitation. By the 1660s it included Tangier in the Mediterranean, Bombay and other holdings in India, the island of St. Helena in the south Atlantic, islands in the Caribbean, territories along the east coast of America stretching from Newfoundland in the north to South Carolina, and, of course, Ireland. By the late eighteenth century, according to Sir George McCartney, the County Antrim-born statesman, diplomat, and governor of Grenada, Madras, and the Cape Colony, the First English Empire was 'this vast empire on which the sun never sets and whose bounds nature has not yet ascertained'.[4]

Empire had a long history in Ireland. England had first invaded Ireland in 1169, leading Friedrich Engels to observe in a letter (1856) to Karl Marx that 'Ireland may be regarded as the first English colony'. Engels continued: 'which because of its proximity is still governed exactly in the old way, and here one can already observe the so-called liberty of English citizens is based on the oppression of the colonies'.[5] How then did the English empire actually function in early modern Ireland and how did this change over time? What did access to European empires mean for people living in Ireland? This book answers these questions by interrogating four intercon-nected themes: first, that Ireland formed an integral part of the English imperial system with its land and labour fuelling English expansionism; second, that people from Ireland operated as agents of empire(s); third, that Ireland served as laboratory in and for the English empire; and, finally, it examines the impact of empire(s) on people living in early modern Ireland.

Issues of identity permeate the book. What did it mean to be 'Irish', 'English', and even 'British' in an era of intense colonisation and mobility? 'Irishness' meant a variety of things to different people.[6] Strictly speaking, only the Gaelic-speaking Catholic natives regarded themselves as being 'Irish'. Those of Anglo-Norman ancestry consistently stressed their 'Englishness' often at the expense of their 'Irishness'.[7] Aidan Clarke's sem-inal work on the political connections and cultural makeup of this 'Old English' community clearly demonstrates that throughout the first half of the seventeenth century they perceived themselves as the Crown's loyal and devoted servants and argued that their Catholicism in no way jeopardised their fealty to a Protestant prince nor their ability to serve him as their ancestors had done.[8] Studies largely by Gaelic literary scholars, especially Breandan Ó Buachalla, suggest that, after the defeat in the Nine Years' War (1594–1603) and the 'Flight of the Earls' in 1607, the native Irish, while acknowledging the centrality of Catholicism to their identity, increasingly adopted the same conciliatory, *politique* attitude towards the Crown which had traditionally characterised the Old English.[9] Despite prohibitions against it, extensive intermarriage and cultural cross-assimilation had occurred between the native Irish and the Old English, with the result that many members of the former had become anglicised and the latter gaeli-cised. Predictably this blurred boundaries between 'Irishness' and 'Englishness' and allowed Catholics, especially members of the elite, to juggle identities. The conversion to Protestantism of leading native Irish and Old English lords complicated matters further.

The 'New English' settlers, Catholic and Protestant alike, who colonised Ireland from the 1530s, flaunted their 'Englishness'.[10] However, as Toby Barnard's insightful study of the collective mentality of the Protestant com-munity demonstrates, the onset of the First English Civil War after 1642 forced Protestants living in Ireland to choose between king and parliament and caused something of an identity crisis for many. Those who opted for Charles I continued to tout their 'Englishness'; while those who sided with parliament and later Oliver Cromwell viewed themselves primarily as Protestants of Ireland. Increasingly, religion became 'the surest touchstone of reliability', preparing the ground for the Protestant Ascendancy of the eighteenth century.[11] To complicate matters further, these nuances around identity were lost on external observers, who increasingly labelled anyone from Ireland as 'Irish' and often used 'Irish' to denigrate and imply disloyalty. In other contexts 'Irishness' was equated with Catholicism and Protestantism with 'Englishness'.[12] Equally misleading are later assertions that the English empire was exclusively Protestant, even if confession did drive, to some degree, the imperial mission.[13]

Like identity, nomenclature is slippery and can bedevil, especially as meanings changed over time and early modern people used terms less familiar today. It is critical to be clear by what is meant in this book by 'empire' and 'imperialism' and related—but not interchangeable—terms, 'colonisation', 'colony', 'colonialism', and 'plantation'. 'Imperialism' derives from the Latin word 'imperium', which signified the power and authority to command and came to denote those subject to Rome through military conquest.[14] According to Niccolò Machiavelli, the sixteenth-century philosopher, historian, and diplomat, imperialism was when a prince held territory by annihilation, by colonisation, or by rule through 'locally entrenched groups'.[15] Machiavelli's definition works well for early modern Ireland, as do more recent ones. In *Culture and Imperialism*, Edward Said defined imperialism simply as 'the process or policy of establishing or maintaining an empire' when an 'empire' comprises extensive territories or sets of territories under the control of a single ruler.[16] John Darwin concurs, adding that imperialism may 'be defined as the attempt to impose one state's predominance over other societies by assimilating them to its political, cultural, and economic system'.[17] This aligns with Jürgen Osterhammel's understanding of imperialism as a process of territorial acquisition initiated by military conquest, which is followed by the implementation of formal and informal structures of rule that resulted in a relationship of domination.[18]

Closely linked to 'imperialism' is 'colony', which derives its name from 'colonia', the Latin word for farmer, which, according to the *Oxford English Dictionary*, signified by the early modern period an area settled by 'a body of people...forming a community subject to or connected with their parent state'.[19] Osterhammel suggests that a 'colony' is a new political organisation

created by invasion, conquest, or settlement; 'colonisation' designates a process of territorial acquisition; and 'colonialism' is a system of domination, in
this case between England and Ireland.[20] Early modern people frequently
used the words 'colony' and the verb 'to colonise' often interchangeably
with 'to plant' or, from the 1610s, 'plantation', meaning the settlement of
people.[21] 'Colonialism' is a more recent construct with usage dating from
the later eighteenth century. So too is the word 'anglicisation'. Instead, contemporaries used words like 'civility', 'to civilise', 'improvement', and 'to
improve' to describe the English mission in Ireland.

   Just as language and meanings changed over time, so too did the context,
the nature of imperialism, and the intensity with which it was executed.
Moreover, colonisation was not a single occurrence but an iterative and
durable process that impacted different parts of Ireland at different times
and in different ways. In fact, during these years Ireland was repeatedly colonised, making for messy models and moving targets that defy easy definition
and simplistic analysis. One thing is clear, imperialism was about the exercise of political and economic power, about violence, and about coercion.
Strategies about how best to turn conquest into profit, to marshal, mobilise,
and control Ireland's natural resources, especially land and labour, varied but
the reality of everyday life did not change and provoked a wide variety of
responses ranging from acceptance, accommodation, assimilation, and
innovation to resistance and rebellion.

   Even though the focus of this book will be on Ireland and the English
empire, people from Ireland were trans-imperial and engaged with all of the
early modern imperial powers. It is therefore critical, where possible and
appropriate, to look to other European and global empires for meaningful
comparisons, contrasts, connections, and entanglements in this era of expansionism and economic exploitation.[22] Given the expansive nature of the
topic, this book makes no claim to be comprehensive but aims instead to
stimulate further research, discussion, and respectful debate.

Acknowledgements

This book derives from the 2021 Ford Lectures on 'Ireland, Empire, and the Early Modern World'. It was a great honour to be invited to deliver the annual James Ford Lectures in Irish and British History at Oxford University. I am grateful to the electors for the invitation and especially to Professor Steven Gunn. The list of previous Ford Lecturers reads like a 'Who's Who' of British and Irish history and includes three distinguished Irish historians, Marianne Elliott, Roy Foster, and the late F. S. L. Lyons.

Instead of delivering the Fords in person in Oxford, I recorded them without an audience in Dublin in January and February 2021, at the height of the Covid-19 pandemic. I would like to thank my colleagues at the Trinity Long Room Hub Research Institute in the Arts and Humanities for allowing me to film in the Neil Hoey lecture theatre and especially Caitriona Curtis, Aoife King, Giovanna Lima, Francesca O'Rafferty, Eve Patten, and Elspeth Payne for their support. The final two lectures were recorded in Iveagh House on St. Stephens Green in Dublin, once the town house of the Guinness family, and today home of Ireland's Department of Foreign Affairs and Trade. I am deeply grateful to Minister Simon Coveney, the then Secretary General Niall Burgess, Ambassador Adrian O'Neill, and colleagues for facilitating the filming in line with the restrictions imposed by the pandemic. Thanks to Neil Leyden and Dermot Horan, the recordings of the six lectures now sit on the RTE website (https://www.rte.ie/history/2021/0304/1201023-ireland-empire-and-the-early-modern-world-watch-the-lectures/) where roughly 20,000 people from around the world have downloaded them. I am grateful to those of you who have viewed these lectures and for your questions and comments.

I am also indebted to the Warden and Fellows of All Souls College for their kind offer of a visiting fellowship in spring 2021, which the pandemic prevented me from taking up. Instead, I spent a very productive time in the autumn of 2021 as a visiting fellow at Merton College and am grateful to the Warden and Fellows, especially Steven Gunn and Richard McCabe, for the very warm welcome. Ian McBride and Dmitri Levin organised a lively

'Fords vs Carlyles' seminar at All Souls College where Mark Goldie, who had delivered the 2021 Carlyle Lectures (also online), and I had an opportunity to reflect with a live audience on our respective lectures. In November 2021 Ambassador Adrian O'Neill hosted in the Irish Embassy in London a delightful evening, where I presented a distilled version of the Fords, my first 'real', in person, lecture since March 2020. After nearly two years of virtual interactions, the conversation, conviviality, and companionship over the autumn of 2021 was particularly welcome. I'd like to thank for their hospitality Judith Buchannan, Susan Brigden, Marianne Elliott, Roy Foster, Charles Hansard, Sadie Jarrett, John Kennedy, Paulina Kewes, Brian Kingham, Michael Lonergan, Adrian O'Neill, Sinead Pentony, Glyn Redworth, Louise Richardson, the late Hamish Scott, and Julia Smith. A special word of thanks to Debby Guthrie and James Wise, who welcomed me into their hearts and London home.

Ireland and Empire is a topic that has long fascinated me. I have been working on aspects of it for nearly 30 years—from my early work on the MacDonnells of Antrim and my contribution in 1998 to *The Oxford History of the British Empire*, to my ongoing collaborative work with Richard Ross and Phil Stern on anglicisation in and through the law, and another project on women and sexual violence with Rosemary Byrne and Stephanie McCurry. My 2021 Ford Lectures, as they looked at Ireland and Empire through the lens of early modernity, attempted to bring together some of these threads.

On a more personal note, I was born in Kitwe in Zambia (then a British protectorate named Northern Rhodesia). My father, a South African originally from Lithuania, worked in the copper mines in Kitwe where he met my mother, a McGucken from County Tyrone, who was a teacher. We moved to Belfast in 1969, the year after the Troubles broke out. The war dominated my childhood and teenage years and like so many of my generation I left at the first opportunity to travel, to study, and to pursue a career that in 2003 brought me back to Ireland, to Trinity College Dublin.

Over the course my life I have travelled extensively and taken with me my fascination with empires, ancient and modern. I have been fortunate to visit the remains of historic empires: the Aztecs, Egyptians, Greeks, Mughals, Ottomans, Romans, and Vijayanagaras. I have spent most time in countries that once formed part of the British empire: Australia, Canada, Egypt, Hong Kong, Israel, Kenya, Malaysia, Myanmar/Burma, Singapore, South Africa, Sri Lanka, Zimbabwe, and, above all, India.

Initially, it was in my role as the founding Vice President for Global Relations at Trinity College Dublin (2011–14) that regularly took me to India. During these trips I seized any opportunity to visit historic sites, to spend an afternoon in a municipal library or archive, and to meet local scholars. We had much to discuss and, thanks in part to the British empire, shared much in common. Though the cultures and histories of our countries were so different, I found very familiar the educational and legal systems, the civil services and bureaucracies, the built environment and architecture, the roads and railways, and, of course, the language—English—through which we conversed. Wherever I went in India there were constant reminders of a shared imperial past. Undoubtedly those experiences of seeing and engaging have helped me to better understand the nuances and complexities associated with the study of empires. I learned much from my conversations during extended research trips to India in 2015, 2017, and 2018 with Jyoti Atwal, the late Rajat Datta, Cyrus Guzder, Irfan Habib, Najaf Haider, Sucheta Mahajan, Aditya and Mridula Mukherjee, Bodh Prakash, Shireen Moosvi, and Malabika Sarkar. It was a privilege to engage with colleagues and students at the Centre for Historical Studies at Jawaharlal Nehru University and Ashoka University, where I co-taught a course to Young India Fellows on 'Ireland, India, and Empire'.

A research fellowship in February and March 2022 at the Centre for Humanities Research at the University of the Western Cape allowed me to explore Irish experiences of empire in the context of South Africa. For this I am indebted to Heidi Grunebaum, Premesh Lalu, and Maurits van Bever Donker and the amazing team at the Centre for Humanities Research. I would also like to thank Patricia Hayes, Ajay Lalu, Valmont Layne, Adam Asmal, the staff at the Zeitz Museum of Contemporary African Art, and the Spences. From Cape Town I travelled to California, where a research fellowship at the Huntington Library in San Marino in March and April 2022 allowed me to conduct further research on the impressive, but often overlooked, early modern Irish holdings and to participate in an international conference on 'Ireland and the Wider World'. I am grateful to Steve Hindle for this opportunity and to Michael Ballagh, Jim and Elizabeth Chandler, Tim Harris, Mary Robertson, and Jennifer Wells for their insights and fellowship.

Over the summer of 2022 I delivered a revised version of the Ford Lectures as a course for graduate students at the University of São Paulo in Brazil. I am grateful to Laura Patricia Zuntini de Izarra for making possible this rewarding and fascinating experience and to Munira Mutran and colleagues associated with the Yeats Chair for their warm welcome. Maria Rita Drumond Viana and Larissa Lagos kindly invited me to speak at the Federal University of Ouro Preto at Mariana, a colonial settlement dating from the late seventeenth century, in the state of Minas Gerais, where more people were enslaved to work in the gold mines than anywhere else in Brazil. I also took the opportunity to visit Recife, settled by both the Portuguese and Dutch, and nearby Olinda, one of the first towns in the country, dating from 1535. Brazil is a country—like Ireland—where imperial after lives loom large and I learned a tremendous amount, especially from my students. The actor Stephen Rea happened to be in Brazil for the launch of 'Secrets from Putumayo', a documentary about Roger Casement's time in the Amazon, and joined the final class, where he read from Brian Friel's *Making History*.

Since delivering the Ford Lectures in spring 2021 I have given papers on themes related to them at various seminars: the Early Modern Seminars at Oxford and Trinity College Dublin, the British History Seminar at the Institute of Historical Research in London, the Irish Studies Seminars at the Princess Grace Library in Monaco and Magdalene College, Cambridge, a seminar on the Irish in the early modern Atlantic held in Seville, and a workshop (also in Seville) on the role played by elites in shaping early modern European empires. Two conferences, where I was honoured to deliver keynotes, deserve special mention for the new ground they are breaking: '"Where Do We Go from Here?" Revisiting Black Irish Relations and Responding to a Transnational Moment', organised in November 2021 by Kim DaCosta, Miriam Nyhan Grey, and Kevin Kenny at Glucksman Ireland House, New York University, and 'Ireland, Museums, Empire, Colonialism: Collections, Archives, Buildings and Landscapes', organised in April 2022 by Dominic Bryan, Emma Reisz, and Briony Widdis at Queen's University Belfast. I am indebted to the organisers of all these events, seminars, and conferences for the opportunity to discuss my research and to the participants and students for their constructive criticism and comments.

Librarians and archivists are often the unsung heroes of books like these. My debts are many: to the librarians at Trinity College Dublin, especially Mary Higgins, Sean Hughes, Jane Maxwell, Laura Shanahan, and Helen Shenton; at the British Library; at the New York Public Library; at the Huntington Library, especially Vanessa Wilkie; at the Bodleian Library in Oxford, especially Michael Webb; and at the National Archives in London, especially Neil Johnston, in Belfast, and in Dublin. Faber and Faber kindly granted permission to quote from Brian Friel, *Making History*. A generous grant from the Grace Lawless Lee Fund has made possible the maps and funded the reproduction of the illustrations and for this I am grateful to Ruth Karras and colleagues in the History Department at Trinity.

I would like to thank colleagues at Oxford University Press, who have been a pleasure to work with, Stephanie Ireland, Cathryn Steele, Saraswathi Ethiraju, and Tom Stotter, as well as the copy-editor, Michael Janes, and indexer, Gillian Northcottliles. I would particularly like to thank the anonymous OUP reviewers and Micheál Ó Siochrú, who read a final draft of this book, for their constructive comments and invaluable suggestions for improvement.

Over the years I have had the good fortune to collaborate with some gifted early career researchers who have worked as research assistants: the late Marie Sophie Hingst, Grace Hoffman, James Leduc, Daryl Hendley Rooney, and Caoimhe Whelan. In different ways each has contributed to this book and I am indebted to them and the students at Trinity College Dublin who, over the years, have challenged and inspired me. I am deeply grateful to many colleagues and friends who have offered advice and support, shared references and insights, and contributed in so many different ways to this book: Robert Armstrong, Tom Bartlett, Guy Beiner, Homi Bhabha, Matteo Binasco, David Brown, Rosemary Byrne, Nicholas Canny, Dan Carey, Clare Carroll, Sandro Carvalho, Marion Casey, Peter Crooks, Sarah Covington, Gaye Cunningham, Linda Cullen, Coleman Dennehy, Mary Doyle, Susan Flavin, Roy Foster, Patrick Geoghegan, Eileen Gillooly, David Harris Sacks, Cathy Hayes, Leslie Herman, Brendan Kane, Jimmy Kelly, Louise and Caroline Kennedy, Kevin Kenny, Phil Kilroy, Mona and Rasid Khalidi, Connie Kelleher, James Kelly, Paulina Kewes, the late Shay Lawless, Ian McBride, Stephanie McCurry, Bríd McGrath, Andrew MacKillop, James Maguire, Annaleigh Margey, John Morrill, Elaine Murphy, Terry Neill, Bríona Nic Dhiarmada, Thomas O'Connor, Finola O'Kane, Hussein Omar, Ciaran O'Neill, Terry Neill, Igor Perez Tostado, Glyn Redworth, Brian Rooney, Richard Ross, Sinead Ryan, the late Hamish Scott, Brendan Smith, Phil Stern, Stuart Switzer, Micheál Ó Siochrú, Ciaran O'Neill, Patrick Walsh, John Walter, and Olivia Waters. My family—Shirley, Richard, Jamie, and Hannah—remain a constant source of support and I am eternally grateful for their love.

Today I divide my time between Dublin, where I'm privileged to work with fabulous colleagues and students in the History Department at Trinity, and our family home on Cruit Island in County Donegal, part of O'Donnell's Tyrconnell and not far from Friel's imagined townland of Baile Beag/

Ballybeg. My neighbours on Cruit are the wonderful nieces of Brian Friel, Finn McMahon and Christa Darrall, and Stephen Rea. Indeed, I wrote the Ford Lectures and much of this book on Cruit during the 2020–1 pandemic and found invaluable conversations, particularly with Stephen about Field Day and *Making History*, which I had seen performed at the National Theatre in London in 1989.

This book is dedicated to the memories of four much loved and much-missed mentors—Margaret MacCurtain (1929–5 Oct. 2020), Lindy Guinness, Lady Dufferin (1941–26 Oct. 2020), Aidan Clarke (1933–18 Dec. 2020), and Hamish Scott (1946–6 Dec. 2022)—who taught me so much about empire and about history.

Jane Ohlmeyer,
Cruit Island, County Donegal
and Trinity College, Dublin

Table of Contents

Maps and Figures

Abbreviations

BL	British Library, London
BL, IOR	India Office Records
Bodl.,	Bodleian Library, Oxford
CSPD	Calendars of State Papers, Domestic Series, Second Series (23 vols., London, 1858–97)
CSPI	Calendar of State Papers relating to Ireland (24 vols., London, 1860–1911)
DIB	James McGuire, James Quinn (eds.), Dictionary of Irish Biography: From the Earliest Times to the Year 2002 (9 vols., Cambridge, 2009)
Gilbert (ed.), Irish confederation	J. T. Gilbert (ed.), History of the Irish Confederation and the war in Ireland, 1641 [–1649] containing a narrative of affairs of Ireland, by Richard Bellings. With correspondence and documents of the confederation and of the administrators of the English government in Ireland, contemporary personal statements, memoirs, etc. Now for the first time published from original manuscripts (7 vols., Dublin, 1882–91)
Gilbert (ed.),	Contemporary history J. T. Gilbert (ed.), A Contemporary history of affairs in Ireland from AD 1641 to 1653 …(3 vols., Irish Archaeological Society, Dublin, 1879)
HL	Huntington Library, San Marino, USA
HMC	Historical Manuscripts Commission
HMC, Ormonde	Calendar of the Manuscripts of the marquess of Ormonde, preserved at Kilkenny Castle (Old and New Series, 11 vols., London, 1895–1920)
IMC	Irish Manuscripts Commission
NA	The National Archives, Dublin
NHI, III	T. W. Moody, F. X. Martin, and F. J. Byrne (eds.), A New History of Ireland. III Early Modern Ireland 1534–1691 (Oxford, 1976, reprinted, 1978)
NLI	National Library of Ireland, Dublin

ODNB	*Oxford Dictionary of National Biography* (Oxford University Press, 2008)
PRONI	Public Record Office of Northern Ireland, Belfast
TNA	The National Archives, London
TNA, CO	Colonial Office
TNA, PROB	Probate

I

Making history

Making History, a play by Brian Friel which was performed in 1988, was set at the end of the sixteenth century on the eve of the Nine Years' War, which began in 1594 and ended in 1603. For the most part it takes place in Dungannon in County Tyrone in Ulster, which was the most geographically remote—from London—of the four Irish provinces. In the play Brian Friel, who was born in County Tyrone but who spent much of his life in neighbouring County Donegal, where he now lies, tells the story of Hugh O'Neill, earl of Tyrone, and hereditary overlord of Ulster, who led the Irish war effort against Elizabeth I and went on to become the symbolic hero of Irish nationalism.[1] The play opened in 1591 with the elopement and marriage of O'Neill, now aged 41, to his third wife, Mabel Bagenal, who was barely 20. This focus on intermarriage—between native and newcomer, Catholic and Protestant—immediately complicated understandings of what it meant (and means) to be 'Irish' and 'English'. Friel conjured up O'Neill's intense relationship with Mabel and her sister, Mary, daughters of the local Protestant planter, Sir Nicholas Bagenal, and their brother, Sir Henry, who was the 'Queen's Marshall' from nearby Newry, and leader of the 'New English' community in Ulster.[2]

Issues of gender, family, and identity are to the fore. Some of the strongest dialogue in the play is between the two women as they discussed what constituted 'improvement' and 'civility'. Mary explained how her father had drained bogland, ploughed it, fenced it, and planted it with trees—apple, plum, damson, and pear—brought over from Kent; she talked of their beehives, vegetable patches, and the herb garden.[3] Mary then chided her sister Mabel: 'You talk about "pastoral farming"—what you really mean is no farming—what you really mean is neglect of the land. And a savage people who refuse to cultivate the land God gave us have no right to that land'.[4] In another intense exchange Mabel defended her decision first to marry

Hugh O'Neill, and then to convert to Catholicism. She converted, she says: 'Out of loyalty to Hugh and to his people. As for civility I believe that there is a mode of life here that is at least as honourable and as cultivated as the life I've left behind. And I imagine the Cistercian monks in Newry didn't think our grandfather an agent of civilization when he routed them out of their monastery and took it over as our home'.[5]

Making History vividly imagined the world of Gaelic Ulster, just as the English state set out to conquer, colonise, cultivate, and 'civilise'. Ulster was one of three geographic zones, where multiple colonisations occurred (see Map 1.1). The first was an area that comprised Dublin, the Pale, most of Leinster, and East Munster, which had been an English colony since the twelfth century. Englishness prevailed but intermarriage and acculturation had occurred between Gael and Anglo-Irish, much to the consternation of officials in London, who dubbed this 'degeneracy'. The second zone, the western part of Ireland, had never been as intensively settled and retained its Gaelic character even if leading powerbrokers, like the earls of Clanricard and Thomond, had committed to 'anglicising' (or 'civilising') policies and lived under the authority of a Crown-appointed lord president. The third zone, Ulster and inaccessible areas like the Wicklow mountains, had resisted English rule for centuries.[6] As a result Ulster was, according to one English official writing in 1609, 'heretofore as unknown to the English here as the most inland part of Virginia is yet unknown to our English colony there'.[7]

Like all frontier societies throughout pre-modern Europe, much of Ulster remained sparsely populated, with widely dispersed settlements, few towns, and difficult internal communications. Frontier zones did not constitute homogeneous units as religious, linguistic, cultural, and economic factors criss-crossed with political ones to create complex, overlapping patchworks of frontier zones within and across frontier zones. This is well illustrated by Gaelic Ireland and Scotland which were united by the sea and, to all intents and purposes, formed part of the same political ethos and cultural entity, with bards composing works aimed at audiences on both sides of the North Channel.[8] Migration across the North Channel, a mere 12 miles at the closest part, spawned extensive informal settlement in Ireland, especially in East Ulster where the rise of the MacDonnells of Antrim, nominally loyal to the Scottish Crown, complicated the political make-up of Elizabethan Ireland, as did the eagerness of Clan Campbell to interfere in Irish affairs. Indeed, Red Hugh O'Donnell's mother, Ineen Dubh or Finola, was the daughter of James McDonnell of the Isles and proved a very effective broker of power

Map 1.1 Map of Ireland showing 'frontier' zones.

thanks in part to the Scottish mercenaries (known as 'redshanks' or 'gallow-glass') she retained.[9] According to her son's biographer, Lughaidh Ó Cléirigh, 'she had the heart of a hero and the mind of a soldier'.[10]

In *Making History* Friel invited us to eavesdrop on O'Neill's discussions with Red Hugh O'Donnell, his closest ally and son-in-law, who had recently escaped from Dublin castle where he had been incarcerated for nearly five years.[11] Friel rightly emphasised the importance of lineage, kinship, foster-age, and marriage alliances. In the case of O'Neill extensive fosterage and marriage links ensured that this was a complex and extensive matrix that connected him to the McDonnells, O'Donnells, O'Cahans, O'Hagans, and O'Quinns.[12] Writing in the 1580s Sir Nicholas Bagenal described O'Neill 'as so allied by kindred in blood and affinity as also by marriages and fosters and other friendships as if he should be ill-disposed might hap put the crown of England to more charges than the purchase of Ulster should be worth'.[13]

The Gaelic economic order, based on pastoralism, exchange, and redistri-bution, was foregrounded in the play.[14] Mabel was in awe of the size of her husband's herds of cattle, the source of his wealth: 'All I could see was mil-lions of them stretching away to the hills. I mean, I never saw so many cows in one place in all my life'.[15] O'Neill used cows as currency and so cattle raiding, especially in the long winter evenings, formed an integral part of the local redistributive economy. A successful cattle raid often resulted in the submission of a territory which enhanced the military and political standing of a given lord and brought him increased riches in the form of tribute. O'Neill and O'Donnell were amongst a small number of powerful overlords who not only controlled their own territories but also collected tribute—in the form of military service, food, lodgings, and agricultural labour—and demanded submission from neighbouring lordships. Little is known of the lower orders over whom O'Neill and O'Donnell lorded it but osteoar-chaeological analysis of nearly 1,300 skeletons, a third of which were of juveniles, excavated in 2003/4 from Ballyhanna in south County Donegal, has provided some extraordinary insights into the everyday life of a Gaelic lordship. Economic hardship, gruelling work, a limited diet, physical impair-ments, and poor health characterised the lives of these modest arable farmers, labourers, and crafts people. Few lived beyond the age of 50, with the majority dying before reaching 35. Disease, chronic infections, vitamin deficiencies, food shortages, and famine appear to have caused most deaths with rela-tively few from interpersonal violence.[16]

That said, it was a highly militarised society. Scottish mercenaries—the 'gallowglass' or 'redshanks'—supplemented the Irish swordsmen who fought for O'Neill and O'Donnell. Between the 1560s and 1590s some 25,000 mercenaries found employment in Ulster.[17] External observers struggled to comprehend what they perceived to be the apparent lawlessness. They were, in the words of another character in the play—Peter Lombard, Archbishop of Armagh—'Constantly at war—occasionally with the English—but always, always among themselves'.[18] Mabel went further when she told O'Neill that 'You are not united. You have no single leader. You have no common determination. At best you are an impromptu alliance of squabbling tribesmen'.[19]

If 'fighting' served as one central pillar on which Gaelic society rested, 'feasting' was the other, something captured in John Derricke's woodcut image of the feast, with the chief of the MacSweeneys, close allies of the O'Donnells, seated at dinner, entertained by a bard and a harper (see Figure 1.1). Feasting was a public display of a lord's power over his followers and mattered hugely to O'Neill, as did those traditions associated with musicians, harpists, bards, and storytellers that enhanced his standing and status within his lordship. These customs and traditions were clearly very strange, even alien, to Mabel who spoke no Irish. But they were non-negotiable for O'Neill. Just as Gaelic culture was core to his identity, the fact that he had fathered many sons and continued to keep mistresses played to his masculinity and status as a Gaelic chieftain. Despite Mabel's complaints, O'Neill refused to dismiss his 'harlots', as Mabel dubbed his lovers; she then justified their presence to her sister on the grounds that this was 'part of his culture'.[20]

Equally insightful were O'Neill's deliberations about 'Englishness' both with Mabel and his trusted friend, foster brother, and private secretary, Harry Hovenden, who unlike O'Neill and O'Donnell, was of 'New English' descent but also Catholic. Even though Friel suggested that O'Neill was educated in England, he was in fact raised 'amongst the English' of the Pale, first in the Dublin household of Sir Henry Sidney (1556–9), to whom John Derricke dedicated his *Image of Ireland*, and later with the Hovenden family, hence the close bond with Harry.[21] As a result of this upbringing in Sidney's household, O'Neill had acquired the necessary trappings of 'civility'. According to Friel, O'Neill spoke with an 'upper-class English accent' and 'like those Old English nobs in Dublin'.[22] In the play, O'Donnell teased him about his 'excessive jacket', later adding 'I bet you that's a London job'.[23] In reality, O'Neill and his children did wear English apparel. In 1599

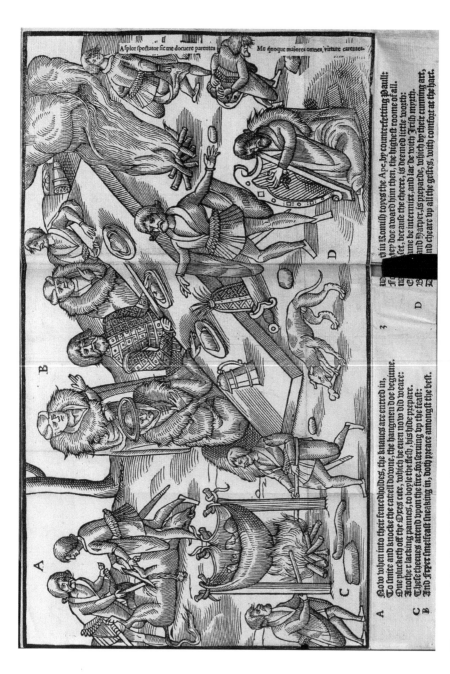

Figure 1.1 John Derricke's woodcut image (*The Image of Irelande, with a Discoverie of Woodkarne* (1581)). Reproduced courtesy of the University of Edinburgh.

Sir John Harington visited O'Neill's camp and noted that his sons, Hugh and Henry, were both 'dressed in English clothes, with velvet jerkins and gold lace'. Harington added that the boys were already 'acquainted with the English tongue'.[24] In a letter to the administration in London O'Neill claimed that he had married Mabel to 'bring civility into my house'.[25] O'Neill enjoyed friendships with many of the families who settled in the Pale, especially Garrett Moore of Mellifont Abbey, who had fostered one of his sons.[26] O'Neill, by his own admission, made himself indispensable to Crown soldiers and settlers as they attempted to colonise East Ulster. He also did what he could to bring 'in' O'Donnell, Maguire, and other local lords.[27] For as Mabel reminded O'Neill in the play: 'Queen Elizabeth made you an earl. And you accepted that title. And you know that that title carries with it certain duties and responsibilities'.[28]

For her part, Elizabeth I once described O'Neill as 'a creature of our own'.[29] She understood the importance of securing the support of magnates like O'Neill if she was to exercise any influence over Ulster. The maps drawn during these years vividly evoke Ulster as a *terra incognita*, replete with inaccessible landscapes devoid of habitations bar a few coastal strongholds populated by fierce, well-armed warriors. This meant that, even after his defeat in the Nine Years' War, O'Neill was able to negotiate terms, something that the earl, well versed in the *realpolitick* of Tudor government, truly understood. For as he explained to O'Donnell in the play: 'Because she [Elizabeth I] knows that the only way she can rule Ireland at this point is by *using* someone like me. She hates me—but she can rule through me provided she has control over me'.[30] Friel underscored the point by quoting from O'Neill's letter of submission to the queen. In it O'Neill humbly begged 'Her Majesty to restore me to my former living and dignity where as an obedient subject I vow to continue hereafter loyal to her royal person, to her crown, to her prerogatives, and to her English laws . . . Particularly will I help in the abolishing of all barbarous Gaelic customs which are the seeds of all incivility'.[31] However surrender in 1603 also meant that O'Neill had no alternative but to engage with the Crown's local agents, men like Henry Bagenal. After all, as O'Neill reminded Mabel, 'it's the plodding Henrys of this world who are the real empire-makers'.[32]

From the 1570s English soldiers and bureaucrats, like Bagenal, held a royal mandate to exercise brute force in Ulster, building forts and garrisoning men in strategic locations and launching fire and sword campaigns often under the guise of martial law. Towards the beginning of the play O'Donnell outlined the aggressive English military strategy in Ulster: 'Do you know what the hoors are at? They're going to build a line of forts right across the country from Dundalk over to Sligo'. O'Donnell continued: 'That'll cut us off from the south. . . . The second stage is to build a huge fort at Derry so that you and I will be cut off from each other . . . when Donegal and Tyrone are isolated, then they plan to move in against each of us'.[33] This is, of course, exactly what happened. Derry's formidable walls are still intact and other remains of these early seventeenth-century castles and fortified houses litter the border landscape, from Newry to Enniskillen, and are vividly represented in the maps by Robert Bartlett and other early modern cartographers.[34]

O'Neill detested Bagenal whose ambitions to be lord president of Ulster threatened his preeminent position in the region. He branded Bagenal a 'Staffordshire mongrel' and 'a bloody upstart'.[35] Confident in his social and cultural superiority, O'Neill focused on Bagenal's unworthiness, inhumanity, and poor breeding. The name-calling continued as Bagenal lambasted O'Neill's disloyalty and Catholicism. Henry laid bare (both in the play and in reality) his humiliation and shame that his blood 'should now be mingled with so traitorous a stock'.[36] Mary concurred and held O'Neill to be 'evil incarnate', the 'Northern Lucifer—the Great Devil—Beelzebub!'[37]

Denigration of the 'other' came with an imperative to replace everything Irish with everything English: the landscape was to be shired; primogeniture was to determine inheritance practices; and English law was to replace Brehon and customary law. In the play, Hovenden recounted to O'Neill the details of a cattle raid on the Devlins, who paid tribute to and expected protection from O'Neill, and reminded him that 'if Hugh O'Neill cannot offer them safety and justice under the Brehon Law, they'll have to look for protection under the new English Law'.[38] Even though violence was endemic and omnipresent throughout the play, the significance of the English victory, first at the battle of Kinsale (in 1601) and then, two years later in the Nine Years' War, is muted. It was Mabel who reminded Hugh that 'This is a war that England must win because her very survival is at stake'.[39]

England's desperation to win explained—but in no way excused—the tactics deployed. In the play there were fleeting—but nonetheless intense—images of the destruction wrought on Donegal by English troops. O'Donnell, still reeling from the news that O'Neill had married outside the tribe and wed the sister—'that Upstart bitch'—of their arch enemy, struggled to contain his rage at an atrocity committed by New English troops:[40]

> Do you know where the Butcher Bagenal was last week? In the Finn valley. Raiding and plundering with a new troop of soldiers over from Chester—the way you'd blood young greyhounds! Slaughtered and beheaded fifteen families that were out saving hay along the river bank, men, women and children. With the result that at this moment there are over a hundred refugees in my mother's place in Donegal Town.[41]

Later in the play, O'Donnell recounted how 'Everywhere you go there are people scavenging in the fields, hoking up bits of roots, eating fistfuls of watercress. They look like skeletons'.[42] The English scorched earth policy, which included unrestricted violence against non-combatants especially women and children, and the use of famine tactics, coincided with the coldest decades of the sixteenth century and a run of bad harvests between 1591 and 1597.[43] The consequences for Ulster were devastating with widespread starvation and depopulation. It has been estimated that two-fifths of the population died thanks to the destruction of the Nine Years' War.[44] Reports, albeit by English observers associated with Lord Mountjoy, of alleged cannibalism circulated with graphic descriptions of children eating the roasted flesh of death mothers.[45]

Even if Friel's focus is the local, he never lost sight of the wider contexts of England, Scotland, and especially Spain and the papacy, from where O'Neill and O'Donnell secured support for their Catholic 'crusade'. Archbishop Peter Lombard embodied these connections with Catholic Europe. Lombard reminded O'Neill:

> I've spent a lot of time in Madrid recently, Hugh, and I can tell you that Europe is looking more and more to us as the ideal springboard for the Counter-Reformation... The initial shock of the Reformation is over. Catholic Europe is now gathering itself together for a Counter-Reformation. And the feeling is that culturally, geographically and with some military assistance we could be the spearhead of that counter-attack.[46]

Lombard was a distinguished theologian and, as O'Neill's first biographer, began the cult of O'Neill as national saviour.[47] In the play most of O'Neill's exchanges with Lombard—first in Dungannon and later in Rome—focus on the meaning of history and allowed Friel to complicate the nationalist myth of O'Neill as the symbolic hero of Irish nationalism.[48]

Time and again, O'Neill insisted that Lombard must tell the 'truth', especially about his relationships with Mabel and with Harry. Lombard fobbed him off with 'I'm not even sure I know what the historian's function is—not to talk of his method...Maybe when the time comes my first responsibility will be to tell the best possible narrative. Isn't that what history is, a kind of story-telling?' 'Is it?' asked O'Neill. Lombard replied: 'Imposing a pattern of events that were mostly casual and haphazard and shaping them into a narrative that is logical and interesting. Oh, yes, I think so'. O'Neill continued:'And where does the truth come into all this?' Lombard answered: 'I'm not sure that 'truth' is a primary ingredient—is that a shocking thing to say? Maybe when the time comes, imagination will be as important as information. But one thing I will promise you: nothing will be put down on paper for years and years. History has to be made—before it's remade'.[49]

Nearly 25 years do pass; history is made and remade. In the final scene of the play O'Neill, having left Ireland in 1607 as part of what is now known as the 'Flight of the Earls', was in Rome with Lombard. Broken and blind, O'Neill again insisted that the archbishop tell his life story exactly as it happened. 'I need the truth, Peter. That's all that's left. The schemer, the leader, the liar, the statesman, the lecher, the patriot, the drunk, the soured, bitter émigré—put it all in, Peter. Record the whole life—that's what you said yourself'.[50] Again, Lombard pushed back:

What are you so miserable about? Think of this [book] as an act of pietas. Ireland is reduced as it has never been reduced before—we are talking about a colonised people on the brink of extinction. This isn't the time for a critical assessment of your 'ploys' and your 'disgraces' and your 'betrayal'—that's the stuff of another history for another time. Now is the time for a hero. Now is the time for a heroic literature. So I am offering Gaelic Ireland two things. I'm offering them this narrative that has the elements of myth. And I am offering them Hugh O'Neill as a national hero.[51]

Of course, by putting it all in—'the schemer, the leader, the liar, the statesman, the lecher, the patriot, the drunk, the soured, bitter émigré'—*Making History* challenged the myth of 'Hugh O'Neill as a national hero'.

Instead Friel portrayed O'Neill as a complex man, redolent with ambiguity, who flitted between two very different and competing worlds. He was a powerful Gaelic lord—the O'Neill—who valued his kin, lineage, culture, and religion. He was also an English earl, comfortable with the language and trappings of England, a friend to English men, a lover of English women, and a servant of an English queen. Friel also imbued O'Neill with qualities—ambition, ruthlessness, hybridity, pragmatism, passion, charm, and charisma—that made him accessible and human.[52] Finally, Friel rendered O'Neill as a leader who was willing to negotiate, to accommodate, to compromise, to survive, and to reconcile.

As even this brief overview of the play makes clear, *Making History* is grounded in the historical record. The dialogue included direct quotations from key documents and, interestingly, Friel's portrayal of O'Neill resonated with contemporary depictions of the earl even by his enemies. For example, Lord Mountjoy's secretary, Fynes Moryson, suggested that O'Neill was 'of a meane stature, but a strong body, able to indure labors, watching, and hard fare, being with all industrious, and active, valiant, affable, and apt to man-nage [sic] great affaires, and of a high dissembling subtile and profound wit. So as many deemed him borne, either for the great good or ill of his Countrey'.[53] Friel also drew inspiration from Seán O'Faolain's very popular biography, *The Great O'Neill*, first published in 1942, which according to Hiram Morgan, was characterised by 'wild inaccuracy' and 'crass romanti-cism'.[54] As a result, the play, at times, has a confused internal timeline, events are conflated, and composite characters created. In other words, Friel strays from the known 'facts'. O'Neill was not reared in England but 'amongst the English' of the Pale. According to O'Neill, the lord deputy 'vigorously' urged him to have his 'eldest son [Hugh] attend the newly established College of the Holy and Undivided Trinity in Dublin', adding 'I'm told he's trying to get all the big Gaelic families to send their children there'. Yet Trinity was only founded in 1592, the year after the exchange occurred.[55] While O'Neill met Lombard in Rome, the archbishop, originally from Waterford, never visited Ulster, spending most of his life on the Continent. Mabel's biographers simply tell us that she died in 1594 'without issue'.[56] There is no evidence to prove that she died in childbirth, as is suggested in the play, though this was certainly possible. However, to focus on factual infelicities misses the point of the play, which is about language, identity, colonialism, and the relationship between history and myth.[57]

It is important to note that *Making History* was not the only insightful play written about Hugh O'Neill. In May 1969 *The O'Neill* by Tom Kilroy, another remarkable Irish playwright and close associate of Friel's, premiered in Dublin with a larger cast of 26 (there were only six actors in *Making History*). Set in London and Ireland before, during, and after O'Neill's vic-tory at Yellow Ford (1598), *The O'Neill* addressed many of the same issues: the challenges associated with conquest, colonisation, and anglicisation; the 'civilising' influence of women; the corrosiveness of commercialisation; ethnic and sectarian tensions and how these shaped identity formation. The bardic poet in *The O'Neill* satirised O'Neill's 'English ways', adding he enjoyed 'Three marks of the foreigner: gaudy clothes, a strange language, and the desire to build houses'.[58] Teasing aside, O'Neill was quick to vilify the low-born arrivistes. According to O'Neill the Bagenals 'are the breed of a Newcastle tailor. They will give them titles but that is all colonials will ever be—tailors. They patch up the holes in the overcoat of the Empire'.[59] Yet O'Neill was willing to intermarry with the daughter of an imperial tailor, confident that she would assimilate. As O'Neill reminded Mabel 'You are Irish. I am Irish. Madam, we are only separated by time, blood, religion. These are small things. History will not be able to tell the difference between us'.[60] Though he may not have been aware of it, Kilroy, as we shall see in Chapters 3 and 6, had found his mark. *The O'Neill,* however, did not engage local audiences and communities to the extent that *Making History* did during its first major run. Part of the explanation for this lies in the context, especially the time and the place in which *Making History* was performed.

I Contexts

Three contexts and related historiographies are discussed in this section: the first, that in which *Making History* was set—the turn of the seventeenth century; the second, that in which it was performed—the late 1980s;[61] and, finally, the context of the moment, the early 2020s.

First, the context in which the play is set. Since the seventeenth century is examined at length in the next five chapters, the focus here is the historiographical debate that is of particular relevance, even if it is a rather tired one, on whether Ireland was a kingdom or a colony or a hybrid combination of both.[62] The passage of the Kingship Act in 1541 transformed Ireland's status from a patchwork of feudal lordships into an imperial kingdom. This 'constitutional revolution' redefined relations between the English king and his subjects, especially those of Irish provenance who were now accorded the same rights as those of English origin.[63] Ireland now formed part of a 'composite monarchy' in the context of an English empire that from the late sixteenth century had expansionist ambitions.[64] After 1603 and the accession of James VI and I to the throne of the three kingdoms, Irish Catholics, of Old English and Gaelic provenance, proclaimed their loyalty to the house of Stuart and celebrated in poetry, plays, and polemics their status as a kingdom.[65] The Ulster poet Eoghan Ruadh Mac An Bhaird, who had eulogised Red Hugh O'Donnell and later shared Continental exile with Hugh O'Neill, welcomed James VI and I as Ireland's spouse and depicted Ireland as a distinct kingdom in the context of James's 'three crowns'.[66] Writing in Rome Archbishop Peter Lombard dedicated his *Episcopion Doron* (1604) to James and in the preface congratulated him on his accession as Ireland's legitimate ruler.[67]

From this moment on the majority of Catholics, especially those of Old English provenance, accepted the extent to which kingship underpinned the exercise of political power together with the centrality of Irish parliamentary sovereignty, something that the Protestant community also took on board during the later decades of the seventeenth century. The celebrated Galway lawyer and MP Patrick Darcy articulated this in his address to the Irish parliament in June 1641 when he called for Ireland's legislative independence as a separate kingdom within the Stuart 'composite monarchy'.[68] The following month the Irish House of Commons declared: 'The subjects of this his majesty's kingdom are a free people, and to be governed only according to the common-law of England, and statutes made and established by the parliament in this kingdom of Ireland, and according to the lawful customs used in the same'.[69] Events surrounding the 'Wars of the Three Kingdoms' (1639–53) and especially the rise of the Westminster parliament as an alternative source of power fundamentally challenged and then changed these assumptions.[70]

Ironically, however, Darcy had prepared the constitutional song sheet for the Protestant ruling elite.[71] His *An Argument* (Waterford, 1643) stated that an Irish kingdom was 'to be governed only by the common lawes of England, and the statutes of force in this kingdome', as is the case in England, 'to be their birth-right, and best inheritance'.[72] First William Domville, Irish attorney general for much of the Restoration period, and then his son-in-law William Molyneux borrowed and recycled Darcy's arguments. Matters came to a head in the 1690s. Molyneux, wrote his influential *The Case of Ireland Being Bound by Acts of Parliament Stated* (1698), arguing that only the Irish parliament could legislate for the kingdom of Ireland. The English parliament and prominent figures condemned and contested Molyneux's assertion. For example, Sir Isaac Newton, the renowned scientist and warden of the royal mint, argued that 'Ireland is one of the English plantations and though it has changed the title of lordship to that of kingdom yet it still continues annexed to the Crown of England like the other plantations'. He added that Ireland 'ought to be inferior to this kingdom and subservient to its interests'.[73] In short, to the English, Ireland remained a colony, and the Declaratory Act (1719–20) confirmed the island's legislative subordination and enshrined Poynings' Law (1494).[74] Poynings' Law had mandated that no parliament could meet in Ireland unless licensed to do so by the king and that the king and his English privy council approve all legislation to be submitted to an Irish parliament, thereby restricting the legislative function of the Dublin parliament.[75]

Ireland's colonial status has invited comparison with other English colonies, especially in the Atlantic world, both by contemporaries and by later historians, most importantly by D. B. Quinn and Nicholas Canny.[76] A generation of scholars from a variety of disciplines—archaeologists, geographers, literary specialists, and historians—have offered nuanced case studies illustrating the interconnectedness of the Atlantic world and the challenges and opportunities that a comparative and diasporic approach affords.[77] A collection of essays published in 2009 to commemorate the 400th anniversary of the plantation of Ulster suggested that the plantation 'became the city of London's and England's first successful attempt at empire…providing a template for future colonial expansion in the Americas, the Caribbean and the Indian sub-continent'.[78] Some have taken issue with this 'colonial model'. Alison Games in *The Web of Empire* sees Ireland as a 'parallel and simultaneous colonial experiment' that occasionally 'provided a model' for English imperialism.[79] Others have suggested that the nature of rule in Ireland was very different to the Caribbean and the mainland American colonies and that comparisons with other European 'composite monarchies' are more appropriate.[80]

There can be little doubt of the importance of taking a 'three kingdoms' or 'four nations' approach to the study of empire even if this has also ruffled feathers.[81] For example, Antoinette Burton, an authority on Britain and empire in the nineteenth and twentieth centuries, labelled the growing body of 'four nations' scholarship as 'sophisticated parochialism', something that Andrew MacKillop took issue with. MacKillop, author of the groundbreaking *Human Capital and Empire: Scotland, Ireland, Wales and British Imperialism in Asia, c.1690–c.1820*, suggests that 'The four nations model has, unquestionably, helped to complicate the colonizer'.[82] In particular, Ireland, where 'resistance to and involvement in empire' went hand in hand, 'provides such a crucial lens' through which to view imperialism.[83] MacKillop has built on foundations laid by John MacKenzie, who did so much to promote a 'four nations' approach to the history of empire.[84]

Equally insightful are concepts associated with borderlands and frontiers. Medieval historians—Robert Bartlett, Jim Lydon, Robin Frame, and Katharine Simms—have fruitfully examined the role that the 'frontier' played in shaping medieval Irish society, culture, and politics.[85] Writing in the 1970s, Michael Hechter has shown that the internal frontier within the British Isles constantly fluctuated as domestic and external forces interacted, pushing, especially in Ireland and Scotland, the political frontier gradually westward.[86] Recent studies of early modern Russian and American borderlands and frontiers, formulated in response to F. J. Turner's controversial 'frontier thesis', have offered insights that could be usefully explored in an Irish context.[87] For example, the focus of Allan Greer's book is land, possession, and the dispossession of the indigenous peoples who lived in early modern Mexico (New Spain), New England, and Canada (New France). He looks at the 'empire effect' or the 'profoundly destabilizing impact of imperial penetration that ran far beyond the zones of conquest and settlement' which paved the way for new empires that aimed to dominate people as well as land.[88] An excellent example of exactly this is *The Comanche empire* where Pekka Hämäläinen tells the story of how the Comanche effectively conquered and colonised the Apache peoples who lived along the northern frontier of Spanish New Mexico. In his book he offers a compelling account of indigenous agency and the part played by native people in the making and unmaking of colonial worlds during the eighteenth century.[89] In short, these approaches—the colonial, the composite monarchy/four nations, and the frontier—are not mutually exclusive. Indeed, all are relevant to discussions about Ireland and empire.

The second context to be explored is that in which the play was written and performed, that of the 'Troubles' of the 1980s, one of the key legacies of empire in Ireland. The war began in 1968 in the wake of the Civil Rights Movement and ended 30 years later with the Good Friday Agreement (1998). By deconstructing and humanising a nationalist hero at the height of the 'Troubles', Friel offered a message of reconciliation and invited his audiences to use their history to imagine another future.[90]

On 20 September 1988, at a moment of grisly political deadlock in Northern Ireland, the Field Day Theatre Company premiered *Making History* in the guildhall—the seat of British rule—in Derry, or Londonderry, as the plantation town developed by the city of London is also known.[91]

It is hard to overstate the symbolism. Strategically sited on the banks of Lough Foyle, the town of Derry (the anglicisation of 'Daire' or 'Doire') came under English control at the turn of the seventeenth century. In 1610 King James VI and I obliged the city of London to develop the town, to build the formidable walls, which are extant, and to colonise the entire county of Londonderry in an effort to bring capital and economic prosperity to what it perceived to be a commercial backwater.[92] A Protestant stronghold for much of the century, the city was besieged, between 1688 and 1689, by forces loyal to the Catholic King James II. Its relief in August 1689 has been celebrated for centuries, giving rise, as Ian McBride reminds us, to 'a cycle of myths concerning the seventeenth-century struggle between Protestant and Catholic, settler and native, for supremacy in Ireland'.[93]

From Derry *Making History* was performed in Dungannon, O'Neill's heartland and close to his inauguration site at Tullyhogue, which Lord Mountjoy had destroyed in 1602. The play, with a cast of six, then toured Ireland, with 59 performances in 21 towns over ten weeks, before opening in London at the National Theatre. The actor Stephen Rea played O'Neill. Rea and Friel had founded Field Day in 1980 as an intellectual response to the Troubles and they were quickly joined by Seamus Heaney, Seamus Deane, Tom Paulin, Davy Hammond, and Tom Kilroy, author of *The O'Neill*. The 1980s were bleak. Bloody sectarian war gripped the north. South of the border, recession mired the economy, outward migration reached high levels, and Catholic doctrine continued to prevail. From the outset, Field Day determined not to privilege one tradition over the other, to use arts and culture to engage and energise local communities, to nurture the notion of a 'fifth province'—that of the mind—and to invite people to imagine inclusive possibilities.[94] The plays opened up new ways of thinking about identity and often had clear political messages as in the case of *Making History*, which humanised O'Neill and offered a more nuanced account of the earl.

Now lauded for having made a remarkable cultural intervention, Field Day was not without its critics.[95] Field Day's 'insistence that Irish problems were inextricable from British imperialism' complicated further matters for some at home. But this also linked Ireland to global debates around post-colonialism.[96] Over the course of the 1970s and 1980s, Edward Said had redefined and reframed the relationship between literature and empire and put the emphasis on the colonised rather than the coloniser.[97] Post-colonial theories developed by Said, Homi Bhabha, and others took Irish literary criticism by storm.[98] Their works addressed 'historical and political conditions in Africa, India, Algeria, and the Middle East rather than in Ireland' but as the poet Dennis Donoghue noted 'these concepts travel well' and resonated with people from Ireland.[99] It was as if Friel, in writing *Making History*, accepted Bhabha's invitation to break down simple binary opposition between colonised and coloniser, to engage different kinds of powers and resistances, and to explore the ambivalent relations of hybridity and 'in betweeness'.[100] By the 1990s it was impossible to conceive, some have argued, of Irish literature (but not history) 'outside of the history of colonialism, decolonisation, and nation-making'.[101] Ultimately, however, post-colonialism had the unintended consequence of perpetuating Eurocentrism and the more current world systems approach to literature has, in the words of Ronan McDonald, 'moved attention away from nation states as discrete entities, towards more comparative and global perspectives'.[102]

Yet the use of the word 'colony' had became politicised, as did discussions around Ireland's involvement in the British empire and the extent to which the Republic of Ireland was 'post-colonial' and Northern Ireland 'colonial'. This helps to explain why historians had difficulty in engaging with post-colonial studies and left discussions of empire to others to address.[103] Things began to change from the 1990s with the publication in 1998 of the five-volume *Oxford History of the British Empire*, the first volume of which was edited by Nicholas Canny, and a bespoke volume on *Ireland and the British Empire*, edited by Kevin Kenny, which appeared a few years later.[104] The 1998 James Ford Lectures by Rees Davies appeared in 2002 as *The First English Empire: Power and Identities in the British Isles 1093–1343*.[105] The pioneering scholarship of D. B. Quinn and Nicholas Canny fixed attention on the Atlantic world, emphasising exploration and migration.[106] Other volumes—collections of essays and an important 2012 monograph by Ivar McGrath—focused on Ireland and empire in the years after 1690.[107]

The turn of the twenty-first century was very much the era of the 'New Imperial History'.[108] According to Stephen Howe the emphasis now shifted from traditional accounts of empire to ones 'centred on ideas of culture and, often, of discourse; ones with strong attention to gender relations and/or racial imaginings; ones which emphasize the impact of colonialism's cultures on metropole as well as on the colonized, and tend also to urge its continuing effects after the end of formal colonial rule'.[109] Welcome though these new trajectories undoubtedly were, Ireland rarely featured even if a few acknowledged Canny's contribution to Atlantic history.[110] It was as if, to quote Joe Cleary, Ireland was 'a case apart' or an anomaly of some sort.[111] With the passage of time the silence became deafening despite the best efforts of Canny and others. A few recent examples illustrate this. L. H. Roper, *Advancing Empire: English Interests and Overseas Expansion, 1613–1688* (Cambridge, 2017) ignores Ireland's position as an English colony and the role that Irish people played as active agents in the Anglophone empire. Priyamvada Gopal in *Insurgent Empire: Anticolonial Resistance and British Dissent* excludes discussion of 'the many important crises generated by Irish resistance' on the grounds that these are well known.[112] There is no mention of Ireland in *The Oxford Handbook of The Ends of Empire* (2018) and no acknowledgement of the transformational role that the Irish example of successful resistance played in the demise of the British empire in the twentieth century.[113] Reflecting on this silence the editors of a 2019 collection honouring John MacKenzie wondered if British historians approach Ireland with trepidation 'as if the green-flag-waving nationalists will descend upon them in a fit of republican wrath for daring to dip a toe into their historiographical waters', something that Stephen Howe had flagged a decade earlier.[114]

Clearly then any attempt to situate Ireland in a colonial framework remains problematic.[115] In 2013 Audrey Horning, an archaeologist, acknowledged in the preface to her book how the Troubles influenced her research. How 'memories of the plantation are routinely invoked by partisans of both traditions' and how the unionist community finds the word 'colony' 'challenging'.[116] In a 2015 article on 'Comparative Colonialism' Horning elaborated:

> Understandings (and misunderstandings) of the character of the relationship between Britain and Ireland lie at the root of today's contemporary dichotomous identities (Protestant/Unionist on the one hand, Catholic/Nationalist on the other). Different understandings of the actualities and legacies of the past not only inform but also are foundational to contemporary identity and contemporary conflict.... Everyone in Northern Ireland is, one way or another, entangled in some form of colonial narrative.... History is not agreed upon.[117]

Increasingly, interest is—albeit slowly—shifting from the political master narrative to multiple narratives that embrace the social, economic, environmental, and cultural histories of the peoples living on the island, along with those who left, and of Ireland's relationships with the wider world including, of course, Britain, its nearest neighbour. Of particular importance was the call for a 'circum-Atlantic' approach to history that allows us to escape territorial and national boundaries and to adopt transnational and global frameworks.[118] The wider emphasis on transnationalism and global history is empowering Irish scholars to engage with issues of identity, migration, and empire in a more inclusive, interdisciplinary, and comparative way and with a recognition that it is impossible to separate imperial history from national history. 'Entangled', 'connected', and 'interconnected' historical frameworks have also allowed for the analysis of the transfer and operation of imperialism albeit in very different contexts.[119] These approaches acknowledge differences—of geography, scale, culture and history—which often resulted in local accommodations.[120] Nevertheless, the challenge remains of how to write imperial, global, or transnational history without losing sight of the significance of the local or of individual human agency.[121] In an effort to address this MacKenzie has pointed to the value of 'glocaliza- tion' or 'glocalism', that interface between the global and the local, where he seeks to find 'answers to large questions in small places'.[122] The termin- ology may sometimes be awkward but these fresh frameworks invite us, as historians of Ireland and empires, to change the questions we ask. In this book every effort is made to examine the global through the prism of imperial actors, women, Irish land and labour, and exotic commodities with a view to disrupting the existing metanarrative and, to paraphrase MacKillop, to complicate the coloniser. Or, in the words of Archbishop Lombard in *Making History*, this is 'the time for a critical assessment' and for 'another history' of our time.[123]

This brings me to the third context: how should *Making History* be read today? The Ireland of the 2020s is a very different country to that of the 1980s, something that the referenda on same sex marriage (2015) and abor- tion (2018) highlight but issues of language, identity, and the relationship between history and myth are as important as ever. Most importantly, Ireland is at peace, even if Brexit (2020) and the rise of English nationalism, and the accompanying glorification of the imperial past and nostalgia for empire, threatens the stability of the peace process. The historic visit to Ireland (2011) of Queen Elizabeth II was a moment to bow to the past without being bound by it and ushered in, as Guy Beiner notes, a period of 'new commemorative inclusiveness'.[124] During a decade of centenaries (2012–23) a number of very significant events have been marked, including the First World War (1914–18), the most imperial of conflicts; the 1916 rebellion, which helped to trigger the unravelling of the British empire and inspired freedom fighters in other European empires; and the partition of Ireland (1920), which served as the template for the later partitions of India and Pakistan and Israel and Palestine.

This period of commemoration, combined with the campaigns, especially in the USA and UK, that foreground issues of race and ways of contesting the past are forcing a fundamental re-examination of our history, how we remember, and how we forget.[125] For example, white supremacists in the USA misleadingly suggest that Irish indentured servitude in the seventeenth-century Caribbean equated to white chattel slavery and thereby distort the true meaning and misery of black slavery.[126] Around the world statues of individuals associated with imperialism and slavery have been targeted. Over the past 100 years most of the imperial statues in the Republic of Ireland have been removed. Keen to dissociate themselves from an imperial past, republicans blew up, amongst others, the statue of William of Orange on College Green in 1929 and Nelson's Pillar in 1966, while the statue of Queen Victoria was removed from outside the Dáil in 1948 and later gifted to Australia.[127] Yet, even though we are not always fully aware of it, the legacy of the British empire lives on in street names, in Ireland's built heritage (plantation towns, big houses, government buildings), in the collections in libraries and museums, in fashions, folklore, and foodstuffs and, of course, the English language.

On 25 February 2021 President Higgins gave a lecture that examined the motivations and practices of British imperialism and of resistance to it. This was part of a series of reflections (*machnamh*) on the years between 1920 and 1923, including the war of independence from England, the civil war, and partition of the island, where the president—invoking Hannah Arendt and Richard Kearney—placed emphasis on 'ethical remembering' and facing the past to avoid being trapped in it.[128] President Higgins wrote in the *Guardian* that:

> As I reflect on the topic, I am struck by a disinclination in both academic and journalistic accounts to critique empire and imperialism. Openness to, and engagement in, a critique of nationalism has seemed greater. And while it has been vital to our purposes in Ireland to examine nationalism, doing the same for imperialism is equally important and has a significance far beyond British/ Irish relations. Such consideration *also* helps explain a reluctance in former imperial powers to engage now with their imperialist past and to examine that past with descendants of those previously colonised, many of whom still live with the complex legacies of that colonialism.[129]

While much of what he wrote also applies to the early modern period, the president's focus was more recent history.

In the preface to an important recent book on Ireland and the Caribbean Sir Hilary Beckles noted: 'As England's first colonials the Irish were an experiment in racial and cultural categorization'. He continued: 'Time heals and hurts; it conceals and reveals. Ireland is now a prime site for the re-examination of the complexity of racism and the hatred it houses'.[130] Events that occurred in the sixteenth and seventeenth centuries remain very much part of the DNA and are core to the identity of people living in Ireland today. Until recently few fully appreciated the significance of Ireland's imperial past but this is changing and there is a growing awareness of the importance of informed discussion and respectful debate. The fact that the much celebrated Irish philosopher George Berkeley (1685–1753), the Church of Ireland bishop of Cloyne, owned slaves caused considerable concern. In the 1720s Berkeley resolved to emigrate permanently to Bermuda and establish a college 'for the moral regeneration of the American colonies'.[131] In the event he never made it to Bermuda. Instead, he settled in Newport, Rhode Island, where in 1730 he purchased two slaves, Philip aged 14 and Edward aged 20, and the following year he baptised 'three of his negroes, Philip, Anthony, and Agnes Berkeley'.[132] In April 2023 continued disquiet resulted in Trinity de-naming the 'Berkeley' library. The revelation that John Mitchel, a revered nineteenth-century Irish patriot, supported slavery also made national headlines.[133] As a Young Irelander, Mitchel led strong opposition to empire as well as falling victim to it when he was transported to Van Dieman's land. On his escape he fled to America where during the 1850s he continued to oppose empire, but also became an apologist for slavery and the confederates. The eighteenth-century statesmen Edmund Burke was a vocal critic of the East India Company and compared Ireland and India on the basis that they were 'similarly victimised'.[134] On the one hand, Burke thought that empire was morally indefensible; while, on the other, he and his brother had interests in sugar and slaves in the Caribbean and as MP for Bristol (1774–80) Burke looked after the interests of the slave-trading merchant community.[135]

More controversial still was the role men from Ireland played at the Amritsar Massacre at Jallianwala Bagh in the Punjab. On 13 April 1919 up to 1,500 Indian men, women, and children were butchered at what is now known as the Amritsar Massacre. When this was aired across Irish radio as part of the 2019 commemoration of the massacre, people struggled to comprehend the bloody role played by the commanding officer that day, Colonel Reginald Dyer, educated in Middleton in County Cork, and his superior, the lieutenant governor of the Punjab, Michael O'Dwyer, a Catholic from County Tipperary who, as recent research has shown, considered himself to be an Irish nationalist. Stories like this challenged and complicated the master narrative of the Irish as victims of empire, not active perpetrators of it.[136]

Clearly these discussions can be politically charged at the best of times but social media has exacerbated matters by giving voice to small and anonymous groups of racist extremists and facilitating their venomous attacks.[137] Despite this, Priya Satia has suggested in *Time's Monster: History, Conscience and Britain's Empire* that the UK's 'Culture Wars' and campaigns connected to 'Black Lives Matter' will 'change popular views of colonialism' and, as part of other programmes focused on reparations, repatriation, and restitution, will help to decolonise institutions.[138] They have certainly found their mark in Ireland where there appears to be a real appetite for understanding the complexities of empire. In May 2020 there was an unprecedented response to George Floyd's death in Minneapolis but this became even more poignant after the death of George Nkencko in Clonee, near Dublin, in December 2020. As part of a wider attempt to confront racism in Ireland, there have been discussions about how to diversify Irish history and to engage with colonial after lives in our universities and cultural institutions.[139]

Like it or not, empire and colonialism have profoundly impacted Ireland and the Irish, as they have so many other places. For as John Darwin, one of the most influential historians of the British empire, put it: 'the world we live in was so largely made by empires (and not just those of Europeans), that to deny their influence is merely futile'.[140] Similarly, in a collection of essays entitled *Imperial Debris*, Ann Laura Stoler examines how 'colonial situations bear on the present... how those histories, despite having been so concertedly effaced, yield new damages and renewed disparities'.[141] These 'colonial situations' often date back to early modernity. Hilary Beckles, whose research on the Caribbean in the early modern period has informed the reparations movement there, argues that reparations are 'a moral, legal and political response to the crimes against humanity committed during the European imperial project'.[142] Jean-Frédéric Schaub has suggested that it is impossible to understand Latin America today without examining the legacy of the Spanish and Portuguese empires. From the early modern period political, religious, and social structures and processes were formed, imperial systems for trade and education were established, indigenous nations destroyed, and enslaved African people—'the indispensable fuel of the colonial motor'—bought and sold.[143] Zoltán Biederman in his analysis of Sri Lanka, formerly Portuguese/Dutch/British Ceylon, argues that the after life of colonialism 'remains disturbingly alive in the post-colonial nation'.[144] Much like Ireland, Sri Lanka experienced a brutal war, lasting nearly 40 years (1983–2009) and resulting in the deaths, often in the most brutal of circumstances, of at least 100,000 people.[145]

II Challenges

The challenges of the present are very real and so too are the limitations of the past. The nature of the archive is a particular issue, as is the danger of relying on English-language sources which 'often reproduce the cultural assumptions of the colonizers and distort those of the colonized', along with more practical issues of linguistic ability.[146] That said, the oppressed in Ireland retained memories of the injustices suffered.[147] To some extent the *Field Day Anthology of Irish Writing*, five meaty volumes compiled in the 1980s and 1990s, became an 'alternative archive'.[148] Of particular importance is the archive of the Folklore Commission, which recorded stories from across the island from the 1930s, and vividly illustrates how memories of what happened and what people believed to have happened during the early modern period have remained alive in social memory.[149] Every effort has been made in this book to interrogate available evidence in whatever language and form. Written records—state papers, legal and taxation records, surveys, correspondence, diaries, pamphlets, treaties, and inquisitions—all offer insights, as do material culture and visual sources—portraits, engravings, maps, and architecture. Works of poetry, prose, and performance help to recapture emotions and more nuanced senses of identity in early modern Ireland. Given that the majority of people living in early modern Ireland spoke only Irish or were bilingual, sources in Irish, especially the poetry and prose but also verse and song, are of particular value—something that the research of Vincent Morely has highlighted.[150] In addition to literature, insights have been gleaned from related disciplines of archaeology, anthropology, folklore, geography, gender and legal studies, and digital humanities.[151]

While much can be done to avoid perpetuating stereotypes and to invert Anglocentric narratives, the silences are more difficult to interpret. This is particularly the case for 'ordinary', non-elite people men and especially women. For example, from the early decades of the seventeenth century indentured servants left Ireland in significant numbers, destined primarily for the Caribbean though some did travel to the mainland colonies as well. Two-thirds were men, mostly under the age of 25, who were from the lowest socio-economic sector of society, typically unskilled or semi-skilled servants or vagrants. Roughly one-third were women about whom we know very little despite their importance for the labour market.[152] Even when the records are apparently silent we can draw inspiration from the pioneering work of Marisa Fuentes who, in *Dispossessed Lives*, offers, despite the limited evidence, vivid insights into the lives of enslaved women in Barbados.[153] Or that of Jenny Shaw who uses legal and other disparate records to recover the stories of an African woman who bore children to her slave master in Barbados in the 1670s and 1680s.[154]

Ann Laura Stoler, in her extensive corpus of work on empire, invites us to look again at how we interrogate our archives, to examine 'archive-as-subject' rather than simply extract information ('archive-as-source') and to read 'colonial archives "against their grain"'.[155] She looked at the Dutch archives but her methodology is equally relevant to other colonial archives which are also sites of knowledge production capable of distorting the past.[156] Of particular relevance here are the '1641 Depositions', which is a single-purpose and contested archive in the library of Trinity College Dublin.[157] Regarded by scholars as 'documents of conquest',[158] the 1641 Depositions, which comprise c.8,000 witness statements given by men and women, from a wide variety of social backgrounds and especially the non-elite, that recount their experiences of a rebellion and a bloody decade of civil war that began in Ireland in October 1641. They record the names of over 90,000 victims, assailants, bystanders, and observers—men, women, and children—and include references to every county, parish, and barony in Ireland. The deponents were mostly Protestant planters from England, Wales, and Scotland who from the late sixteenth century had settled in Ireland. The '1641 Depositions' record mass killing and extreme violence, along with the loss of homes, property, and livestock, and vividly capture the distress, fears, and trauma of those caught up in the insurrection, alongside details of their pre-war lived experiences. They document how the war tore apart families and communities and how it exposed the inner workings of a society, making visible women who were previously hidden, albeit often in plain sight. For centuries politicians, propagandists, and polemists seized on the more extreme stories related by Protestant colonists to distort the past and to inflame sectarianism.[159] Yet, if we acknowledge their biases and read the 1641 Depositions 'against the grain', they provide important insights into otherwise hidden or forgotten pasts of those who resisted or of non-elite women (see Chapter 3), and how they negotiated everyday life during times of peace and war.[160]

Challenging though it inevitably is, Stoler also calls for the history of comparison and suggests that we study the connections between empires to better understand how they monitored and learned from each other.[161] Here Stoler's work dovetails with the monumental study by Jane Burbank and Frederick Cooper, *Empires in World History: Power and the Politics of Difference*. Their focus on empire allows for the revision of 'conventional chronologies and categories and helps us see how, when, and where world history took new directions'.[162] To provide coherence for a global study that embraces two millennia, Burbank and Cooper identified five major themes: (1) differences within empires; (2) imperial intermediaries; (3) imperial intersections; (4) imperial imaginaries; and (5) repertoires of power.

Since these resonate with what happened in the English empire and the experiences of colonial Ireland, it is worth dwelling on the five themes and mapping them on to Ireland. First, in an effort to secure loyalty and compliance, empires 'employed the politics of difference' that allowed 'for the recognition of the multiplicity of people and their customs' but also sought to create difference. In empires from across Eurasia pragmatism often prevailed as rulers used a variety of methods to govern and to ensure that local intermediaries enjoyed a stake in 'the imperial edifice'.[163] In the case of the composite Tudor-Stuart monarchy a lack of resources—human and financial—resulted in pragmatic policies that ranged from conciliation and reform to outright war along with the development of ethnocentric policies that aimed to 'other' and prevent the 'degeneracy' of the colonial elite. Second, successful empires depended on 'imperial intermediaries'—agents of empire, local elites, or settlers—who secured 'contingent accommodation'. These agents of empire are discussed at length in Chapter 4 but both Hugh O'Neill and Henry Bagenal are good examples. In short, Elizabeth I, as we saw above, did whatever was necessary to secure the continued support of O'Neill and other regional power brokers. This vertical focus on the relationship between ruler and agent is often downplayed in favour of emphasis on those between coloniser and colonised.[164]

Third, the relationships between and among empires 'provoked competition, imitation, and innovation' usually over the control of resources in both war and peace. The Irish used to great effect these 'imperial intersections', as they flitted between the overseas empires of the early modern European powers (see especially Chapter 4).[165] They were, in fact, trans-imperial and often highly innovative especially in frontier regions.[166] Fourth, engagement with empire both 'opened up political imagination and constrained it' and ensured that empires were sites of debates over political legitimacy and sovereign power. Certainly, in colonial Ireland 'imperial imaginaries' varied depending on the lens through which a person looked. Hugh O'Neill's perspective differed from that of his wife Mabel or that of Queen Elizabeth I; Peter Lombard's from that of Henry Bagenal.[167] What is striking, however, is the extent to which after 1603 the Catholics of Ireland, both Gaelic and Old English, loyally embraced the house of Stuart. It was the relationship with the king's parliament in Westminster that caused such consternation for Catholics and Protestants alike (see Section I above).

Fifth, rulers had access to repertoires of power and this 'political flexibility could give empires long lives'. Some parts of an empire might be ruled directly. Others indirectly via settlement colonies; via local elites, who often retained great autonomy (proprietorial colonies); or via private corporations, with some—like the East India Company—enjoying partial sovereignty. Of course, as the example of 700 years of English/British rule in Ireland illustrates, power relations changed and were redefined over time.[168] Ireland was colonised repeatedly and different, sometimes overlapping and unstable, models of colonial governance operated in Ireland at the same time. By the seventeenth century there were settlement or Crown colonies in Munster and Ulster where the Crown empowered 'imperial intermediaries' to combine public gain with private profit; proprietorial ones in the palatinate lordship enjoyed by the Butlers of Ormond; and the corporate model, overseen by the Irish Society, in county and city of Londonderry.

More explicit comparisons might be made across the early modern European empires.[169] Recent research suggests that the Spanish Habsburgs ruled their dominions in South America and interacted with their political elite there much as the Stuarts did in Ireland.[170] The similarities are striking between the 'undertakers' in the Munster and Ulster plantations and between the 'captaincies' of early Portuguese Brazil, the 'patroonships' of

New Netherland, and the 'proprietors' of some of the English Atlantic colonies. Public interest and private enterprise characterised each as these regions as men colonised, commercialised, cultivated, and mobilised human and natural resources in return for grants of lands and sometimes titles.[171] One also has to wonder whether 'ordinary', non-elite planters in (and from) Ireland had much in common with colonists in the Iberian empires. Many left their homes in England, Scotland, and Wales, as they did in Spain and Portugal, because they were too poor, unlikely to inherit, and were in search of a better life.[172] Of course social status and economic 'push' factors also applied to those from Ireland who later settled in the Atlantic and even Asia. Another fascinating study of the colonial civilising processes in Dutch Formosa (modern day Taiwan), between the 1620s and 1640s, suggests some possible intriguing parallels with colonial Ireland. In Formosa the Dutch Vereenigde Oostindische Compagnie (VOC) colonised, commercialised, and did all they could to 'civilise' and Christianise. In other words the VOC aimed to make Formosa Dutch and to impose the Dutch language, religion, and way of life on the indigenous peoples of the island and the migrant Chinese labourers they encouraged to settle there. For the Dutch, Formosa was also a 'colonial laboratory', much as Ireland was for the English (see Chapter 5).[173]

Identifying differences is as important as examining the similarities. For example, prior to the 1690s the fact that many people in Ireland practised a religion different from that of their king would not have been tolerated elsewhere in contemporary Europe (save the Dutch Republic). In later seventeenth-century Ireland the Crown effectively accepted religious pluralism, arrangements more akin to those made in the Ottoman, Safavid, and Mughal empires.[174] From the mid-sixteenth century (the reign of Akbar) until the mid-seventeenth century (and the reign of Aurangzeb), de facto religious toleration characterised Mughal rule in India as the Muslim emperor did what he could to accommodate the majority Hindu faith. This included intermarriage with Hindus.[175] As in Ireland, the Mughal nobility was a composite body, comprising Muslims and Hindus and a variety of ethnic groups: Muslims from Central Asia who had come to India in the early sixteenth century, native Indian Muslims, the Rajput (Hindu rulers of Punjab), and other native lords. This service nobility was loyal to the regime and always ready to serve the emperor on the battlefield or as trusted officials, much as the Stuart peers were.[176] Of course, in other respects, especially their financial dependence on the emperor, the Mughal nobility was very different from its Irish counterpart and there was nothing in Ireland comparable to the land-revenue assignment system (*jagir*).[177] The fact that, in theory at least, the Mughal nobles held no hereditary titles or lands also allowed the emperor to exercise greater authority over them than the Tudor-Stuart Crown could. But whether in India or Ireland, there is much to learn from looking at the operation of early modern empires, even if the scales of such empires might be very different.

III Chapters

How then did the English empire actually function in early modern Ireland and how did this change over time? What did access to European empires mean for people living in Ireland? This book answers these questions by interrogating four interconnected themes, which Friel aired in *Making History*: first, that Ireland formed an integral part of the English imperial system with its land and labour fuelling English expansionism; second, that people from Ireland operated as agents of empire(s); third, Ireland served as laboratory in and for the English empire; and, finally, the impact of empire(s) on people living in early modern Ireland.

Chapters 2 and 3 examine colonial Ireland as an integral part of the English imperial system. Chapter 2 begins with Hugh O'Neill and the conquest, colonisation, 'civilisation', cultivation, and commercialisation of the island itself and explores these five 'cs' under the umbrella of anglicisation. Alongside discussion of religion and rebellion and extreme violence, exploitation, and expropriation, there are also stories of negotiation, assimilation, acceptance, survival, and tolerance that need to be told. These are explored in Chapter 3, where a focus on Mabel Bagenal and her sister, Mary, allow for traditional configurations of kingdom, colony, and empire to be examined through the prism of women and marriage.

Chapter 4 looks at empire makers, Friel's 'plodding Henrys', both Protestant and Catholic, who played active roles in global expansionism. By 1680 people from Ireland were to be found in North and South America, across the Caribbean, in North and West Africa, in India and elsewhere in Asia where they joined colonial settlements, forged commercial networks, and served as clergy. How did these trans-imperial encounters and experiences shape their identity and how did others perceive and represent them?

Equally, how might this hibernocentric perspective challenge, disrupt, and even change received understandings of empire, especially the English one?[178]

Chapter 5 explores the extent to which Ireland served in the early modern and modern periods as laboratory both for imperial rule and for resistance to that rule. Processes and practices of government, especially legal and landed ones and others relating to anglicisation, characterised the implementation of English imperial authority in Ireland and across the empire from the mid-sixteenth century. In addition to analysing influences and actions distinctive to English rule in Ireland, it is important to recognise those shared more generally by early modern empires and acknowledge that Ireland was one of several locations where the English learned the business of empire. Equally challenging is how we draw insights across time and make meaningful connections from the early modern into the modern period, rather than reading history back from the present and thereby losing sight of the context.[179]

Finally, Chapter 6 focuses on the impact of empire on Ireland. Given the interconnectedness of the early modern world, how did empires shape the lives of those who remained in Ireland? How did imperial commodities (especially food, drink, clothing, and furnishings) and representations of empires—in novels, plays, prose, images, travel literature and maps—form and influence ideas, identities, mindsets, tastes, fashions, and landscapes? How is Ireland's engagement with and experience of the English empire remembered (or not), represented, and misrepresented? While some in Ireland continue to celebrate connections with the British empire, which they date back to the plantations of the seventeenth century, many have either conveniently forgotten our imperial past or are simply ignorant of it. This book suggests that the moment has come to revisit the history of empire, if only to better understand how it has formed the present, and how this might shape the future.

2

Anglicisation

In 1892 Douglas Hyde, later Ireland's first president, passionately called for 'de-anglicising', for reversing his country's perceived cultural impoverishment and degradation by reclaiming Irish language and literature instead of mimicking England's.[1,2] Anglicisation in Ireland had a long history. Writing in the early decades of the seventeenth century an Ulster poet called Fearflatha Ó Gnímh lamented how conquest, colonisation, and commercialisation had transformed Gaelic Ireland into 'this new England called Ireland'.[3] In his poem Ó Gnímh described the processes associated with making Ireland English. Others used the language of 'civility' or 'improvement' to describe what we understand to be 'anglicisation', a term that was first coined in the nineteenth century.[4]

In the play *Making History*, Brian Friel had much to say about anglicisation and resistance to it. Hugh O'Neill, earl of Tyrone, represented himself as an upholder of English civility.[5] O'Neill dressed in the latest English fashions; was fluent in the language; married briefly the daughter of an English Protestant planter; was highly regarded at court in Dublin and London; and, when it suited him, served the English Crown. Throughout the play O'Neill debated the merits of an English education, of English law, of the shiring of Ulster, and of the role to be played by zealous English soldiers and administrators. Of course, at the same time, O'Neill was a great Irish overlord, inaugurated at Tullyhogue, who never lost sight of his Gaelic inheritance, power base, kin, religion, and culture. Then, during the Nine Years' War, he led resistance to English rule.

The fact O'Neill flitted with apparent ease between two very different worlds also made him a threat.[6] From the English perspective his very hybridity and the way he crossed boundaries diluted their authority and so commentators repeatedly focused on his ungrateful treachery. A local English commander dubbed him 'obstinate, perfidious, and barbarous'.[7]

During the 1590s and 1600s English poets ridiculed, satirised, and deni-grated O'Neill as a traitor and his allies as sly serpents, venomous toads, 'savages', 'dunghill gnats', and 'rebellious swine'.[8] Representations on the London stage in the closing decade of the sixteenth century reinforced these pejorative stereotypes of the Irish as animals, as subhuman, and stoked English fears and anxieties about Ireland and Irishness.[9] At worst the Irish were perfidious traitors, at best 'potential dissemblers', something personi-fied by Captain MacMorrice, a character in Shakespeare's *Henry V* (1599). MacMorrice, an Irish soldier in the service of England, famously wondered: 'Of my nation? What ish my nation?'[10]

This worked both ways. Shakespeare captured in MacMorrice the hybridity that the Flemish painter, Marcus Gheerhaerts, created on canvas with the extraordinary portrait of the English soldier, Captain Thomas Lee (1594), which hangs in the Tate Gallery in London (Figure 2.1). Of English gentry stock and well connected at court, Lee had for much of his career served with the English army in Ireland where he became a confidant of O'Neill and advocated for a compromise solution in Ulster. In this extraor-dinary composition Gheerhaerts depicted Lee as the combination of an English soldier and a bare-legged Irish wood kern. Lee wore a loose tunic, patterned with Tudor roses, with a lace collar, an English jacket over which appears to be draped an ornate orange cape, suggestive of a mantle. In his right hand Lee held an Irish throwing spear (a 'dart'); a pistol nestled into his waist. A Latin inscription (on the tree behind him) by Livy referred to a soldier who tried to secure peace with the enemy while remaining loyal to Rome.[11] Lee represented visually 'Englishness' and 'Irishness' but the mes-sage was clear: Lee may have tried to broker peace with Irish rebels but that in no way compromised his loyalty to the Tudor Crown, nor his Englishness. He had not succumbed to degeneracy.[12]

By portraying Lee as a 'shape shifter', someone who manipulated identity and acted as a mimic across cultural boundaries, and by blurring the lines between Englishness and Irishness, Gheerhaerts captured the fluid and hybrid nature of life and identity in colonial Ireland.[13] Andrew Hadfield and Willy Maley have argued that 'Ireland was both a mirror and a hammer— reflecting and fragmenting images of England' which threatened to under-mine the stability of Englishness.[14] At the heart of English discourse on Ireland, and central to English constructions of 'Englishness' and 'Irishness', then, there lay a paradox: the simultaneous recognition and disavowal of similarity. It was a move that betrayed a profound anxiety, one that,

Figure 2.1 Captain Thomas Lee (1594) by Marcus Gheerhaerts. Reproduced courtesy of the Tate Gallery in London.

as Homi Bhabha long ago argued, characterised all colonial discourse: the inability to fully suppress the Other, that figure that lingers and haunts the coloniser, always unsettling the coherence and integrity of his identity.[15]

Complex and unstable though identity undoubtedly was, discussions of hybridity should not deny the power relationships that underpinned imperialism.[16] The English empire in Ireland had medieval origins, discussed so eruditely by the late Rees Davies in his 1998 Ford lectures and more recently by Peter Crooks.[17] Rees Davies argued that England's first empire was a medieval one and traced the intrusion of the English state across Britain and Ireland from the late eleventh century, culminating with the Anglo-Norman invasion of Ireland after 1169. While acknowledging the waxing and waning of the imperial mission in Ireland, Crooks argued that from the 1360s 'the English crown engaged in a concerted effort to resuscitate its colony in Ireland'.[18] He concluded that 'England's long Irish experience proved formative', adding: 'The men who experimented in this "laboratory" of the early modern empire were versed in the foundational ethnographic texts of Gerald of Wales, and sought to learn from the trial and error of Ireland in the late Middle Ages'.[19] In short, the first English empire of the early modern period was built on medieval foundations.

That said, the overlapping and interconnected processes that drove anglicisation to new levels really began after 1541, by which point the Anglo-Norman colonists had become fully integrated and were known as the 'Old English'. In an article on 'Anglicisation of and through Law: British North America, Ireland, and India Compared, c. 1540–c. 1800', it is argued that anglicisation can be seen as part of the 'life-cycle' of colonialism.[20] Though the focus of this collaborative article is the law, the argument it makes can be applied more generally to all aspects of anglicisation. The 'life-cycle' had three stages, each of which is clearly visible in Ireland. In the first, colonial settlements were vulnerable and adaptive. This phase in Ireland, which had its origins in the twelfth century, really took off in the period between the passage of the Kingship Act (1541) and the accession of the Stuart king, James VI and I in 1603. During these years anglicisation was geographically limited to Dublin, the Pale, and other enclaves; the king's writ operated alongside Brehon law; and a series of aristocratic revolts challenged the Crown's authority.

The second stage of the 'life-cycle' was one of consolidation. Anglicisation became more possible, both in principle and in practice, in colonies that survived stage one (and many did not).[21] The establishment of stronger and more stable forms of government, judicature, policing, and defence also allowed for the imposition of various forms of English law. This second stage began in Ireland with the completion of English military conquest at the end of the Nine Years' War (1594–1603). Thanks to an aggressive policy of plantation, anglicisation gained momentum during the early decades of the seventeenth century but shifted gear again during the mid-seventeenth century. The reconquest of Ireland by Oliver Cromwell after 1649 saw unprecedented military commitment—60,000 troops and a massive war chest of tens of thousands of pounds, much of it in gold—and was very different from the more piecemeal approach of the Tudors and their predecessors.[22] With the completion of the Cromwellian reconquest and the revolution in Irish landholding of these years a new order founded on English legal, administrative, political, landed, and economic structures, the English language, and English culture had become established. The Williamite settlement (after 1690) copper-fastened the Protestant Ascendancy.

The third stage of the life-cycle, which grew out of the consolidation phase, coexisting with it and drawing strength from it, displayed what one might call the anglicisation of resistance. Anglicisation, in a sense, became the victim of its own success. Protestant colonial leaders more than the displaced Catholic elite, the original 'targets' of anglicisation, deployed English legal arguments in resistance to Britain. This irony contains more ironies within. Catholics, as shall be shown throughout this chapter, often lamented and resisted the changes wrought by anglicisation. Yet, interestingly, during the 1640s when Ireland enjoyed a decade of independence from English control, the leaders within the Confederation of Kilkenny made no attempt to de-anglicise or to re-introduce Brehon law, the Irish language, and Gaelic agricultural practices. The Catholic Confederates instead proclaimed their loyalty to the Stuarts and took over the pre-war legal and political infrastructure. Catholic lawyers, trained at the Inns of Court during the pre-war years, became key figures within the Confederation of Kilkenny. One of the most influential, the Galway lawyer Patrick Darcy, drew on contemporary English as much as Irish precedents when arguing that Irish subjects enjoyed common-law procedure but that no English statute bound Ireland unless enacted by the parliament in Dublin.[23] The silencing of Catholic voices like those of Darcy from the mid-seventeenth century meant that effective challenges to the anglicising agenda of king and parliament thereafter came from the Protestant ruling elite. From the 1690s they revived the claim that

Ireland was a distinct and self-governing kingdom united to England only by the link of the Crown. The lawyer William Molyneux wrote his influential *The Case of Ireland Being Bound by Acts of Parliament Stated* (1698), arguing that only the Irish parliament could legislate for the kingdom of Ireland. To the English, however, Ireland remained a colony, and the Declaratory Act (1719–20) confirmed the island's legislative subordination.[24]

This 'life-cycle' approach should not, however, suggest that anglicising processes occurred in a linear way, nor that the outcome was predestined. On the contrary, stages in the life-cycle often occurred in different places within Ireland at different times. Moreover the drive for English domination was regularly challenged and fiercely resisted. The operation of imperialism in Ireland became a case of learning by doing, with failure as its constant companion. The haphazard, messy, and clumsy nature of the processes surrounding anglicisation and imperialism and the limitations on central power were very real, if now muted by the passage of time and the nature of the historical record. While humanist thinking and, more sinisterly, ethnocentricity undoubtedly shaped the practice of government, the fact that English imperialism in Ireland lacked any overriding, coherent, and consistent framework allowed some Catholics, together with many Protestants, to co-opt the colonial processes to strengthen their regional power bases and even to subvert the original anglicising agenda.[25] Very often pragmatism and the need to engage local elites forced the Crown to negotiate with regional power brokers and to foster networks that were not entirely dependent on imperial largesse. These were the 'imperial intermediaries' identified by Burbank and Cooper and discussed in Chapter 1. As a result, multiple colonisations, occurring at a variety of levels, took place at different times and with varying degrees of intensity throughout this era. However, from the mid-seventeenth century commerce and aggressive economic imperialism, rather than colonisation, drove anglicisation, in part because Irish land now fuelled English expansionism around the globe (see Chapter 4).[26]

It is also critical to remember that extreme violence underpinned anglicisation throughout the early modern period. The Irish theatre of war was one of the bloodiest in Europe.[27] During the Nine Years' War (1594–1603) English forces used scorched earth tactics and starvation to secure submission.[28] The Irish conflict of the 1640s, with an estimated population loss of 20 per cent, was on a par with the destruction experienced by Bohemia during the Thirty Years' War (1618–48).[29] In particular, large numbers of non-combatants, especially women and children, suffered death (from war, exposure, famine, and disease), dislocation, and extreme violence during the 1590s, 1640s, and 1690s.[30] In short, the daily reality of anglicisation was for many people extraordinarily grim, robbing them of their homes, their livelihoods, their dignity, and even their lives.

The goal of this chapter is to examine anglicisation as an instrument of English imperialism.[31] In Sections I, II, and III anglicisation as process is explored from three interconnected perspectives: first, the cultural and religious; second, the political and legal; and, third, the landed and economic. Resistance to anglicisation—ranging from revolts and rebellions to agrarian, political, and intellectual protest, to a continued commitment to Catholicism—is a thread running across the three sections. For as Antoinette Burton reminds us 'disrupting imperial authority was a workaday practice for many ordinary colonised peoples'.[32]

I Culture and religion

Early modern people never used the word 'anglicisation', preferring the language of 'civility', but it nonetheless represents a central component of what today we might term 'cultural imperialism'. In an interesting article on 'Violence, Civil Society and European Civilisation', Stuart Carroll notes that the verb 'to civilise' was an English invention. Initially it referred to attempts to return 'the Irish lords to good government (*civilitas*) by dismantling their feuding culture'. By the 1570s, as more radical solutions were being adopted in Ireland, it took on an all-encompassing meaning and was used in other colonial contexts.[33] Intermittent attempts to 'civilise' Ireland or at least keep the English settlers from turning Irish dated back to the Norman conquest of 1169. Most notably the Statutes of Kilkenny of 1366 insisted on the exclusive use of English law, language, dress, and names, while forbidding fosterage and intermarriage with the Irish.[34] The statutes, however, had little impact and by the sixteenth century (if not long before), the Anglo-Normans, or the Old English as their descendants were known, and the Gaelic Irish had intermarried and effectively shared many aspects of the same political culture.[35] Rather than being the upholders of civility, critics held these lords to be responsible for the degeneration of Ireland into lawlessness as they pursued violent vendettas and became embroiled in factional feuding.

From the sixteenth century and the onset of the Protestant Reformation things changed and the Crown set out with renewed vigour to civilize and to anglicise. Legislation that promoted the English language, dress, and culture became law in 1537.[36] This act also outlawed the Irish language, the wearing of glibs (or long fringes) and Irish garments, such as mantles. Later legislation prohibited other Gaelic agricultural, social, political, and cultural practices. The removal of Irish-speaking 'poets, story-tellers, babblers, rymours, harpers, or any other Irish minstrels' also became a priority.[37] The attorney general and legal imperialist Sir John Davies later suggested that these laws had 'reclaymed the Irish from their wildenesse, caused them to cut off their Glibs and long Haire, to convert their Mantles into Cloaks; [and] to conform themselves to the maner [sic] of England in al[l] their behaviour and outward formes'.[38]

More than anything else, the mantle symbolised Irishness. Edmund Spenser in *A View of the Present State of Ireland* described the mantle as:

a fit house for an outlaw, a meet bed for a rebel, and an apt cloke for a thief...when it raineth it is his pentice; when it bloweth it is his tent, when it freezeth it is his tabernacle; in summer he can wear it loose; in winter he can wrap it close; at all times he can use it; never heavy; never cumbersome...it is light to bear, light to throw away, and being (as they commonly are) naked, it is to them all in all...besides all this he or any man else who is disposed to mischief or villainy may, under his mantle, go privily, armed without suspicion of any.

For women the mantle served as a 'coverlet for her lewd exercise', then covering her pregnancy, and swaddling 'her bastard'.[39] Spenser's vilification of and anxieties about the mantle played out on the London stage, where in 1613 Ben Johnson represented the Irish converting—quite literally and as Davies had forecast—their mantles into cloaks. In *The Irish Masque* four 'wild' Irish servants danced to harp music only to remove their mantles and reveal themselves as anglicised courtiers.[40] The message was clear: the Irish were no longer dangerous rebels but clownish figures, jockeying for royal favour.[41] Earlier attempts had been made by Elizabeth I herself to appropriate the mantle and make it 'English', something also seen in the portraits of Sir Thomas Lee and the earl of Kildare (Figures 2.1 and 2.2). And while thousands of mantles were shipped to Bristol, for clients mostly in London, and were prized gifts, anxieties remained that wearing the mantle would make an Englishman 'Irish' and lead to degeneracy.[42]

Figure 2.2 George FitzGerald, sixteenth earl of Kildare (*c.* 1612–60). Reproduced courtesy of the trustees of the Castletown Foundation.

Of course, what a person wore made a powerful statement about who he or she was and, in early modern and later empires, clothing 'was contested and regulated'.[43] The 'great emperor', as he was named, of the Chesapeake region, Powhatan, was presented with an English cloak, much as Irish chieftains were. For his part, Powhatan gifted one of his old mantles, now in the Ashmolean museum in Oxford, to the English adventurer, Christopher Newport.[44] A portrait that hangs in the National Portrait Gallery in London of Powhatan's daughter—variously known as Pocahontas, as Matoaka, and, on conversion to Christianity, as Rebecca—depicted her as a pale-skinned English woman, wearing a tailored bodice with lace cuffs, an ornate ruffed neck, a hat with gold brocade, and drop pearl earrings.[45] At that moment the Indian princess had become English. In other words, to paraphrase Ulinka Rublack, clothing spoke its own language and statements about social status and ethnic background.[46] In a fascinating article Audrey Horning discusses how colonialism shaped the relationship between identity and clothing at the turn of the seventeenth century. Central to her argument was a rare archaeological discovery of an Irish mantle, an English doublet, Highland tartan trews, and leather 'brogue' shoes from a bog near Dungiven on land associated with the O'Cahan lordship. Horning suggests: 'The Dungiven costume is clearly ambiguous in its cultural associations—but perhaps deliberately so…the product of a combination of static cultural identities, the outfit also speaks to hybridisation as a process'.[47] As well as illuminating anglicisation, the apparel signals commercialism. During these years imports of luxury cloth and clothing increased, something that the Bristol port books highlight.[48] By the early decades of the seventeenth century 'the better sort' were, according to one observer, 'apparelled at all points like the English'.[49]

Writers reflected on the meaning of these changing fashions. Barnaby Rich opened *The Irish Hubbub* with the lines: 'For want of a better cloake whereby to shelter these indeavours of my untutored penne, I have borrowed an Irish Mantle'. Rich then criticised English upstarts for filling 'Ireland so full of new fashions, by their strange alterations in their Ruffes, in their Cuffes, in their huffes, in their puffes, in their Muffes, and in many other vanities, that Ireland was never acquainted withall, till these women brought them up'.[50] The bardic poets concurred. The Monaghan poet Laoiseach Mac an Bhaird lambasted those who cut off their glib (or long fringe) when he wrote 'O man who follow English ways, who cut your thick-clustering hair'.[51] Another anonymous verse ridiculed the Butlers of

Mountgarret for their determination to keep up with the latest London fashions, wearing shirts with fancy collars, 'broad-brimmed' hats, 'narrow shoes', 'cambric blouses', lace and silk fabrics, and elaborate hair adornments.[52] Another entitled 'Woe is me, These Fashions of Ireland', by Brian Mac Giolla Phádraig, scorned the cloak, coat, spurs, stockings, curls, rapier, scarf, cuff, garter, and bracelet:

> O how woeful this new fashions in Eber's plain: each beggarwoman's son has curled locks, bright cuffs around his paws and a golden ring…Each churl or his son is starched up around the chin, scarf tied thrown around him and a garter on him, his tobacco-pipe in his gob and he puffing away at it, and his hand from joint to joint bedecked with bracelets.[53]

Similar processes were at work in the Spanish Atlantic. Amelia Almorza Hidalgo has shown how colonists, especially women, 'sought to reproduce in America the way of life of the European elites' but also used Spanish dress and jewellery to enhance and elevate their status as well has flaunting their wealth. Contemporary commentators ridiculed their ostentation and their crass attempts to climb the social ladder.[54]

With the outbreak of rebellion in 1641 Irish insurgents vowed to abolish 'English fashions' and insisted that 'all the women in Ireland should as formerly go only in smocks, mantles and broughs [brogues]'.[55] During the 1640s assailants actively targeted 'English fashions' and regularly stripped their victims. Motivated in part by the value of the apparel or the valuables hidden in it, stripping also aimed to humiliate, dehumanise, and, quite literally, to denude their adversaries of their 'civility' and to 'make all savage'.[56]

Along with the obligation to dress like the English came the imperative to speak English, something that Friel addressed brilliantly in *Translations*. The play was set in an Irish-speaking community in the 1830s and was about language: 'We should all be learning to speak English. That's what my mother says. That's what I say. That's what Dan O'Connell said last month in Ennis. He said the sooner we all learn to speak English the better'.[57] 'Language', as Patricia Palmer notes, 'was intimately bound up with the ideologies that legitimised colonisation and shaped its unfolding'.[58] During the early decades of the seventeenth century the use of English increased substantially; by the mid-century bilingualism appears to have been common and it is likely that one person literate in English lived in each community.[59] There are examples of English verse containing Irish words or awkwardly translated phrases from Irish (and vice versa), a fact that illustrates the crossover between the two languages.[60] Davies suggested that exposure to English law had encouraged the Irish to 'conform themselves to the manner of England in all their behaviour and outward forms...[and] they do for the most part send their Children to schools especially to learne the English language'.[61] This logic inspired Daniel Gookin who during the later decades of the century wanted to establish schools for the Indians in the 'praying towns' of Massachusetts so that they could learn English 'and thereby learn civility and religion'.[62] As he reflected on 'an approved experiment' Gookin made explicit comparisons with Ireland:

> the changing of the language of a barbarous people, into the speech of a civil and more potent nation that have conquered them hath been an approved experiment, to reduce such a people unto the civility and religion of the prevailing nation. And I incline to believe, that if that course had been effectually taken with the Irish, their enmity and rebellion against the English had been long since cured or prevented.[63]

The increased use of English infuriated poets like David Ó Bruadair, who in 'How queer this mode' lambasted those who 'utter nothing but a ghost of strident English/Woe to him who cannot simper English'.[64] While English did predominate in council chambers and courts and was the language of commerce, a significant proportion of the population, especially ordinary people, continued to speak only Irish for much of the early modern period.[65] The 1641 Depositions provide interesting instances of deponents, especially during the early 1650s, who spoke no English and required an interpreter.[66] There are also examples of bilingualism and the coexistence of the English and Irish languages.[67] Jane Cooke, a Protestant woman from County Armagh, escaped assault in 1642 'because she spoke Irish and sayd she was an Irish woman'.[68] In other instances the insurgents killed a woman 'because she could speak Irish and would discover their acts, wants and words if they suffered her to live'.[69] In both instances bilingualism seemed, in the words of Patricia Palmer, to 'destabilise identity'.[70]

Language and clothing, along with religion and law, were repeatedly signalled as badges of identity. A tract dating from 1598 noted that 'every conqueror bringes, ever three things with him to establishe his conquest: Religion, the lawe, and the language of his owne country'.[71] Protestantism undoubtedly served as a further key indicator of 'civility'.[72] After 1603 James VI and I set out both to revitalize and to reform the Church of Ireland with a view to persuading, rather than coercing, the Catholic population to conform.

By 1641 the Church of Ireland had a full complement of bishops who attempted, under the watchful eye of Archbishop Laud, a root-and-branch reform of the fabric and personnel of the church.[73] It remained, however, woefully under-resourced with an insufficient number of ministers to service the church's *c*.2,500 parishes. In contrast the Catholic church went from strength to strength, albeit operating as an underground and clandestine organization. There were 30 Catholic dioceses and in 1641 15 bishops lived in Ireland.[74]

The threat from a resurgent Catholic church was very real and the Crown did everything possible to secure high profile conversions from Catholicism, which could result in cultural reorientation and the introduction of anglicising initiatives in a region, especially if the convert tried to persuade immediate family members to switch faith and thereby add credibility to the person's conversion. Of particular importance was the policy of 'surrender and regrant'. From the 1540s the Crown negotiated 'surrender and regrant' agreements with leading Gaelic chieftains. Land held by a non-English title was surrendered to the Crown and regranted to its holder with title and tenure good in English law. The lord agreed to renounce his Gaelic title for an English one, to accept primogeniture as the basis for succession and inheritance, to recognise the king's writ and courts, and to anglicise his territories.[75] By 1547 some 40 Gaelic chieftains had surrendered their lands including some of the most powerful magnates. Henry VIII demanded that the most influential travel to court in London to receive their titles, much to the disgust of the *literati* who castigated them: 'unworthy is your altered rank, you weak misguided crowd, henceforth say nothing but shame'.[76]

The particular willingness of Gaelic lords to collaborate and compromise with the Crown highlights the extent to which they were 'in fact pragmatists concerned with maximizing their power and enhancing their reputation at minimum risk'.[77] David Edwards's pioneering study of the FitzPatricks of Upper Ossory, a middle-ranking Gaelic dynasty, offers a series of fascinating insights into Gaelic attitudes towards English rule and Tudor reform. In 1541 Brian Fitzpatrick willingly surrendered his chiefly title and lands, agreed to end the use of Gaelic practices, adhere to the English common law (including primogeniture), to encourage his followers to use the English language and dress, and permitted his son Barnaby to be reared at court with Edward VI, where he embraced Protestantism. Brian was the first Gaelic chieftain to take his seat in the House of Lords. Yet, despite the rhetoric of the agreement 'the barons of Upper Ossory remained cattle lords in the classic Gaelic tradition'.[78] They embraced Tudor reforms as a means of minimizing English interference and of bolstering their own position within the lordship. In the short term collaboration proved a very effective survival strategy for the FitzPatricks as it had for Hugh O'Neill.

Dubbed by some as 'imperialism-on-the-cheap',[79] the effectiveness of these policies need to be measured over time, as the example of the O'Briens of Thomond illustrates.[80] Henry VIII had through a surrender and regrant agreement elevated the Gaelic chieftain Murrough O'Brien to the earldom of Thomond in 1543, but it was not until the late sixteenth century that his great-grandson, Donough, fourth earl, who had been reared at the English court, embraced Protestantism. According to the Franciscan writer Antonius Bruodin, the poet Tadhg mac Dáire Mhic Bhruaideadha served as his tutor and accompanied him to court but could not prevent the young earl's conversion.[81] This was attributed to the influence of Thomas Butler, tenth earl of Ormond, who along with Barnaby FitzPatrick was educated with Edward VI and who also converted.[82] During the course of the fourth earl's lifetime, he transformed his vast Munster patrimony, nurtured urban development, and encouraged English and Dutch tenants to settle on his estates. He improved his lands by promoting tillage; he introduced new breeds of cattle; he promoted the English language, dress, and legal system; and he educated his sons at Eton and Oxford. In addition, he attempted to convert his kinsmen to Protestantism by offering to educate them; and encouraged members of his extended family to intermarry with Protestant planters in the hope this would help to 'civilise' them.

By the early seventeenth century a form of English county government operated on the Thomond estates in County Clare. This included incorporated market boroughs and the machinery of English common law operating at the local level (courts, petty officials, bailiffs). When the town of Ennis received its charter of incorporation in 1612 Thomond ensured that only New English Protestants—and no Gaelic Irish—were made burgesses.[83] Little wonder that his followers held Thomond to be 'more English than Irish'.[84] A senior government official in Ireland paid a further tribute to him: 'In the ordering of his house or governing of his country, his course has always been English, striving to bring in English customs and to beat down all barbarous Irish usages, that he might in time make his country civil, and bring the inhabitants in love with English laws and government'. Another hoped that 'the example of the earl . . . will within a few years alter the manners of this people and draw them to civility and religion both'.[85] Eager to

expand their territorial empires and to secure royal goodwill, many members of the Catholic elite followed the example of Thomond and became
enthusiastic exemplars of civility even if personal agendas, local circumstances, and patronage and kin links often tempered their civilising fer-
vour.[86] The bardic poet Pádraigín Haicéad felt particularly let down by
those who had converted to Protestantism. In one poem dating from the
1640s he named two prominent converts and challenged their identity: 'ask
if Inchiquin and Thomond/stay faithful to their own'.[87] These men, as
Nicholas Canny noted, were regarded as being 'neither truly Irish nor truly
Catholic'.[88]

This process of cultural reorientation was very real but it took time and
even enthusiasts like the fourth earl of Thomond retained many of the vest-
iges of a traditional Irish lord. He may have been an improving and anglicising magnate yet Thomond, like his ancestors, remained a patron to the
Gaelic literary and professional classes.[89] The bards marked his passing in the
traditional manner, though English words—like 'crown' and 'president'—
peppered the elegy written by Tadhg Mhic Bhruaideadha, hereditary poet
to Ui Bhriain (or O'Brien).[90] In a similar vein, Caitilin Dubh's elegy on the
fourth earl incorporates, as Marie Louise Coolahan notes, his 'anglophile
commitments in Gaelic terms'.[91] In his will, the earl reminded his heir to
nurture his native Irish followers as well as the newcomers. Yet, significantly,
none of his successors shared the fourth earl's concerns for 'the gentlemen
and inhabitants of Thomond'.[92] By the 1670s Henry, the great-grandson of
the fourth earl, urged his own heir 'to cherish the English uppon his estate
and driue out the Irish'.[93] Thus 130 years after the original surrender and
regrant agreement had been signed, the state had finally succeeded in anglicising this leading native dynasty, much to the disappointment of the early
eighteenth-century poet Aogán Ó Rathaille, who criticised the Thomonds
for embracing English ways.[94]

As the examples of Fitzpatrick and Thomond illustrate, education had
played an important role in promoting anglicisation and Protestantism. Sir
John Bath held: 'One of the chief means to hold the subjects of Ireland in
safe subjection to the crown of England was the breeding and education
which the nobility and gentry had, being sent young by their parents into
England, where they were made familiar with the English manners and
fashions, studied their laws and received the benefit of their studies upon
their return home'.[95] The government dispatched Con, Hugh O'Neill's
youngest son, to Eton, where he was schooled alongside the sons of other

Gaelic and Old English lords (Barrys, Bourkes, and O'Briens) and New English ones (Annesleys, Boyles, and Ropers).[96] Andrew Hadfield has suggested that the colonisation of Ireland began in these classrooms, where a curriculum privileging Latin and Greek and the writings of Aristotle, Plato, and Cicero 'led to an understanding that the establishment and maintenance of colonies was a central element of a responsible government's concerns'.[97]

Given the fundamental importance of education in shaping young minds and securing religious, cultural, and political conformity, the state monitored closely where the sons of leading Irish figures were educated. In 1615 King James required that the heirs of all prominent Catholic lords 'to be brought up in England for a time'.[98] Many resisted any attempt to ship their sons to England for their 'breeding and education', claiming that the boys were too young or too sickly, or the family too impoverished.[99] Back in Ireland the sons of the landed gentry and wealthy merchants attended parochial and grammar schools in Kilkenny, Waterford, Limerick, Drogheda, Dublin, Dundalk, and Galway, where students learned to speak, read, and write Latin and were introduced to Cicero and other classical authors.[100] The Old English writer Richard Stanihurst believed that this sort of education would 'breed in the rudest of our people resolute English hearts' and make them 'good members of this commonwealth'.[101] Davies concurred. Only education, he argued, could guarantee 'that the next generation will in tongue and heart, and every way else, become English; so that there will be no difference or distinction, but the Irish sea betwixt us'.[102]

Elizabeth I had founded Trinity College Dublin in 1592 'to serve for a colledge for lernyinge whereby knowledge and civilitie might be increased by thinstruction [sic] of our people there, wherof many have usually heretofore used to travaille into ffrance, Italy and Spaine to gett lernyinge in such fforraine universities where they may have been infected with poperie and other ill qualities, and so become evill subietts'.[103] Founded to promote 'civility' and to train Protestant clergymen, funding the new college initially fell to the merchants and citizenry of Dublin. Then, as a result of the Ulster plantation, 180,000 confiscated acres was set aside to endow Trinity. Though some Catholics attended Trinity (even if they neither matriculated nor graduated), it proved more appealing to zealous Protestants.[104] The humanities (or 'liberal arts'), especially classics and theology, dominated the curriculum. The fact that so many early provosts were Cambridge-educated 'reforming Puritans', with strong links to Dutch Calvinists, made Trinity particularly attractive to those who had colonised the godly settlements of New England. This explains why John Winthrop, the first governor of Massachusetts, sent his son, also John, to Trinity during the 1620s.[105] Trinity-trained clergy populated Ireland's parishes, where some did their best to promote Protestantism.[106] Other graduates served in the global Anglican empire. Over time Trinity modified its curriculum to serve even more overtly the needs of empire, preparing young men for imperial service, especially in India.[107]

From the Crown's perspective, Oxford, far from the interference of potentially subversive family members and less religiously radical, was an even better destination for young men from Ireland, especially Catholics. During the course of the seventeenth century the heirs of at least 65 resident peers received some sort of university education: 28 of them (nearly half) attended Oxford, especially Christ Church and Magdalen.[108] The Inns of Court in London were important too but for different reasons.[109] Members of the landed elite, especially Catholic families, felt it critical that a family member be able to understand the law, no doubt in order to outwit it. The example of Sir Patrick Barnewall, Mary Bagenal's husband, who attended the Inns in the 1580s and led Catholic resistance to government policies during the early decades of the seventeenth century, illustrates this. Between 1625 and 1641 140 Irish recusants, mostly Old English, attended the Inns.[110] But over time the sons of Gaelic Irish grandees followed.[111] They included Sir Phelim O'Neill, one of the leaders of the 1641 rebellion, and his brother Turlough, who both spent time at Lincoln's Inn.[112] The government encouraged this if only to prevent Catholic boys being educated abroad, which 'makes them strangers to the English law; and being strangers to it they are less likely to obey it'.[113]

Of course, the education of Catholic heirs was contested and many opted to send sons and even daughters to be educated at one of the Continental colleges (by 1800 there were 41 Irish seminaries and convents across Europe). Before attending the Inns in London, Sir Patrick Barnewall was reported to be 'the first gentleman's son of quality...to be brought up in learning beyond the seas'.[114] He later sent his son Nicholas to be educated at the Irish college in Douai. Undoubtedly, these prolonged stays at the Catholic seminaries influenced attitudes and mindsets and at the very least these helped to create an identity for Catholic Ireland that effectively excluded Protestant England.[115] According to Edmund Spenser these Continental sojourns sustained the Catholic faith as an underground religion. In *A View* he suggested that those returning from Continental colleges 'lurking secretly in their houses and in corners of the country, do more hurt and hindrance to religion with their private persuasions than all the others can do good with their public instruction'.[116] The determination of so many to remain true to Catholicism highlights the importance of religion as a tool of resistance to empire.[117]

For its part, the Crown did everything possible to stop this, as the foundation of Trinity and the passage of penal legislation in 1695 simply underscores.[118] In the instances where a lord died leaving a minor or a title was forfeited (in the case of Hugh O'Neill), the Crown enjoyed even greater control. The king became responsible for the heir's education and material welfare.[119] Thus the premature death of a father facilitated the conversion to Protestantism of the heirs to the most prestigious and powerful houses of Ormond and Kildare. When his father died in 1619 his mother placed James, later duke of Ormond, in the Catholic school in Finchley in London. The king removed young James to the care of George Abbot, Archbishop of Canterbury, who raised him as a Protestant. Lord Deputy Wentworth maintained that if Ormond had been reared 'under the wing of his own parents' he would have been Catholic like his brothers and sisters. 'Whereas now he is a firm Protestant, like to prove a great and able servant to the crowne, and a great assistant...in the civill government; it being most certaine that no people under the sunne are more apte to be of the same religion with their great lords as the Irish be'.[120]

In the case of Kildare the king awarded the wardship of the eight-year-old to his favourite, the duke of Lennox. Then the earl of Cork took over Kildare's wardship and in 1630 married his ward to his daughter, Joan, and thereby reinforced the Protestant credentials of the Kildare dynasty.[121] In an unusual portrait (Figure 2.2), reminiscent of the one of Captain Thomas Lee, Kildare wore a luxurious fur-lined scarlet robe over a simple linen shirt with a delicate lace collar. The robe, reminiscent of a mantle, served as a reminder of Kildare's ancestry and Catholic lineage. Despite his Protestantism and his marriage, Kildare continued to take seriously the traditional responsibilities associated with lordship. That said, over time the Kildares, along with most of the leading aristocratic houses, firmly espoused the Established Church and English ways.[122] Little wonder that the Gaelic poets denied their 'Irishness' and condemned as traitors members of the Catholic elite who had converted to Protestantism. They also vented their spleen against the workings of the Court of Wards, along with the central and local courts.[123] Cultural imperialism went hand in hand with political and legal imperialism, something that contemporaries recognised. The goal of anglicisation in Ireland was, according to Sir William Parsons, a leading royal official, to 'change their course of government, apparel, manner of holding land, language and habit of life. It will otherwise be impossible to set up in them obedience to the laws and the English empire'.[124]

II Political and legal imperialism

This was an age of bloodshed, brutality, and bigotry. Imperialism in Ireland ultimately rested on a bed of pikes and the use of force. Fighting became endemic and violence proved ubiquitous.[125] Major aristocratic revolts, triggered by aggressive English imperialism, wrought chaos during the second half of the sixteenth century and three major wars (1594–1603, 1641–52, and 1689–91) defined the seventeenth. Violence, much of it committed by the English state, pervaded and was underpinned by sectarianism, cultural stereotyping, dehumanisation, and expropriation.[126] Over the course of the early modern period the Crown maintained thousands of English soldiers in Ireland and built defensive fortifications along the Irish coastline, first against possible invasion from Spain and then from France. Roughly 36,000 troops served during the Nine Years' War (1594–1603). The expense involved in maintaining a permanent military presence proved prohibitive and helps to explain why the Tudors initially favoured policies of 'limited conquest' rather than all-out war. In the event the Nine Years' War cost Elizabeth I nearly two million pounds, an astounding figure which almost bankrupted the English state. Ireland may have served as a 'testing ground for English military might',[127] but it also drained English resources—both human and financial—from the Continental theatre of war and from overseas expansionism.[128] Significant though this was, the investment in the military machine deployed against Ireland by the Cromwellians was unprecedented: between 1649 and 1651 the English parliament dispatched 55,000 men to serve in Ireland supported by a very significant war chest.[129] Each English victory, especially in 1653, brought with it a fresh wave of expropriation and colonial activity as England exercised military and political dominance.[130] Then, from the 1690s Ireland financed, housed, and maintained a standing army of 12,000 men capable of going to war at home or abroad. In fact,

Table 2.1 Ethnic breakdown of all peers in 1603, 1628, and 1641[131]

	1603	1628	1641
Non-resident English	*0*	*29*	*24*
Resident in Ireland			
Native Irish	5	6	7
New English	0	22	22
Old English	22	30	33
Scots	0	6	5
Welsh	0	1	1
Total (resident)	27	94 (65)	92 (68)

until the 1770s, this army, as Ivar McGrath has shown, formed the backbone of the British military machine, ready to be deployed across the empire.[132]

Important though the army undoubtedly was in maintaining English control and as a source of administrators and colonists, traditionally, the Crown had relied on two dominant factional networks to rule Ireland: the Fitzgeralds of Kildare and of Desmond; and the Butlers of Ormond.[133] However, from the 1530s the burden of implementing imperial policies in Ireland fell instead to English chief governors, government officials, lawyers, soldier-administrators (or servitors)—Friel's 'plodding Henrys'—and Church of Ireland clergy.[134] In Ulster Brutus Babington, bishop of Derry, aimed to 'bring this rude and uncivilised people to some good conformity', while Bishop Knox of Raphoe became known as the 'governor of the red-shanks'.[135] Yet a lack of resources during the early decades of the century effectively forced the Crown to outsource governance to 'imperial interme-diaries', as Burbank and Cooper term them, something typical of other early modern empires.[136] In Ireland a significant number of these 'imperial intermediaries' used royal service to acquire lands and titles as part of a 'ser-vice nobility' or colonial hierarchy loosely modelled on the English aristoc-racy, but in fact more akin to what the Habsburgs achieved in Bohemia and Lower Austria after 1620.[137]

The Tudor peerage was small and had remained relatively stable for gen-erations with dynasties of Anglo-Norman provenance predominating. During the first three decades of the seventeenth century, the Crown embarked on an unprecedented experiment in social engineering and cre-ated a much larger hybrid peerage (see Table 2.1).[138] Between 1603 and 1640, the resident aristocracy more than doubled, from 29 to 69. The num-ber of Protestant peers increased tenfold over the same period, from three

Table 2.2 Religious breakdown of the resident peerage[139]

	1603	1628	1641	1670	1685
Protestant	3	34	36	39	37
Catholic	24	31	32	37	38
Total	27	65	68	76	75

to over 36 (see Table 2.2). Thus the Crown ennobled a new generation of ambitious and avaricious men, largely of English and, to a lesser extent, Scottish extraction, who were determined to make their fortunes in Ireland and to secure public reward and social recognition. Lords, especially members of the traditional social and ruling elite, men like Thomond, were encouraged to serve as exemplars of civility and, whether wittingly or not, they collectively facilitated the implementation of anglicising policies on their estates across Ireland (discussed in Section I above). Yet their involvement in these processes also afforded them an opportunity to negotiate compromises that best suited their personal circumstances and political ambitions. They used these opportunities to acquire land, which in turn underpinned their status as cultural, economic, and political brokers and provided the wealth needed to sustain their status.[140] As a result, the aristocratic hierarchy ceased to be determined simply by the rank held by a peer or by other traditional criteria (such as lineage, regional status, or the number of followers over whom a lord wielded power). Instead, lordship came to reflect a peer's financial prowess, his ability to exploit his landed resources, his success in securing high office, and his capacity to network at court.

Many lords continued to have a military function, with the mightiest using brute force to exercise power locally.[141] This was often done under the guise of martial law.[142] Contemporaries, like Edmund Spenser, held that martial law was an essential tool needed for the anglicisation of Ireland.[143] They advocated for the widespread issue of martial law commissions to local sheriffs, constables, mayors, loyal peers, provosts marshals, and seneschals, giving them the power to execute on sight vagrants, felons, and 'traitors'. For her part, Elizabeth I worried that the use of summary martial law was 'hurting the imperial project' and hindering 'English imperial designs'. Yet it was still widely used as a method of governance from the late 1550s until the 1590s, especially in Ulster.[144] Davies, did his best to stop the use of martial law on the grounds that, rather than civilise, it perpetuated 'plaine tyranny'. The Irish had been 'broken and conquered by the Sword', he argued, and were now protected and governed by the law. It was the law, he noted, that would make Ireland English.[145] Despite his best efforts, martial law operated over the course of the seventeenth century. In 1638 Thomas Wentworth, earl of Strafford, suggested that 'the bad minded Irish are better contained, held in more Fear and better Duty, by one Provost Marshal, and the Terror of his executing Martial Law upon them than by twenty others, be they Justices of the Peace, or Justices of Assize, a Truth as clear in experience as can any be'.[146] No wonder historians have suggested that the arbitrary use of martial law contributed to the outbreak of rebellion in 1641.[147] Yet, as a result of these experiences in Ireland martial law was repurposed and then deployed across the English colonies in America, the Caribbean, and Bombay (discussed in Chapter 5).[148]

Of course the law underpinned the legitimacy of the state, allowing it to suppress challenges to its authority.[149] In *Solon his Follie* Richard Beacon, the Munster planter, believed in the implementation of English law and suggested that 'the more often princes shal[l] acquaint their subjects with the discipline of the lawe the more great obedience shall the subjects yeelde'.[150] Lord Chancellor William Gerrard concurred: 'For can the sword teache them to speake Englishe, to use Englishe apparel, to estrayne them from Irish exaccions'. No, he argued, 'it is the rodd of justice' that would make Ireland English.[151] As it was a system of courts replicated the English judicial hierarchy. The four central courts—exchequer, chancery, king's bench, and common pleas—functioned effectively and were located in Dublin castle, along with the court of castle chamber, which was the judicial arm of the Irish privy council. The central courts were widely used and the Dublin Chancery attracted a disproportionately large number of Catholic Gaels in the process of mediating English common law and Gaelic custom.[152] A parallel structure of prerogative courts—the court of wards and the commission for the remedy of defective titles—emerged in part as a response to the uncertainties associated with a period of war and plantation. Assize and presidency courts were established as part of the surrender and regrant process and provided justice in the localities alongside manorial courts. By 1624 the country had, one scholar suggested, a 'full establishment of justices of the peace, constables, sub-sheriffs, bailiffs, gaolers, portreeves, recorders, sovereigns and other local functionaries essential to the task of carrying out litigation'.[153]

Provincial councils, in Connacht and in Munster, also offered effective governance. With an army and a large number of officials at his disposal, the lord president enjoyed absolute authority in his own province and his commissions gave extensive powers, embracing civil, criminal, and ecclesiastical jurisdiction and the use of martial law. The council book for the province of Munster survives and vividly recaptured the extent to which the council acted as a 'civilizing' agent as it brought law and order to the province, inculcated English tenurial, economic, educational, cultural, and social practices, and promoted Protestantism.[154] In 1615 the king ordered the council of Munster and Lord President Thomond to cherish 'the reformed and civill sorte of subjects' and to instruct the 'ignorant and disobedient... to imbrace knowledge and civillitie'.[155] The earl of Clanricarde, lord president of Connacht, received a similar set of instructions.

Over the course of the early seventeenth century, anglicisation in and through the law took hold in Ireland, something that the Gaelic poetry captured. According to Brendan Kane, one poet, Donnchadh Mac Chaoilfhiaclach, 'bewailed the enslaving effects of interconnected English courts—including the Court of Wards, Exchequer, Star Chamber... King's Bench, the Bishop's Court... and assizes'.[156] In a long and very influential poem ('Tuireamh na hÉireann'), dating from the 1650s, Seán Ó Conaill, reiterated the transformational impact of English laws and the legal system:

> Dark were the laws made to afflict us,/ The court sessions with their cruel words:/ *Wardship livery* and the Court of *Exchequer*,/ ...Bonds, fines, unjust indictments,/ ...Sheriff, seneschal, and the deceitful mareschal,/ Every little law was made to convince the Gaels/ To make a *surrender* of their rights./ That's what put Conn's half in confusion:/ The Gaels took up these arms though they killed themselves with them.[157]

The sheer contempt in which some insurgents held the English, their courts, and their legal practices is reflected in mock trials which occurred during the 1640s.[158] For example, in 1644 Thomas Johnson from Mayo deposed that the insurgents brought 'the English breed of Cattle' before a man pretending to be a judge. The pretend judge asked the cattle 'if they could speake English'. The animals were then given a book to read and, when 'they stood mute & could not read', the judge condemned them to death.[159] Elsewhere, according to another deponent, 'cattle and sheep of English straine' were first tried and then slaughtered.[160] Bizarre as these animal trials may seem, this performative ridiculing of Englishness and legal imperialism gave voice to the deep-seated resentments and emotions held by ordinary people, who otherwise leave no imprint on the historical record.[161] These cow and sheep trials also formed part of a long history of ritualised violence against animals in Europe, North America, and Ireland and other depositions testify to the cruelty inflicted on these animals.[162] In this case cattle and sheep were targeted in response to changes in the Irish landscape caused by 'commercialised pastoralism', discussed in the next section.[163]

III Irish land and English economic imperialism

Edward Said argued in *Culture and Imperialism* that 'The actual geographical possession of land is what empire in the final analysis is all about'.[164] Friel captured this in an Irish context in the words of Red Hugh O'Donnell: that the land 'is the goddess that every ruler in turn is married to'.[165] A 1569 'Act for Shiring Ireland' signalled 'the arrival of English property law', the primacy of primogeniture, and the introduction of a culture of 'improvement'.[166] It is hard to overstate the significance of these developments as land, rather than control over people, became the basis for political power. Land, inherited through the practice of primogeniture when property passed from a father to his legitimate male heir, also provided the wealth that sustained a lineage. One government official, writing in the early seventeenth century, predicted that 'the love of [money] will sooner effect civility than any other persuasion'.[167] He had a point. The dissolution of the monasteries in the 1530s and 1540s, the rebellions of the sixteenth century, and the wars of the seventeenth century resulted in large swathes of Irish land being expropriated and redistributed by the Crown to favourites, to clients, to the 'deserving', and to those who needed to be paid off. In addition numerous opportunities—informal land transfers through widespread mortgages and sales—allowed for the purchase of cheap land and facilitated upward social mobility. Greedy speculators of all creeds and backgrounds grabbed lands whereever they could, which allowed for the creation of vast estates. The widespread adoption of entails, whereby land was settled on a number of persons in succession so that it could not be bequeathed at pleasure by any one possessor, created relatively stable landed bases and allowed for the emergence of powerful and enduring landed dynasties.[168]

In the medieval Irish system, land belonged to the sept rather than to individuals and partible inheritance (known as 'gavelkind') was the norm, rather than male primogeniture, which had resulted in the atomization of landholding. The creation of a landed elite in Ireland represented a significant departure from the past when status and influence were determined by the number of followers who owed loyalty to a lord and the herds of cows he owned, rather than the size of his estates.[169] Over time, surrender and regrant arrangements (discussed above in Section I) became increasingly sophisticated. Throughout the 1570s and 1580s, the state pressured leading powerbrokers to accept 'composition' agreements, which sought to demilitarize the local magnates by appealing directly to their principal followers and enhancing the power of the state in the process. Thus the 'Composition of Connacht' (1585) promoted anglicisation in the lordships of Clanricarde and Thomond and paved the way for moderate reform. Ultimately, however, it weakened—rather than strengthened—the position of the lesser landowners and enshrined in English law the 'essential characteristics of the traditional lordships'. Thus, as Bernadette Cunningham has shown, these reforming arrangements not only protected, at least in the short term, the estates of leading lords from confiscation but also represented an effective form of 'unconscious colonization'.[170]

Demands for more formal colonial enterprise and the expropriation of native lords dated from the later Middle Ages. Although rarely defined, the word 'plantation' was used freely at this time and often interchangeably with 'colony' or 'colonisation' and came to describe English policy in Ireland.[171] Early attempts at plantation during the 1550s in King's and Queen's counties, today Laois and Offaly, failed. Similarly in Ulster, efforts by Sir Thomas Smith (in the Ards) and the earl of Essex (in Clandeboye) to establish private military settlements, which would provide bulwarks against the destabilising influences exerted by the MacDonnells, ended in disaster.[172] Though unsuccessful, Smith developed a number of innovations which influenced later thinking both in Ulster and in Virginia. These included the use of promotional pamphlets and the application of a joint-stock company principle as a means of financing the colony.[173] In his writings Smith wanted to bring civility and improvement to the barbarous Irish and for him civility and economic development went hand in hand. Ireland was, according to Smith, 'a lande that floweth with milke and hony, [with] a fertile soile... whether it be manured to corne, or left to grasse...a country full of springs, riuers and lakes bothe small and greate, full of excellent fishe and foule'.[174]

After the outbreak of the Munster rebellion, plantation became an instrument of royal policy and private enterprise was put to work for the purposes of state. In 1585, shortly after the first abortive English attempt to colonise the New World, the government announced an ambitious scheme which aimed to recreate the world of south-east England on the confiscated Munster estates of the earl of Desmond. Grants of land, ranging from 4,000 to 12,000 acres, were awarded to 35 English landlords who undertook to introduce English colonists and to practise English-style agriculture based on grain growing. By the end of the sixteenth century roughly 12,000 adult settlers were actively engaged in farming.

The most avaricious and best-documented Munster speculator was Richard Boyle, later first earl of Cork.[175] A brief examination of his activities provides a glimpse of what other men on the make were doing across the Ireland, albeit not on the same scale. In 1588 Boyle arrived in Ireland virtually penniless and thanks to the patronage of Sir Geoffrey Fenton, whose daughter Boyle later married, he secured easy access to land being disposed of at rock-bottom prices.[176] Cork did all he could to improve his vast estates. He managed his natural resources carefully, especially his woodlands and waterways, and leased farms to many English tenants.[177] They in turn attracted English subtenants, who built stone or timber houses and improved their holdings. These men and women brought with them the English language, dress, social customs, technology, and agricultural practices.[178] They helped to make parts of Munster English. Yet continuity of landholding amongst established Catholic lineages is striking, even in those counties that formed part of the Munster plantation. In west Cork 40 per cent of the earl's tenants were Catholic and Irish; in Kerry the majority were.[179] Praised as a model planter, Cork undoubtedly promoted civility and anglicisation on his sprawling estates but self-interest ensured that his approach was pragmatic and measured.[180] In other words, hybridity characterised Cork as much as it did Captain Thomas Lee and Hugh O'Neill.[181]

In the wake of English victory at the end of the Nine Years' War and the Flight of the Earls (1607), Ulster met a similar fate to that of Munster. The king now had an opportunity, as one astute contemporary observed, 'not only to pull down for ever these two proud houses of O'Neill and O'Donel, but also to bring in colonies of the English to plant both countries, to a great increase of His Majesty's revenues'.[182] The state confiscated vast tracts of Ulster encompassing present day Counties Armagh, Tyrone, Fermanagh, Londonderry, Cavan, and Donegal.[183] After 1610 nearly four million acres were allocated in relatively small parcels (ranging from 1,000 to 2,000 acres) to three classes of grantees: the undertakers, the servitors, and the native freeholders. The chief responsibility for plantation fell to the 100 Scottish and English 'undertakers' and c.50 'servitors' (largely English army officers who had settled at the end of the war, together with servants of the state) in the hope that they would create a British type of rural society. The undertakers were to take possession of their holdings by late 1610 and were obliged to plant 24 adult males (English or lowland Scots) representing at least ten families for every 1,000 acres they held. Undertakers, who were to be resident for five years, and their tenants had to take the oath of supremacy and no land was to be leased either to any Irish or to any person who refused to take the oath (this changed in 1622 when the Irish were permitted to become tenants on one quarter of the undertakers' holdings). All articles concerning building, planting, and residence were to be fulfilled within five years. The servitors received land on the same conditions as the undertakers but could let land to Irish tenants since there was no requirement to plant. The third group of grantees, the native Irish freeholders (or 'deserving Irish' who had served the Crown during the Nine Years' War), held their land in the same precincts and on the same basis as the servitors but were required to farm in accordance with lowland practices. The 'deserving Irish' included cadet branches of the O'Neills and Hovendens. Additional acres were set aside to endow key 'civilising' institutions—the church, towns, schools, and Trinity College Dublin. Finally, the king obliged the City of London to colonise the entire county of Londonderry in an effort to bring capital and economic prosperity to what it perceived to be a commercial backwater.[184] This initiative occurred under the auspices of the Irish Society, a joint-stock company modelled on the 1600 charter of the East India Company and, interestingly, the membership of the Irish Society overlapped with that of the Company for much of the seventeenth century.[185]

Contemporaries made frequent comparisons between the colonisation of Ulster and North America. Lord Deputy Chichester noted in 1610 that 'I had rather labour with my hands in the plantation of Ulster, than dance or play in that of Virginia'.[186] Many shared Chichester's preference for Ireland and, certainly, the colonisation of Ireland during the early decades of the seventeenth century progressed at a faster pace than the settlement of North America. It has been estimated that prior to 1641, 100,000 people migrated to Ireland from Britain (30,000 Scots largely to Ulster and 70,000 Welsh or English migrants), which helps account for the presumed rise in the population of Ireland.[187] While the precise male/female breakdown is unknown, historians have suggested that the proportion of women was high.[188] It could well have been higher than female migrants to New Spain, where Spanish women were seen as 'civilisers' and as being key to the formation of permanent stable settlements. By the end of the sixteenth century between 28 per cent and 40 per cent of all immigrants to New Spain were female.[189] Yet the reality of plantation failed to match the king's intentions. Many settler landlords did not construct the required number of buildings, or exploited their holdings for a quick return. Colonists such as John Rowley, initially chief agent for the Londoners, and Tristram Beresford, mayor of Coleraine, illegally exported timber and illicitly felled trees for pipe staves, which they then sold. They set up breweries, mills, and tanneries without licence, alienated church lands, and rented holdings at extortionate rates to native Irish tenants. More importantly, from the government's perspective, the settlement did not generate substantial revenue, and during the reign of Charles I the wranglings over how the plantation in County Londonderry should be administered alienated members of the London business community at a time when the king desperately needed their support against his increasingly belligerent English parliament.[190]

These unintended consequences should not obscure the fact that the Crown actively encouraged Ireland's transformation from a redistributive economy to one based on money, markets, and consumption. As part of its civilising mission it promoted the development of towns which also hosted weekly markets and annual fairs and created urban networks. According to Edmund Spenser 'nothing doth sooner cause civility in any country than many market towns, by reason that people repairing often thither for their needs will daily see and learn civil manners of the better sort'.[191] Between 1600 and 1640 the Crown issued patents for 560 markets and 680 fairs. Sixty-five new patents were issued for new markets and fairs in south Munster and in Ulster 153 patents for markets and 85 for fairs were handed out.[192] Plantation thus brought a wave of Protestant corporate culture to Munster and then Ulster. The Fermanagh planter Thomas Blennerhasset captured this in his *A Direction for the plantation of Ulster* (1610) when he called for subscriptions to a joint-stock company that would oversee the plantation of Ulster (and not just Londonderry) and for the incorporation of Irish towns. As it was, during the early decades of the seventeenth century, Ulster's rate of incorporation (28 corporate towns) was second to that of England and levels of urbanization lurched from lowest to highest almost overnight. Phil Withington suggests that Ulster served 'not so much a 'laboratory' of empire [but] as a red hot crucible for precisely the kind of "civil society" that already characterized much of provincial England'.[193]

In addition to the formal Crown-sponsored plantations, an informal plantation occurred in East Ulster. In 1605 James Hamilton, first Viscount Clandeboye, and James Montgomery, first Viscount Montgomery of the Ards, both royal favourites, carved up the estates of Con O'Neill, lord of Upper Clandeboye and the Great Ards, in a tripartite agreement with O'Neill. In doing so, they created a 'Scottish Pale'. In 1625 the cartographer Thomas Raven vividly captured the progress of the plantation on Hamilton's holdings in his exquisitely detailed coloured maps of the Clandeboye estates (Figure 2.3).[194] Raven portrayed the varied nature of the land (meadow, pasture, moor), how it was farmed and divided, and showed the location of roads, the castle, gardens, deer park, orchards, houses, cottages, mills, harbour, and the prospering towns of Bangor (with 70 houses), Killyleagh (with 75 houses), and Newtown (later Newtownards with 100 houses), together with other natural features, especially bogs and woods. He depicted Scottish towers alongside English manor houses with their gables, chimneys, upper and lower storey windows, turrets, and porches.[195] Montgomery also worked hard to establish a thriving plantation, using kin and clientage links to attract settlers to the region, and to maximise local natural resources. Skilled work-men—'smiths, masons, carpenters'—built stone houses in Grey Abbey, Newtown, and Donaghadee, the main market centres of Montgomery's plantation. Trade with Scotland flourished as both entrepreneurs developed the infrastructure—harbours, mills, mines, and towns—to develop commer-cial activity along with arable and pastoral farming. As Alison Cathcart has pointed out, the early successes of the Hamilton-Montgomery plantation, while often overlooked, far exceeded that of the 1607 Jamestown plantation, and eclipsed the failed attempts to settle Roanoke, North Carolina, during the late 1580s. Moreover, the Hamilton-Montgomery plantation was 'sig-nificant in shaping the king's perspective, ensuring plantation took central place in James' civilising agenda for the North Channel context with the aim of benefiting his entire three kingdoms'.[196]

In neighbouring County Antrim, informal plantations also flourished. With an estate of over 190,000 plantation acres, the Catholic earl of Antrim was the largest landholder in Ulster and one of the largest in Ireland. The first earl's meteoric rise was largely due to his enthusiastic support for James VI and I's schemes for the plantation of Ulster. He would have been familiar with this concept because he had been fostered on the Scottish island of Arran (hence his name Randal Arranach) and thus exposed to James's unsuccessful attempts to 'plant' the troublesome Highlands with Scottish lowlanders.[197]

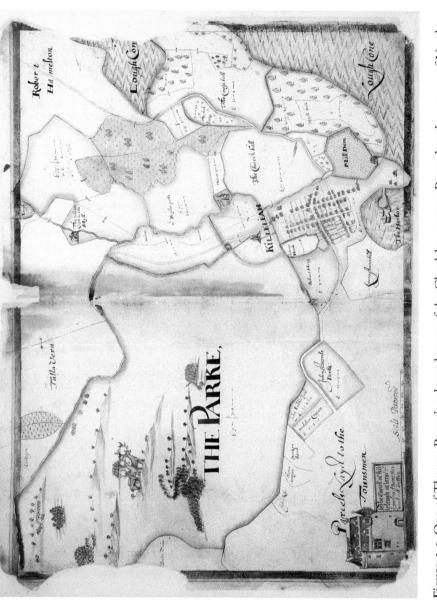

Figure 2.3 One of Thomas Raven's coloured maps of the Clandeboye estate. Reproduced courtesy of North Down Museum.

Like Gaelic lords elsewhere in Ireland, Antrim recognised the economic advantages of the English system of landlord–tenant relations and of a commercial economy, both of which were introduced with the plantation. Between 1609 and 1626 he leased considerable amounts of land to lowland Scots and within a relatively short period of time there was a thriving colony of Scottish Protestants living in the baronies of Dunluce and Glenarm.[198] A 1611 report suggested that the nearby town of Dunluce comprised 'tenements after the fashion of the Pale' and the earl built a Protestant church close by. An archaeological dig has recovered part of the town, which was clearly planned and laid out on a grid with two cobbled streets that were ten-metre-wide streets with drains at each side. There was a large courthouse, rows of stone and timber houses, a large masonry two-storey house with a gable fireplace, glazed windows, and indoor privy.[199] The earl's farsighted policies soon paid off and in 1629 it was noted that he 'hath good tenants and is very well paid his rents'.[200] The elaborate nature of the settlement and the scale of the first earl's investment was a tribute to private enterprise, something that his son, the second earl and later marquis continued. On numerous occasions the king thanked him for 'his services in improving those barren and uncultivated parts of the country, and planting a colony there'.[201] The Antrims were not the only Catholic lords to colonise, commercialise, and 'civilise'. His neighbour—Sir Henry O'Neill of Clandeboye who had married Martha, daughter of Francis Stafford, a local English official, extended and renovated their medieval tower house at Edenduffcarrick in County Antrim.[202] Rose O'Neill, his heir and daughter, later married as his second wife the marquis of Antrim.

Antrim and O'Neill were typical of many Catholic Gaels who quickly realised that, in order to survive and be considered 'worthy subjects', they had no alternative but to accept the new commercial economic order inherent in the Crown's civilising and improving initiatives. Many borrowed heavily, using their estates as collateral, to finance their new lifestyles. On the eve of the Irish rebellion of October 1641, indebtedness plagued people—native, newcomer, Catholic, and Protestant—across the country.[203] When asked why he had wanted to rebel Lord Maguire, one of the leaders of the 1641 rising, attributed his action to the 'the smallness of my estate', which was diminished as a result of plantation, and the fact that he was 'overwhelmed in debt'.[204] Maguire, like so many others, had engaged in excessive conspicuous consumption during the early decades of the seventeenth century and had mortgaged his estates to fund his spending.[205]

Similarly, Robert Hovendon, who had received lands on the grounds that he was 'deserving' (despite his brother Harry's associations with Hugh O'Neill), along with his stepson Sir Phelim O'Neill, borrowed heavily to fund an anglicised lifestyle. Their borrowings, secured by mortgages, were recorded in the statute staple and a number of '1641 Depositions' mentioned outstanding debts in excess of a hefty £10,000. O'Neill, like Maguire, had little to lose and everything to gain by leading the rebellion that broke out on 22 October 1641.[206]

The 1641 rebellion, which resulted in a decade of independence from English rule, had many long- and short-term causes, including a desire to reverse the processes, policies, and trappings associated with anglicisation. According to Gerard Boate, author of *Irelands Naturall History* (1657), 'those barbarians, the natural inhabitants of Ireland' wanted to use the 1641 rebellion to 'extinguish the memory' of the English 'and of all the civility and good things by them introduced amongst that wild nation'. So the insurgents demolished recently built houses, gardens, orchards, enclosures, ironworks and killed English breeds of cows and sheep.[207] The '1641 Depositions' bear witness to grass-roots attempts to reject every aspect of anglicisation. They recorded the frustration that the Irish language was being eroded, that Irish place names were being replaced with English ones, that commercialisation had resulted in widespread indebtedness, and that some members of the elite had converted to Protestantism.[208]

In his deposition Dr Robert Maxwell from Armagh recounted how Sir Phelim O'Neill had explained to him what the insurgents hoped to achieve by rebelling. They wanted liberty of conscience and asked that all tithes paid by Catholics should support the Catholic clergy. They requested that the lord deputy, privy councillors, judges, and justices of the peace be of 'the Irish nation'; that all plantations since 1603 be voided; and that 'All strangers (meaneing brittish) to be restrayned from comeing over'. They asked that the standing army should be stood down and all fortifications and strongholds surrendered to the Irish; that an independent parliament should repeal Poynings' Law and all anti-Catholic legislation. In addition, Sir Phelim requested for himself 'the Earledome of Tirone', along 'with all the antient patrymonie and priviledges belonging to the o Neales'.[209] In short, according to Maxwell, Sir Phelim wanted to turn the clock back to the turn of the seventeenth century and to pick up where Hugh O'Neill had left off. Even though Sir Phelim O'Neill's voice was refracted through Maxwell's deposition, it nonetheless rang true and resonated with later confederate calls for freedom of religion, the opportunity to serve the Crown in trusted legal, military, and civic roles, and an independent parliament no longer shackled by Poynings' Law.[210]

As a member of the elite and as a former MP, O'Neill's commitment to the institution of parliament comes as no surprise. More radical was *Pairlement Chlionne Tomáis* (the parliament of Clan Thomas), a complex work of bawdy satire written during the early decades of the seventeenth century. The first part featured rural labourers from Clan Thomas at imagined parliaments held in County Kerry in 1632 and 1645. The second part, written by a different author in the early 1660s, described a fictional parliament of labourers, small tenants, and tradesmen from Leinster and eastern Munster, that sat near Mullingar during the 1650s and showed unbounded admiration for Oliver Cromwell. The authors ridiculed everything and everyone associated with England: the upwardly mobile pretensions of the lower orders, those who wore English fashions, bought up land, educated their children, smoked tobacco, spoke English, used English courts, engaged in conspicuous consumption, and curried favour with English patrons. They mocked parliamentary proceedings, the drafting of legislation, and the operation of the ecclesiastical and civil courts: 'We reject the sheriff's court,/the court-leet and great sessions,/all except the cottier-royal's court,/that sits at the feast of Christmas'.[211]

This scathing response to anglicisation resonated with the writings of the *literati*.[212] Geoffrey Keating in *Foras Feasa* sought to refute the negative representations of the Irish propagated by Giraldus Cambrensis and other hostile commentators (discussed below in Chapter 5). Keating compared them to a dung beetle:

> For it is the fashion of the beetle, when it lifts its head in the summertime, to go about fluttering, and not to stoop towards any delicate flower that may be in the field, or any blossom in the garden, though they be all roses or lilies, but it keeps bustling about until it meets with dung of cow or horse, and proceeds to wallow in it.[213]

Many members of the traditional learned classes, like Keating, reeling in the wake of political (but not intellectual) collapse, clearly abhorred the changes wrought by colonial processes and did what they could to challenge colonial authority.[214] Two Ulster poets, Fearghal Óg Mac an Bhaird and Eoghan Ruadh Mac an Bhaird, closely associated with O'Neill and O'Donnell, bore witness to their exile and used this as a metaphor for the wider political and cultural crisis and trauma Gaelic Ireland experienced in the wake of the displacement caused by the flight of the earls.[215] Lochlainn Ó Dálaigh, a poet from Bréifne (modern-day Cavan) recorded how 'a proud and impure swarm of strangers' divided the land 'into acres' and turned 'dark thickets of the chase...into streets'.[216] Others vented their spleen against the new-comers, whom they regarded as low-born thugs and as 'English-speaking bastards' who were drawn, according to John Lynch, 'from the barbers' shops, and highways, and taverns, and stables and hogsties of England'.[217]

Rather than turning the clock back, the 1641 rebellion paved the way for military conquest and after 1649 England subjected Ireland to an unprecedented level of political and economic control. The Cromwellians executed Charles I and abolished the Irish parliament; instead 30 MPs from Ireland sat in an imperial parliament in London. They transported thousands of Catholic soldiers to Continental Europe for service in European armies. They ordered that all persons regarded as dangerous to the state, together with paupers and vagabonds, be transported to English colonies in the Atlantic.[218] Large numbers of Catholics and royalists were transplanted west of the River Shannon and others sought refuge on the Continent as part of the royalist court in exile.

The land settlement of the 1650s represented another ambitious attempt to plant Ireland. The Adventurers' Act (March 1642) began the process of expropriation by offering Protestant speculators, adventurers, 2,500,000 acres. Legislation the following year allotted parliamentary soldiers serving in Ireland land in lieu of their pay on the same terms as the adventurers. In order to recompense these soldiers and adventurers the English parliament stipulated in the Act of Settlement (August 1652) that virtually all land held by Catholics should be confiscated and that many of the dispossessed should be transplanted to Connacht.[219] The revolution in Irish landholding, which began with the plantations of the early seventeenth century and culminated with the Cromwellian and later the Restoration land settlements, resulted in the wholesale transfer of land—roughly eight million acres in all—from Catholic to Protestant hands and was one of the key developments that shaped the face of modern Ireland. Catholic landholding dropped from about 54 per cent in 1641 to 23 per cent in c.1670.[220] Control of land, people, and natural resources allowed the state to promote with even greater impact English tenurial and agricultural practices, along with proto-industrialisation. Moreover, Irish land—and the private enterprise that it spawned—funded English imperialism in Ireland and beyond, something discussed at length in Chapter 4.[221] Ireland was well and truly embedded in an economic structure that was oppressive and one that came to characterise the later British empire and emerging capitalist structures of power.

A new order founded on English economic, legal, administrative, political, and landed structures, the English language, and English culture had been established. From the mid-1650s London emerged as a major financial and commercial centre; trade increasingly became a determining reason of state; and Ireland's colonial status became more apparent still. Priorities shifted from conquest, colonization, cultivation, and civilization to economic protectionism but the reality of English imperialism in Ireland remained firmly grounded on English economic and political domination.[222] The Navigation Acts, especially of 1651, 1660, 1663, and 1696, created, in the words of Peter Marshall, 'an imperial trading system that remained essentially in force until the nineteenth century'.[223] Only English ships engaged in colonial trade and European goods destined for England's colonies had to pass through London.[224] To the English economist and politician Charles Davenant, the subjugation of Ireland and other colonies to England, the 'mother country', was non-negotiable, as was the regulation of all aspects of trade.[225]

Writers, like the poet Fearflatha Ó Gnímh, who at the turn of the seventeenth century lamented that Ireland had become 'a new England in all but name', may have been appalled by the changes wrought by military conquest and colonisation but they were powerless to stop them, never mind to reverse them.[226] Ó Gnímh was closely associated with the O'Neills of Clandeboye whose kinsman, Sir Neil O'Neill of Killyleagh in County Down, was painted by John Michael Wright, probably in 1680 when the artist visited Dublin.[227] In an intriguing portrait (Figure 2.4) Wright depicted O'Neill as an Irish chieftain in a loose white tunic, red 'trews' with an exquisite fringed, stylised 'mantle' wrapped around his body. He held a 'dart' (or spear) in his right hand, his left hand rested on a circular shield, and a sword was at this waist. Behind him, to the left, an unidentified attendant held similar weapons. Beside him stood an Irish wolfhound, a highly prized hunting dog. A rare suit of Japanese armour lay at this feet which may, as some have suggested, signified O'Neill's commitment to Catholicism but also invited us to imagine the exotic. The portrait evoked the 1580s and John Derricke's stereotype woodcut of an Irish chieftain, with a mantle over his stitched tunic and conical hat, dart in his hand with his attendant at his side and another holding his horse (Figure 2.5). It also exudes Englishness

Figure 2.4 Sir Neil O'Neill by John Michael Wright. Reproduced courtesy of Tate Britain in London.

Figure 2.5 John Derricke's woodcut image (plate 1) of the Irish chieftain (*The Image of Irelande, with a Discoverie of Woodkarne* (1581)). Reproduced courtesy of the University of Edinburgh.

and civility: the ornateness of the intricate embroidery on the tunic, the richness of the fabric, the plumed headgear, and the rather delicate shoes. Just as Gheerhaerts had done with Lee, Wright captures O'Neill's hybridity. The artist presented O'Neill as an anglicised nobleman yet one who valued his religion, his heritage, and his Irishness. What is missing is any indication of his relationship with the Crown but O'Neill's death at the Battle of the Boyne in July 1690 in the service of James II underscored his loyalty to the house of Stuart.[228] For O'Neill, like so many others, devotion to the king was also core to his identity.

In conclusion, it is important to note that the processes that underpinned anglicisation in Ireland were not unique. In seventeenth-century Formosa (modern-day Taiwan) the Dutch Vereenigde Oostindische Compagnie (VOC) colonised, commercialised, and did all they could to 'civilise' and Christianise.[229] 'Hispanicisation' and the imposition on indigenous peoples of a language, way of life, religion, legal authority, and intrusive forms of government characterised the Spanish colonial world.[230] Anglicisation—and the cultural, linguistic, legal, and economic imperatives associated with it—also characterised English and later British imperialism in their other colonies in the Atlantic, Asia, and Africa (discussed in Chapter 5). And, of course, in Ireland anglicisation did not end in 1690 with the establishment of the Protestant Ascendancy and the implementation of penal legislation against dissenters, but remained a feature of life in Ireland despite efforts by cultural nationalists, including Douglas Hyde, to 'de-anglicise' Ireland.

3

Assimilation

In *Making History* Brian Friel placed great emphasis on the domestic and gave strong voices to women, especially Mabel and her sister, Mary. The play opened with the marriage in August 1591 of Hugh O'Neill, earl of Tyrone, to his third wife Mabel Bagenal, the daughter of a Protestant military governor based in Newry but originally a tailor from Staffordshire. O'Neill had married outside his tribe and below his rank. Twenty years his junior, Mabel too crossed ethnic, social, cultural, and religious boundaries by wedding a Catholic Gael, vilified by her people for being 'wild and barbarous'. Her family disowned her. In a letter back to London, Henry, her brother, acknowledged his sense of shame 'that my blood which in my father and myself hath often been spilled in repressing this rebellious race, should now be mingled with so traitorous a stock and kindred'.[1]

In *Making History* Friel imagined the response of O'Neill's closest kin and allies to the news of the marriage, which was conducted by the Protestant bishop of Meath. His son-in-law, Red Hugh O'Donnell, exploded: 'Hold on, Hugh—wait now—wait—wait. You can't marry into the Upstarts! And a sister of the Butcher Bagenal! Jesus, man'. He continued, 'Keep her for a month, Hugh—like that McDonald woman—that's the very job—keep her for a month and then kick her out...She won't mind, Hugh, honest to God. That's what she'll expect. Those New English are all half tramps. Give her some clothes and a few shillings and kick her back home to Staffordshire'.[2] Equally aghast, Peter Lombard, Catholic archbishop of Armagh, reflected on the political fallout in Madrid and Rome of the 'association'. Furious with them both, O'Neill responded:

> I have married a very talented, a very spirited, a very beautiful young woman. She has left her people to join me here. They will never forgive her for that. She is under this roof now, among a people she has been reared to believe are

wild and barbarous. I am having a celebration tonight when I will introduce her to my people. I particularly ask you to welcome her here. But if that is beyond you, I demand at least civility.[3]

The symbolism of the marriage—between a Gaelic prince and upstart Protestant planter—and Friel's attempt to create a space for people from different communities and classes to come together, to compromise, to forge shared cultural identities, and to reconcile, would not have been lost—in 1988—on audiences who had already experienced twenty years of bitter and bloody war in Northern Ireland.

Unlike the playwright, historians have paid little attention to the role women, children, and the family played in empire, focusing instead on a political narrative that privileges the stories of men of power and influence.[4] As Philippa Levine and others have noted, empire was predominately a masculine space and one that obscured colonial women and colonised peoples.[5] Yet gender is of central importance in understanding the complex processes at work even if the archives leave women in the shadows. The challenges associated with the nature of the historical record have been tackled in the pioneering work of Ann Laura Stoler, who has put great emphasis on reading colonial archives 'against their grain'.[6] Marisa Fuentes, who looks at enslaved women in Barbados, takes the conversation a step further by suggesting that we need to read the sources 'along the bias grain' and to mine 'archival silences'.[7] While the importance of 'dethroning inter-pretive paradigms' that privilege the masculine and colonial perspective has long been acknowledged,[8] scholars of early modern Ireland, with a few notable exceptions, have paid little attention to the study of women, children, and marriage.[9] The recent focus on elite women in Ireland, with some of the most important studies by literary scholars, is welcome but what of more 'ordinary', non-elite women?[10] This neglect has been attributed to the nature of the historical sources, an excuse that no longer suffices, especially in the light of the riches available as a result of digitisation and the growing impetus to interrogate evidence from 'colonial' archives 'against the grain'.[11]

Women in colonial Ireland are the focus of this chapter, which explores assimilation and integration, together with the everyday relationships between colonised and coloniser. Two works of literature—the first Irish play, *Landgartha*, and the first Irish novel, *Vertue Rewarded*—bookend the chapter. Sections I and IV use these remarkable works to review the trad-itional configurations of kingdom, colony, and empire through the prism of women.[12] Though *Landgartha* touches on it, marriage across ethnic, social, and religious boundaries and the extent to which this fostered integration and assimilation is explored in greater depth in Section II. Section III examines the lived experiences of 'ordinary', non-elite women during times of peace and then during the bitter colonial war of the 1640s. It suggests that warfare, when all cultural norms were suspended, exposed the inner workings of a society and made visible women who were previously hidden, albeit often in plain sight.[13] By exploring more everyday issues—of literacy, landholding, and labour as well as material culture and moneylending—it moves beyond the 'colonised'/'coloniser' stereotypes and recognises that women, from all ethnic and religious backgrounds, were often the social glue that held together families and communities. Throughout, the emphasis is on assimilation but this chapter never loses sight of how women experienced endemic violence and intense warfare or the expropriation and exploitation that characterised early modern Ireland.

I The first Irish play

The seventeenth-century equivalent of *Making History* was a play called *Landgartha. A Tragie-Comedy, as it was presented in the new Theater in Dublin, with good applause, being an Ancient story* by Henry Burnell, a Catholic playwright. It was, as Deana Rankin points out, a play about reconciliation in which 'diverse ethnic and confessional groups might be united, even subsumed in a shared notion of the public good'.[14] The performance in Werburgh Street Theatre on St Patrick's Day 1640 coincided with the opening session of the Dublin Parliament, which had taken place the day before.[15] It was also the first Irish play by an Irish playwright and remarkably included two Latin poems, one in hexameters and one in elegiac couplets, by Eleanora, Burnell's daughter.[16] *Landgartha* was a tragicomedy set in the Scandinavian multiple monarchy, where a group of Norwegian Amazons (who represent the Old English) were at war with the king of Denmark (representing England) and Sweden (representing Scotland).[17] It was staged in 1640, during the final 'Swedish' phase of the Thirty Years' War (1618–48) then raging on the Continent and on the eve of the colonial war in Ireland, which broke out in October 1641.[18]

Like *Making History*, *Landgartha* featured strong women, the Amazons, led by Landgartha. It immediately tapped into Greek mythology, where the

Amazons formed a community of fiercely independent and courageous women, but also wider global imaginaries that were being played out by people from Ireland living in the Amazon (discussed in Chapter 4) and by publications like *Discoverie of Guiana* (1596), by the Munster planter and English adventurer, Walter Raleigh. This circulated widely and featured female Amazon warriors living in Guiana, 'a country that hath yet her maidenhead'.[19] The play opened with Frollo, the king of Sweden, raping one of the Amazons. Having taken the woman's 'maydenhead', Frollo—this 'blacke devill'—denigrated the Amazons as 'Furies and plagues: these wild, wild bloudy whores'.[20] Landgartha, leader of the Amazons, though power-less to stop Frollo, dismissed him as 'libidinous Woolfe, foule Tyrant'.[21] Landgartha then married King Reyner of Denmark, reminding the audi-ence of the Old English commitment to the Stuart king, Charles I. Almost immediately Reyner deserted Landgartha and committed bigamy by marry-ing Vraca, a daughter of Frollo, the Swedish king and rapist. Landgartha responded by telling Reyner that she was his 'only lawfull wife'.[22] At the end of the play Landgartha again reminded Reyner, who had now repledged his faithfulness, of how he had wronged her. She also refused to reconsummate the marriage and warned him of the limitations of her loyalty: 'my heart shall still receive you; But on my word, / The rest of my body you shall not enjoy, sir'.[23]

The messages for the audiences who watched, and later read, *Landgartha* were threefold. First, Burnell made it clear that Ireland was England's only loyal wife. Here Burnell could have been invoking the famous 'I am the husband' speech that King James VI and I gave in 1603 to the Westminster parliament.[24] Interestingly, some of the bardic poets used this metaphor of James as Ireland's rightful spouse,[25] as did Richard Bellings, the Old English lawyer and politician, when he wrote *A Sixth Booke to the Countesse of Pembrokes Arcadia* (Dublin 1624), a sequel to Sir Philip Sidney's *Arcadia*.[26] The Galway lawyer and MP Patrick Darcy did likewise in his 1641 address to the Irish parliament. In his *Argument* (later published in Waterford in 1643), Darcy stressed the importance of trust between husband and wife and called for Ireland's legislative independence as a separate kingdom in the Stuart composite monarchy: 'The trust betweene the King and his people is threefold; First as betweene Soveraigne and Subject, Secondly, as betweene a Father and his Children... Thirdly, as betweene Husband and wife, this trust is comprehensive of the whole body politicke'.[27] Darcy argued that despite a series of disappointments and betrayals—namely the failure of the

Crown to approve concessions to Catholics (known as the 'Graces') and the high-handed nature of the administration in Ireland during the 1630s under Thomas Wentworth, earl of Strafford—the Catholic Irish remained the king's trustworthy servants. This loyalty was, however, conditional, something that Landgartha had made clear and the outbreak of rebellion in October 1641 underscored.

The second thing that is so striking about *Landgartha* is how Ireland is feminised, a well-established trope later seized upon by Irish nationalists as they developed the image of 'Mother Ireland'.[28] The opening scene and troubling image of rape is significant given that the 1640 parliament addressed the matter of rape when it revisited a decree of 1613.[29] Moreover, bardic poets had for decades invoked images of defenceless Ireland being violated by foreigners. In one of Aonghus Ó Dalaigh's poems Ireland is viewed 'as a harlot' because 'every man is raping her', leaving her as a 'woman who has children with no father'.[30] Less graphic is the *aisling* poetry of the eighteenth century, where Ireland was depicted as a beautiful woman expecting deliverance from a foreign country (in this case, France).[31] The metaphor of Ireland as a virgin 'waiting fertilisation or penetration by English colonists' was, according to Mary O'Dowd, common in colonial discourse as Raleigh's discussion of Guiana illustrated.[32] In *A Discourse of Ireland* (1620) the English administrator, Luke Gernon, suggested that Ireland 'wants a husband' who would embrace her and hedge and ditch her landscape.[33] This feminisation of conquered territory was part of a conscious effort to justify territorial expansion on the grounds that the colonised nation was incapable of ruling itself, lacking the necessary masculine attribute of responsible governance.

No doubt many in the audience—both during the 1640 performance in Dublin and later reading the version published in 1641—would also have been familiar with the acts of extreme sexual violence committed by the Swedes and other protagonists in Germany, where interestingly cities were feminised.[34] Pamphlets, like the *Lamentations of Germany* (1638), replete with graphic images designed to stir emotions, circulated widely. They became particularly relevant in an Irish context with the publication in 1642 of James Cranford's *The Teares of Ireland*. In one harrowing woodcut a soldier pinned against a wall a young girl, with her legs spread and skirts raised, and the caption explained how the insurgents 'deflowered her one after another'.[35] Another broadsheet from 1647 entitled *A prospect of bleeding Irelands miseries* depicted a woman at prayer with her hair and clothing dishevelled

Figure 3.1 Broadsheet from 1647 entitled *A prospect of bleeding Irelands miseries.*
Reproduced courtesy of the British Library in London.

and her breasts exposed, suggesting that she had been violated (see
Figure 3.1). She was surrounded by corpses and speech bubbles testify to the
sorrow she feels at having lost her children and loved ones. The woman
represented Ireland, a country now bereft and despoiled, with families and
communities completely shattered. Even if the context was different, the

image of Ireland as a violated woman persisted into the eighteenth century. In *The Story of the Injured Lady*, Jonathan Swift's 'lady'—defenceless Ireland— was shabbily treated by her lover who acted 'like a Conqueror' and exploited her estate.[36]

By focusing on Landgartha and her Amazons and by featuring his daughter's Latin poems, Burnell, according to Nessa Malone, put centre stage matters 'relating to family and womanhood, namely bigamy, wifehood, daughterhood and virtue'.[37] Discussions of bigamy were to the fore in 1640. Five years earlier, in 1635, the Irish parliament had passed legislation that made bigamy a criminal offence, undermining as it did the legitimacy of primogeniture, legal rights to property, and the very stability of colonial Ireland.[38] Burnell also used *Landgartha* to respond to some of the most negative representations of Irish women. As Clare Carroll reminded us in her pioneering work, *Circe's Cup*, during the early decades of the century the New English portrayed Irish women as 'bewitching, sexually seductive, and morally debilitating'. These writers used the image of 'Circe's cup' as a metaphor for the loss of human identity, as men were turned into swine through intercourse with a female goddess. This, in turn, justified English domination.[39] Edmund Spenser's *A View of the Present State of Ireland* represented the country, according to Carroll, as 'a feminized, culturally barbaric, and economically intractable society that must be subjected to complete cultural and economic destruction and reorganization by the English colonists'.[40] In his epic poem, *The Faerie Queen*, which had been framed by his experiences in Ireland, Spenser told the story of Radigund, a rebellious Amazonian queen, whom the English determined to civilise.[41] It is tempting to suggest that Burnell's Landgartha was a direct response to Spenser's Radigund, a work that Burnell would undoubtedly have been familiar with. Certainly the person of Landgartha—virtuous, loyal, honest, and strong— challenged hostile portrayals of Irish women as filthy, rude, barbaric, promiscuous, and politically subversive.[42] By focusing on Reyner's bigamy, the play confronted those commentators who had systematically vilified the Irish for their sexual practices, including allegations of bigamy, which flew in the face of English insistence on primogeniture and the legitimacy of marriage.[43]

This brings us to the third key message of the play: the significance of marriage as a force of integration and assimilation. Burnell used the play to celebrate the coming together of native Irish and Old English especially in the Pale. At the wedding celebration for Reyner and Landgartha he introduced the character of Marfisa, who wildly performed the whip of

Dunboyne, a well-known dance from Burnell's home in Fingal, north of Dublin.[44] In other words, the playwright—himself the son of a Gaelic-speaking mother and an Old English father—used the play to celebrate the cultural assimilation that had occurred between the Gaelic Irish and Old English. Burnell consolidated his links to the Old English elite with his marriage to Frances Dillon, sister of the second earl of Roscommon, who had conformed to Protestantism, and whose son, later third earl, married the youngest daughter of Lord Deputy Thomas Wentworth, earl of Strafford.

This level of cultural assimilation was not unusual, as the example of the FitzGeralds, earls of Kildare, Ireland's premier aristocratic family, also illustrates. The ninth earl of Kildare's library contained 61 Gaelic manuscripts, mostly devotional; only seven works were in English.[45] Upon her arrival at Maynooth castle his English bride learned Irish to the point where she could read, write, and speak the language fluently, something celebrated in the 'Primer of the Irish language', which was prepared at the request of Queen Elizabeth I.[46] Similarly, another leading Old English family from the Pale—the Nugents, barons of Delvin—may have dispatched Christopher (1544–1602) to Cambridge and his brother, William, to Oxford—but they supported the Gaelic school of poetry run by Ó Cobhthaigh bards at Uisneach near Delvin. Mícheál Mac Craith has shown how the poetry of William Nugent is 'remarkable in its fusion of Gaelic culture with Catholicism and in its assumption that this Gaelic Catholic patrimony belongs to both those of Gaelic origin and those of Old English stock'.[47] On the face of it, the onset of the Protestant reformation complicated the situation. It was one matter to marry across ethnic boundaries, but quite another to cross religious ones. Yet the evidence suggests that mixed marriages were remarkably widespread, especially amongst the elite, and readily accepted by contemporaries.[48] Commentators, both Catholic and Protestant, repeatedly highlighted the very real links of kinship—together with friendship and mutual indebtedness—that united Irish society on the eve of the 1641 rebellion.[49]

In a radical departure from earlier denunciations Sir William Petty, writing in the early 1670s, suggested that marriages between Irish men and English women would result in 'the transmuting one People into the other, and the thorough and lasting union of interests upon natural and lasting principles'. Petty viewed women as the key influencers over the next generation and argued that they would teach their children the English language, culture, manners, and, ideally, religion.[50] In other words these English

women would 'civilise' the male population. As the father of political economy, Petty touted a disturbing and radical form a colonialism that literally
exploited the body for colonial and economic purposes. English subjects
would dissolve into the majority population but retain and foster their
identity, while the indigenous population would reach an advanced level of
'civilisation'.[51] It is quite remarkable that Petty seemed incapable of imagining that his scheme could work the other way around, making the English
women more Irish, as the examples of the Bagenal sisters illustrate (Section II
below).[52]

Unlike Petty, most New English writers of the day saw intermarriage as
a route to degeneration. Fynes Moryson, secretary to Lord Mountjoy, suggested 'friendship and marriages' between the Old English and 'the mere
Irish', resulted in 'dayly more degenerating from the English' and the acquir-
ing of 'the Customes, manners, language, and apparell of the mere Irish'.[53]
Spenser concurred and in *A View of the Present State of Ireland* suggested that
fosterage and marriage 'are two most dangerous infections'.[54] It was women,
he argued, who had 'the trust and care of all things both at home and in
the fields'.[55] He suggested that the 'Childe that sucketh the milk of the
[Irish-speaking] nurse must of necessity learne his first speech of her'. Even
if the child was later taught English, 'the smack of the first will always abide
with him and not only of the speech, but also of the manners and conditions. For besides the young children be like apes, which will affect and
imitate what they see'.[56] Another English commentator, Barnaby Rich,
agreed and added that wives and mothers were the guardians of Catholicism
and that their babies were 'nuzeled from their cradles in the very piddle of
Popery'.[57]

Fears that Irish women would result in cultural degeneration also crossed
the Atlantic. In the 1620s the lord deputy of Ireland, Henry Cary, Viscount
Falkland, stipulated that all female immigrants to English colonies should be
English, 'speake onlie the pure Englishe tounge', and be Protestant. He continued that well-educated English women 'will maintaine the language to
ther children & then it is noe great matter of wha[t] nation the men bee soe
the women bee Englishe'.[58] This emphasis on English women as agents of
'civility' resonated with Sir William Petty's ideas about transmutation.
Interestingly, Iberian officials held that women were 'civilisers' and key to
the formation of permanent stable settlements in the Atlantic.[59] As a result,
from the 1530s, an increasing number of women left Spain for the Atlantic
colonies, reaching 16.5 per cent in 1560 and increasing to 40 per cent by the

end of the century. In all, between 1500 and 1700, Susan Socolow has suggested that '2,900 Spanish women arrived in America each year'. The number of Portuguese women migrating to Brazil was lower but still significant and 'probably more than 100,000 Portuguese women made their way across the Atlantic, an average of about 500 per year'.[60]

In a book entitled *Colonial Intimacies* Anne Marie Plane suggests that marriage formed part of a 'colonial toolkit' in early modern New England even if no marriage is known to have occurred between an English settler and Indian before 1679.[61] With the major exception of the marriage in 1614 between the English adventurer, John Rolfe, and the Algonquin princess, Mataoka (or Pocahontas, as many know her), the same held true for Virginia. Mataoka was the favourite daughter of Chief Powhatan who had been captured by the English and who later converted to Christianity, taking the name Rebecca.[62] As it was, worries about degeneracy and invoking God's ire for marrying 'strange wives', as the sons of Levi and Israel have done, plagued Rolfe prior to his wedding.[63] In contrast, as John Elliott and others have shown, in New Spain the Crown sanctioned inter-ethnic marriage to 'help realize Spain's mission of bringing Christianity and civility to the peoples of the Indies'.[64] That said, some, like Spenser in Ireland, feared that the use of Indian wet nurses in Creole homes could have negative consequences since the child would learn Indian habits 'imbibed with the milk'.[65] It was the nineteenth century before discussions about inter-racial unions and anxieties about degeneracy, which became 'fears of white impoverishment', developed fully but they had their origins in these earlier exchanges where the experience of Ireland featured.[66]

II Intermarriage

Stepping back from the hostile rhetoric, this section focuses on the actual experiences of marriages that crossed confessional, ethnic, and social boundaries. If intermarriage is, as sociologists suggest, both an index and a method of assimilation between ethnic and religious groups, the importance of marriage in early modern Ireland cannot be overstated. Consider by way of example the marriages of Mabel Bagenal and her sisters.[67] Mabel was born in Newry, County Armagh, the youngest of 11 children and the sixth daughter of Sir Nicholas Bagenal and his Welsh wife, Eleanor Griffith of Penrhyn. Clearly infatuated with O'Neill, Mabel willingly eloped with him from her sister's home at Turvey in north County Dublin in July 1591. On 3 August the Church of Ireland bishop of Meath married them. Cast out by her family and denied her dowry of £1,000, details of Mabel's married life are sparse but O'Neill's fourth wife, Catherine Magennis, later complained about his drunken abuse.[68] In 1595 Mabel, who had converted to Catholicism, died childless, after four short years of marriage. Peter Lombard in *De Hibernia Commentarius* noted her piety: 'Whatever may have been the religion in which she was brought up by her own people, it is certain that having wedded this prince, she was so well instructed in her home by Catholic priests that she lived most piously and died a most holy death'.[69]

Of Mabel's five sisters, the marriages of three are documented. Anne Bagenal married first Sir Dudley Loftus (1561–1616), who served as lord chancellor, and then Dominick Sarsfield, Viscount Kilmallock.[70] Sarsfield was a lawyer and judge, who nominally conformed but whose heir was a practising Catholic. Two of Mabel's sisters married high-profile Catholics, albeit of Old English, rather than Gaelic provenance. One (unnamed) sister wed the distinguished lawyer and MP, Sir Christopher Plunkett (1568–*c*.1636) of Donsoghly, County Dublin, who led Catholic opposition in the 1613 parliament. She bore him five sons, one of whom studied for the priesthood in Douai and another served in the Spanish Army of Flanders. Finally, Mary, who featured in *Making History*, in 1582 married Sir Patrick Barnewall (?1531–1622), a bachelor then in his early 50s. Sir Patrick had remained loyal to the queen during the Nine Years' War but led Catholic opposition to government policies during the early decades of the seventeenth century. The couple lived at Turvey, in north County Dublin, and they had three daughters and a son.[71] Their son and heir, Nicholas, named after his maternal grandfather, later became Viscount Kingsland (1592–1663). Nicholas had been educated at Douai in the Spanish Netherlands and in 1611 entered Gary's Inns in London. In 1617 Nicholas married Brigid (d. *c*.1661), the widow of Rory O'Donnell, earl of Tyrconnell, brother of Red Hugh O'Donnell, and a daughter of Henry FitzGerald, twelfth earl of Kildare. When Rory fled to the Continent in 1607 he had left behind Brigid, who was heavily pregnant. It is not clear whether the son and heir Brigid bore to Nicholas Barnewall was called Henry after his uncle. However, it seems likely since Sir Patrick held the wardship of Arthur, Henry's mentally disabled son, who became his heir when he died in 1598.[72] Interestingly, Brigid and Nicholas named one of their daughters Mabel. In 1637 young Mabel married Christopher Plunkett, second earl of Fingal, head of one of the most important Old

English families of the Pale.[73] Lady Mabel Fingal was an ardent Catholic, something that her willingness to offer refuge to a priest during the 1650s underscored.[74]

To all intents and purposes these Bagenal women, daughters of a Protestant planter, had become part of the established ruling Old English elite and embraced Catholicism with real zeal. There is a fascinating exchange, probably dating from the late 1640s, between Lady Brigid Barnewall, Mary Bagenal's daughter-in-law, and Susanna Stockdale, a Protestant kinswoman. In an undated deposition Susanna related how, when the rebellion broke out, her 'neere kindred', the Catholic Barnewalls of Turvey, had fled for safety to Wales (Nicholas's maternal grandmother was a Welsh Protestant), returning only after the conclusion of the ceasefire in September 1643. Lady Barnewall welcomed Susanna to their house in Castle Street, in Dublin, and invited her to join their household. When Susanna refused, Lady Barnewall replied 'in some angrie & scornfull words' that: 'Noe, noe, I am glad of it, for god would never blesse the howse if you were in it in regard of your Religion'. Lady Barnewall's priest, Father John, who was also present added that there was no point in trying to convert Susanna: 'she hath been long enough in handleing, but none could convert her'.[75]

The marriages of the Bagenal women are also interesting examples of upward social mobility. Within a generation the daughters of Thomas Kilroy's 'imperial tailor' turned soldier from Staffordshire had entered the ranks of the Irish nobility, with Mabel and his granddaughter, also Mabel, becoming countesses. This was not untypical. Across Ireland recently ennobled Protestant lords married off their daughters to members of the ancient but usually impoverished Catholic nobility. Many did so in the hope that the next generation—now infused with aristocratic blood and landed estates—would be raised as anglicised Protestants.[76] Certainly marriage, together with the policy of wardship, secured for Protestantism the great aristocratic houses of Kildare, Ormond, Thomond, and Inchiquin. Matches with members of the established titled nobility added particular lustre to the new dynasty, while old families, strapped for cash, also sought out parvenus like the Boyles of Cork. The first earl Cork wed five (of his seven) daughters to Irish lords.[77] In the case of Alice, she married in 1621 the first earl of Barrymore, who also happened to be Cork's ward. Ultimately, what mattered to Cork was the fact that the son of their union would be heir to this 'noble and anciently hon[oura]ble house' which, imbued with Boyle blood, would regain 'its former lustre and greatness'.[78] It was with the same ambition that in 1630 Cork wed Joan to the heir of the house of Kildare. The earl was determined to create a Boyle dynasty and within two generations Boyle tentacles embraced many of Ireland's titled houses.

Like Cork, the great political powerbroker after 1660, Arthur Annesley, earl of Anglesey, matched his daughters with prominent, but impoverished, Catholic lineages. Elizabeth married Alexander, heir of the marquis of Antrim. Since she died without producing a male heir, Annesely's return on his investment was a poor one.[79] More productive was the match in 1654 between his eldest daughter, Dorothy, and Richard Power, fifth baron Le Power and Curroghmore (Annesley had served as guardian to Richard's 'lunatic' father). Annesely provided the couple with an English nurse for his grandson, an English cook, and a Protestant chaplain.[80] The examples of the Annesleys and the Boyles are particularly well documented but these sorts of arrangements were replicated across Ireland as the elite used marriage to build and consolidate their dynastic fortunes and to bolster their social status. Englishness in a bride was highly prized by Irish lords. Over the course of the seventeenth century one-third of resident peers in Ireland married English women or the daughters of recent migrants, especially as their first wives. They aimed to increase their social status by uniting with members of the English nobility, landed gentry, or even prosperous merchant families.[81] In particular, Irish Catholic lords, especially those from the higher ranks (viscounts and above) sought English wives. These women perpetuated the family line, infused it with new blood, helped to define a dynasty's identity, and, for many Catholic houses, secured the political survival of the lineage at a particularly turbulent moment. Though contested and resented in some quarters, marriages across social, ethnic, and religious boundaries undoubtedly helped to forge economic, social, and cultural assimilation.[82]

Some looked on in horror at those who married outside their social rank. An account of Ireland, presented in 1619 to Philip III of Spain, condemned the policy of placing Catholic noble children in the care of English and Scottish guardians who often pressured the young man to 'marry with the daughter or maid [of the guardian], or other of low fortune without lineage, nor quality of blood', which he contended would 'diminish the Irish nation'.[83] At the other end of the social spectrum, the rise of the lower orders alarmed the Gaelic *literati* who felt that these unions subverted the established order and hierarchy. Anonymous works like *Pairlement Chlionne Tomáis* poured scorn on Gaelic arrivistes who were upwardly mobile as a result of collaborations with the newcomers. In *Pairlement Chlionne Tomáis* the descendants of Tomas Mór, who were peasants, had accumulated wealth at the expense of the Old English nobility by wedding 'women of higher rank'.[84]

What then of women of lesser rank and social status? The '1641 Depositions' provide an alternative lens through which to look at intermarriage and related issues of identity, especially amongst non-elite women from the 'middling sorts'.[85] However, given the controversy that surrounds them, it is important to first evaluate the historical worth of the '1641 Depositions'.[86] They comprise over 8,000 witness testimonies, examinations, and associated materials in which men and women of all backgrounds told of their experiences following the outbreak of violence on 22 October 1641. As in any legal document the format of each deposition was fairly standard and included basic biographical information: the woman's name, address, marital status, and, in some cases, her age, and her husband's occupation. After relating any losses, the deponent first provided an account of what she had seen and experienced—her eye-witness evidence—followed by what she had heard from others, her hearsay evidence. The eye-witness testimony usually included the names of her assailants, their actions, and their words and so these became deeply personal narratives. The hearsay evidence tended to be vaguer and often included more sensational claims and rumours. The woman then signed her deposition or left her mark. The names of the commissioners were recorded along with the date.

Though it is hard to detect, the depositions also provide evidence of marriage across religious and ethnic boundaries and invite us to ask how this shaped identity. In 1653 John Crowe from Tipperary deposed that he 'hath credibly heard & beleeveth that where the Irish mett with any English man married to an Irish woman or any Irish man married to an English woman those villaines for their hatred to the English would hang such married parties which they frequently did in the Countie of Tipperary'.[87] This was not always the case though. One widow from Macroom in County Cork survived because she had married 'an Irishman' and presumably a Catholic, while her Protestant mother and siblings all perished at the hands of the insurgents.[88] Ellen Matchett from County Armagh deposed that in 1642 Mrs Dun, 'being an English gentlewoman and a Constant protestant secretly entertained' her displaced neighbours. Ellen added 'that poore gentlewoman *Mris Dun* [suffered] for her Religion' and that Frances, one of her young daughters, said that 'shee hoped ere long that some of the Irish would giue her mother a swinge for her Religion'.[89] The volatile mix of Englishness,

Irishness, and confession in the Dun household, at a moment of sectarian conflict, forced the refugees to move on.

How did these women perceive themselves and their senses of identity? A case study of the widows suggests that over one-fifth (22 per cent) described themselves as 'British protestants' and included women probably born in Ireland. The wide-scale use of the descriptor 'British' by ordinary women is significant since not even 40 years had passed since the union of the Crowns in 1603. The efforts of the Stuarts, especially James VI and I, to create a 'British' state had clearly had some impact throughout Munster, Dublin, and the parts of the Pale (unless, of course, the commissioners put these words in the mouths of the deponents, which is also possible and something that we need to be mindful of). Interestingly, few women from Ulster used the term 'British' to describe themselves, preferring 'English protestant'. One widow from Wicklow hedged her bets and described herself as a 'British, English protestant'. Some described themselves as 'Irish Protestant' and could well have been converts from Catholicism.[90] For example, Margery Bellingham was a widow who had been living in County Carlow with her adult son, Henry. She related in her deposition that her brother, Patrick White, 'formerly a protestant and now revolted papist', had refused to help them after insurgents attacked their home.[91] Margaret Fagon of Clonduffe in County Dublin deposed that the insurgents hanged her husband, Robert, because he refused to attend Mass even though 'he was an Irish man'.[92] In a deposition dating from 1644 Jane Smith explained that her stepson, Michael, 'was a protestant minster but now is revolted & is turned papist'. This suggests that the Smiths, like the Bellinghams and the Fagons, might have been converts.[93] Teasing out the meaning of these stories will enable scholars to explore the potent forces—marriage but also religion, social status, geography, birth, kinship, fosterage, language, and culture—that formed identity and shaped representation and so better understand what 'Irishness', 'Englishness', and 'Britishness' actually meant on the eve of the 1641 rebellion.

What is clear is that ethnic categories were complex and unstable.[94] Undoubtedly, the war of the 1640s tested to the limit relationships—between husband and wife, parent and child—that crossed religious and ethnic divides. However, the fact that in 1651 and 1653 the Cromwellian authorities prohibited intermarriage between Catholics and Protestants and in 1658 the Catholic synod did likewise suggests that mixed marriages continued to be widespread.[95] This did not change with the passage of time, something highlighted by legislation preventing Protestants from marrying Catholics in 1697, 1725–26, 1746, and 1750 and insisting that the children of mixed marriages be educated as Protestants.[96] Dagmar Freist's study of early modern Germany, where each denomination (Catholic, Lutheran, and Reformed) also discouraged mixed marriage, offers some interesting points of comparison. It challenges assumptions about religious toleration after the Peace of Westphalia (1648) by focusing the lens on the practical lived experiences of those who married across confessional boundaries and how this played out between spouses, the state, and the church. Freist concludes that 'regardless of daily compromises in practice, people remained aware of and committed to their confession' though tensions inevitably flared around the faith in which children were to be raised.[97] Yet, as Benjamin Kaplan has shown, mixed marriages and conversions should not be equated with religious toleration but instead point to 'a pattern of interaction between people of different faiths that involved high degrees of integration and assimilation'.[98] Though the full extent and scale is hard to discern with precision, integration and assimilation clearly occurred in colonial Ireland. The challenge is how best to capture this without trivialising the endemic violence, the periods of intense warfare during the 1590s, 1640s, and after 1688, and the expropriation and exploitation that characterised the century.[99] The next section on lived experiences attempts to do this.

III Lived experiences in colonial Ireland

The intricate engraving by Wenceslaus Hollar from Sir James Ware's *Equitis Aurati de Hibernia* (1658) depicts *Hibernia*, or Ireland, as both shepherdess and huntress, with bees—the symbols of industry and colonisation—circling her head and highly prized Irish wolfhounds at her side (Figure 3.2). Her apparel and hair styling speaks to her 'civility', as do the cultivated arable and pastoral lands in the foreground where English breeds of horned cattle graze. These images of 'Englishness' contrast with the wild forests in the background, no doubt replete—in the imagination of the reader—with wolves, 'wild' wood kerns, and 'meere' Irish women, so vilified by English observers as threats to political stability and the social order.[100] It is critical, however, to move beyond these binary 'colonised'/'coloniser' stereotypes and recognise that women, from all ethnic and religious backgrounds, were often the social glue that held together families and communities and to examine the

Figure 3.2 Wenceslaus Hollar from Sir James Ware's *Equitis Aurati de Hibernia* (1658) depicting *Hibernia*. Reproduced courtesy of Marsh's Library in Dublin.

key role that Catholic and Protestant women from diverse social and economic backgrounds played as mothers, sisters, daughters, wives,[101] widows,[102] heads of household, moneylenders,[103] entrepreneurs, and landholders.

Though predominately given by Protestant women and very much a 'colonial' archive, the '1641 Depositions' nonetheless provide valuable insights into lived experiences of women. In all there were 959 female deponents (see Table 3.1), which meant that roughly one eighth of all deponents were women, which by early modern standards was an exceptionally high proportion. Hundreds more women were named in the depositions given by men. Of the female deponents, 512 (or 53 per cent) were listed as widows, 297 (or 31 per cent) as married, and 65 as single (described as 'spinster' or unmarried). Thus 'ever married' women (i.e. wives and widows) accounted for at least 84 per cent of all female deponents and 'never married' women for seven per cent.[104] Widows formed the majority, a high number no doubt inflated by the war, though Amy Erickson has noted that in early modern England, only about one-third of all adult women were married at any given time.[105] There is a subset of 'pre-war widows'—180 (or 19 per cent of the total) —which means that one in five of all female deponents was a widow prior to the outbreak of war in 1641.[106]

These women lived in urban and rural places and came from every province and every county. As the figures in Table 3.2 show, the greatest number of female deponents (324) gave a Leinster address, with at least 55 from Dublin, 310 from Munster, and 265 from Ulster, with largest numbers coming

Table 3.1 Status of women who deposed (as recorded in '1641 Depositions')

	Women Total	Unknown	Married	Widows	Unmarried	'Spinster'
Total	959	85 [9%]	297 [31%]	512 [53%]	26 [3%]	39 [4%]

Table 3.2 Geographic origin of depositions given by women (as recorded in '1641 Depositions')

	Total	Unknown	Married	Widows	Unmarried	'Spinsters'
Ulster	265	13	91	144	9	8
Leinster	324	35	96	167	11	15
Munster	310	32	87	176	5	10
Connacht	60	5	23	25	1	6
Total	959	85	297	512	26	39

from the troubled counties of Cavan and Fermanagh. Only 60 gave a Connacht address, something attributed to the difficulty of travelling overland from the west to Dublin. In Ireland the majority of women who deposed were Protestants, and scrutiny of the surnames suggests that they were the wives, sisters, and daughters of colonists who had settled in Ireland from the 1530s but arrived in significant numbers during the Munster plantation of the 1570s and then during the Ulster plantation of the early seventeenth century. Evidence for the geographic origins of the women is rarely revealed and always indirect. For example, during a siege of her castle in King's County, Grace Smith gave instructions to her servant Ann, in 'the Welsh tongue', suggesting that both were relatively recent migrants.[107]

While the marital status of a woman (single, married, widow) is usually recorded in the depositions, her occupation and social status is rarely stated though specific tasks she undertook might be noted. The occupation and/ or social status of her husband was listed in over a third of depositions given by all women and in 50 per cent of those provided by married women. The language used to describe status and occupation in the depositions was identical to that used in early modern England, which should come as no surprise since the Crown had consciously set out to recreate the English social order in Ireland.[108] As the data in Table 3.3 shows, the largest group—one quarter (or 89)—of the husbands of women were craftsmen or tradesmen: blacksmiths, button makers, brewers, carpenters, carriers, chapmen, coachmakers, clothiers, fishmongers, founders, grocers, innkeepers, joiners, locksmiths, saddlers, skinners, tailors, tanners, vintners, and weavers. Alongside the tradesmen were merchants and those

Table 3.3 Occupation of the husbands of women who deposed (as recorded in '1641 Depositions')

	All women[109]	Married	Widows
Gentry	88	22	66
Yeoman	49	28	21
Husbandman	18	7	11
Soldier	47	27	20
Clergy	24	4	20
Merchant, professional	26	10	16
Craft/trade	89	46	43
Servant	4	1	3
Total	345 [959]	145 [297]	200 [512]

offering professional services (26 or eight per cent): doctors, clerks, and teachers. The church was well represented (24 or seven per cent): clerks, deans, ministers, parsons, and vicars, which reflected the fact that the commissioners, all Church of Ireland clergymen, sought out their own. While some of the clergy, merchants, doctors, and tradesmen lived in towns and cities, the majority made their homes in smaller nucleated settlements, where they leased or owned small farms.

Wives of members of the landed gentry (earls, knights, esquires, and gentlemen) deposed, which comprised 26 per cent (or 88) of husbands. Moving down the landed hierarchy there were 49 yeomen and 18 husbandmen, who farmed on a smaller scale. Thus at least 45 per cent, or nearly half, of these husbands can be closely associated with the land. Of the 47 soldiers listed, one-third were officers (major, lieutenant, captain, and coronet) and presumably came from a landed gentry background. With the exception of Ladies Antrim and Westmeath who both deposed, members of the titled nobility were entirely missing. Representatives of the lower orders of society—servants, apprentices, and labourers—were also under-represented. Instead the bulk of husbands were drawn from the gentle and 'middling sort', something that makes the '1641 Depositions' so extraordinary. These are the people who are so absent from history, especially in Ireland.[110]

Each deponent either signed her deposition or left a mark. Since reading was generally taught as a skill before writing, analysis of the depositions might shed light on levels of literacy in Ireland, at least amongst Protestant women.[111] Only 85 (out of 512) or 17 per cent of all widows signed their names at the end of their depositions; the majority (378 or 74 per cent) left their mark (see Table 3.4). How typical are these findings? Working with a comparable body of English legal evidence but with a larger group of women (3,331 female witnesses) over a much longer time period (1550–1728), Alexandra Shepard found that 86 per cent of women endorsed their deposition with a mark 'suggesting that they did not have the ability to write'.[112]

Table 3.4 Signature of widows vs mark (as recorded in '1641 Depositions')

Signature	85	17%
Mark	378	74%
NS	49	9%
Widows	512	100%

Even though the figure for Ireland is lower, where the sample is smaller and time frame shorter, it broadly accords with Shepard's and other findings for early modern England, where research on signatures suggested that on the eve of the outbreak of war a tenth of all women—and not just the 'middling sort' examined here—could sign their names, with literacy levels highest amongst the social elites and in urban areas.[113]

When the ability of a widow to sign her name is correlated with the occupation/status of her husband, some interesting patterns emerge (Table 3.5). Amongst the widows of tradesmen and craftsmen only three could sign, with 36 leaving a mark; amongst the widows of merchants and professorial men the number able to sign was higher, nine, with six making a mark. Of the widows of clergy ten (out of 22) signed and 12 left a mark. The widows of the landed gentry had the greatest ability to write, with 34, nearly half, able to sign their name and 31 leaving a mark. Of the widows of soldiers, eight could sign and these were the women who had married officers. Only the widows of three (of 18) yeomen could sign and the widows of all 11 husbandmen left marks. An absence of evidence means that this sample is biased towards Protestants. Of the dozen Catholic women who deposed only one (Lady Westmeath) signed her name which might reflect the importance of orality in Irish culture.

The '1641 Depositions' contain detailed inventories of losses recorded by predominately Protestant women and provide a glimpse into their 'worth' and the material culture of their worlds.[114] These laundry-like lists allow us to re-imagine the contents of their wardrobes, kitchens, and farms.[115] Many women mentioned their rugs, drapes, linens, and woollens;

Table 3.5 Status/occupation of husband and the signature/mark of the widow (as recorded in '1641 Depositions')

	Sign	Mark	NS	Total
Soldier	8	10	3	22
Gentry	34	31	5	70
Clergy	10	12	—	22
Merchant, professional	9	6	3	18
Yeoman	3	18	—	21
Craft/trade	3	36	3	42
Husbandman	—	11	—	11
Servant	—	4	—	4
Total	67 [32%]	128 [61%]	14 [7%]	210 [100%]

their pewter, iron, and brass goods; their kitchen and other utensils used for brewing and cooking, including mortars and pestles, brass pots and pans, and pewter vessels; along with items of furniture—stools, chairs, tables, cupboards, chests, along with wooden and brass beds and feather pillows and mattresses. They recorded lost items of clothing—linen, silk, satin, woollen, delicate fabrics, and home-spun cloths. They mentioned precious jewels, gold and silver rings, plate and books, along with swords, firearms, and fowling pieces. The lists of ordinary and precious goods situated these women in their localities, but mentions of silks and spices also allow us to imagine their wider connections. Given the detailed nature of these accounts, comparative research with Spanish women in the American colonies—whose clothing and material culture has been carefully analysed by Amelia Almorza Hidalgo—might provide further insights into the significance of clothing and personal goods as moveable assets and how this related to female identity and social status.[116]

The women were just as familiar with the contents of their farmyards where many would have worked, alongside their children, menfolk, and servants. They listed their livestock: horses, geldings, different breeds of cattle, including 'English' varieties, heifers, sheep, swine, oxen, poultry, and hives of bees. The depositions by women described the goods that they produced for domestic consumption, for barter, and for the marketplace: wheat, hay, malt, turf, vegetables, fruit, and honey. They were careful to distinguish between corn 'in the haggard' (or the barn) and 'winter corn in the ground'. Farming tools and implements were noted alongside carts and coaches. They were quick to record how the insurgents had destroyed property, especially buildings that they and their husbands had constructed or any damage to their gardens and orchards. They often noted improvements to their holdings—how they had enclosed land with fences and hedges and dug ditches and drains. Similarly, the womenfolk of craftsmen, tradesmen, and merchants listed the loss of specific stock, along with the tools of their trade.

In all 411 widows (of 512) from across the country recorded losses accrued as a result of the 1641 rebellion and ensuing war. These ranged from £1 (or 20 shillings) to over £20,000 (Table 3.6) and encompassed a wide range of women. The commissioners noted the losses of Ann Cappar from Dublin (£5),[117] Jane Mansfield from Meath (£6),[118] and Isabell Staples from Cavan (£8)[119] and described each of them as being 'olde', 'old and sickly', and 'not able to worke'. At the other end of the spectrum, a few made considerable livings from arable and pastoral farming, food processing, and more specialised

Table 3.6 Widows' losses (as reported in '1641 Depositions')

	Connacht	Ulster	Munster	Leinster	Ireland	*pre-war widows*
less £100	4	35	71	56	166 [40%]	*78 [48%]*
£101–£500	8	44	65	44	161 [39%]	*59 [36%]*
£501–£1,000	1	9	12	18	40 [11%]	*14 [9%]*
£1,001–£3,000	2	12	8	12	34 [8%]	*7 [4%]*
over £3,000	0	2	2	6	10 [2%]	*5 [3%]*
Total	15	102	158	136	411	*163*

activities, especially milling and tanning. Consider the example of Lady Jane Forbes, whose deposition, dating from 1642, provided a vivid snapshot of the family's fortunes after a 20-year sojourn in Ireland and after a decade of widowhood (her second husband Sir Arthur died in 1632). Lady Forbes claimed losses of £4,314, which included 'beasts and cattle', horses and mares, sheep and hogs, and household goods and clothing. She noted the 'charge of building and making the howse of Castleforbes with the bawn and other houses gardens and orchards' amounting to £1,000 and the lost profits from 600 acres of land in County Longford, plus three 'plantation' houses, mills, the tan house and its contents. She recorded the loss of rental from 500 acres in County Leitrim and 1,000 acres in County Cavan which were her jointure lands by her first husband, worth £200 per annum.[120]

As this example illustrates, the importance of landed income for these women cannot be overstated.[121] While specific mentions of jointures or dowers predominately occurred in the depositions of pre-war widows who, like Lady Forbes, had been married to men of substance, others were quick to note any income from land. Thus the '1641 Depositions' provide a wealth of information on the property held by women, the rentals they secured from it, how they improved and laboured on it, all of which is worthy of further detailed investigation, especially in conjunction with analysis of data provided in the Down Survey maps, dating from the 1650s, and the Books of Survey and Distribution, the Irish equivalent of the Domesday Book for Ireland, which capture the revolution in landholding that the country experienced during these years.[122] Drawn up in the wake of the Restoration of Charles II and the victory of William III, in part for taxation purposes ('quit rent'), these contain a wealth of information. The names of landholders, including women, in 1641, in *c.*1670, and again in *c.*1704 appear in columns together with the number of plantation acres (profitable and non-profitable) and the county, barony, and parish where the land was held. Some entries contain information on mortgages, jointures, and dowers.[123]

Landed income also featured in testimonies provided by women working in textile production or specialist trades. Women like Mary Ward from County Monaghan, whose late husband was a weaver and whose deposition, of 2 April 1642, listed losses totalling £274. Some of these losses spoke to Mary's trade—clothing that was for sale and 'weavers loomes and instruments' (£6)—together with hay in haggard (£26) and corn (£12). The couple had also invested £60 in improvements and fencing and had lost £68 'in debts due from English men who were robbed and dispoyled by this rebellion'.[124] The widows and wives of craftsmen, tradesmen, and merchants listed the loss of specific stock (tobacco, hides, herrings, etc.), along with the tools of their trade, their boats, and fishing tackle. Fifty-year-old Agnes Windsor had been married to William, a tanner from County Fermanagh. On 5 January 1642 she claimed losses of £1,032, including 'in the Tanyard in hyds, leather and Barke' worth £380, £100 of debts, and £40 in ready money, along with corn, cattle, hay, household goods, and income from leases.[125] This suggests that Agnes and her late husband had owned a thriving tanning business and a small farm. Jane and Thomas Stewart ran a shop in Sligo. In her testimony of 23 April 1644 Jane noted that the couple had lived 'in very good estate and condicion' for the past 26 years, 'haveing contynually furnished the Inhabitants... with all sorts of wares and marchandize'. With the support of the local grandee, O'Connor Sligo, they continued trading after the outbreak of the rebellion until insurgents murdered Thomas and incarcerated Jane.[126] Margery Hazard, of Youghal, was a prosperous pre-war widow who described herself as a 'merchant' and 'British protestant' when she deposed on 6 February 1643. Her losses totalled £950 and these included herrings worth £660, 40 barrels of which were on a captured ship, along with £80 in debts due from 'rebels' and other debts of £210.[127] The deposition of 24 February 1645 by Sarah Roades, whose late husband had been a Dublin beer brewer, claimed losses of £1,152. These related to properties which had either been abandoned by the tenants or destroyed and to 'just debts' of £509 (or the equivalent of 44 per cent of her total losses).[128]

The '1641 Depositions' thus provide vivid insights into tasks undertaken by women and their roles as heads of household, managers of their estates, producers, providers, and entrepreneurs, as well as modest farmers, labourers, and craftswomen (milling, malting, brewing, tanning, spinning, sewing). The current literature on women's roles in the early modern economy empha-sises that labour, while gendered, was cooperatively undertaken.[129] The extent to which this applies to Ireland remains to be fully determined but preliminary research suggests that women were, to quote Jane Whittle, 'active economic agents', much as they were in England and elsewhere.[130] In Ireland women were involved in spinning, sewing, service, washing, car-ing, and wet-nursing and worked, often alongside their children, in the fields and farmyards and ran—either with their husbands or independently—their family business, purchasing items, accessing credit, managing their estates and property.[131]

The '1641 Depositions' are especially important for what they reveal about the relationship between debt, credit, and widowhood in an era before banks and in a country where coinage was scarce.[132] As has just been noted, recorded amongst the losses of many widows was 'ready money' and debts owed, which provide a fascinating insight into the operation of moneylending at a very local level since the widows usually listed everyone, sometimes with their address and occupation, to whom they had loaned money and when.[133] The pattern is clear: relatively small amounts were lent to a variety of people, both native and newcomer. A detailed look at 50 widows (Table 3.7), the majority from the southern province of Munster, who recorded 'debts' amongst their losses suggests that pre-war widows (i.e. those widowed before the outbreak of war in 1641) actively engaged in moneylending, with six widows testifying that debts formed more than 50 per cent of their total losses.[134] Moneylending was how these widows made their living and the war reduced them to penury. For the majority, however, debts accounted for less than this but with interest rates of between eight and ten per cent, even small loans could have represented a meaningful income stream, providing of course the debtor paid up. The widows thus formed a critical element in the maintenance of small-scale rural credit, especially important given the limited coinage that circulated in Ireland.[135] These conclusions resonate with the findings of Jane Whittle and Craig Muldrew for England and Cathryn Spence for Scotland about the role that widows played in moneylending, with Whittle showing that 'money-lending was the only occupation carried out more frequently in widows' house-holds than in the households of married men'.[136]

What, then, do the '1641 Depositions' tell us about the lived experiences of Catholic women? There are only a few examples of depositions dating

Table 3.7 Debts as percentage of total losses
(as recorded in '1641 Depositions')

	Total widow	Pre-war widow
75%+	4	4
50%–75%	3	2
25%–49%	15	7
15%–24%	12	8
under 15%	16	9
Total	50	30

from 1640s by women who were identified as Irish Catholics.[137] Twenty others, who deposed between 1651 and 1654, appear from the context or from their name—Barnewall, Birne, Browne, Butler, Ferrall, O'Donovan and those with the prefix 'Ni'—to have been Catholic. Despite the passage of roughly a decade, their testimony was particularly important because depositions by Catholic women were so rare. Few list any losses, which is unfortunate since these would have shed light on their material culture and how they deployed their labour. Instead most testify to the brutality they suffered at the hands of the government forces. Consider by way of example an examination, dating from 1653, by Grainne Ni Mullan, a young recusant widow from Inch in County Down. Grainne related how in February 1642 John Irwin, her neighbour, and a party of Scots came to her house and attacked Mary Mullan, her mother. Grainne, who was a teenager when the atrocity occurred, recalled how Mary had begged for her life:'dear John doe not kill me for I never offended you'. Unmoved, John stabbed Mary, along with Evelyn, Grainne's grandmother. Clearly cold-blooded brutality and the targeting of women and children was not the preserve of the Catholic insurgents and from the latter part of the sixteenth century characterised English warfare in Ireland.[138] Archaeological evidence, especially skeletal remains at Carrickmines castle and King John's Castle in Limerick, bear witness to extreme violence and offer stark insights into the slaughter of women and children, of both faiths, during sieges dating from the 1590s and 1640s.[139]

The '1641 Depositions' also illustrate the limits of assimilation, providing graphic examples of where relationships had broken down. They have much to say about the violence committed by Irish women and that suffered by Protestant women, thereby tapping into the negative rhetoric of earlier hostile commentators (discussed in Section I above).[140] In their deposition

Elizabeth Gilbert and Rebecca Hill, from Kilkenny, testified that their husbands, William Gilbert and Thomas Hill, were killed and decapitated when they refused to 'become papistes'. Their heads were taken to the market place in Kilkenny 'as trophies' and set up on the market cross, where 'whorish women' and 'lewd viragoes' stabbed them.[141] These women thus challenged the masculinity of the English colonists and their 'barbarism' was used to inspire fear.[142] Other reports, especially the 'massacre pamphlets' dating from the early 1640s, featured the suffering experienced by Protestant women and children.[143] In one graphic woodcut from James Cranford's *Teares of Ireland* (1642) Irish insurgents impaled an infant on a pike in front of a group of distraught mothers and terrified children. Elsewhere equally disturbing images—of foetuses being ripped from the bellies of pregnant women or of infants having their brains bashed out or of children being roasted on spits— aimed to instil fear and to provoke emotional responses. Audiences would have been familiar with the biblical story of mass infanticide carried out by King Herod in order to eliminate possible threats to his power by the new-born King of the Jews ('The Massacre of the Innocents') and with atrocity works that circulated widely.[144] These included John Foxe's *Actes and Monuments*, commonly known as the *Book of Martyrs* and first published in 1563 and reprinted six times by 1610, Jean Crespin's *Histoire des martyrs* (Geneva, 1554), and Bartolomé Las Casas' *Mirror of Spanish Tyranny*, where children were also impaled, first published in 1552 in Spanish but reprinted in English, Dutch, and German translations.[145] These works both informed and provided the context for the atrocity literature about the conflict in Ireland.

The 'massacre pamphlets' were followed by longer histories that adopted similar tactics.[146] Consider the most influential example of Sir John Temple's *The Irish Rebellion* (1646), which published carefully selected extracts from 88 of the '1641 Depositions', 31 (or 35 per cent) of which were given by women. Temple selected depositions that included extreme violence against women and children and for maximum emotional impact he shortened the length and included only the most disturbing component of the violence, which was often based on hearsay rather than eyewitness testimony. According to Temple, Protestant women were blessed with qualities—valour, loyalty, and honour—normally the preserve of men.[147] In contrast, he demonised the 'meere' Irish women, whom he represented as being as brutal and barbarous as their menfolk.[148] Sarah Covington reminds us that Temple's use of the depositions 'offers an important means of understanding the process by which collective or social memory is forged; that is, by asserting its truth and legitimacy through the law—or the depositions—and by locating it in turn within a religious frame of meaning whose biblical references early modern readers would have readily understood'.[149]

The selective use of the '1641 Depositions' and the determination to vilify meant that Temple and other reporters simply ignored accounts where Catholic women helped their Protestant neighbours. For example, in February 1653 the Coleraine commissioners examined Alice, countess dowager of Antrim, a daughter of Hugh O'Neill, earl of Tyrone, who in 1604 had married Randal MacDonnell, first earl of Antrim. Despite their Catholicism, her husband, who had died in 1636, like her son the first marquis, were royal favourites (indeed, Randal had married the widow of the duke of Buckingham).[150] Father and son had actively promoted plantation and anglicisation on their vast estates in East Ulster, something that the rebellion and war totally disrupted and which Lady Antrim's deposition bore witness to. With the outbreak of rebellion, Lady Antrim, by her own account, offered refuge to the families of local millers, craftsmen, and tradesmen. She claimed that her house in Ballycastle 'was full of Irish Scotch & English'.[151] Elsewhere other Catholic women protected Protestants from the excesses of the insurgents. An undated examination by Jane Roberts recounted how Donnell Boye O Lennan, from Louth, murdered her husband and their two teenage sons. Four days later she encountered Donnell Boye and when he drew his knife to kill her, Donnell's wife intervened 'and saide unto him (seeing a tender infant att her brest) you have killed her sonne (which is enough) doe not kill her too'. Thanks to 'his good wife and some good people', Jane escaped and lived to tell her story.[152]

In a very long and detailed deposition, dating from August 1642, Dr Robert Maxwell recounted his incarceration at the home of Sir Phelim O'Neill, one of the leaders of the 1641 insurrection, who had been raised by his stepfather Robert Hovenden. Maxwell recounted how Sir Phelim's mother, Katherine Hovenden, 'preserved 24 English & scotts in her owne howse and fedd them for 37 weekes out of her owne store and . . . [how] she left both them and this deponent to theire libertie, and gave them free leave to escape. Many more she would haue saved but that while she lay sick 10 weekes of an Ague'. Maxwell added that Katherine's son, Alexander, escorted convoys of refugees to safety and on two occasions prevented the insurgents from burning the town of Armagh, along with its cathedral.[153] Alexander's grandfather was Harry Hovendon, Hugh O'Neill's confidant and private secretary. While Harry lived out his life in Rome, his son Robert had become a member of the 'deserving Irish'. Allocated lands in County Armagh, Robert engaged in commercialisation, supported Sir Phelim during his time at the Inns of Court, and borrowed heavily to fund an increasingly anglicised lifestyle.[154] Why Katherine, a daughter of a Gaelic lord, Turlough MacHenry of the Fews, acted as she did was not stated. However her actions highlighted her agency, her economic independence (she fed the refugees 'out of her owne store'), her bravery, and her humanity. In an important work on religious conflict and toleration Benjamin Kaplan suggests that toleration was a pragmatic necessity that helped to contain conflict. Despite the richness of the literature on religious coexistence for elsewhere in early modern Europe, the significance of acts of humanity and compassion and the role that women played as peace makers or in promoting tolerance in Ireland has received little scholarly attention.[155] Yet this clearly contributed to the survival of many women in colonial Ireland. Moreover, it offers glimpses into how women from different faiths interacted on a daily basis, something lacking in other regions of Europe.[156]

IV The first Irish novel

This chapter began with a discussion of *Landgartha*, the first play by an Irish writer. It concludes with a brief discussion of the first modern Irish novel, *Vertue Rewarded; or, The Irish Princess*, which told the story of strong women and explored marriage, assimilation, and integration in Ireland and in the Spanish empire.[157] Set in Clonmel, County Tipperary, in 1690 *Vertue Rewarded* was the account of Miranda, a beautiful woman from a humble Protestant planter family who eventually found love with an impoverished European prince, whose religion is never stated (and makes us wonder if he might have been Catholic). Published in 1693, in the immediate aftermath of the Williamite wars, it wove into the narrative a story of an Irish holy well and Cluaneesha, the daughter of the king of Munster. It also recounted the Spanish conquest of Peru and the story of Faniaca from a noble, but savage, Amazonian tribe, who fell in love with a Spanish conquistador called Astolfo. When they first met Faniaca explained to Astolfo that her father 'was an Indian Priest in the Province of Antis, which Countrey having never been conquered by the Incas, kept up the ancient Barbarity, not being Civilized by their Laws, as those nations were, who had yielded to their Government'.[158] Exchanges like this must have both resonated with readers whilst also firing their imaginations with exotic encounters from the Amazon, just as Raleigh's travel account had done a generation earlier or Aphra Behn's novella, *Oroonoko*, did after 1688.[159]

After much intrigue and heartache, the novel ended with Miranda marrying her European prince, and her cousin, Diana, who interestingly self-identified as an 'Irish-woman', marrying his aide, an English Protestant officer, called Celadon. The Amazonian princess, Faniaca, wed Astolfo after tracking him down to Clonmel and converting to Christianity. Their story evoked an earlier real-life marriage between the English adventurer in Virginia, John Rolfe, and the Algonquin princess, Mataoka (discussed above).[160] There are sufficient similarities in the stories of Mataoka and Faniaca to suggest that the anonymous author may have wanted to link them in the minds of the readers. What is clear is that the author draws heavily on George Story, *An impartial history of the wars in Ireland* (1693) and Paul Rycaut's 1688 translation of Garcilaso de la Vega's *The Royal Commenataries of Peru*. Interestingly, de la Vega was a 'mestizo' or of mixed race, the son of an Inca princess and Spanish soldier, who left Peru in 1560 to settle in Spain where he wrote the first history of Peru before the conquest.[161] Some have suggested that Rycaut, a distinguished diplomat who had been chief secretary of Ireland between 1685 and 1687, might have been involved in the publication of *Vertue Rewarded* or was even the author. Others posit that it was written by his friend and the career diplomat Robert, later Viscount Molesworth, whose daughter Mary was also known as Miranda.[162]

Whoever the author, the ending of *Vertue Rewarded*, according to Daniel Roberts, elided 'complex religious and cultural differences, and envisage[d] the successful integration of hitherto disparate elements within the promised harmony of the Williamite settlement'.[163] *Vertue Rewarded* offered more nuanced understandings of identity and what constituted 'civility' and 'barbarism' and thereby challenged the very negative representations by Spenser and other English writers of the Irish, especially of Irish women.[164] The novel certainly invites us to reflect on matters of marriage across ethnic, social, and religious boundaries, on upward social mobility, and on cultural and political assimilation. It also allows for an exploration of the complex relationships between colonised and coloniser abroad, in Spanish America, and at home through appropriating the tale of Cluaneesha and suggesting that Miranda was her worthy successor as an Irish princess.[165] In other words, the anonymous author of *Vertue Rewarded* was trying to achieve in this novel what Burnell aspired to do in *Landgartha* 50 years before and what Brian Friel did centuries later in *Making History*.

A number of more general conclusions can be drawn about the role women played in colonial Ireland. First, with a few notable exceptions, historians have undervalued or simply ignored the agency and varied experiences of women living in a society undergoing profound economic, political, and cultural transformation as a result of colonisation. Instead it largely fell to novelists, playwrights, and literary scholars to recover how women responded to transformative processes—proto-globalisation, state formation, confessionalisation, warfare, commercialisation, environmental change, and so on—and to tease out how these shaped and complicated their senses of identity. Second, reading existing historical sources 'against the grain' suggests that women have been hiding in plain sight all along. Some operated as colonial actors committed to making Ireland English, others resisted imperial incursions, and others focused on living and surviving. In many communities women served as the glue that held families together and thanks in part to marriages across confessional and ethnic boundaries fostered integration and assimilation. Third, whether as carers, producers, moneylenders, or entrepreneurs female labour made a significant, if little understood, contribution to the operation of the economy at all levels. Moreover, despite legal restrictions and patriarchal norms, the story of land and moveable property was also a story of women's lives. Fourth, whether as victims or viragoes, women negotiated the war and violence of these years in different ways and adapted, often in extreme circumstances, in order to survive. It might even be argued that some women used periods of intense warfare, when all cultural norms were suspended, to advance their role and in some instances to improve their position. In short, women's agency and their lived experiences provide an alternative lens through which to interrogate the history of colonial Ireland and to better understand the complex operation of imperialism.

4

Agents of empire

Midway through *Making History* there is a heated exchange between Hugh O'Neill, earl of Tyrone, and his wife Mabel about her brother Henry. Hugh roared:

> It's always the Henrys, the menials in the middle, who get the kicks, isn't it?...Our Henry? Nobody better. London couldn't have a more dutiful servant than Our Henry. As you and I know well—but as London keeps forgetting—it's the plodding Henrys of this world who are the real empire-makers.[1]

Sir Henry Bagenal, like his father Sir Nicholas, had served as the marshal of the army and as a member of the Irish privy council. Chapter 2 focused on anglicisation and drew on the life and experiences of Hugh O'Neill, earl of Tyrone, and Chapter 3 looked to his wife Mabel and her sister Mary, as it explored assimilation and the particular significance of marriage. This chapter uses the careers of their brother Henry Bagenal and O'Neill's close ally Red Hugh O'Donnell as points of departure from which to discuss empire and enterprise. Bagenal and O'Donnell, one a member of the Protestant 'New English' community and the other a Catholic Gael, came from very different cultures and beg the question of what it meant to be 'Irish' at the turn of the seventeenth century? Strictly speaking only the Gaelic-speaking Catholic natives regarded themselves as being 'Irish'. The 'Old English' (or those of Anglo-Norman ancestry), many of whom were Catholic, consistently stressed their 'Englishness', often at the expense of their 'Irishness'.[2] The 'New English' settlers, the majority of whom were Protestant who colonised Ireland from the 1530s, flaunted their 'Englishness'.[3] However, as will be shown in Section IV below, these nuances were often lost on external observers who labelled as 'Irish' anyone from the island.

From Bagenal Castle, his stronghold in Newry, Henry spearheaded government offensives into Ulster while also colonising local acres. In Ireland—like so many colonies in the early modern world—private warfare and colonial enterprise went hand in hand. By the turn of the seventeenth century, land was at the heart of the colonial endeavour in Ireland and of the English empire abroad. The land, according to Red Hugh O'Donnell in *Making History*, 'is the goddess that every ruler in turn is married to'.[4] Red Hugh's death, as a political exile in Simancas in 1602, also serves as a reminder that involuntary migration characterised the movement of thousands of Irish men and women during the seventeenth century. In 1607 O'Neill, along with many of his followers, sailed from County Donegal during 'the Flight of the Earls', dying in relative poverty and isolation in Rome in 1616. Then, over the course of the seventeenth century, thousands of Irish soldiers served in Continental armies. From the early decades of the century indentured servants also left Ireland in significant numbers, often involuntarily, while the Cromwellian transportations of the 1650s saw thousands more, from both Ireland and Scotland, shipped to the Caribbean and North America.[5]

It is difficult to overstate the trauma associated with forced migration, displacement, and engagement in empire as a result of expropriation, themes that are explored here. This chapter also examines the agency of people from Ireland as they interacted with empires across the early modern world and notes the ease with which some flitted across these empires and created considerable economic opportunities. Section I focuses on the English empire and the importance of cosmopolitan London, and explores who these agents—'the plodding Henrys'—were, what they did, how, and why. Section II develops the notion of trans-imperialism and of an 'Irish global empire' built on the back of other European powers. Section III examines the Irishness of the English empire in the Atlantic and Asia and aims to complicate the dominant coloniser narrative. Section IV asks what being trans-imperial meant for senses of identity, especially for 'Irishness', 'Englishness', and 'Britishness'.

I Agents of empire

Those most active in empire were often younger sons or high achievers from humble backgrounds, who were usually unscrupulous and invariably great risk takers. A self-made man, Richard Boyle, earl of Cork, is an excellent example of a colonial entrepreneur even if he did his best to hide his imperial tracks. A complex web of relationships embedded the earl in the English imperial system. One of Cork's closest business associates,

Daniel Gookin, migrated to Virginia in 1621 but returned frequently to oversee Boyle's commercial interests in the old world. Gookin's factor in Virginia was William Tucker, a close associate of Maurice Thomson and his brothers, who monopolised the tobacco trade during the boom years of the later 1620s and 1630s. From 1631 cargoes of tobacco were shipped from Montserrat to Virginia and from there to Cork, thereby avoiding customs duties and enriching Cork and his associates. Cork was also linked to the Caribbean through Phane Beecher, whose father had developed the town of Bandon as part of the Munster plantation, and who had left Ireland in 1627 to become the governor of St. Kitts (or St. Christophers), one of the Leeward Islands. Beecher brought with him financial investment from Cork and later large numbers of indentured servants. The Barrys, kin of the earls of Barrymore and of Cork, his father-in-law, were also early investors in Barbados.[6] Thanks to the fact that Sir Nathaniel Rich had surveyed Ireland in 1622, Cork enjoyed close connections with his brother Robert Rich, earl of Warwick, who was the most enterprising and colonial of English peers and held multiple interests across the English Atlantic, especially in Bermuda and Virginia. In 1641 Cork's youngest daughter Mary married Charles, later earl of Warwick, and thereby strengthened further the connection.[7] Finally, Cork manufactured cheap iron bars that served as the currency used to buy African slaves.[8]

Though Cork may have stood back from direct engagement in colonial enterprise, operating through trusted intermediaries, he understood better than any the importance of these social and political networks and of the opportunities afforded by Irish land, woodlands, and labour. Little wonder then that the earl drew attention to the rich pickings that might be had in the wake of the 1641 rebellion and suggested to Warwick that Catholic lands should be confiscated and settled with Protestants: to 'root the popish parte of the natives out of the kingdome, and to plant it with English protestants'. This would secure Ireland for the king and make the Crown a fortune.[9] Others concurred. One noted in April 1642 that 'a man with one hundred pounds in his purse shall purchase that [land] here [in Ireland], whereupon he may live better than he that hath 100 per annum in England'.[10]

Of course, this is exactly what happened (see Chapter 2 above). The revolution in Irish landholding, which began with the plantations of the late sixteenth century and culminated with the Cromwellian and later the Restoration land settlements, resulted in the wholesale transfer of land from Catholic to Protestant hands. During the 1640s and 1650s alone the English state expropriated and reallocated 2,500,000 acres and over the course of these years roughly eight million acres changed hands, more than anywhere else in early modern Europe.[11] As a result of this Catholic landholding dropped from about 54 per cent in 1641 to 23 per cent in *c.*1670. It was one of the key developments that shaped the face of modern Ireland and ensured that land was 'the goddess'.[12] The mid-century revolution in landholding afforded particular opportunities to an influential oligarchy of London merchant adventurers (or 'venture capitalists'), along with a few from Amsterdam who during the 1640s secured these Irish acres at rock-bottom rates.

In a pioneering monograph David Brown has made visible this group of roughly 20 men, led by Maurice Thomson. They organised themselves as a corporate body and enjoyed strong links to Westminster MPs, to local civic bodies across London, to England's social and political elite (especially the earl of Warwick), and to the English army and navy. Brown has shown how the adventurers used Irish land to fuel their global expansionism. Irish estates formed part of a portfolio of investments that extended from the fisheries of Newfoundland to the Virginian tobacco plantations, from the sugar colonies in the Caribbean to the trade of spices, coffee, and calicoes in India, and of enslaved peoples in West Africa.[13] For the adventurers, Ireland, with its temperate climate, cheap land, and growing population, was a perfect source of raw commodities for manufacture in England, along with a ready supply of labour.[14] Contemporaries recognised this. According to the Old English author and cleric John Lynch, Donough O'Brien, fourth earl of Thomond, compared the economic exploitation of Ireland with the Caribbean (or West Indies). Thomond may have confused the 'West Indies' with India but his observation nonetheless rang true: 'Ireland is another India for the English, a more profitable India for them than ever the Indies were to the Spaniards'.[15]

With the onset of the wars of the three kingdoms in the 1640s, the adventurers became indispensable to the parliamentary cause funding the war effort, securing Indian saltpetre, which was essential for gunpowder manufacture, transporting goods and men, and supplying armies, especially in Ireland. By the early 1650s, the adventurers, led by the Thomson clan, had taken over control of all of England's external trade, including that of the East India Company. In a nutshell, the adventurers traded enslaved Africans for Spanish silver and sugar from Barbados. They then used this silver to buy Indian textiles, which could, in turn, be exchanged for more slaves.[16] In 1656 alone Maurice Thomson dispatched, on his own account, 11 ships to

India and five to Africa under the auspices of the Guinea company, while never losing sight of business interests in Ireland, Newfoundland, Virginia, and across the English Caribbean.[17] One of his close allies, Martin Noel, who had acquired vast estates in Ireland and also operated as a privateer, traded with the Levant in the Mediterranean and across the English Atlantic (New England, Virginia, Nevis, Montserrat, Barbados, and later Jamaica).[18] These same men then went on to play a key role in facilitating the Restoration of King Charles II, who, in turn, guaranteed their Irish landed windfalls.[19] In short, Irish land underpinned English expansionism around the early modern world.

Legislation, in the form of the Navigation Acts, which the adventurers spearheaded, confirmed their pre-eminence and privileged the English economy over the Irish one by creating a political economy of dependency centred on London. The passage of the Navigation Act in 1651 represented, according to Brown, 'a complete victory for the Adventurers' and served as 'the foundation of English imperial policy for the next century'.[20] The adventurers had created on their own doorstep—in Ireland—a subservient economy, something later endorsed by Sir William Petty when he defined the Irish by their function as reliable producers, providing sustenance and revenue for the English state.[21]

It is hard to overstate the importance of London as a city where anglicising policies were formulated, where lawyers and imperial agents were trained, where joint-stock companies were founded, where credit was secured, and where peoples from across the early modern world interacted, networked, and did business. That said, whether in parliament or on the London stage, the Irish were ridiculed, vilified, and even feared, especially at moments of crisis—the Nine Years' War (1594–1603), the 1640s, the Popish Plot (1678–81), and after 1688.[22] This hostility did nothing to stem the flow of migrants. Cosmopolitan London was for many people from Ireland—from all faiths, ethnic identities, and social backgrounds—a gateway to the early modern world.

As the century passed wave after wave of migrants, including large numbers of refugees during the 1640s and 1690s,[23] moved to London and by the 1780s roughly 23,000 Irish people lived there.[24] A considerable proportion were apprentices and domestic servants who established themselves in the eastern part of the city. Roughly one-third of all vagrants in London were Irish.[25] Those better off came together in close-knit communities linked by bonds of kinship, marriage, sociability, and commerce. The Inns of Court had attracted men from Ireland since the sixteenth century; some returned to Ireland but many established themselves at court or in the city.[26] These professional lawyers worked closely and often intermarried with doctors and members of the merchant community, who settled in significant numbers from the mid-seventeenth century. From their bases in Cheapside, Irish Catholic merchant families—the Arthurs, Blakes, Bodkins, Frenches, Kirwans, Lynches, and Skerretts—connected Ireland with Continental Europe and with the Asian and Atlantic worlds.[27] Many made considerable fortunes trading sugar and enslaved peoples and developed extensive and trusted trading networks that moved resources around the globe as they traversed the empires of the European powers, especially France, Spain, and Portugal.[28] By the turn of the eighteenth century, the London firm of Fitzgerald, originally from Waterford, was one of the most important Irish mercantile houses, with large tobacco interests.[29] Protestants from Ireland also prospered.[30] Whatever their faith, the men and women from Ireland who made London their home shaped its development, something that has been explored for the eighteenth century and the later period, but not for the pre-1700 years.[31]

One of the most influential commercial entrepreneurs from Ireland during the later seventeenth century was Arthur Annesley, earl of Anglesey (1614–86), a major political figure in Restoration Ireland and England where he held the office of lord privy seal. The marriage of his daughter to John Thomson (1648–1720), son of Maurice, afforded Anglesey immediate access to an exclusive and extraordinary wealthy and influential group. He described Maurice Thomson as 'my brother' and shamelessly promoted the interests of his son-in-law at court.[32] Back in Ireland Anglesey was the greatest beneficiary of the Restoration land settlement and his holdings increased tenfold from 14,972 acres in 1641 to an incredible 144,546 acres, 129,432 of which were deemed to be profitable, making him the fourth largest landholder in Ireland.[33] He used his new-found wealth to speculate. As entries in Anglesey's diary record, whilst in London he regularly attended meetings at the 'African Company', the 'Gambia Company', the Committee of Trade and Plantations, or with commissioners from New England, Jamaica, and Tangier.[34] During the 1670s and early 1680s, Anglesey entertained other entrepreneurs who shared his imperial business interests. His dining companions included an interesting mix of Catholic and Protestant grandees from Ireland: Lords Cecil Calvert of Baltimore (1605–75),

Thomas Butler of Ossory (1634–80), William O'Brien of Inchiquin (c. 1640–92), and Francis Aungier of Longford (c. 1632–1700).

Anecdotal as they are, the varied colonial activities of Baltimore, Ossory, Inchiquin, and Longford offer insight into the nitty-gritty operation of imperialism during these years and illustrate the *modus operandi* of agents of empire from Ireland. Anglesey dined with Lord Baltimore on 4 October 1675, the month before he died. Despite his Catholicism, Baltimore's father, George Calvert, had been a favourite of the duke of Buckingham and had acquired over 9,000 Irish acres in Counties Wexford and Longford together with an Irish peerage during the early decades of the seventeenth century. In 1628, keen to promote plantations 'in those remote parts of the world', he transferred his interests from Ireland to the New World, first to Newfoundland (he had obtained a charter to found a colony in 1623)[35] and later to Maryland (the charter was issued in 1632).[36] In 1628 Baltimore's brother-in-law, Sir Robert Talbot of Kildare, and about 40 other Irish settlers, travelled to Newfoundland in order to 'builde and sett and sowe' and exploit the fisheries.[37] Harsh climatic conditions drove the colonists south, where Cecil, who had been schooled in Waterford, founded a proprietary colony in Maryland, which his younger brother Leonard later governed.[38] Maryland became a base for Catholic missions into neighbouring Virginia and later Pennsylvania and attracted Irish Catholics, sometimes from the Caribbean as well as further afield. The first few generations of Calverts were seasoned colonists and highly entrepreneurial, with investments in the East India Company as well as in the Atlantic, but Maryland as a 'Catholic colony' ultimately failed after 1688, partly for the want of leadership.[39]

On 29 August 1679 Anglesey supped with the earl of Ossory at Windsor Castle.[40] As the eldest son of the duke of Ormond, who governed Ireland for much of the later seventeenth century, as a distinguished veteran of the Continental wars, and as a great favourite at court, Ossory had extensive political experience and influence. In July 1680 he was appointed as governor of Tangier, dubbed by some as a 'failed colony'.[41] In the event Ossory's premature death prevented him from taking up his post in Tangier, which, like Bombay, had formed part of Catherine of Braganza's dowry on her marriage to Charles II in 1661.[42] Had he lived Ossory would have replaced another of Annesley's dinner guests, William O'Brien, second earl of Inchiquin, who in 1659 had been captured by Barbary pirates but went on to serve in 1674 as governor of Tangier and captain general of the king's forces.[43] Catholic O'Briens—Murrough, first earl of Inchiquin (d. 1674), and his brother Christopher—had served briefly in Tangier during the early 1660s, along with John Fitzgerald, a former Irish confederate and the deputy governor, who according to Samuel Pepys was dishonest, dishonourable, and sought to 'raise the Irish and suppress the English interest there'.[44] This fortified city, strategically situated as a gateway between Europe and North Africa, operated as free port, unfettered by the Navigation Acts, as a base for the Royal Africa Company, and as a royal colony. During the 1660s the Crown invested heavily (£75,000 per annum) in developing the port, fortifications, and creating a cosmopolitan colony. By the later 1670s Tangier had over 2,000 inhabitants, of whom at least 270 were 'Irish men and papists', 18 'Portugal priests' and 'Irish fryers... [who] keep the Catherdrall church and another smale church', and a significant community of Jews together with Portuguese, Dutch, Italian, and especially French merchants.[45] Irish names included senior figures like Inchiquin, Fitzgerald, and Thomas Dongan, later governor of New York, together with Cusacks, Farrells, Glyns, MacKennys, Molloys, O'Briens, Roches, Walshs, and Whites.[46] Many were Irish speakers and during the siege of 1680 the Irish soldiers used Irish to communicate with each other.[47] Despite the unprecedented investment—two million pounds over a 20-year period and more than any other colony—the absence of a corporate structure, the decision to exclude Tangier from Atlantic trade, and relentless Moroccan aggression meant that the colony was abandoned in 1684.[48]

This shambles in North Africa did not prevent William III appointing, in 1689, Inchiquin as governor of Jamaica, which England had taken from Spain in 1655 (as part of Oliver Cromwell's 'Western Design') and developed as a 'sugar and slavery' colony. Inchiquin died there in 1692 and his will reflects both his Irish interests, his slave trading, and his imperial priorities.[49] His extensive ancestral patrimony in County Clare, which his Catholic father Murrough had managed to cling onto after the Restoration, passed to his eldest son William. The second earl's younger son James, who had accompanied him to the Caribbean, received an annuity of £250 (from the manor of O'Brien's Bridge in Ireland), his father's estate in County Cavan, 'all money and other effects and revenues in the Assiento [i.e. the slaves sent to New Spain] and... his estate in America', together with the earl's interest in a ship called the *Adventure* (and her cargo).[50]

Back in London, Anglesey was as interested in Asia as he was in the Atlantic and Mediterranean. Another associate was Francis Aungier, first earl of Longford, whose brother, Gerald Aungier (*c.*1640–77), enjoyed a prominent career with the East India Company. Aungier's grandfather Francis, Lord Longford, had served as master of the rolls in Ireland, had played an active role in the plantations of Ulster, Wexford, Leitrim, and Longford, and was associated with Anglesey's father, Lord Mountnorris, a prominent official and avaricious planter. In 1669 Aungier became president of Surat and governor of Bombay, which the Portuguese had ceded, along with Tangier, to England as part of Charles II's marriage settlement. Unlike his royal colony in the Mediterranean, the king asked the East India Company to develop Bombay on his behalf, which may have accounted for its long-term success (and Tangier's failure).[51] As governor Aungier colonised Bombay as his grandparents had Ireland and laid the foundations for its later development. Bombay, like Tangier, may have been an 'English' colony but extant censuses, dating from the 1670s, revealed the presence of soldiers with Irish Catholic surnames: Butler, Barnewall, Kennedy, Talbot, and O'Neill. During these years Aungier increased significantly the export of Indian textiles that fed the 'calico craze' of the 1670s. A hugely successful businessman, he regularly remitted money to his brother Longford, who developed Dublin's first suburb—along Aungier Street—on the back of this Indian treasure.[52]

As these brief vignettes illustrate, Anglesey's imperial network, thanks to the Irish and Thomson connections, had a global reach, stretching from Newfoundland to the Chesapeake, from Tangier to West Africa to the Caribbean, and from English India back to London and Dublin. Though Anglesey did not record their names in his diary, he was certainly acquainted with William Penn (1644–1718), who spent much of his life on his family estates in County Cork and in London before converting to Quakerism and securing in 1680 a charter to found Pennsylvania. Certainly Anglesey dined on 7 August 1676 with Penn's close (and Munster-born) friend, Sir Robert Southwell (1635–1702), who had served as ambassador to Portugal and in 1675 became secretary of the newly formed but all important board of the Lords of Trade and Plantations.[53] Anglesey may also have known Thomas Dongan (1634–1715), governor of New York between 1682 and 1688 and the nephew of the Richard Talbot, later duke of Tyrconnell.[54] A decade later Richard Coote (1636–1701), baron of Coloony and earl of Bellamont, who was involved in transatlantic trading ventures, became governor of Massachusetts, New York, and New Hampshire.[55] No doubt Anglesey would have been acquainted with him and certainly knew his father Richard and his uncle Charles, first earl of Mountrath.

Three general observations can be made about the agents of empire associated with Anglesey. First, it was a religiously and ethnically diverse group comprising Anglicans, Catholics, and Quakers, from a variety of ethnic backgrounds (Gaelic Irish, Old English, and New English) who were committed to securing religious toleration for their respective colonies.[56] The Calverts of Baltimore made no secret of their commitment to Catholicism and of wanting to create in Maryland a safe haven for Catholics by promoting a religiously tolerant society.[57] In 1649 Lord Calvert persuaded the Maryland general assembly to pass legislation that provided religious toleration for the colony's Christian settlers.[58] In Jamaica the significant Irish Catholic population effectively enjoyed liberty of conscience.[59] Pennsylvania quickly attracted c.440 Irish Quakers.[60] In 1686 Dongan passed a charter of liberties ('Dongan's Charter'), which provided for freedom of religion. Religious toleration characterised Aungier's Bombay and it quickly became known as a place where 'none shall speake evill of the English religion, nor shall they speak evill of other religions'.[61] Some were motivated by faith and others by a recognition that toleration and religious pluralism were good for business, allowing fledgling colonies to attract talent and investment. Even in Ireland, where Catholics received rough justice, the Crown during the later decades of the seventeenth century effectively accepted religious pluralism.[62] This, of course, changed in Ireland after 1690, with the introduction of the penal laws. In short, it was easier for the Stuarts to achieve the religious pluralism, even the toleration, that they desired across their colonies than in England.

Second, these men engaged with a variety of 'colonial' models, which given their Irish connections would have been familiar to them, and which might explain why men, including Catholics, from Ireland made for effective early colonial governors in frontier settlements in Bombay, Tangier, the Caribbean (St. Kitts, Nevis, Montserrat, and Jamaica), and the mainland colonies (Maryland, Pennsylvania, New York, and South Carolina).[63] Third, these imperialists from Ireland, all members of the social elite, were often closely interconnected, meeting in London, but also coming together as they also circulated around the British Isles, Europe, and the English empire. Figures like Inchiquin and Dongan moved from Ireland to service on the Continent, where they had formed part of the royal court in exile, to Tangier, where Dongan served as Inchiquin's deputy, and from there to the New World (Jamaica and New York). For his part, Anglesey plugged these men into the powerful and exclusive network of merchant adventurers, led by the Thomsons, based largely in London but with strong links to Amsterdam and Lisbon. In short, relationships forged in London could well determine the success—or failure—of men from Ireland with imperial ambitions.

Finally, it is worth noting the broad similarities between the imperial patchwork of colonies that comprised the English empire. The proprietorial colonies in the pre-war English Caribbean, Maryland, Carolina, and even Pennsylvania, where the proprietor exercised regional sovereignty or feudal powers, were similar to the palatinate lordship enjoyed by the Butlers of Ormond, which was only abolished in 1715 by the County Palatine Tipperary Act, and to some arrangements with leading 'undertakers' and power brokers in Ireland who combined private interest with public service. The trading or corporate model in early Virginia or that of the East India Company shaped the plantation of the county and city of Londonderry by the Irish Society.[64] Though the precise nature of governance varied across these colonies, charters (or letters patent), as Ken MacMillan noted, 'set the rules of empire'. The Crown might delegate considerable authority yet all colonists recognised the ultimate sovereignty of the king with whom many, especially from amongst the elite, enjoyed a personal relationship. This changed over time. The drive for more direct rule from London, often propelled by trading and economic imperatives, came first to Ireland in the 1650s before being extended across the English Atlantic to the Caribbean colonies and New York. Increasingly, after 1675, the king became more vigorous and systematic in enforcing his authority and strengthening powers of royal governors, many of whom were from Ireland.[65]

II Trans-imperialism and global empires

Described as that 'famous island set in a Virginian sea', Ireland formed an integral part of the Atlantic world.[66] Yet the diverse nature of Irish experiences—as servants, soldiers, subversives, and slave masters—across the early modern globe makes for fragmented, but nonetheless compelling, narratives. The absence of evidence can, of course, be frustrating. Nini Rodgers has suggested that the Irish failure to found a colony in the Caribbean meant that they are rarely considered as part of official accounts. 'Working within the empires of others, they left behind no distinctive state structure, language or architectural style', yet Rodgers continues that 'the Irish have been a changing but constant presence in the history of the Caribbean'.[67] The same held true for the mainland American colonies, from Newfoundland to the Carolinas, and for Bombay in India.

A people 'without an empire',[68] men from Ireland instead piggybacked on the empires of others.[69] Recent scholarship has highlighted this trans-imperialism and the extent to which people, both Protestants and Catholics, from Ireland contributed to the imperial activities of the Portuguese, the Spanish, the French, the Danish, and the Dutch global empires, as well as the English one. They participated in the voyages of discovery. William Eris (or Ayres) from Galway allegedly sailed with Christopher Columbus on his historic voyage of 1492 to the Americas (in 1477 Columbus had stopped in Galway as he voyaged from Portugal to Iceland).[70] Three Galway sailors were with Ferdinand Magellan on his circumnavigation of the globe between 1519 and 1522. The first Irish people to travel to Chile were 'Guillermo' and 'Juan' from Galway, who arrived in 1520 with Magellan's expedition, and discovered the strait that bears his name.[71] Others, for whom no record survives, could well have sailed with Vasco da Gama, who after 1497 opened the direct sea route to Asia.

The buccaneering of English adventurers attracted mariners from Ireland who sailed with Sir Francis Drake when in 1585 he raided Spanish bases in the Caribbean.[72] The early decades of the seventeenth century—and the opening up of the New World—was the heyday of piracy in Ireland. From their bases along the south-west coastline of Munster, pirates ranged as far as Harbour Grace in Newfoundland, to Mamora in North West Africa, to Tunis and Algiers in the Mediterranean.[73] Abroad they formed part of an international network and at home they operated in cahoots with smugglers and entrepreneurs based along the Munster coastline, including the ubiquitous Boyles of Cork.[74] Others, especially merchants and sailors, fell into the hands of Barbary pirates with some converting to Islam.[75] Then in 1631 Barbary pirates sacked the town of Baltimore in West Cork and enslaved at least 100 people. The lucky few were ransomed. For example, in 1646 19 Irish women were redeemed from slavery in Algiers. Six came from Youghal. Two others—Ellen Hawkins and Joan Brabrook—had been seized from Baltimore 15 years earlier.[76] Involvement in privateering continued as the century passed, with Wexford and Waterford serving as privateering hubs during the 1640s. With the completion of the Cromwellian reconquest these privateers and pirates relocated to Continental ports and to safe havens in the Caribbean, especially Jamaica.[77]

By the 1660s Irish people were to be found in the Spanish, French, and Dutch Caribbean, the Portuguese and later Dutch Amazon, across New Spain, and in English settlements from Newfoundland to the Chesapeake in North America, the Caribbean, India, and the Mediterranean, at Tangier in North Africa. At sea, they served in royal and company navies, slave ships, or as pirates and privateers. On land, they joined colonial settlements, forged commercial networks, worked as administrators, soldiers, educators, priests, preachers, servants, and labourers. By the 1680s Irishmen, involved in the trade of enslaved people, were also based in West Africa.[78]

In the Amazon the Irish operated as entrepreneurs and colonists from 1609 when Philip Purcell, who traded tobacco, recruited 14 men to establish 'an Irish colony'. According to Joyce Lorimer this was 'the earliest example of independent Irish colonial projects in the New World'.[79] Purcell was later joined by Bernardo O'Brien and others (de Courcy, Gayner, Moore, Mulryan, and O'Malley) who worked as tobacco and timber merchants in the Dutch Amazon during the early decades of the seventeenth century. Though they mastered the languages of the region, amongst themselves O'Brien and his compatriots communicated in Irish.[80] The Dutch connection may be linked to the relationships forged back in Ireland when the earl of Thomond encouraged Dutch tenants to settle on his estates. O'Brien later claimed that he was the son of 'Sir Cornelio Obrien...a noble gentlemen of the house of Thomond' and that his motivation to travel was 'the desire he had to see countries and strange things'. In 1621, aged 17, he left for London in search of adventure.[81] It is even possible that O'Brien formed part of the shipment of settlers dispatched to the Essequibo River in Guiana by the Anglo-Dutch merchant, Sir William Courteen, a close ally of the Thomsons.[82] In the Amazon, O'Brien, according to his own account, 'earned the friendship of the [Tupi] cannibals. He learned their language and went more than 200 leagues inland, surveyed the rivers, mountains, drugs and secrets of the Indians and brought an Indian province to his alliance'.[83] He also understood how to navigate the complex waterways at the mouth of the Amazon. No wonder the Dutch were keen to do business with him even if he was Catholic and also worked alongside the English.[84]

Later accounts by O'Brien and his compatriot Jaspar Chillan offer incredible stories of exploring the interior, and of keeping the peace amongst the Indians who laboured on their tobacco 'plantation'.[85] A suggestive account of a meeting between O'Brien and 'an Amazon queen' resonated with Burnell's portrayal of Langartha.[86] A Spanish memo of 1631 claimed that the

Irish 'know the language and customs of those savages', adding that they were 'well received by the said savages'. However, suspicious of their relationships with English 'heretics', the Spaniards refused to work with them.[87] During the 1640s Irish Catholics, eager to exploit the rich resources of the Amazon—tobacco, dyes, timber, and sugar—offered to establish colonies in other areas under Portuguese and Dutch control. A proposal by Peter Sweetman to bring 400 Irish, most of them married couples, from St. Kitts to Belém in northern Brazil, came to nought.[88] However, as a result of these negotiations, William Brown arrived in Pará, close to Belém, in 1647 with 'nine boatloads' of Irish people, many of whom claimed to be married. It is not clear what became of them but three years later the Jesuits suggested sending hundreds of Irish families to the captaincies of São Paulo and São Vicente in southern Brazil.[89] The Dutch did not hesitate to commission William Gayner of Leitrim in County Longford to relocate and settle on the island of Tobago (or Nieuw Walcheren). Years later Gayner's Dutch widow Christian petitioned the Dutch government for the recovery of losses he had incurred in their service.[90] Though the details are sparse, other men from Ireland served the Dutch in the Caribbean. In 1665 there were 26 Irish men living on the Dutch island of Saba and others on the neighbouring island of St. Eustatius.[91] As these examples highlight, the economic and commercial considerations of the Dutch consistently overrode religious concerns.[92]

Yet religion mattered. O'Brien later claimed that 'amongst the Irish [in his Amazonian colony] were 4 good scholars and Latinists who resolved to bring the knowledge of God to the Indians'.[93] It is not clear if these men were priests but it is likely. As members of religious orders, Irish Catholics travelled to the remotest corners of the known world as educators and missionaries. Franciscans and Jesuits from Ireland served in Spanish and Portuguese stations, especially across Latin America, and were seen to have an advantage over their Iberian co-religionists because they could often speak English and therefore counter the work of Dutch and English missionaries. One of the earliest was Achilles Holden, active in Santo Domingo in Hispaniola in 1525. A few decades later Richard Arthur became the bishop of Santiago de Cuba and vicar general of Florida.[94] The Limerick-born Jesuit, Thomas Field (1546/9–1625), who had been educated at Douai then Louvain, arrived in Brazil in 1577, mastering the Tupi language and later writing a catechism.[95] He spent a decade there before moving on to Argentina and Paraguay, where he established a province in 1587, and taught indigenous languages to other young Jesuits.[96] The Jesuits were first to proselytise in the New World but the Franciscans dispatched larger numbers of priests as they circulated around the globe. During the early decades of the fourteenth century, James of Ireland, a Franciscan friar, accompanied Odoric of Perdenone to Asia. They sailed 'from Ormus to India, landing at Thane', near Mumbai before travelling to Ceylon, Sumatra, Java, and China. They spent three years in Dadu (Beijing) returning to Italy overland through central Asia.[97] Three hundred years later Waterford-born Luke Wadding, OFM, rector of the Irish College in Rome, kept in close touch with Franciscan missions around the world and especially in Latin America (Peru, Columbia, Bolivia, and Ecuador).[98] His cousin Michael (or Miguel Gódinez) spent 34 years living in Mexico, first amongst the indigenous peoples in Sonora and Sinaloa and then teaching at the university,[99] and his nephew, Francis Harold, later wrote books on the church in Peru.[100]

Most priests travelled to the New World from Continental Europe, which had been an important destination for Irish missionaries, merchants, and migrants for centuries. From the early decades of the seventeenth century, an average of 500 men per annum migrated to Continental Europe; and if women and children are included the figure probably stands at 700, which was a far higher number than for those who crossed the Atlantic.[101] Those migrants who took up arms for the kings of Spain and France are particularly well documented, especially the thousands of 'Wild Geese' of the post 1690 era. Significant numbers also fought east of the Elbe, in Scandinavia, and in the global armies of European powers.[102] Thus Irish troops were an important component of the military machines during the Seven Years' War (1756–63), fought between Britain and France for global supremacy. French and British armies battled it out in Europe, North America, the Caribbean, West Africa, and in India. During the 1750s Count Thomas Lally, the son of a Jacobite soldier, commanded the French forces in India, where he fought against Eyre Coote, a Protestant from Limerick, whose military victories paved the way for British control over Bengal.[103]

Many Irish opted to soldier, while others studied in Europe. Between 1578 and 1680, 29 Irish Colleges were established across Continental Europe, from Paris in the north to Rome in the south and from Lisbon in the west to Prague in the east.[104] The levels of interaction, and the nature of the contact between scholars, soldiers, sailors, and merchants from Ireland and those of their host nations were diverse, ranging from transient visits to permanent settlement, and often involved extensive internal mobility and migration in multiple geographies.[105] As the seventeenth century progressed, permanent settlements emerged often around merchant communities, such as those in Belgium (Ostend and Bruges),[106] in Spain (Cadiz, La Coruña, Málaga,[107] Seville, and Bilbao),[108] in Portugal (Lisbon),[109] and in France (Bordeaux, La Rochelle, and Cognac). Detailed case studies of these communities collectively constitute innovative first steps towards recapturing the diverse and often complex nature of the experiences of the Irish abroad, the processes of assimilation and appropriation that these migrants underwent, and their varied senses of 'Irishness'.[110]

The range and diversity of Irish experiences is illustrated by the example of the Lamport siblings—Catherine, John, Gerald, and William—who left Wexford during the early part of the seventeenth century. Catherine found a new life on the Continent as a nun. Gerald served as a soldier in the army of Philip IV of Spain. John became a Franciscan friar in Madrid and later served in Mexico, ministering to indigenous peoples.[111] William attended the Irish College at Santiago de Compostela before crossing the Atlantic to Mexico, where he went on to claim the throne of New Spain, alleging that he was the legitimate heir of Philip III. He wrote the first proclamation of Mexican independence in 1642 (the year after the 1641 rebellion had broken out in Ireland), which advocated for the freedom of African slaves and the return of lands to the indigenous Indian population.[112] Later captured, Lamport was tried by the inquisition and in 1659 burned alive for heresy and sedition.[113] In death Lamport became a national hero in Mexico, just as Bernardo O'Higgins, whose father had been born in Sligo, would later be celebrated for helping to secure Chilean independence. Similarly, Admiral William Browne, from County Mayo, is seen as father of the Argentinean navy and Daniel O'Leary of Cork, who served during the early nineteenth century in the wars of independence in Venezuela and Colombia, is revered in both countries.[114] Lamport may have been the first but the Irish presence in Latin America, especially as resistance leaders as well as missionaries and colonists, had a long history.

As well as illuminating celebrated figures like Lamport, the Spanish Inquisition records capture, as Thomas O'Connor's important book reveals, the life stories of more ordinary people accused of heresy. They included John Matthews, a 30-year-old from Kinsale, who managed a sugar estate in Bogotá, and Robert Walters, a 20-year-old from Limerick. Walters served on the 1629 English expedition to St. Kitts and later entered the Spanish navy, fighting against the Dutch in Brazil.[115] Particularly intriguing was the case of John Drake (Gales/Welsh/Cox), aged 48, who appeared before the Cartagena Inquisition in 1647. The son of an English soldier, who had served in Ireland during the Nine Years' War, and an Irish Catholic mother, John was apprenticed to his mother's uncle in Ghent. He preferred to fight and in 1618 joined the imperial army, then the English navy, and during the 1640s served in the royalist army. With the defeat of Charles I, John joined a Dutch ship that brought him to the Caribbean where he hopped from one Irish settlement to the next before ending up in Caracas in Venezuela, where he settled down with a Spanish woman.[116]

There are also fleeting glimpses in the Spanish records of Irish women. For example, during the late 1620s Maria Nele/O'Neill and her husband, Captain Cornelio Cornelius, originally from Waterford, had settled in St. Kitts with their son. According to Maria's later account, they had prospered, owning land, silver, jewellery, and 16 enslaved people (worth 300,000 reales). In 1639 the family fled, first to Santo Domingo and then to Cartagena, where Maria sought refuge in the home of another Irish-born woman, Maria Roche. Maria Roche, wife of Governor Melchor de Aguilera, had travelled to New Spain with her daughter and husband, an official in the Spanish government who previously served in Italy and France. Their daughter, Teresa (b. 1613), had been educated in a Milanese convent before moving to Cartagena, where she met and married the governor of New Mexico. Maria Roche's willingness to help Maria O'Neill suggests that her Irishness may have meant something to her but it would appear that her daughter Teresa was fully Hispanicised.[117] Other material in the Spanish archives, as Kirsten Block and Jenny Shaw have shown, charts Irish migration from the English Atlantic to territories controlled by Spain (Portobello, Cartagena, Santo Domingo, Margarita, Puerto Rico, and Veracruz). For example, in 1642 Richard Hackett, who held land on Barbados, travelled as a refugee to Hispaniola and asked that he be given command of the 350 Irishmen there which he had 'outfitted and armed at his own cost'. His offer was refused but other Irish troops helped to defend Hispaniola from the English onslaught in 1655.[118]

Though initially suspicious of 'foreigners', some Irish women and more Irish men had by the turn of the eighteenth century become embedded in the Spanish empire. The career of Ricardo Wall (1694–1774), 'of the Irish nation' and originally from Limerick, offers a compelling illustration of this. In 1754 Wall became secretary of state in Spain, secretary for the Indies, and briefly secretary for war and used his offices to support Irish mercantile interests in the Canaries, Bilbao, and Cadiz and to favour Irish soldiers, including Ambrose O'Higgins, who rose to prominence in Chile, and Alexander O'Reilly in Cuba.[119] O'Reilly (1723–94), a native from County Meath, who at the age of 11 joined the Hibernia regiment in Spain, fought all over Europe before being sent to Cuba, where he overhauled and reformed the army and rebuilt Cuba's fortifications along with those in Puerto Rico. He went on to be governor of Cuba and Louisiana. O'Reilly's passage to Cuba was via Madrid; however, others migrated within the Caribbean.[120] Irish transplantees from the English colonies of Barbados and Jamaica later migrated to Cuba. For example, Juan Duany, from Connaught, helped to construct the fortifications in Santiago, in south-eastern Cuba, and his descendants went on to play an important role on the island through-out the seventeenth and eighteenth centuries. Many others, including Juan's son, Ambrosio, made their fortunes in sugar production. Ricardo O'Farrill y O'Daly (c.1677–1730), from Montserrat and before that County Longford, also came to Cuba and became one of the most notorious Irish figures involved in the Atlantic slave trade. As a result of this migration Irish names litter the Cuban landscape.[121] Calle O'Reilly is one of the main streets in Old Havana and the 'palacio O'Farrill' is a heritage hotel there.

The Atlantic ports—Cadiz,[122] Nantes,[123] Bordeaux—afforded Irish mer-chants, soldiers and sailors easy access to colonisation, to slave trading, and to sugar production in the New World. David Dickson has shown how from the 1660s the French purchased, via European entrepôts or covertly, Irish salt beef for their Caribbean colonies.[124] Of the 550 families involved in the French slave trade, 17 had Irish surnames.[125] Between 1734 and 1749 the Riordans, originally from Cork, 'purchased and traded some 3,000 enslaved people spanning eleven voyages'.[126] One of the most successful Irish slavers was Antoine Walsh, the son of an Irish merchant who had settled in France in the later seventeenth century and married Marie O'Sheil/Shiell, whose grandfather had settled in France.[127] Over the course of his career Walsh, based in the Atlantic port of Nantes, made 40 slaving trips and shipped more than 12,000 enslaved Africans.[128] With his profits Walsh purchased a planta-tion for himself in the French colony of St. Domingue (modern day Haiti), which supplied up to 70 per cent of all of the sugar sent to France.[129] Walsh was not the only Hiberno-French family to prosper and of the 12 Saint-Domingue representatives attending the 1789 French National Assembly, three were of Irish descent.[130] The Irish also formed communi-ties in St. Kitts, which the French shared with the English until 1690, and

Guadeloupe and Martinique, which were settled after 1635. Irish priests visited periodically and one reported back in 1669 on the scale of Irish settlement: 200 in Martinique and 800 in Guadeloupe. A few prospered; the majority eked out existences in the remotest parts of the island.[131] According to William Stapleton, governor of the Leeward Islands, 'they live much as they do at home [in Ireland], in little huts, planting potatoes, tobacco, and as much indigo as will buy them canvas and brandy, and never advance so far as a sugar plantation'.[132]

Eager to develop their own sugar colony, the Danes purchased the island of St. Croix from the French in 1733. In return for religious toleration and access to land, Catholic Irishmen helped to develop sugar and slavery activities for the Lutheran Danish empire. Orla Power's research has illuminated the Irish presence on St. Croix, especially the activities of Nicholas Tuite (1705–72), who migrated there from Montserrat. On Montserrat, Tuite had a plantation of 100 acres with 41 enslaved Africans and, on St. Croix, he owned seven plantations and was part owner of seven others, all geared for sugar production.[133] By the mid eighteenth-century the Irish community on St. Croix numbered 250 people, along with over 22,000 enslaved people, and today the landscape of St. Croix bears names of Irish estates: Enfield Bog, Bog of Allen, Butler's Bay, and Castle Bourke.[134] As the example of St. Croix illustrates, a confessional analysis of migration to the Atlantic— though it might work for Spain and even France—obscures the reality of what actually happened elsewhere.[135]

The fact that enterprising figures like Nicholas Tuite relocated from Montserrat to St. Croix also highlights the level of mobility across empires within the Caribbean and the importance of following people, rather than being constrained by national borders, to better understand Irish activities in the New World. Though there has been some pioneering research done on trans-imperialism by a new generation of scholars, much work remains to be done. Rigorous interrogation of the archives of the Dutch, Portuguese, Spanish, French, Danes, and the records of the Inquisition and religious orders will allow us to better appreciate the scale of the Irish contribution to these early modern European empires, along with their lived experiences.[136] It might also allow for a better understanding of why people chose to migrate. 'Pull' factors—seeking adventure, a better life, or a fortune— clearly influenced the decision-making of some, along with 'push' factors associated with political exile, warfare, economic adversity, and expropriation. There is also evidence of 'chain migration', as the example of the

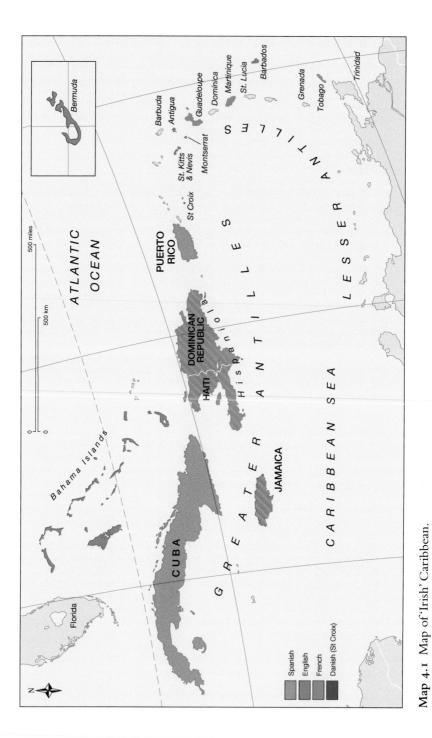

Map 4.1 Map of 'Irish' Caribbean.

Blakes, the Lynches, and the Frenches—all from Galway—highlights.[137] According to Louis Cullen, by the later seventeenth century, the Irish constituted 'the largest single flow of white migrants to the seventeenth-century West Indies', forming the majority of non-African workers.[138] Their Catholicism and, above all, the poverty of the majority has ensured that accounts of their lives are now largely lost from the historical record. As a result, the Irish remain marginal in histories of the region.[139]

III The 'Irish' empire

Spain had dominated the Caribbean for a century before England muscled in, first taking St. Kitts (1624) and using it as a base to settle the other Leeward islands of Nevis (1628), Montserrat (1632), and Antigua (1632), along with Barbados (1627) and later Jamaica (1655), see Map 4.1.[140] Their objective was to cultivate tobacco and sugar, which required a considerable labour force. Unable to gain access to the West African slave markets until the 1660s, England turned to Ireland for human capital.[141] From the early decades of the seventeenth century indentured men and women, predominately Catholic, left Ireland, especially Munster, in significant numbers.[142] The flow began in the 1620s and gathered momentum as the demand for tobacco and later for sugar increased. In the 1650s the Cromwellian authorities shipped thousands of Irish Catholics directly to the English colonies in Barbados and Jamaica.[143] During the later decades of the century the flow of indentured servants from Ireland lessened, but did not cease, as the trade of enslaved Africans satisfied the demands for labour in the sugar plantations.

Though some merchants migrated, the majority were indentured servants under the age of 25 who were from the lowest socio-economic sector of society, typically unskilled or semi-skilled servants or vagrants. The investor covered the cost of the indentured servant's passage, food, clothing, and shelter on the plantations in return for up to seven years of contracted labour (ten years in the case of convicts). On termination of the indenture masters were legally bound to offer 'freedom dues' in the form of a small parcel of land and a sum of money or its commodity equivalent.[144] Unlike the enslaved person, the indentured servant had some legal rights even if it proved challenging to exercise them.[145] However, during the period of indenture the person was, like an enslaved person, at the mercy of their master. Richard Ligon, who wrote a history of Barbados first published in

1657, distinguished between the categories of servitude: 'The slaves and their posterity, being subject to their masters forever, are kept and preserv'd with greater care than the servants, who are theirs but for five years'. Ligon described the life of an indentured servant: their basic housing, clothing, and diet; their long and hard working day, and the punishments they received. 'Truly I have seen such cruelty there done to servants, as I did not think one Christian could have done to another', wrote Ligon.[146] Of course, experiences did vary across the Caribbean and, according to Richard Dunn in *Sugar and Slaves*, indentured servants were better fed, clothed, and housed than enslaved people.[147]

Nearly one-third of these indentured servants were female. The 1678 census of the Leeward Islands (Table 4.1) shows that 660 women from Ireland lived in the islands, alongside 1,776 men, and 1,040 children. Nearly 40 per cent of migrants were female, largely Catholic with a significant number of Irish speakers, yet we know very little about them despite their importance for the labour market. As well as bearing and caring for considerable numbers of children, some worked as domestic servants but many of these women also laboured in the sugar plantations at least until the end of the seventeenth century when white women were pulled

Table 4.1 William Stapleton's census of the islands in 1678[148]

		Nevis	Antigua	St. Kitts	Montserrat	Total
White men						
	English	1,050	800	370	346	2,566
	Irish	450	360	187	769	1,766
	Other	34	76	138	33	281
White women						
	English	700	400	409	175	1,684
	Irish	120	130	—	410	660
	Other	8	141	130	6	158
White children						
	English	920	400	543	240	2,103
	Irish	230	120	—	690	1,040
	Other	9	8	120	13	150
Total		*3,521*	*2,308*	*1,897*	*2,682*	*10,408*
Black men		1,422	805	550	?	3,177
Black women		1,321	868	500	?	2,989
Black children		1,106	499	386	?	2,283
Total		*3,849*	*2,172*	*1,436*	*1,894*[149]	*9,351*[150]

out of agricultural production. What evidence we have for their lived experiences is anecdotal and indirect but the various censuses compiled during these years provide invaluable insights into the levels of migration and lived experiences.[151]

The 1678 census was the work of William Stapleton. By the 1670s the Tipperary-born Stapleton had amassed governorships of all the English Leeward islands and married a rich English heiress from Nevis (when he died in 1699 he left 183 enslaved Africans).[152] Stapleton's 'colonial counting', a tool widely used across the English empire (discussed in Chapter 5), provides a wonderful snapshot of the Irish living on the islands of Nevis, Antigua, St. Kitts, and Montserrat.[153] As the figures in Table 4.1 show, across the Leewards there were 10,408 whites, over a third (3,466) of whom were Irish. The community on Nevis, where Colonel James Russell, 'a native of Ireland', served as governor, comprised 800 people (450 men, 120 women, and 230 children) which equated to 23 per cent of the white, mostly English, population.[154] On neighbouring Antigua there were 610 Irish (360 men, 130 women, and 120 children) or 26 per cent of the white population.

Phane Beecher of Bandon had been the founding governor of St. Kitts which, by 1638, numbered 'six hundred Irish of both sexes'. Many only spoke Irish and probably included those who had been forcibly transplanted during the 1620s.[155] Though this figure could well have been inflated, the community shrank with the passage of time as settlers died or relocated to other settlements in the region. The 1678 census suggested that only 187 Irish men (but no women or children) lived scattered across the island (Table 4.1). Gaelic surnames associated with Munster and the west of Ireland (McSweeney, Murphy, O'Brien, O'Connor, O'Donovan, O'Driscoll, and O'Sullivan) predominated, along with Old English names (Butler, French, Lynch, and White). The absence of Irish women is striking given the reported numbers in 1638 and the high number of English women in 1678 (409).[156] Perhaps this was an oversight and the figures had been conflated or maybe significant intermarriage had occurred with English men, thus rendering for statistical purposes the Irish women 'English'. Interestingly, the census of 1707–8 of St. Kitts did not list ethnic origin but names like 'Honor Murphy' suggest the presence of Irish women.[157] A significant number of the Irish men served as rank-and-file soldiers in the 'English' forces in St. Kitts, Nevis, and especially Montserrat and, according to Stapleton, 'there is great difference between them and the English in trust and valour'.[158]

Only on Montserrat were the Irish in the majority with 1,869 people (769 men, 410 women, and 690 children) or 70 per cent of the white population. Little wonder Montserrat was described in 1634 as a 'noble plantation of Irish Catholiques' and in 1668 as 'almost an Irish colony'.[159] Anthony Briskett, a Protestant from County Wexford, arrived in 1632 and became the colony's first governor. When he died in 1646, Roger Osburne, born in County Waterford, took his place. Elizabeth, Osburne's sister, had first married Briskett and then Samuel Waad, described as an 'English gentleman'. Waad owned a plantation called Newark with 'one of stateliest sugar works' in the Caribbean, a tobacco plantation, a 'stately built stone house' along with fine furniture, 70 cattle, 500 sheep, hoggs, 30 'Christian servants', 50 'slaves young and old', and a great stock of tobacco and sugar.[160] Elizabeth had married well but Osburne and Waad feuded. According to a later account Osburne orchestrated, using his 'Irish complices', the 'barbarous and most inhuman murthering' of Waad. Osburne's henchmen allegedly included five 'barbarous Irish', Nathanael Read, married to 'an Irish woman', and 'one Dabram an Irish papist'. The publication of a broadside in 1654, which vilified the Irish and pitted them against the English, was an effort to hold Osburne to account. The authorities summoned him to Barbados but Osburne was never charged or punished for the murder.[161]

While Osburne appears to have nominally conformed, he allowed priests to operate on the island. Matteo Binasco, building on the pioneering scholarship of Aubrey Gwynn, has charted the activity of Irish priests in the Caribbean. During the first mission in 1638 to St. Kitts, two Irish priests, based on the French part of the island, ministered to people who only spoke Irish.[162] The Irish Jesuit, John Stritch of Limerick (1616–81), later used St. Kitts as a base from which to tend to the Irish communities in Montserrat.[163] The very presence of Catholic priests ensured that sectarianism and 'othering' continued with the Irish on Montserrat being branded as 'a bloody and perfidious people to the English Protestant interest'.[164] In spite of this Irish Catholics—mostly from Connacht and Munster—rose to positions as elected assemblymen and came to hold numerous offices of importance in Montserrat alongside English colonists and others of Irish Protestant background.[165] A closer look at the data underpinning the 1678 census (Table 4.1) paints an interesting picture of the Irish community where a high proportion of men (769) were married with children, living in households of between four and eight people. Many owned at least one enslaved person, while the more prosperous colonists owned more slaves.[166] Merchants, like

Henry Blake of Galway, amassed small fortunes often on the back of sugar produced by his 38 enslaved Africans. By 1676 he had made enough to go home, purchasing two estates, one in County Mayo and another in County Galway.[167] During the 1670s another prominent planter, David Galway, recorded on his census return that over 300 (of 1,869) Irish and 74 (of 992) enslaved Africans lived on his estate.[168]

The 'Wars of the Three Kings' (1688–91), as the conflict between William III, James II, and Louis XIV is known, played out in Montserrat—and across the Leewards—with the Catholic Irish, supported by the French, siding with James II. In July 1689 it was reported that the 'Irish Papists . . . have of late been very turbulent and rebellious'.[169] The defeat of James II did little to abate the fear that the Irish posed. In 1701 it was reported back to London that:

> Mountseratt is in far greater danger than any by reason of ye few Protestant inhabitants in that place, there being twinty Roman Catholics to one Protestant; and unless they quickly find out how to stop ye progress of the Irish among them, who daily grow thicker (being drawn thither out of Ireland and other parts by some relations or acquaintance of ye same opinion) they seem to be disposed, as soon as they'll find an opportunity (I mean ye Papists there, who would soon overpower ye others) to deliver the Island into ye hands of ye French, or any of their Popish confederates.[170]

Despite this the Irish plantations prospered and 'chain migration' from Ireland continued with people 'being drawn thither out of Ireland and other parts by some relations'.[171]

A very detailed census dating from 1729 provides a fascinating snapshot of the Irish community in Montserrat.[172] At one end of the spectrum was the planter, Colonel John Daly, who owned five houses, a windmill, a cattle mill, 100 cultivated acres, 100 uncultivated acres, plus 100 'sugar' acres, two horses, 28 mules, 40 sheep, two hogs, five firearms, and 115 enslaved men and women (50 and 40, respectively), and children (15 boys and 10 girls). His household comprised his wife, his 'little girl', five adult men—presumably kinsmen—and four male servants. Less well-off was John Blake, listed as a merchant, who lived in St. Anthony's district where he owned a house (but no land), 16 enslaved people (five men, three women, five boys, and three girls), a horse, a goat, two cows, five guns, and a sword. His household comprised two adult women, a boy under the age of nine, and a girl under the age of eight, and two 'white' servants (a man and woman). A significant number of women were listed. Some were clearly widows but were described as 'planter' or 'merchant'. Thus Cathleen Lynch, a 'planter', owned her house, a cattle mill, one acre of land, two horses, six firearms, and two swords, along with 16 enslaved people (11 men, one woman, three boys, and one girl). Living as part of Cathleen's household were two men and two women, possibly adult children or kin, one 'big girl' (under 14), two 'little girls' (under eight), and two 'white' male servants. St. Peter's or Northward District was a poorer area with the largest number of labourers, masons, carpenters, and fishermen. Yet even here Daniel O'Donnell, a 'labourer' and father to a 'little boy' and a 'little girl', owned a house, two acres of land, two cows, a gun, a sword, and ten enslaved people (four men, three women, two boys, and a girl). By 1729 Irish families owned the majority of the 5,855 slaves on Montserrat. Donald Akenson's case study of Montserrat shows that the Irish, 'schooled in early English imperialism', became aggressive and expert imperialists and slave masters themselves.[173] The landscape bears witness to Irish colonisation: the Galway estate, Cork Hill, and Kinsale,[174] as do the archaeological remains and the local telephone book, which lists families of Allens, Dalys, Farrells, Kirwans, Lynches, Rileys, Skerrets, Sweeneys, Tuites, Roches, and Ryans.[175] Others remained impoverished. Over time those who settled in the north of the island, where the soil was less fertile, often took African spouses and became known as the 'black Irish'.[176]

Though much attention has been paid to the Leewards and especially Montserrat, Barbados and Jamaica became important destinations for indentured servants from Ireland. Barbados exported 60 to 70 per cent of all sugar from the English Caribbean and by 1640 it had the largest white servant market in the English Atlantic. During the first half of the seventeenth century, Old English merchants—the Blakes, Bourkes, and Rices—bought plantations.[177] In 1636 Captain Thomas Anthony shipped men and women from Kinsale, three died en route and 53 more were sold over two days for 500 pounds of tobacco apiece. Anthony's 'shipment' included women between the ages of 17 and 35, two of whom were pregnant, and another who had syphilis.[178] Infamously, it was the destination for many of the Cromwellian transplantees during the 1650s; they were 'barbadosed'.[179] For

Table 4.2 Censuses of Leewards (1708), Jamaica (1673), and Barbados (1684)[180]

	Leewards, 1708	Jamaica, 1673	Barbados, 1684
White	7,311	7,768	19,568
Black	23,500	9.504	46,502

example, in 1655 Robert Molesworth, a Dublin merchant, secured a licence to transport 1,000 vagrants to Barbados, where his brother served on the council. Molesworth, along with other merchants and local officials, some of whom had links to the Thomsons and Martin Noel in London and many of whom had kin in Barbados, managed the trade that saw hundreds of men and women shipped from Dublin, Wexford, Cork, and Kinsale.[181] There is no consensus over the total number transported but in 1655 the planters on Barbados estimated that there were '3,000 Irish and 4,000 Scots, formerly prisoners of war and ready to rebel'.[182] David Brown suggests that 'hundreds, and perhaps thousands' were transported. He has analysed the only extant burial records for two parishes in Barbados, which 'show an eightfold increase in Irish deaths from 1652 to 1654, a level that was then sustained while the transports were at their height'. Mortality rates were around 50 per cent.[183] In 1669 a Catholic priest, John Grace, suggested that there was a community of 8,000 Irish, which—if accurate—would have meant that the Irish comprised nearly half of the white population of the island (the 1684 census simply recorded that there were 19,568 white people and 46,502 black people, see Table 4.2).[184]

Hilary Beckles, whose research on the history of Barbados and the region is pioneering, suggested that 'Irish servants and freemen suffered the most intense day-to-day discrimination and humiliation on the labour market. They were kept in slave like conditions and rarely given employment that conferred prestige'.[185] John Scott who visited Barbados during the 1650s noted that the Irish were 'derided by the negroes, and branded with the Epithet of white slaves'.[186] Writing in 1676 the English governor noted that the bulk of indentured servants arriving on the island 'come from Ireland and prove very idle; three blacks work better and cheaper than one white man'.[187] In short, according to Beckles, English masters 'considered their Irish servants as belonging to a backward culture, unfit to contribute anything beyond their labor to colonial development'.[188] Given the pre-eminence of labour in this society, the repeated references to the 'laziness' of the Irish indentured servant begs the question of whether labour was intentionally withheld as a form of passive resistance?

The Catholicism of the Irish, their poverty, the fear that they would ally with the enslaved Africans, and their propensity for rebellion (in 1649, 1655, 1675, and 1692) reinforced their subordinate status.[189] As the descendants of indentured servants these poor whites, dubbed the 'red legs', lived in isolated communities in the areas with least fertile land.[190] That said, some managed to prosper.[191] Over time, their whiteness did accord the Irish some advantage even if their poverty rendered them contemptible.[192] The extant wills of people with Irish names who died in Barbados deserve close scrutiny and will provide glimpses of the material wealth, social status, kinships links, economic relationships, and networks.[193] For example, Cornelius Bryan, who had arrived in the 1650s and invoked the ire of the authorities for his 'mutinous' anti-English speech had by 1680 acquired a modest estate of 22 acres in St. James parish, Barbados. He died seven years later, in 1687 leaving a feather bed, a cedar chest, a black horse, and 13 enslaved Africans.[194] Nicholas and George Rice arrived in the 1660s and by their deaths (in 1677 and 1686) left money for the church and the poor in Limerick and a bequest for the establishment of a hospital in Barbados.[195]

As the seventeenth century progressed, Jamaica became an important destination for Catholics and Protestants from Ireland. Today Irish surnames—Lynch, Murphy, McCarthy, O'Brien, O'Connor, O'Reilly, and O'Hara—are common on the island. Place names also testify to the presence of early Irish settlers: Irish Town, Dublin Castle, Irish Pen, Sligoville, Athenry, Bangor Ridge, Leinster Road, Leitrim Road, Longford Road, and Kinsale Avenue.[196] An Irish poet, Seán Ó Conaill, memorialised Jamaica in 'The Dirge of Ireland' when he wrote 'Transport, Transplant go to Jamaica'.[197] Until the 1660s privateering drove the Jamaican economy and employed around 1,500 men, including the infamous Philip Fitzgerald and other men from Ireland. Plunder offered quick returns but peaceful commerce proved more sustainable.[198] During the 1660s Irish men and women were relocated from the Leeward Islands and promised up to 20 acres of land on the condition that they re-indentured themselves for two or three years. Relegated to marginal areas in the interior of the island, these poor Irish were perceived to be unruly, rebellious, and loyal to the French.[199]

In 1690 William O'Brien, second earl of Inchiquin, became governor of this sugar and slave colony, landing in Port Royal with his wife, close family, and his 'menial servants'. 'After escaping great dangers of the sea and a malignant fever', Inchiquin arrived to find 'the animosities here far greater than I imagined'. He attributed the problems not to the recent war—the 'late transactions'—but to poor leadership and the fact 'people have lived without law or justice, to the great encouragement of malefactors and to the strengthening of pretensions to martial law'.[200] Shortly after he arrived 'all the negroes on Mr. Salter's estate in the mountains in the middle of the Island broke out into rebellion'. Inchiquin managed to quell it but later reflected: 'This rebellion might have been very bloody, considering the number of negroes and the scarcity of white men. There were but six or seven whites in that plantation to five hundred negroes, and that is the usual proportion in the Island, which cannot but be a great danger'.[201]

William III had instructed Inchiquin to govern Jamaica in accordance with the laws, and to promote godliness and commerce, reminding him that the island needed a 'constant and sufficient supply of merchantable negroes at moderate rates in money or commodities'.[202] The king also urged him to reduce the period of indentured service to four years, to pass a law 'for the restraining of any inhumane severity' towards Christian servants, and to encourage 'the conversion of negroes to the Christian religion'.[203] In speeches to the Jamaican Assembly, dating from June and July 1691, Inchiquin called for the settling of 'private piques and animosities' amongst the planters and reminded them of 'great disquiet' in New York, Virginia, and Maryland, and the 'the deplorable condition of Ireland' after the recent war.[204] Inchiquin died in January 1692 'after long indisposition through fever and ague, which ended in a flux...and was buried that night in St. Catherine's Church at St. Jago de la Vega'. His secretary, George Reeve, outlined his achievements:

At his coming he found the most considerable people divided into parties eagerly bent upon the destruction of each other. These he composed, and did all he could to make the Island considerable and the people happy. Last summer he sent out a strong squadron of ships which so humbled the French in these parts that until they receive recruits from France we need not fear them. He left us in a quiet and flourishing condition.[205]

Reeve did not mention the role Inchiquin played in reviving the Spanish slave *asiento*, which was masterminded by Genoese bankers, especially the Grillos, working with a global network of intermediaries that included the Thomsons and Martin Noel.[206] In his will the earl left to his younger son 'all money and other effects and revenues in the Assiento [i.e. the slaves sent to New Spain] and all other his estate in America', together with the earl's interest in a ship called the *Adventure* (and her cargo).[207]

Of the 717 property owners in Jamaica, at least ten per cent were of Irish extraction and they included members of the Assembly and other officials.[208] John Bourden, a Protestant plantation owner from the parish of St. Catherine, was born in Coleraine in 1633 and later served as acting governor.[209] The Munster-born John O'Neill, whose father had died for the confederate cause leaving his eight-year-old son an orphan, also prospered. A parliamentary soldier adopted John, who then spent 30 years at sea before settling in Jamaica where he owned a sugar factory and 40 slaves.[210] During the 1680s Redmond McGragh secured a plantation of 1,000 acres and John Stapleton, William's brother, also settled briefly before relocating with his family to French colony in Saint-Domingue. Others were small landholders, artisans, or traders. Irish names appear in inventories uncovered by Nuala Zahedieh: 'Michael Farrell, a millwright; John Casey, a tavern keeper; Jane Fitzgerald, a garment trader; Michael Hanigan, a tailor; and Conn Connelly, a bricklayer and builder'.[211] During these years ships from Ireland—from Cork, Dublin, Limerick, New Ross, Waterford, and Wexford—regularly docked in Port Royal, bringing with them food (meat, cereals, butter, dairy, herrings, and salmon), linens, and more settlers hoping to make their fortunes.[212] In 1731 the governor of the island complained to London of the numbers of Irish migrants, 'native Irish papists…pouring in upon us in such sholes [shoals]'.[213] Some, especially those trained as lawyers, like Edmund Kelly who became in 1714 attorney general, made good.[214]

From the perspective of Ireland, the Caribbean, was the 'hub' of the Atlantic trading system but many also travelled to the mainland colonies either from the Caribbean or directly from Ireland. Planters from Ireland— Humphrey Gilbert, Sir Walter Raleigh, and Ralph Lane—had played key roles in attempting to establish colonies and Irish men had been involved— primarily as soldiers and sailors—in the early settlements in Virginia.[215] Over the course of the seventeenth century, as the research of Elodie Peyrol-Kleiber has shown, 3,000 indentured servants and 1,000 free people migrated to the Chesapeake colonies of Virginia and later Maryland, where they mostly cultivated tobacco.[216] As in the Caribbean the majority were unskilled and under the age of twenty-five, with a high number under the age of fifteen with evidence that children as young as five were being sold as indentured servants. Roughly one third of these migrants were women.[217] In the early 1620s Sir Edward Blayney, a Welsh planter who had made his home in Ulster, transported 153 men and 50 'maids and young woemen' from Ireland to Virginia. Each person was worth 150 pounds of tobacco, which was to be paid to Blayney upon delivery.[218] The Cromwellians, eager to rid Ireland of vagrants, orphans, and criminals regularly issued licences. In 1653 alone Sir John Clotworthy, the County Antrim landowner and parliamentarian, secured permission 'to transport to America 500 natural Irishmen';[219] David Selleck, a Boston merchant, 'to take in 400 Irish children, and transport them to those plantations';[220] and Richard Netherway, a Bristol merchant, 'to transport from Ireland to Virginia 100 Irish tories'.[221] Of these a minority were skilled. Writing in 1655 Munster-born Vincent Gookin claimed that of every hundred Irishmen five or six were carpenters or masons 'more handy and ready in building ordinary houses and much more prudent in supplying the defects of instruments and materials than English artificers'.[222]

Maryland, founded by the Catholic Calverts, became known as 'a place pestered by hundreds of...Irish families'. Interestingly, out of 415 Irish indentured servants that Peyrol-Kleiber has identified in Virginia and Maryland, at least 30 came with kin and so travelled in family groups.[223] On arrival these Irish migrants faced a hostile environment and reception. Mortality rates were as high as 40 per cent in the early years.[224] County court records document significant levels of anti-Catholicism and particular fear of those arrivals who only spoke Irish. Despite legislation aimed at curtailing the behaviour and mobility of Irish indentured people, anxieties soared at moments of crisis, especially after 1689, along with more general fears that 'Irish servants...may confederate with the Negros'.[225] Being treated as second-class citizens did not deter other Irish Catholics from migrating to the Chesapeake and to the Carolinas, founded as a propriety colony in 1663.[226] Well-known landmarks occasionally reflect their presence. For example, Florence O'Sullivan, the first Carolinian surveyor general in the 1670s, gave his name to Sullivan's Island. One of South Carolina's early governors was Sir Richard Kyrle, a Cork merchant. Well prepared for life on the frontier, others—Browns, Dohertys and O'Briens—traded with the Cherokee Indians and even intermarried with them.[227] Some prospered. In addition to the Calverts of Maryland (see Section I above), was their kinsman, George Talbot, who amassed by the end of the seventeenth century an estate of 32,000 acres and over a 12-year period imported 640 indentured servants.[228] The Carrolls of Maryland, originally from County Offaly, made their fortunes in the late seventeenth-century Chesapeake on the back of enslaved Africans.[229] In 1688 Charles Carroll became the attorney general of Maryland and when he died in 1720 he owned 48,000 acres worth £20,000, together with 112 enslaved Africans across five plantations. His son, also Charles, was the only Catholic to sign the Declaration of Independence in 1776.[230]

In the middle and later decades of the eighteenth century, Protestants from Ulster, who were largely of Scottish provenance and known as the

'Scots Irish', crossed the Atlantic in substantial numbers (by 1775 as many as a quarter of a million had left Ireland).[231] On 10 July 1741 the *Philadelphia Gazettee* announced the arrival of a ship from Cork with 'a parcel of likely servants used to country work' along with a wider variety of tradesmen that included bakers, barbers, carpenters, cobblers, coopers, joiners, smiths, tanners, tailors, rope makers, and weavers.[232] They settled across the Thirteen Colonies with the largest numbers moving to Pennsylvania, which had been founded in 1680 by William Penn, who brought with him his Irishness.[233] There was a Dublin Township in the centre of Philadelphia County, which ran alongside Dublin Creek.[234] During his only visit to America (1682–4), Penn established his colony's government and disputed its boundaries with the governors of neighbouring colonies, including New York.

New York, formerly New Amsterdam, became an English colony in 1664 and in 1683 Thomas Dongan became the first—and only—Irish-born Catholic governor of the city.[235] In many ways Dongan was a man ahead of his time. As soon as he arrived in New York he called the freeholders of the province to a general assembly, granting a charter of liberties, which attempted to make them coequal and independent of the English parliament, promising no taxation without representation, and guaranteeing liberty of conscience. Dongan also spearheaded the transformation of New York into a thriving commercial town. In 1686 he presented the city with a new charter ('Dongan's charter') which has remained the basis of the municipal laws, rights, privileges, public property, and franchise in the city.[236] He also grew taxation and carefully controlled land purchase. Writing in 1687 Edward Randolph claimed that Dongan 'has squeezed the people of New York that they are hardly able to live, and as many as can leave the place'. In his dealings with French Canada, Dongan used English Jesuits to defend the English empire. However, this, combined with his policy of religious toleration, his promotion of Irish Catholics to key military, legal, and administrative posts, and his generosity in rewarding them with patents to land undoubtedly stirred up jealously, fear, and prejudice amongst the Protestant settlers.[237] No doubt their politicking was part of the reason why James II dismissed him in 1688. Within the decade, a Protestant from Ireland, Richard Coote, earl of Bellamont, became governor of New York (1697), along with Massachusetts and New Hampshire.[238] Unlike Dongan, he had no time for his compatriots. In 1700 he complained bitterly that 'The recruits that came from Ireland are a parcel of the vilest fellows that ever wore the King's livery, the very scum of the army in Ireland, and severall

Irish Papists among 'em, who have stirr'd up a generall mutiny among the souldiers'.[239]

The prevalence of so many Catholics, both in the English mainland colonies and especially in the Caribbean, prepared the ground for Irish Catholic 'episcopal imperialism' in the nineteenth century.[240] Their presence also challenged any notions of a 'Protestant Atlantic' even if a 'Protestant International' of trade, familial, and scholarly networks was superimposed over the Atlantic by the larger Protestant diaspora, of which the Huguenot migrations were a part.[241] In Ireland attempts to convert the population to Protestantism had floundered as the English, in the words of one contemporary, 'took more Pains to make the Land turn Protestant than the People'.[242] Yet missionary zeal did drive some. As a director of the New England Company, Robert Boyle, the scientist and the earl of Cork's youngest son, had a strategy for 'gospellizing' the indigenous peoples in America (and later India) that mirrored his plans for Ireland, where he supported translations into Irish of the Bible, Book of Common Prayer, and catechism, and promoted other evangelical activity through the medium of Irish.[243] Anglesey and Ormond were also directors of the New England Company but only Boyle served for 27 years, working hard to put theological and moral questions at the heart of English expansionism.[244] In so doing he laid the foundations for the growth of the spiritual empire associated with the later British empire.[245]

Many of the adventurers in Irish land were also 'reforming Puritans' with strong links to Dutch Calvinists and to the godly settlements of New England and especially to John Winthrop, the first governor. A letter dating from 1621 revealed that Winthrop wished 'oft God would open a way to settle me in Ireland', where his uncle had settled in County Cork.[246] His son, also John, attended Trinity College Dublin during the 1620s before spending time in the Netherlands and later becoming one of the founding governors of Connecticut (from 1659 until his death in 1676).[247] He brought his Irish links with him to New England. Interestingly, when John later developed ironworks in Connecticut he copied Sir Charles Coote's 'business model' and attracted some of the same investors.[248] The fact that so many of Trinity's early provosts were 'reforming Puritans', with strong links to Dutch Calvinists, made Trinity particularly attractive as a destination to those who had colonised the godly settlements of New England. Equally, those associated with Trinity received a warm welcome in New England. One of the best-known was George Berkeley (1685–1753), the Church of Ireland bishop of Cloyne and celebrated philosopher. In the 1720s Berkeley resolved to emigrate permanently to Bermuda and establish a college 'for the moral regeneration of the American colonies'.[249] The Bermudan University would 'maintain ten savages and ten whites', and in addition 'half a dozen of the most agreeable and ingenious men of our college [Trinity] are with me in this project'.[250] In the event he never made it to Bermuda. Instead, Berkeley settled in Newport, Rhode Island, and from here influenced the development of universities in the American colonies, especially King's College in New York (later Columbia University), Yale, and Harvard. He bequeathed books to the libraries at both Harvard and Yale, where a college is named after him.[251] In 1868 the first campus of the University of California—Berkeley—was named in his honour.

So far the focus of this chapter has been on people from Ireland operating in the Atlantic world, which also reflects scholarly interest on engagement with 'westward enterprises'. This needs to be combined, however, with discussion of Irish contributions to 'eastward enterprises' as members of the Ostend East India Company, French East India Company, and especially the English East India Company.[252] Closely linked to this is the intimate interplay between commerce and colonisation and the importance of challenging, much as Philip Stern has done, the traditional distinctions between the commercial and colonial eras in British India, as well as distinct notions of a colonial Atlantic world and a 'trading world' of Asia.[253] What becomes immediately apparent in any wider study of the Atlantic colonies and the Indian city colony of Bombay, never mind Ireland itself, is the extent to which colonisation and commerce went hand in hand.[254] Thus, historians of early Virginia and Bombay could, as Stern has suggested, learn a lot from each other, and the inclusion of Ireland in that conversation might provide fresh insights into Atlantic history and provoke debate around our understanding of colonial processes in the early modern period.[255]

As we look east, it is important to bear in mind two things. First, Indian textiles were used to purchase enslaved Africans, so it was essential to enjoy access to a supply of textiles. Second, and linked to this, was the extent to which the London merchant adventurers had, by the early 1650s, taken over control of the East India Company along with Irish land. By the 1660s and 1670s, of the 73 men who served as directors of the East India Company, over half (37) had subscribed to the Adventurers' Act (of March 1642), which offered Protestant speculators 2,500,000 Irish acres, and to subsequent schemes that underpinned the revolution in Irish landholding of the 1650s.[256] For some directors of the East India Company Ireland simply

formed part of a portfolio of global investments. For others the Irish links
were stronger and at least ten directors had close family members living on
Irish estates.[257] For example, Sir Joseph Ashe, a West Country textile indus-
trialist, was one of the most influential directors of, and largest investors in,
the East India Company.[258] During the early decades of the seventeenth
century Ashe's father's cousins had acquired ecclesiastical office and lands in
Counties Meath, Cavan, and Londonderry.[259] Then, during the 1640s, Ashe's
brothers, Edward and John, invested £1,200 and received 1,200 acres in
County Tipperary, where his nephew later settled.[260] The strongest links of
all were held by the polymath Robert Boyle, a Company director, who was
well placed to build on trusted relationships developed by his father and his
brother Roger Boyle, Lord Broghill, who in 1655 secured a licence to ship
300 Irish prisoners to Antigua.[261]

Thus, a significant cohort of directors of the East India Company would
have been familiar with how colonisation in Ireland operated and some had
direct knowledge of it. One can imagine that these experiences, along with
other imperial encounters especially in the Caribbean and North America,
informed their thinking as they debated about how best to proceed in
Bombay. A royal charter of 1669 established Charles II's absolute sovereignty
over the island and specified that the inhabitants of Bombay were 'our liege
people, and subject to our imperial crown'.[262] But the king entrusted Bombay
to the East India Company on the condition that they guaranteed freedom
of worship to the Portuguese Catholics living there, something that had been
stipulated in his marriage treaty to Catherine of Braganza. For its part the
East India Company welcomed the acquisition of Bombay, which had been
a Portuguese settlement since the 1530s. It was an H-shaped island that
formed part of an archipelago of seven islets and enjoyed an extraordinary
natural harbour. Though never developed as a trading hub by the Portuguese,
the English immediately realised Bombay's potential to become a major
commercial centre in the wider Indian Ocean trading world.

From the outset the Company had ambitious plans for Bombay and
determined to make it 'an English colony' and encourage 'free burghers in
trading, building and planting'.[263] The Company asked that a town might
'be laid out, in the most commodious manner, to be walled and fortified'
and that the commercial infrastructure needed to encourage trade—a dock,
crane, wharf, storehouse, customs house, and mint—be put in place. The
buildings, of stone and brick, were to be in a 'regular forme' and modelled
on those in the city of London.[264] Others have suggested that Portuguese

patterns of town planning influenced Bombay, which, given its history, is plausible. Whether shaped by London or Lisbon, Bombay—like Portuguese Goa and Cochin in Southern India and Dutch Batavia—was a colonial port-fort city that was developed in order to extract and distribute products not available in Europe and to consolidate local economic and political power in English hands.[265] Bombay was the Indian equivalent to the city of Derry. In 1609 King James VI and I had charged the London livery companies with developing the city and colonising the entire county. This initiative occurred under the auspices of the Irish Society, a joint-stock company modelled on the 1600 charter of the East India Company.[266] Indeed, there were overlaps in membership between the two. For example, during the 1660s and 1670s, Sir Theophilus Biddulph (d. 1683), draper,[267] John Lawrence (d. 1692), haberdasher and alderman,[268] and Sir William Turner (d. 1693), merchant,[269] were governors or deputy governors of the Irish Society and directors of the East India Company. As Ian Archer has shown, the amounts invested in Ulster were modest (£60,000 by 1616) compared to two million invested in Tangier during the 1660s and 1670s (Section I above).[270] As it turned out, the investment in Ulster proved to be a long-term one; it was the later seventeenth century before the London companies began to see a meaningful return on an outlay made generations before.[271]

The same held true for Bombay and it was the later eighteenth century before Bombay emerged as the largest port in Western India.[272] In the seventeenth century, the East India Company made the bulk of its profits at Surat, 'the most fam'd emporium of the Indian empire'.[273] Black pepper, from Bantam and Malabar, was a staple import from Surat, along with coffee (from Yemen), cinnamon, cardamom, and other spices. By the later seventeenth century, the Company profited from importing Indian textiles and the 1670s, when Gerald Aungier was president, were the boom years of the 'calico craze'.[274] Initially, the focus was for household consumption— tablecloths, bed linens, and floor coverings—but the demand for cotton items of clothing for both men and women grew.[275] Aungier also oversaw the increased production of the coarser textiles—gingham, cotton, dungarees—used in the slave trade. The profits to be made on successful voyages were huge. The Company paid out generous dividends of between 10 and 20 per cent to its shareholders and the value of stock rose significantly from £90 in 1661 to £245 in 1677.[276]

Riches aside, it seems clear that Aungier took much from his years living in Mughal Surat, including examples of best commercial practice, an extensive mercantile network, and an understanding of the importance for business of religious pluralism and cosmopolitanism. Contemporaries noted how he developed an appreciation of the region's religions, languages, and cultures, perhaps thanks to the influence of his uncle, also Gerald, who was skilled in oriental and other languages.[277] Aungier secured rare Persian texts, many from the local Parsi Zoroastrian community, which he sent to Thomas Hyde, librarian at the Bodleian in Oxford.[278] Aungier's enthusiasm for the religions and cultures of others should not detract from his zealous Protestantism. As the John Winthrop of India, Aungier worked closely with lawmakers to eradicate sin, promote godly discipline, and secure moral regeneration amongst the European colonists.[279] He also did what he could to proselytise and, much as Boyle had advocated, secured translations of the Lord's Prayer, creed, and commandments into Portuguese, Hindi, Arabic, and Persian.[280]

IV Identities and empires

Tangier serves as an interesting case study for what empires meant for senses of identity, especially for 'Irishness' and for 'Englishness'. In 1679 an anonymous English informant provided a detailed assessment of the royal colony at Tangier, where he argued that the Irish within the walls of the city were as much of a threat as the Moors who attacked it. The problem, according to his account, began with the governor, the earl of Inchiquin, who was 'an Irish man & supposed papist though he goes to the English church'. Inchiquin's deputy, Colonel Dongan, was 'an Irishman'. So too were Captain John White, Major Maurice Glyn, who opened and shut the gates to the city, and Captain Makenny, commander of the cavalry, along with 230 rank-and-file soldiers. In all, the informant identified 270 persons in Tangier's army 'that will never be for the English'. In addition, he believed that three (of six) of the city's alderman were 'professed papists', two of them Irish, while the mayor was more 'papist than protestant'. He recounted an anecdote 'by one Ensigne Cusack who is an Irish papist' who allegedly said that any true-born Irish man 'hated an Englishman naturally'. The informant agreed and cited as evidence the 1641 rebellion and 'their bloody massacring the English in Ireland soe fresh in memory'. Based on Cusack's story, the informant concluded that the Irish 'doe naturally hate [the] English . . . and are better lovers of Spayne then [sic] their own King'.[281] Accounts like this, articulating anxieties about Catholicism, anti-Englishness, and disloyalty, were typical. Across the Caribbean and mainland American colonies, English governors and planters repeatedly banged the sectarian drum. Where possible they punished any anti-English sentiment or actions. They also othered their Irish labourers and servants, branding them as idle, drunken, rebellious, and inferior and devised restrictive anti-Irish laws and codes to minimise 'degeneracy' and to control mobility. Thus, anti-Irishness and anti-Catholicism helped to consolidate senses of 'Englishness' and cultural superiority, something that came to characterise the British empire in the nineteenth century.

How then did people from Ireland, who operated on the world stage, describe themselves? And, how were they perceived by their contemporaries, who were often oblivious to any nuances around identity? Some self-identified as of 'the Irish nation' or were labelled as 'Irish' by others. Across the Atlantic world, significant numbers of men and women from Ireland formed communities, encouraged their kin to migrate, and intermarried with other people from Ireland. Catholicism was widely practised in the Atlantic world and members of the Catholic elite educated their children in the Irish Colleges on Continental Europe or sent them home to Ireland.[282] Language, like religion, was an important badge of identity and was widely spoken amongst the Irish community living in the Atlantic world. Vincent Gookin attributed the degeneracy of the Anglo Irish in the Middle Ages to 'The frequent use of the Irish language in all commerce and the English habituating themselves to that language, was one great means of Irishifying the English colonies'.[283] Concerns of 'Irishifying' transferred to the New World, where some migrants only spoke Irish while others—in Tangier, the Amazon, across the Caribbean, and mainland colonies—used it as a secret language to communicate amongst themselves in order to prevent others from understanding.

However, when it came to matters of faith, the majority appear to have been pragmatic, playing down their Catholicism in interactions with the Dutch and English and emphasising their zealousness when dealing with Spain and France. Linked to this was the question of loyalty. Ireland's very proximity to England could compromise the position of Irish Catholics eager to secure favour abroad or to serve Catholic princes.[284] In these instances, being devout Catholics, anti-English, and 'disloyal' did define the Irish and signalled their resistance to English imperialism. Yet what is so striking about these years was the deep devotion so many Irish Catholics displayed to the house of Stuart, especially during the 1640s and 1650s, and after 1688. Of course, this attachment to the Stuarts did not sit well with the ruling Cromwellian and later Williamite regimes, who used this to further vilify Irish Catholics. Even if the English focused on the 'disloyalty' and 'barbarism' of the Irish, by the eighteenth century their 'whiteness' also afforded them some privilege and the Irish found, 'that they had far more in common with their former English masters than they did with newly arrived enslaved Africans'.[285]

In an insightful article on 'Ireland in the Atlantic World', William O'Reilly dismissed as misleading any attempt to represent 'the Irish in the Atlantic as a diasporic community' united by Catholicism. Instead, he argued the majority actively engaged in an international labour market, determined to make better lives for themselves and their families. 'Any sense of identity in the pre-modern period', he continues, was 'both place-specific and time specific'.[286]

Thus, Irish Catholics, like William Stapleton, used every opportunity—especially marriage, education, and social interactions—to downplay his Catholicism in case it was interpreted with suspicion, and to make himself English. Like members of the landed elite back in Ireland, Stapleton supported with enthusiasm the imperial venture by building parish churches, maintaining Anglican clergy, and taking every opportunity to demonstrate his loyalty to Charles II.[287] He also used his position to lobby the king for lands back in Ireland—'his birth right'—which had been allocated to 'Lady Demsy'.[288] Similarly, Nicholas Tuite may have made his fortune on the Danish colony of St. Croix but he was also quick to settle in Richard's Court, off Lime Street in London, and live as a member of the English gentry.[289] That said, his will also reflected his Irish connections. When he died in 1772, Tuite left 'sundry lands plantations [and] negroes' worth 'a considerable amount' to his son, wife, and daughters, who were now settled in England but the surnames of their husbands (Stapleton and McCarthy) suggest that at least two married into Irish families. Tuite also remembered in his will his kinswomen in Ireland—Mary Cahill and Ann McNammarra—and Biddy Reily, 'a dwarf', who lived at Granard in County Longford.[290] Writing in 1655, Henry Cromwell, son of Oliver, who served as governor of Ireland during the 1650s, maintained that the transportation of Irish to the Caribbean would turn them into Englishmen.[291] To some extent this did ring true for the Tuites and Stapletons though neither compromised their faith and each left generous bequests to the Catholic church in their wills.

What of the poor Irish, known as the 'red legs', whose loyalty was always regarded with suspicion, or those of mixed heritage, 'the black Irish', or others born to enslaved mothers?[292] These people are hard to track down but Anthony French's will of 1787 made a number of bequests including to his 'meulatto children in the islands of St. Kitts', whom he named—Anthony, Martin, Bridget, Mary, and Helen French—the 'sum of £200 of the currency of that island each'. Anthony also asked that John Lynch 'my old servant' distribute his 'appareal amongst my two sons [Anthony and Martin] as he may think proper'.[293] Anthony clearly held his children in some affection and gave them familiar names and the French surname. There is no reference to their mother (or mothers) in Anthony's will or to them in the wills of Anthony's close kin. The absence of evidence is frustrating but here we can draw inspiration from the pioneering work of Marisa Fuentes who, in *Dispossessed Lives*, offers vivid insights into the lives of enslaved women in Barbados.[294] Or that of Jenny Shaw who uses legal and other disparate records to recover the lives of Susannah Mingo and the children she bore to a wealthy and influential English slave master, John Peers, in Barbados in the 1670s and 1680s.[295]

Identity formation for Protestants from Ireland who lived abroad was also complex and complicated by the fact that, like their compatriots in Ireland, many saw themselves as 'English' but when it suited also acknowledged their 'Irishness'.[296] For their part, the English, ever fearful of cultural degeneracy, regarded with suspicion Protestants from Ireland and gave preference to English Protestants. Thus, after the Indian revolt of 1675 in New England, Daniel Gookin, who had been born in Munster of a Kentish father before migrating first to Virginia and then Massachusetts, was perceived to be sympathetic to the Indians, which resulted in him being branded as disloyal and an 'Irish dog'.[297] In the case of Gerald Aungier, his links to Ireland remained strong despite his cosmopolitism and global interactions in India. Though he may have seen and described himself as an 'Englishman',[298] his Irishness was closely held, something that his superior in the East India Company touched on when he congratulated him on his 'English' but added in parentheses '(I was going to say Irish) fortitude and forbearance'.[299] The exchange captures the extent to which Aungier's Englishness was refracted through the lens of Ireland. Of course, strictly speaking, Aungier was a member of the 'New English', as people from England who settled in Ireland from the 1530s became known. Yet he was born and raised in Ireland, as were his parents. He had close kin links to other New English families and the Old English house of Kildare, many of whom were Catholic. Indeed, he was named after his great uncle Gerald FitzGerald, fourteenth earl of Kildare.[300]

In a similar vein, Robert Hedges, son of another Munster planter, who made his fortune in Bengal at the turn of the eighteenth century was accused by a colleague in the East India Company, Sir Edward Littleton, of cooking the books and defrauding the Company of £50,000 sterling. In an ethnocentric diatribe, Littleton described Hedges as the 'devising Irish boo[k] keeper', adding that even an Irishman deserved punishment although 'some thinke such crimes naturall to them'. Littleton added insult to injury by invoking 'Lilliburlero', an anti-Catholic and anti-Irish ballad, particularly popular during late 1680s, and thereby suggesting that Robert had Jacobite sympathies. In fact, the Hedges—committed Protestants and active colonists—had been staunch Williamites and would have seen themselves as English gentlemen.[301] There is no record of how the County Down doctor, Sir Hans Sloane, whose Jamaican plantations funded his collecting and who spent most of his life in London, self-identified. Certainly, he enjoyed deep ties to Ireland, illustrated by his life-long friendship with Sir Arthur Rawdon (1662–95), who also lived in County Down. Sloane's librarian, Thomas Stack, boasted in 1728 at the height of his influence in London: 'What glory . . . for Ireland to see one of its sons so crowned'.[302] Colin Kidd has suggested Protestants from Ireland, especially after 1690, adopted 'dual strategies combining both appropriation and denigration of the indigenous culture as a means of ensuring territory-specific legitimacy'. In this they resembled the Creole population in New Spain who acknowledged their Hispanic ancestry and appropriated 'a mythical Aztec past as part of their civic identity'.[303]

While it is always tricky to generalise about identities, which can be slippery, multi-faceted, and change according to time and place, a number of conclusions can be drawn. First, the presence of so many people from Ireland disrupts the dominant narrative that Englishness and Protestantism drove the First English Empire or to paraphrase Andrew MacKillop, it complicates the coloniser.[304] Clearly, the English empire was neither exclusively English nor Protestant, and even associating Protestantism with Englishness and Catholicism with Irishness is problematic.[305] Second, important though religion undoubtedly was to the identity of people from Ireland living in early modern Asia and the Atlantic world, an overly narrow focus on confession obscures the extent to which lived experiences and social and kin networks became entangled and traversed religious, political, and imperial boundaries.[306] Third, it was not unusual for upwardly mobile colonial elites, whether in Calcutta, Cork, or the Carolinas, to share a common sense of 'Englishness' that could be adapted to suit local circumstances. This harkened back to anglicising processes taking place back in Ireland and those, in the words of Laoisioch Mac an Bhaird, 'who follows English ways' (see Chapter 2 above).[307]

Where did all of this leave 'Britishness'? People from Ireland operating on the world stage during the early modern period never described themselves as 'British' and those living in Ireland rarely did. It is only in more recent times that a segment of the population living in Northern Ireland claim 'Britishness' as being core to their identity.[308] John MacKenzie, who did so much to promote a 'four nations' approach to the history of empire, concluded that the empire never succeeded in becoming 'British', despite all of the propaganda. 'In many respects', he argued, 'it remained four empires, those of the English, Irish, Scots and Welsh'. MacKenzie continued that they 'all took on global significance and came to frame aspects of their ethnic integrity in terms of their worldwide connections'.[309] There is much truth in Brian Friel's assertion that 'the plodding Henrys of this world' were 'the real empire-makers'.[310] But where Ireland was concerned, 'the plodding Henrys' were male and female and came from diverse faiths, ethnic groups, and social backgrounds as they traversed—as migrants, menials, merchants, and mercenaries —the empires of the early modern world.

5

Laboratory

The Brian Friel play that best speaks to this chapter is *Translations*, which premiered at the Guildhall in Derry on 23 September 1980. The play tells the story of the Ordnance Survey of Ireland conducted by Royal Engineers between 1824 and 1846. This was the first detailed mapping of the entire country since Sir William Petty's Down Survey of the 1650s but went further than Petty's in that land boundaries were redrawn and place names further anglicised. Set in the imagined townland of Baile Beag/Ballybeg in County Donegal, *Translations* narrated the interactions between members of an Irish-speaking community and a detachment of Royal Engineers. Over the summer of 1833 Yolland, a young English-speaking surveyor, fell in love with Marie, who only spoke Irish. The relationship did not end well in part because this was a world in which people married 'within the tribe' and did not 'cross those borders casually'.[1] *Translations*, like *Making History*, is a play about language, culture, and identity, which confronts the tribalism that plagued Northern Ireland during the Troubles and, to some extent, still does.[2] The play is also a powerful reminder of the importance of mapping as a tool of empire in Ireland and elsewhere.[3] Indeed, Yolland reflected on how his father had wanted him to join the East India Company but when he missed the boat he had been sent to Ballybeg rather than to Bombay.[4]

By the nineteenth century Ireland undoubtedly was a 'crucial sub-imperial centre for the British Empire' but this chapter argues that Ireland had served as laboratory of and for empire from the late sixteenth century. This notion is not novel and was first mooted by D. B. Quinn (1945, 1966) and Nicholas Canny (1970s) in relation to the Atlantic world.[5] In the intervening years some scholars have disputed their conclusions or have simply tired of the 'laboratory model', feeling that it has run its course.[6] Karen Kupperman, for example, has stressed how plantations occurred on both sides of the Atlantic at different times, under different models, and with different outcomes.[7] Audrey Horning concurs and suggests that any similarities 'lie in process and persona, whereas differences are rooted in historical, political and cultural contexts as well as geography'.[8] Alison Games acknowledges that English engagement in Ireland may have delayed their expansion into the Atlantic and might explain 'cultural expectations about Indians' held by some English but she rejects any notion that the English crossed the Atlantic with the specific intention to 'establish colonies in the Irish model' (not that either Quinn or Canny suggest this). Instead Games views Ireland as a 'parallel and simultaneous colonial experiment' that occasionally 'provided a model' for English imperialism and situates English ventures in both America and Ireland as part of a wider struggle against Catholicism.[9]

Important though these interventions are, they do not undermine the basic premise of the Quinn/Canny thesis and this chapter looks at the English Atlantic through the lens of Ireland. It also extends the narrative geographically to include the English empire in India, and chronologically, beyond the early modern period into the nineteenth century and the heyday of the British empire. It argues that the experiences of Ireland—as a colony, as a testing ground for imperial policies and processes, and as a source of agents of empire—is significant for the wider study of colonialism and imperial history. However, two methodological challenges complicate the argument. The first is how to disentangle what was distinctively 'Irish' versus what was the normal practice in empire across the early modern world. The second relates to periodization.

With regard to the first challenge, it would be false and naïve to suggest that Ireland was the only place where adventurers and colonists learned the business of empire. The need to establish sovereignty, the use of force, the provision of security, law and order, the settlement of colonists, the development of an urban and commercial infrastructure, and the exploitation of human capital and natural resources were all common to other early modern global empires, as well as colonial Ireland where they underpinned the exercise of English imperialism. Equally, figures who shaped imperial administrations and served in the army circulated around the English empire, bringing these various experiences with them as they travelled. They included men from Ireland and others of English or Scottish birth, but with strong Irish connections, who also served as agents of empire. For example, Sir Ralph Lane, an English planter in Munster, who in 1585 led an expedition to Roanoke and then settled in Ireland, brought, according to

Audrey Horning and Rory Rapple, experiences of the New World back to the Old.[10] Techniques developed in America, especially in Puritan New England, returned to Ireland to help define the Cromwellian occupation in the 1640s and 1650s.[11] Later, the English-born Charles Cornwallis found himself in Dublin as lord lieutenant, having served first in America, before becoming governor general of India. Having lost the American war, he suppressed the 1798 rebellion by United Irishmen and oversaw in 1800 the union of Ireland and Great Britain.[12] So, this 'return' and 'lateral' circulation of people and ideas took place alongside a variety of 'outward' initiatives—especially from London but also Dublin—inspired by colonial experiences. So what, then, was novel and distinctive about what emerged out of Ireland? This chapter argues that ethnocentric ideas, anglicising processes and practices of government, especially legal and landed ones, along with the refinement of 'tools of empire', were distinctive to Ireland and went on to characterise the implementation of imperial authority in other early modern English colonies and the later British empire in spite of very real differences in contexts, cultures, and circumstances.

The second challenge is around periodisation. How do we draw insights across time and make meaningful connections from the early modern into the modern period, rather than reading history back from the high point of empire in the mid-nineteenth century, and thereby losing sight of the all-important context? A close analysis of Ireland and India, especially in Sections IV and V below, allows for a comparison of imperial experiences from the mid-seventeenth to the mid-twentieth centuries and reveals several policies that originated in Ireland and shaped the development of empire in both places. While there is no mention in the seventeenth-century records of a grand imperial design for early modern India, the language of 'plantation', 'planters', and 'colony' is repeatedly used in relation to early modern Bombay, something that invites a re-examination of the traditional periodisation of the English empire in India.[13] Of course, colonial India had a rather different timeline to that of colonial Ireland. Historians have traditionally argued that the East India Company 'pursued trade, not territory' until the second half of the eighteenth century when it became a territorial power.[14] This, as Phil Stern and others have noted, is problematic. Stern stresses the intimate interplay between commerce and colonisation and challenges the traditional distinctions between the commercial and imperial eras in British India, as well as distinct notions of a colonial Atlantic world and a 'trading world' of Asia.[15] That said, we nonetheless associate British imperialism in India with the 'second British Empire' and the years after the victory at Plassey (1757), or even post-1857 and the period of the Raj.[16] However, this timeline can be challenged and disrupted, something that Kathleen Wilson has also called for in her study of colonial frontiers in Fort Marlborough in Sumatra, in St. Helena, and in Jamaica.[17]

Bearing these health warnings in mind, this chapter examines Ireland as laboratory of and for empire, a place of testing, where some experiments worked and others failed, where some were directed by the Crown or imperial agents and others emerged organically. Section I examines concepts of empire and how Ireland served as a test bed where ethnocentric ideas were worked out and iterated over time in accordance with changing imperial priorities. Building on the discussion of anglicisation in Chapter 2, Section II explores the imprint of Ireland across the governance, policies, and physical landscape of the English empire. Section III looks at how 'tools of empire' were trialled in Ireland and then adopted, albeit having been adapted to suit local circumstances, throughout the early modern Anglophone world. As the example of the Ordnance Survey highlights, some of these 'tools of empire', especially the law and knowledge collection, transcended from the early modern period into the nineteenth century.[18] In the final two sections arguments developed in early modernity are extended into the modern period using Ireland and India as a case study. Thus the focus of Section IV is on the structural and human links between Ireland and India that continued into the nineteenth and twentieth centuries. Moving from discussions of being servants of empire, Section V looks briefly at the Irish as subversives within it—how Ireland served as an exemplar for resistance to imperial rule and how a colonised people helped to bring down the British empire.

I Concepts of empire

Hiram Morgan has suggested that early modern Ireland 'was a laboratory of Renaissance political ideas'.[19] The example of Sir Thomas Smith illustrates this.[20] One of the leading humanists of the day, Smith looked to classical antiquity and especially Roman models as he developed his own colonial thinking. Smith promoted ideas of social improvement, the cultivation of virtue, the rejection of corruption in private and political life and wanted to break the ties that bound men to their lords and thereby facilitate Ireland's transition to a civil society.[21] Smith both helped to set the colonial agenda in Ireland and then lived it when during the early 1570s his son, also Thomas, attempted to plant the Ards peninsula in East Ulster, an ill-fated venture effectively resisted by the O'Neills of Clandeboye.[22]

Humanist theories about society and governance, as Ian Campbell has shown, were widely taught and understood amongst the elite in Ireland.[23] The New English commentator and veteran of Irish affairs, Barnaby Rich, used the language of disease to describe the state of Ireland. Rich blamed the 'canker' of Catholicism and poor governance, with corrupt and incompetent government and legal officials taking bribes and being motivated by greed and self-interest rather than civic duty and private virtue. In 'The Anatomy of Ireland', written in 1615, he suggested that 'the dysceases of Irelande are many, and the sycknes is growne to that contagion, that is all most past cure' and thus compromises the health of the entire body politic.[24] Over 50 years later, in 1670s Bombay, humanist ideas of social improvement, the cultivation of virtue, and the rejection of corruption in private and political life characterised the correspondence of Gerald Aungier, the most important early governor, who had been born in Ireland, as had his parents. Aungier configured social problems metaphorically as 'diseases' and 'illnesses' that compromised the health of the whole body politic. In his speech at the opening of the law court in August 1672, he suggested that Bombay was like an embryo 'without forme, without life, starved in the womb for want of nourishment, neglected, despised, discouraged by her hard neighbours the Moors and the Portuguese... jealous of her growth and fortune'. Now Bombay was properly 'nourished with faithful tender care, reduced to a comely order in religious discipline, in government civil and military; in wholesome laws, in revenues, in strength by sea and land'.[25]

In a similar vein, the garden as metaphor characterised early seventeenth century humanist writings on early Stuart Ireland, colonial America, and India.[26] Sir John Davies, in *A Discovery of the True Causes why Ireland was never entirely subdued* (1612), compared the Irish to plants, amenable to improvement through industry, and emphasised the skill of the gardener to plant, to weed, and to create order out of disorder.[27] He held colonists to be culturally superior but vulnerable to degeneracy: 'if the number of civil persons who are to be planted do not exceed the number of natives, [they] will quickly overgrow them as weeds overgrow the good corn'.[28] In 1670s Bombay Aungier regularly used the garden as metaphor and through this defined his mission. Aungier invoked Davies when in 1673 he described

Bombay as a 'garden planted with several sorts of flowers promiscuously growing up and among another without order or decorum and having no head or chief among themselves' and proposed bringing order to the garden by establishing the *panchayat* system of representation and arbitration.[29] Aungier compared the Dutch and English models of government in India: the Dutch rule 'by their sword and violence' and would, in his opinion, 'sinke under their owne weight'. The English, however, have a 'plant watered by divine providence, rooted in the affections of all people', which, with investment, can only prosper.[30] Whether in Bombay, the English Atlantic, or Ireland gardens and an ordered landscape, according to John Patrick Montaño, 'became key manifestations of a tamed wilderness, places of peace and order representing the ideal state of a nation'.[31]

Interestingly, there was no discourse of 'civility' and 'barbarism' for late Stuart Bombay. That came later. On the contrary, Aungier, while deeply attached to humanist values and rhetoric, appears to have taken a genuine interest in and has a respect for local cultures and peoples.[32] A discourse of 'civility' and 'barbarism' did, however, underpin English imperialism in Ireland and the Atlantic world. The fact that the political and social organisation, the culture, and the economic practices of Ireland did not coincide with the norms of English society left it open to scorn and led to comparisons with the ancient Britons (whom the Romans had 'civilised') or with the Amerindians of the New World and the 'infidel' or 'pagan' Turks to the East.[33] Giraldus Cambrensis (Gerald of Wales), writing from a colonial perspective in the twelfth century, consistently referred to the Irish as 'a barbarous people', 'a rude people' with 'primitive habits' 'living themselves like beasts'.[34] In his description 'of the character, customs, and habits of this people' in his *Topographia*, Cambrensis argued that Ireland's geographical isolation from the 'civilized nations' ensured that 'they learn nothing, and practice nothing but the barbarism in which they are born and bred, and which sticks to them like a second nature'.[35] Sarah McKibben has identified four claims by Cambrensis that were relentlessly recycled over the centuries: 'the Irish are animalistic in their passions; sinful and ignorant in their irreligiosity; deficient in proper technological advancement, husbandry, and industry; and lacking in proper human cultivation and social relations, all of which signal their properly subordinate status'.[36] Cambrensis was widely read across Europe, where the *lingua franca* of the intelligentsia remained Latin. An English translation of his work was published in Holinshed's *Chronicles* and this ensured that early modern observers appropriated this medieval rhetoric, denigrating everything Irish and promoting everything English. The Italian humanist, Polydore Vergil, eulogised in his *Anglica Historia* (written by 1513; printed 1534) the 'civilising' role of the English in Ireland, reasserting and confirming English *imperium* on the island by casting the battle between 'civility' and 'barbarousness' in world-historical terms. 'Civility' as the direction in which history moved prescribed a just origin, purpose, and end for sovereignty: the triumph over 'barbarousness'.[37] Stuart Carroll notes that the verb 'to civilise' was an English invention that initially referred to attempts to return 'the Irish lords to good government (*civilitas*) by dismantling their feuding culture'. By the 1570s, as more radical solutions were being adopted in Ireland, it took on an all-encompassing meaning and was used in other colonial contexts.[38]

This discourse of 'civility' and 'barbarism', grounded in a shared understanding of the philosophical writings of Aristotle and Cicero, had long underpinned English imperialism in Ireland but, as the sixteenth century progressed, it became the language of superiority. Pre-modern ideologies of ethnic superiority, as Ian Campbell has shown, did not equate with modern notions of racism and while there are some striking continuities it was the nineteenth century before modern racial ideology was born.[39] That said, as Keith Thomas noted *In Pursuit of Civility*, 'racist practice long preceded racial theory'.[40] Nicholas Canny's recent study, *Imagining Ireland's Pasts*, documents how 'apocalyptic authors' first marginalised then subsumed humanist historians.[41] For example, John Derricke's *Image of Ireland* (1581) reinforced—in prose and with graphic woodcuts—negative images of the Irish and vilified them as sub-human, as 'grasshoppers and caterpillars', hogs, and dogs.[42] Other writers did likewise. Experiences of the Nine Years' War fired racial stereotyping. The English poet Gervase Markham, who had served as a captain in Ireland during the conflict, compared Irish with Indian: 'Like brutish Indians these wild Irish live'... 'They are the savagest of all the nation'.[43] For Ralph Birchensa, all Irish were 'rebels' and worse: they were the 'brood of wolves... Haters of truth sworne slaves to rape and spoyle,/ Authors of mischief... Furies of hell, shaking their dog-eard locks/... Breakers of wedlocke, wantons in their lives,/ Most bred up bastards from their very birth:/ Lovers of theft, living by thieving trade,/ Idle in life, like beasts fed in the stall/... Idolators, superstitious men,... sworne slaves unto the Pope... lothsome locusts' and so on.[44] Sir John Davies also portrayed the Irish as barbarians, murderers, and villains who behaved 'little better than Canniballes, who doe hunt one another, and hee that hath most strength and swiftnes doth eate and devoures all his fellowes'.[45] Davies, like so many of his contemporaries, made direct and very negative comparisons between the native peoples of Ireland and America, especially the ritual of cannibalism (as opposed to the necessity of it during the 'starving time' of 1609–10 in Virginia).[46]

The classic exponent of cultural superiority during these years was the poet and planter Edmund Spenser who, in *A View of the Present State of Ireland*, called for the wholesale destruction of the Irish along with their culture, society, and economy, and invited England to enjoy a monopoly over the exercise of violence.[47] David Edwards has suggested that as far as Spenser was concerned 'only terror would civilise Ireland by making the Irish English'.[48] Having purged Ireland of its Irishness, the country would then be colonised with English settlers responsible for the erection of the political, economic, and social framework that was considered the necessary support of a civil life and the Protestant faith. Towns, roads, bridges, houses, gardens, orchards, tillage, enclosure, the clearance of woodlands, and the improvement of wastelands would tame and civilise the landscape and its inhabitants. Predictably, Spenser's aggressive imperialism shaped the mind-sets of others in his immediate circle along with later figures like Sir John Davies and Thomas Wentworth, later earl of Strafford and lord deputy of Ireland, who supported the publication of *A View* in 1633, which prior to this had circulated widely in manuscript.[49] Gerard Boate later noted in his history that the natives of Ireland were called 'wild Irish' because 'in all manner of wildness they may be compared with the most barbarous nations of the earth', while Oliver Cromwell maintained that 'All the world knows their barbarism'.[50]

These ethnocentric ideas permeated the English colonies in the New World. According to Stuart Carroll, 'Ireland was the laboratory for empire, a testing ground for the potential of civilising savages'.[51] Nicholas Canny and D. B. Quinn have shown how English expansionists—including Sir Walter Raleigh and his half-brother Sir Humphrey Gilbert, and Ralph Lane—used their Irish experiences to confirm their assumptions of savagism, paganism, and barbarism and applied these 'to the indigenous popula-tion in of the New World'.[52] Wayne Lee has argued that 'Ireland-New World cross over colonists' also exported extreme violence—scorched earth tactics, starvation, sexual violence—honed in Ireland during the suppression of the Desmond rebellion and later the Nine Years' War, to the New World, even if they were supposed to exercise restraint.[53] David Harris Sacks shows how Gilbert drew on Roman precedents and advocated for brutal and total war in Ireland.[54] According to Eliga Gould, Gilbert and his ilk also justified their brutality in the 1560s and 1570s in Munster 'by drawing on published accounts of the [Spanish] conquest of Mexico, and that experience in turn helped shape the ideology that the English used against the native peoples of Virginia'.[55] Writing in 1624, John Smith acknowledged: 'It is more easy to civilise them [in Virginia] by conquest than faire meanes'.[56]

The 1622 rising in Virginia, when the indigenous peoples attacked the English settlements and killed 347 men, women, and children, explained Smith's hostility and the subsequent demonization of native people. In a pamphlet that aimed to stir emotions, Edward Waterhouse, the resident secretary to the Virginia Company, recorded how the 'perfidious and treacherous Indians' had 'basely and barbarously murthered' the settlers, 'not sparing eyther age or sexe, man, woman, or childe'.[57] He continued that the rising now justified the use of extreme violence against the Indian tribes and the confiscation of their land, which the English quickly put to the cultivation of tobacco.[58] The 1622 rising was the equivalent of the 1641 rebellion which further hardened attitudes towards Irish Catholics and facilitated extreme policies, further waves of expropriation, and, according to Micheál Ó Siochrú, 'genocide'.[59]

Over time, contemporaries made explicit comparisons between the indigenous peoples in both countries. 'The Natives of New England', wrote an English observer, 'are accustomed to build them [sic] houses, much like the wild Irish'. Another, who returned to England from Massachusetts in 1641, later noted that 'the wild Irish and the Indian do not much differ'.[60] The author of *The English Empire in America* suggested: 'The *Indians* are of disposition very inconstant, crafty, timorous, quick of apprehension, and very ingenious, soon angry, and so malicious...very Letcherous...all of them *Canibals*, or eaters of Human flesh, and so were formerly the Heathen *Irish*, who use to feed upon the Buttocks of Boys, and the Paps of Women'.[61] The anonymous author continued that 'they howl at their funerals like the wild *Irish*' and wear robes 'as large as an *Irish* Mantle'.[62] It is important to remember, as Brendan Kane has noted: 'If the Irish were seen as barbarous and savage in custom and practice, the Indians were seen as barbarians and savages in essence. This is to say that in the New World context, the nouns were used—in the Irish context, the adjectives'.[63]

Convictions of moral, intellectual, and spiritual superiority characterised English interactions with the Irish across the Atlantic world. In the English

Caribbean the Irish were treated with contempt and described as 'barbarous and most inhuman' as well as lewd, lazy, and insolent.[64] The Barbados Master and Servant Code of 1661 described the Irish as 'a profligate race', as 'turbulent and dangerous spirits' who thought nothing of 'joining themselves to runaway slaves'.[65] Minister Morgan Godwyn arrived in Virginia in 1665 and suggested that 'the natives of that Kingdom [Ireland], who have been Imported hither [Virginia], are observed to be, in divers respects, more Barbarous than the Negro's'.[66] He added that the Irish were the 'negro's' of the English.[67] In the early 1720s George Berkeley, the Irish philosopher, himself an owner of slaves on his Rhode Island plantation, concurred when he wrote: 'If negro was not negro, Irishman would be negro'.[68]

Of course this 'cultural essentialism', that later became race, was critical to maintaining imperial power.[69] In fact, Ann Laura Stoler argues that race was 'a central colonial sorting technique'.[70] Colonial 'sorting' can be traced back to William Petty, the father of political economy, who suggested that the economic value of Irishmen be assessed 'as Slaves and Negroes are usually rated' with men at £25 and children at £5; by contrast an English man was valued at £70.[71] This othering of the Irish, this dehumanisation as a means of control, persisted well into the twentieth century. In other words, Spenser's *View* became a foundational text, much as the writings of Giraldus Cambrensis had in the earlier period, and influenced policymakers from the seventeenth century. More generally, Clare Carroll in *Circe's Cup*, argues that Spenser's work was an important milestone in:

> an emerging discourse of race. Nineteenth-century racial discourse, economically motivated by the full-blown European imperialist exploitation of Africans, Asians, Arabs and other colonized peoples, certainly takes forms different from that of Spenser's ethnographic description of the Irish. Nevertheless, his use of this ethnography to further his argument for colonization, cultural reorganization, and even extermination becomes a way to constitute the disparate groups within Irish society as a type of unified racial other.[72]

In the construction of otherness, ethnography, travel narratives, and histories were bedfellows. In her important doctoral thesis on 'The evolution of British imperial perceptions in Ireland and India, c.1650–1800', Alix Chartrand has shown how, through the writing of history, imperial authorities exercised dominance. By taking control of another nation's historical narrative, various English administrations sought both to reinforce their own claims to power and, at the same time, to present specific images of their colonial subjects. In the Irish and Indian contexts, English-produced histories also represented an exercise in defining social and/or religious categories in ways that generated new social identities frequently adhering to religious lines. Religion, in particular, served as a dominant source of unease in Catholic Ireland and Mughal India. This demonization, in turn, provided much scope for justifications of greater imperial intervention in both places, while the appropriation of historical events affirmed colonial strength and encouraged further expansion. Events such as the 1641 rebellion and the Black Hole of Calcutta in 1756 also demonstrate how anxieties over the trustworthiness of Irish and Indian colonial subjects coloured British perceptions and policies for decades, even centuries. Sir John Temple's *Irish Rebellion* (1646) needs to be treated as the equivalent for Irish Protestants of John Foxe's *Actes and Monuments*, commonly known as the *Book of Martyrs*, in terms of identity formation and forging a national myth based on the barbarous nature of Irish Catholics and Protestant suffering at their hands. Temple—together with sermons, pamphlets, and other histories—fuelled sectarianism, and was republished at moments of political crisis well into the nineteenth century. These fed into an anti-Catholic narrative that helped to sustain a Protestant Unionist identity, especially in Ulster, something that we still live with, especially in this post-Brexit world.[73]

In a study of English travel writings in early modern India, Rita Banerjee shows how the cartographer and illustrator John Ogilby, who during the 1630s served as dancing master to Wentworth's daughters and after 1661 as master of the revels in Ireland, drew direct parallels with India, which he never visited. In *Asia* (1673) Ogilby's crude image and description of the 'halalchors' (or untouchables in the caste system) bears, according to Banerjee, 'resemblances to the conception of the uncivilized wild man' depicted in John Speed's atlas.[74] Like Temple, Ogilby builds his narrative around a series of treacherous incidents, leading Banerjee to conclude that the 'ingratitude, barbarity, and moral perversity for which both Temple and Ogilby condemn the Irish and the Indians point to a clear ethnocentric bias'.[75] Whatever form it took, this dehumanisation helped to justify English imperialism, something that Irish nationalists later drew attention to.[76] For example, Eamon De Valera, one of the founding fathers of Irish independence, gave a speech in New York in February 1920. He argued that Britain had drained India, like Ireland before it, of capital and people and called for solidarity 'to rid ourselves of the vampire that is fattening on our blood'. He reminded his audience that 'the people of India, we are told by the British apologists, are backward and ignorant, lazy and unable to rule themselves. They have made exactly the same pretense about Ireland at other times. The Indians are "mere Asiatics", we are told. We were the "mere" Irish'.[77] The discourse of 'civility' and 'degeneracy', honed in early modern Ireland, had a long history and a global impact.

II Imprint of Ireland

In a meaty memorandum, dated 6 January 1674, John Locke, the secretary to the Council of Trade and Plantations, reflected on the governance of Barbados. Locke suggested that:

> The Government of the Plantations would be hereby suited to that which hath been allwais observed in Ireland and long experience has approved of there, where the nominacion of the Councill was not thought fitt to be trusted to his Majestie's Lord Lieutenant, though a person allways of eminent dignity, wisdome, loyalty, and estate, and though Ireland be neere at hand, and so all miscarriages capable of a more timely remedy.[78]

Three years later, in 1677, the attorney general was instructed 'to prepare a Bill like Poynings' law in Ireland, directing the manner of enacting laws in Jamaica, the transmitting them, and how to be received after His Majesty's amendments and additions'.[79] Poynings' Law (1494) mandated that no parliament could meet in Ireland unless licensed to do so by the king and that the king and his English privy council approved all legislation to be submitted to an Irish parliament.[80] A few months later the king ordered that 'in future no legislative Assembly be called [in Jamaica] without His Majesty's special directions... That the same method be made use of in legislative matters in Jamaica as in Ireland according to the form prescribed in Poynings' law'.[81] Ireland was again invoked in 1678 during discussions about the establishment of a mint in Jamaica. The minute of the meeting noted a request 'to peruse entries in the Council Books of 1661 touching a mint for Ireland'.[82] As these three examples illustrate, the king and his officials in London not only saw Ireland as a template for colonial governance elsewhere but also used the example of Ireland in an effort to restrict the legislative function of assemblies across the empire.[83]

And with some success. Writing about the nineteenth century, David Fitzpatrick suggested: 'The imprint of Ireland may be detected in virtually every colonial institution'.[84] In an essay on governance in the Atlantic world, Jenny Bannister has suggested that there 'may be no single archetype for Atlantic imperialism, but Ireland offers a useful starting point'.[85] In Ireland a patchwork of 'colonial' models, which later characterised Atlantic settlement, operated over the course of the early modern period: the royal plantations (or Crown colonies) in Munster and Ulster like those in the English Caribbean islands from the 1660s or New York; the palatinate lordship of the Butlers of Ormond akin to the proprietorial ones in Maryland and the Carolinas; and the corporate model in London/Derry.[86] Proposals to create a hereditary peerage in Virginia, and later in Massachusetts and South Carolina, along the lines of the Irish peerage which by the 1620s had become a 'service elite', came to nothing.[87] However, the Council of Virginia chose the presidency model of government, which—though it originated in Wales and in the northern regions of England—had been fine-tuned during the late sixteenth century in Munster and Connacht.[88] One of the best examples of 'imprinting' is plantation, tried and tested in Ireland from the sixteenth century before being rolled out in the Americas, the Caribbean, the Indian sub-continent, and later Africa.[89] As James Walvin notes in *Fruits of Empire*, the plantations that came to Asia in the nineteenth century or to Africa in the twentieth owed much to their Atlantic and Irish predecessors. Whether in early modern Ireland, nineteenth-century India, or twentieth-century Kenya colonists 'beat back the wilderness, drove out, destroyed or frightened away native peoples, discovered ways of creating agricultural bounty . . . devised new ways of disciplining labour'. The success of the system rested on violence and force.[90]

As well as governance and policies, Ireland left imprints on the physical landscapes of early modern empires. From Calle O'Reilly in Cuba to Sullivan's Island in the Carolinas and from Enfield Bog in St. Croix to Dublin Creek in Philadelphia, place names testify to Irish settlement. Leslie Herman, in an important doctoral thesis, examines the built environment and the architectural history of the mainland colonies through the lens of Ireland. The similarities began with Fort Raleigh, built by Sir Ralph Lane on Roanoke Island, something noted by E. M. Jope, an archaeologist, who compared it with Fortwilliam, Belfast. Next came Jamestown which has 'an enclosed, palisade-and-earthwork structure and has the same practical lineaments as the Irish forts'.[91] Emily Mann has compared the militarised landscapes in Ireland and Bermuda during the early decades of the seventeenth century.[92] Ivar McGrath has documented imperial barrack building in Ireland and Jamaica, arguing that 'Ireland became the first testing ground for this new military innovation within the British empire'.[93]

Principles of improvement and civilisation, grounded in classical precedents, also guided the imperial endeavour. Colonists in Ireland and the Americas were, as Nicholas Canny noted, 'given detailed and almost identical, instructions on the erection of houses and churches'.[94] Even if houses in Ireland became increasingly anglicised, they nonetheless retained defensive features. The same held true for homes in Jamaica, the Chesapeake, and later American colonies.[95] Luke Pecoraro, an archaeologist, has identified similarities in fortified architecture on the Gookin estates in Munster, the Chesapeake, and the 'praying' Indian town of Magunkaquog, where Daniel Gookin later lived. In the praying towns of Massachusetts, the Indians, like the native Irish, were expected to live a settled life in permanent houses, to own plots of land as individuals, rather than collectively, and to form defensive communities that embraced civil life. A 1674 survey by Gookin of Natick, one of the praying towns, recorded the extent to which it was an 'English-style town' and here he echoed the 1622 survey of Ulster conducted by Thomas Raven.[96]

Raven's maps of Coleraine and especially Londonderry illustrate how these plantation towns were designed to defend and to support commercial activity, with less emphasis on the religious or civic function.[97] In 1724 Bishop Berkeley wrote to Sir John Percival: 'The city of Londonderry is the most compact, regular, well built town, that I have seen in the King's Dominions'.[98] Berkeley and Percival, who assisted with the Georgia colony, corresponded regularly about the Londonderry plantation and there is evidence to suggest that their thinking did shape the new colony.[99] The layout of Londonderry also fed into plans for Philadelphia, as did the designs of towns and settlements in Munster. The colony's proprietor, William Penn, who grew up on his father's estates at Macroom in County Cork, would have been familiar with plantation towns like Bandon. Penn, a close associate of the Southwells, the Gookins, and the Boyle brothers (Robert, Francis, Viscount Shannon, and Roger, earl of Orrery) had visited Charleville, Orrery's 'big house' dating from the 1660s.[100] Orrery designed Charleville as a fortified mansion that also served as an engine to drive the economic growth of the local town of Charleville, which could well have served as the prototype for Penn's mansion at Pennsbury.[101] Equally distinctive to Ireland was the 'feudal' structure and tenurial practices of these plantation estates, with their manorial courts and privileges, something that Penn, like Calvert before him, brought to the New World.

It has been suggested that London after the 1666 fire was the primary inspiration for Philadelphia but Leslie Herman has definitively shown its 'Irish' character, which she attributes to two primary factors. First, Penn's personal and lived experiences of Munster and, second, his close relationship with Sir William Petty, the father of political economy, who had his own 'Irish colony' in County Kerry where he combined 'improving' and 'scientific' methods with ambitions to make a profit.[102] Throughout the mid-1680s, as Ted McCormick notes, Petty 'attempted to apply the lessons of Irish plantation to America'.[103] He influenced Penn's colonial venture, especially the planning of Philadelphia, his advice honed by the fact he became one of the first investors purchasing a 5,000 acre plot.[104] Thomas Holme (1624–95), a former Cromwellian soldier who had experience of the Civil and the Down Surveys (discussed in Section III below), became the colony's first surveyor general. Working with Penn, Holme laid out Philadelphia on a grid pattern, with a commercial centre, wide main streets, and four parks, similar to St. Stephen's Green in Dublin, in each corner. Holme took one of these prime lots for his new home, which was built by an Irish indentured servant, a carpenter called Edward McVeigh.[105] In short, Leslie Herman has made 'visible a history that has been hiding in plain sight' despite numerous attempts by later scholars to erase the 'Irishness' and replace it with 'Englishness'.[106]

The 'Irishness' of early Bombay is even more opaque yet imprints of Ireland undoubtedly shaped its early development. Between 1669 until his death in 1675, Gerald Aungier, who had been born in Ireland, created an 'English colony' in Bombay.[107] Aungier's views on plantation accorded with those of the East India Company but he placed greater emphasis on the importance of anglicisation and his Irish experiences influenced his thinking and policies in Bombay.[108] Of course, as Phil Stern reminds us, anglicisation was as much about other Europeans—especially the Portuguese—as it was about South Asians. Thus Aungier aimed to eliminate the use of Portuguese, which had become the *lingua franca* of the island, and establish the primacy of English as the language of the church, court, and commerce. The parallels between Aungier's determination to rid the island of Portuguese law, language, and culture and the English government's efforts, albeit a century previously, to suppress Brehon law, Gaelic practices, and the Irish language are striking. Aungier insisted that the inhabitants of Bombay use English weights and measures, be governed by English law, and speak English.[109] As in Gookin's New England and in Ireland, contemporaries recognised the importance of education as a means of anglicisation.[110] The East India Company held that 'an English schoolmaster or two' could 'teach their children English, w[h]ich we looke on as a considerable matter, both in policy for cementing us in affection, and...also in piety, for uniting us in religion'.[111] Aungier built a mint, the first one in English India, and gave the coins English names 'for in this and in all things else we endeavour to entice people to and teach them the English tongue'.[112] To provide for the effective administration of justice, Aungier divided Bombay into two shires (the shiring process was completed in Ireland in the 1560s).[113] There is no evidence to suggest that Aungier, unlike his paternal grandfather, uncles, and brothers, attended the Inns of Court in London but he appears to have had some legal training and,[114] interestingly, the works of Richard Bolton appear in the inventory of the library in Surat.[115] Sir Richard Bolton, the Irish lord chancellor, was a close colleague of both of Aungier's grandfathers and had published *The Statutes of Ireland...* (1621) and *A justice of peace for Ireland* (1638).[116] The latter would have been especially useful to Aungier in Bombay since it was a manual that instructed JPs how to do their job.[117] In 1673 Aungier reported back to London that he had succeeded in establishing 'the English laws on this island as near as wee can reach to the method and form in England'.[118]

The Bombay colony desperately needed settlers, especially women, so that 'the children of all protestant fathers be brought up carefully in the protestant religion'.[119] Aungier did everything possible to encourage tradesmen and their families to colonise the island. He drew inspiration from other 'English' colonies in New England, Virginia, Barbados, and Jamaica, along with examples of successful Portuguese and Dutch colonies in India itself. Aungier maintained that the Bombay colony would only prosper if settlers and their families made a long-term commitment 'to plant and improve'.[120] In so many respects Aungier strove to recreate in Bombay the world into which he had been born and one where his grandparents—one an archbishop and the other an active planter and lawyer—had acted as 'imperial intermediaries' intent on making Ireland English.[121] Of course, anglicisation and the 'civilising mission' did become official policy in India from the 1830s. Thomas Babington Macaulay, in his famous 'Minute on Education' (1835), expounded ideas about creating a body of loyal Indians who would become 'English in taste, in opinions, in morals and in intellect'.[122] Macaulay wanted to recreate in nineteenth-century India exactly what Davies and others had been advocating for in early modern Ireland.[123]

III Tools of empire

'Colonial counting' and the need to catalogue, chart, draw, engrave, map, paint, and survey land, people, and natural resources became a hallmark of English imperialism in Ireland, the Atlantic, and India. Collectively, this served as proof of dominance and signified legal rights of possession and ownership and drew attention to the commercial opportunities the natural world afforded to enterprising colonists.[124] This section looks at how 'tools of empire'—the law, especially how it related to land, together with knowledge collection—were trialled in Ireland and then adopted, albeit having been adapted to suit local circumstances, throughout the early modern Anglophone world.

The operation of the law also provides fascinating examples of imperial interconnectedness. Over the course of the seventeenth century, individuals who had cut their teeth in Ireland repurposed martial law for use initially in Roanoke and Jamestown in Virginia, but later in Maryland, Pennsylvania, Jamaica, Tangier, St. Helena, and Bombay. William O'Brien, second earl of Inchiquin, attributed the problems he encountered in Jamaica during the early 1690s to 'the strengthening of pretensions to martial law'.[125] In a case study of highway banditry in India, Alix Chartrand shows the direct line of influence between Irish toryism, controlled by martial law, and eighteenth-century Indian legal measures against the socially subversive 'dacoits'.[126] In short, the Irish version of summary martial law, though it continued to evolve over time, served widely as an imperial tool.[127] Other initiatives emerged from a dynamic interplay of borrowing from Ireland and adaptation elsewhere. For example, as the research of Jennifer Wells has shown, settlers familiar with the severe repressive techniques used during the Cromwellian conquests in Ireland in the 1650s brought these methods to Barbados to be reworked into controls on servants and enslaved Africans. Their 'usefulness' attracted notice in London, where the East India Company recommended the 'Barbados discipline' as a model for the slave code in its settlements of St. Helena and, later, Sumatra.[128] Aaron Graham has compared the penal laws and slave codes in Ireland and the Caribbean and suggested that local elites in both colonies assembled these 'codes of law for social repression'.[129]

Legal practices also moved 'laterally' from settlement to settlement. Aungier developed a 'legal code' in Bombay (1670–2) derived from his Irish experiences, which the authorities in St. Helena then appropriated for their own purposes.[130] Ireland's example informed how Aungier handled contested land title investigations and repossessions. In 1672 Aungier seized all land in Bombay, forcing the Portuguese incumbents to prove their titles by English law. Three quarters of them failed to do so. Having gained the upper hand, Aungier skilfully negotiated a deal, called a 'composition' (the 1585 Composition of Connacht is discussed in Chapter 2).[131] Aungier now expected that those who benefited from the 'Bombay composition' would commit themselves fully to the king and English rule in Bombay and renounce all Portuguese 'royalties, rights, privileges'. This was the Bombay equivalent of 'surrender and regrant', the policy that the Crown had used with great effect against the Gaelic chieftains during the sixteenth century (see Chapter 2 above). In another move redolent of colonial Ireland, clause 12 of the Bombay composition agreement provided for a survey of the island so 'that the lands and estates of each person be measured'.[132] Aungier had the island of Bombay carefully mapped and surveyed but, unfortunately, Colonel Herman (Blake or) Bake's 'large map of [the] island' is apparently lost.[133] Instead, a 1677 survey offers detailed descriptions of each building, including East India house, the court, the hospital, the customs house, the warehouse, workshops, and private residences for Company officials. These were made of brick or stone with timber or tile roofs, with oyster shell windows and landscaped gardens.[134]

As tools of empire, maps were of special importance, depicting a physical and cultural geography.[135] Tudor administrators, like Sir William Cecil, collected and commissioned maps of Ireland, fully aware of the relationship between power and knowledge.[136] John Speed, who never visited Ireland, developed a convincing pictorial language, indicating towns, villages, rivers as well as fortresses, streets in cities and ports, using always the same stylistic conventions and thus creating a remarkable effect of recognition.[137] Increasingly, English place names (or anglicised versions of Irish ones) were used on these maps, while images of people, townscapes, and ships provided useful topographical and ethnographic details. In particular, the depiction of fortifications led to their iconic representation as contemporary and future symbols of colonial power. Most important of all, before expropriated land could be redistributed, it first had to be surveyed and mapped. Land deemed to be 'profitable' (or not) was recorded, along with forests, bogland, rivers, lakes, waterways, enclosed land, orchards, mills, houses, churches, villages, towns, and so on. Various maps and surveys associated with the plantations of Munster and Ulster are extant, along with the Strafford Survey of Connacht (1636–40), Sir William Petty's voluminous 'Down Survey' (1654–9), the 'Civil Survey' (1654–6) and the Books of Survey and Distribution.[138]

Of particular significance for the English empire was the 'Down Survey'—c.2,000 maps covering all four provinces, thousands of baronies, and over 60,000 townlands—which visualised the claim of the colonial authorities to Irish land. These represented Ireland as anglicised and integrated into the English imperial system.[139] Taken in the years between 1656 and 1658, under the direction of Sir William Petty, the Down Survey was the first ever detailed land survey on a national scale anywhere in the world. It became the prototype for future surveys in the emerging British empire and introduced the English empire to empirical planning.[140] According to Allan Greer, 'Much about the Down Survey seems to foreshadow the transformation of indigenous American territories'.[141] For example, the Down Survey was a model for the 'Map of the Improved Part of the Province of Pennsylvania' (1687), replete with the use of the terms 'province' and 'barony'.[142] It is hard to overstate the significance for the later seventeenth-century English empire of Petty, and his Munster social circle—William Penn, Robert Boyle, Daniel Gookin, and Robert Southwell, who in 1675 became secretary to the newly formed board of the Lords of Trade and Plantations.[143] According to Ted McCormick, 'Political arithmetic' was a 'new kind of governance. Its object was a knowable, measurable, and above all manipulable population. Its essence was not quantification but a new kind of demographic agency, initially intended for the use of the state'.[144] Having completed his political anatomy of Ireland, during the 1670s Petty turned his attentions across the Atlantic and began to compile materials for a political anatomy of New England. In the early 1680s he focused on the colony of Pennsylvania where he urged Penn to survey the land, chart the natural resources, and count every person.[145]

From the later 1670s the Board of Trade and Plantations made Crown policy—from Bombay to St. Helena, to the colonies in the Atlantic world—the mobilisation of information on people and their productivity as developed by Petty in Ireland.[146] For example, the Bombay censuses, dating from the 1670s, named men, women, and children living in the colony, along with those who had died since the previous census. The climate and disease took a heavy toll, with one in four people dying every year, bearing out the adage that 'two monsoons are the age of a man'.[147] As well as serving the needs of state, imperial counting revealed the ethnic diversity of the colonial populations. Analysis of surnames in the Bombay censuses records the presence of soldiers with Irish names: Butler, Barnewall, Kennedy, Talbot, and O'Neill.[148] Bombay—like the other colonies in the empire—was far from 'English'. The numerous censuses associated with the Caribbean, especially those of the Leeward Islands conducted by Sir William Stapleton in 1678 (and discussed in Chapter 4), testify to the intensity of Irish settlement. These censuses recorded addresses and sizes of households, the numbers of men, women, children, servants, and enslaved Africans along with details of livestock, acreage, and natural resources. Over time these censuses became increasingly sophisticated and sometimes included details of ethnic origin, age, status, occupation, whether land was cultivated (or not), what was growing on it (sugar or indigo) and weapons owned.[149]

Initially, in Ireland the measurement of land was given priority over the counting of people. Elsewhere the reverse was true, and the focus was on people. The goal was, however, the same: to make a profit. Thus Petty combined in his writings a mixture of pseudo-scientific assumptions with radical visions of social engineering, all with a specific economic twist. Petty was also a great exponent of 'improvement' and supporter of proto-industrial schemes. He held that through surveying and drainage, building new roads and harbours, and harvesting Ireland's human and natural resources the country could be 'civilised' and made profitable. Governor Aungier had this sort of an 'improving' mindset. He sought during the 1670s to increase Bombay's agricultural output, to reclaim wastelands that were flooded by the sea, and to exploit other natural resources.[150] He experimented (unsuccessfully) with the cultivation of pepper for export. Above all, Aungier did all he could to develop the textile and other proto-industry.[151]

The ideology of 'improvement' later became a feature of the East India Company, especially after 1757 and the Permanent Settlement of Bengal. The mapping of India began in earnest in 1765 with James Rennell's survey of Bengal and over time increased in scale and scope.[152] Barry Crosbie argues that from the 1750s onwards Ireland was a 'crucial sub-imperial centre for the British Empire' in South Asia that provided a significant amount of the manpower, intellectual and financial capital that fuelled Britain's drive into Asia. He has shown how people from Ireland played key roles in 'transferring and adapting systems of knowledge and practice from Ireland's "laboratory" of colonial science to India'. He examines the close relationship between the Ordinance Survey of Ireland, that Friel featured in *Translations*, and the mid-nineteenth-century Great Trigonometrical Survey of India (GTS) and the Geological Survey of India (GSI), which was led by Thomas Oldham, professor of engineering at Trinity College Dublin. It is an interesting coincidence that Thomas Larcom, who worked on the Ordinance Survey of Ireland in the 1820s and 1830s and liaised closely with colleagues in Madras, responsible for the Great Trigonometrical Survey of India, also prepared for publication an edition of the Petty's 'Down Survey'.[153] In India they surveyed and described the natural environment, resources and peoples of conquered lands, just as Petty and others had done in Ireland 150 years before.[154]

This book is primarily about the early modern period; however, the next two sections shift the discussion into the nineteenth and twentieth centuries to test the hypothesis of Ireland as a laboratory in and for empire across time. Taking Ireland and India—England's oldest and largest colonies—as a case study, Section IV explores the structural continuities and human links, an approach that might usefully be applied to other regions colonised by Britain and by other imperial powers. Though the geographic scope of Section V, which focuses on resistance to empire, includes a brief discussion of the Atlantic world, Ireland and India remain the focus.

IV Ireland and India

Although the process of change took place over two different timeframes, land ownership policies in Ireland and India looked strangely similar by the turn of the nineteenth century.[155] Given the importance accorded to land— Friel's 'goddess'—from the early modern period, two questions continuously plagued administrators in Ireland and India: who owned the land, and how? In a ground-breaking monograph, *Imperial Affinities*, S. B. Cook looked at 'how Ireland served as a colonial prototype, a provider of policy precedents that the British drew upon in governing India' during the nineteenth century.[156] Cook examined ideas about land tenures and argued that there were 'similarities in outlook, motive, method, policy and even, to a limited extent, practice between such very different and distant components of empire as India and Ireland'.[157] Building on this, Alix Chartrand has shown how Irish and Indian theories of landownership were deployed to reinforce the ruling administrations' authority over colonial subjects.[158] The revolution in Irish landownership that occurred over the course of the seventeenth century (and discussed in Chapters 2 and 4) resulted in the creation of a Protestant ascendancy and the transfer of millions of acres from Catholics to Protestants. The Permanent Settlement of the 1790s tried to replicate in Bengal the model of the Irish Protestant Ascendancy, with the creation of a class of loyal landowners who owed their position and status to the governing administration. The colonial rulers wanted to maximise the usage of all available arable land in order to provide a steady source of income. They also wanted to create a loyal and stable Irish and Indian land-owning class that owed its loyalty to London.

In order to extract the landed wealth of India, the East India Company and later the Crown needed to control ever-increasing swathes of the sub-continent. Ireland continued to provide prototypes for governance well into the nineteenth and twentieth centuries.[159] The presidency model of government, fine-tuned in Ireland, was transferred to India, where a chief secretary and lord lieutenant represented the Crown. The structure of local government, with resident magistrates bringing law and discipline to local communities, also provided the template for India.[160] The Irish system of elementary education served as a model for India. In the 1830s the British government overhauled primary education in Ireland and established a centrally controlled national school system with an approved series of textbooks which were used throughout the empire. Whether in Ireland or India these educational initiatives formed part of a wider programme of anglicisation reminiscent of what had occurred in the early modern period. Other structural similarities included policing, which often operated in both countries by coercion rather than consent. The Royal Irish Constabulary (RIC), a government controlled force, organised along military lines, was held up as an exemplar and after 1907 all officers of colonial police forces had to attend the RIC depot in Dublin for training.[161] From the 1920s Ireland provided lessons in policing terrorism and counterinsurgency. Men from Ireland or who had served there drew frequently on their Irish experiences—figures like Sir Charles Tegart, police commissioner of Calcutta (1923–31) who was later active in Palestine, or Sir John Anderson, who served as chief secretary for Ireland during the 1920s where he oversaw partition before becoming governor of Bengal in 1932.[162]

As well as policing, Ireland provided a disproportionate number of soldiers for service in India. The East India Company began recruiting Irish soldiers in earnest from the Seven Years' War (1756–63), though Irishmen served in the Bombay garrison from the 1670s.[163] By the 1810s nearly 60 per cent of all privates and 45 per cent of non-commissioned officers were from Ireland, and by the 1890s Irishmen comprised roughly two-thirds of the British army in India.[164] These rank-and-file troops (Rudyard Kipling's 'Rishti') were usually impoverished Catholics, known for their bravery, endurance, and good humour along with their racism and drunken brawling. Their officers were often Protestants of Anglo-Irish provenance who tended to view their Irishness as something of a liability, even an embarrassment.[165] They included figures like Eyre Coote (d. 1783), Arthur Wellesley, duke of Wellington (d. 1852), Lord Roberts of Kandahar (d. 1914), the Lawrence brothers (George (d. 1884), Henry (d. 1857), and John (d. 1870)), and John Nicholson (d. 1857). During India's First War of Independence in 1857, six Irish regiments were involved in the brutal suppression of the insurgents. Of Londonderry stock, Henry Lawrence died from fatal wounds received at the siege of Lucknow and on his deathbed echoed the words of Derry's defenders in 1688: 'No surrender!'[166] The savagery of Nicholson, another Ulsterman, and his use of extreme violence in 1857 did not prevent him from being venerated as a British imperial hero, when in fact he behaved like 'an imperial psychopath'.[167] It is also important to acknowledge the role that men from Ireland—Colonel Reginald Dyer, educated in Middleton in County Cork, and his superior, the lieutenant governor of the Punjab, Michael O'Dwyer, a Catholic from County Tipperary—played on 13 April 1919 at the Amritsar Massacre of 1,500 Indian men, women, and children at Jallianwala Bagh in the Punjab (see Chapter 1).

In addition to soldiers, Irish universities—Trinity and the Queen's Colleges at Belfast, Cork, and Galway—educated servants of empire. By the mid-nineteenth century Trinity offered a wide range of oriental languages—Arabic, Bengali, Gujarati, Hindustani, Marathi, Persian, Sanskrit, and Tamil—together with courses in Indian history and geography.[168] The Trinity Medical School developed an innovative curriculum, training doctors in public health and tropical diseases, and 40 per cent of all medical recruits to the presidencies of Madras, Bombay, and Bengal were from Ireland (the majority from Trinity). Trinity was the first university in the United Kingdom to integrate applied sciences, such as engineering, into the curriculum and in 1841 created a School of Civil Engineering, which initially offered a two-year diploma and where professors like Thomas Oldham trained generations of engineers and surveyors. These courses were aimed specifically at young men from the Irish (Dublin) middle classes who were ambitious for a career in India.[169] Trinity was especially successful in preparing candidates for the Indian Civil Service exams and in the decade following their introduction Trinity produced 16 per cent (86 out of 561) of all graduates. The figure for Oxford was 22 per cent (121) and Cambridge was 15 per cent (85). By 1865 recruits from across the Irish universities accounted for 33 per cent of all graduates, including a growing number of middle-class Catholics, at a time when Ireland made up 20 per cent of the population of the United Kingdom (in the 50 years prior to this, when recruits attended the East India College, Haileybury, only five per cent of the graduates were Irish-born).[170] Whether as administrators, engineers, doctors, missionaries, or soldiers, men and occasionally women from Ireland served the British empire in India over the course of nearly three centuries.

V Resisting empire

'The trouble with British imperial histories', wrote Antoinette Burton 'is that they are not written with dissent and disruption in the lead...Yet the very character of imperial power was shaped by its challengers and the trouble they made for its stewards'.[171] Like Burton, Priyamvada Gopal has argued, in *Insurgent Empire*, that resistance accorded agency to colonial subjects and highlighted the limits of imperial power.[172] Throughout this book, especially in Chapter 2, special attention has been paid to the voice of resistance in Ireland, and the actions associated with it. These ranged from aristocratic revolts in the sixteenth century to major rebellions after 1594, 1641, and 1688 and from agrarian, political, and intellectual protest to a continued commitment to Catholicism, to speaking the Irish language and following Irish ways.

Both Burton and Gopal note how resistance was often transnational, linking protestors in one colony with those in another.[173] Thus strategies for contesting English rule often moved laterally and Ireland served as a laboratory for resisting empire and as a warning of what English colonial rule looked like. Irish objections to Poyning's Law, so well articulated by the Catholic confederate, Patrick Darcy, and later by the Protestant patriots, including William Molyneux, were recycled by colonists in the Atlantic as settlers in Virginia and the Carolinas reacted angrily when the Crown tried to apply to them heavy-handed techniques of governance developed in Ireland.[174] The usually turbulent factions in Jamaica joined together in the later 1670s to prevent the imposition of Poyning's Law, aware of its deadening effect in Ireland.[175] Officials in London hoped to mollify the Jamaican assembly by reassuring them that 'their freedom as Englishmen' would not be violated 'by being governed as Ireland is'. They added that the 'qualities and estates of the King's subjects in Ireland are doubtless much superior to those of Jamaica, and Irishmen are quite as careful to conserve their liberty'.[176] Quips like this would have offered cold comfort.[177] In another move reminiscent of Ireland, the duke of York only agreed to the calling of an assembly in New York on the condition that it granted funding to pay off the public debts and to support the government and the garrison in perpetuity. However, the duke then rejected attempts by Governor Thomas Dongan, no doubt familiar with earlier Irish attempts, to secure a charter that made the New York assembly coequal and independent of the English parliament, that promised no taxation without representation, and that guaranteed liberty of conscience.[178]

The Irish Declaratory Act of 1720, which confirmed Ireland's status as a colony, became such a symbol of the subservience of Ireland that American patriots recognised the ominous implications of the Westminster parliament passing the Declaratory Act of 1766 claiming the right to bind the colonies 'in all cases whatsoever'. Seeking to restrict parliamentary authority to such 'external' matters as defence, foreign affairs, and transatlantic trade, and to challenge its power in internal colonial affairs, the patriots carefully studied Molyneux's *The Case of Ireland Being Bound* (1698), which had argued that only the Irish parliament could legislate for Ireland. According to Molyneux, Ireland's constitutional status was that of a sister kingdom to England rather than a colony. As a sister kingdom sharing the same Crown, Ireland was entitled to legislative and judicial independence. Molyneux's book caused a sensation and his writings were particularly popular with American colonists in the 1760s, especially the call for no taxation without representation.[179] Ultimately, rebellion was their response to imperial rule.[180]

Of course, the Irish had risen in rebellion on numerous occasions during the early modern period, with that of 1641 securing a decade of independence from English rule. Another major rebellion in 1798 resulted in the abolition of the Irish parliament and political union with Great Britain. The maintenance of that union became core to the identity of the Unionist community, especially in the north of Ireland. However, the ending of that union became, from the early nineteenth century, the focus for generations of Irish nationalists. Some hoped to achieve this using constitutional and cultural means, others favoured the use of violence.[181] Whatever the form, Irish resistance of empire had global consequences, especially for India.

In the 1870s and 1880s, Irish radicals attempted constitutional reform of imperial practices in India.[182] Irish MPs at Westminster dominated parliamentary debates on India. One of the most active was Frank Hugh O'Donnell, a Queen's College Galway, who was an early proponent of transforming the empire 'into a commonwealth of equal partners' and formed the Constitutional Society of India.[183] In his maiden speech in the House of Commons in 1874, Frank addressed the government's response to the Bengal famine (1872–3), connecting famines experienced by India and Ireland.[184] Frank was exceptionally well informed thanks to the presence of his brother, Charles, in India as a member of the Indian Civil Service. Charles wrote a number of pamphlets criticising British policy in India. In one, *The Ruin of an Indian Province* (1880), 'he described the plight of the Indian peasantry in the state of Bihar and attacked the feudal system of land tenure. In this and subsequent writings on India over the next thirty years, he was very aware of parallels with Ireland'.[185] Prior to 1900 discussions about the rights of the tenant influenced legislation in both counties and, in the words of S. B. Cook, 'though different in many respects Irish and Indian land legislation reflected similar orientation, ideology and policy'.[186] Indian land legislation provided the precedent for the Land Act of 1870 in Ireland, while the Irish Land Act (1881) in turn provided the basis for the Bengal Tenancy Act (1885), which Irishmen, mostly notably the Catholic Sir Anthony MacDonnell, greatly influenced.[187] Cook has shown how men like MacDonnell were central in ensuring the greater protection shown to *raiyats* (substantial peasants) by the Bengal Tenancy Act, something that caused resentment, especially amongst the *zamindars* (land owners), who dismissed the legislation as the product of 'Home Rulers and Fenians'.[188]

The late nineteenth century was the high point in terms of Irishmen serving in the Indian Civil Service, and by the 1890s Irishmen ran seven (out of eight) of the Indian provinces (including Burma).[189] This coincided with the viceroyalty of Lord Dufferin (1884–8), who was descended from seventeenth-century Scottish planters and viewed India through the prism of his Irish experiences.[190] Dufferin was a Liberal but Prime Minister Gladstone's call for home rule and Irish land acts had alienated him and caused him to regard with suspicion the foundation in 1885 of the Indian National Congress, which he referred to as the 'Indian Home Rule movement'.[191] He wrote in March 1886: 'I cannot help having a strong suspicion that the course of events at home in regard to Ireland has produced a very considerable effect upon the minds of the intelligent and educated section of our own native community. Associations and sub-associations are being formed all over the country'.[192] He wondered how long it would be before 'the perfected machinery of modern democratic agitation', tested in Ireland, would take hold in India.[193] He did not have long to wait.

Even though it was 1914 before Annie Besant, of Irish provenance, established the All India Home Rule League, from the 1880s Indian nationalists watched closely the tactics of parliamentary obstruction honed by Charles Stewart Parnell, the charismatic leader of Irish Home Rulers.[194] M. K. Gandhi later attributed the origin of his own mass movement of peaceful resistance in India to the Irish Land League, which served as a model of agrarian disturbance, and to Michael Davitt, who had pioneered peaceful methods of agitation and passive resistance, including the use of boycott, rent strikes, and the press.[195] Cultural nationalism came together through the friendship of W. B. Yeats and Rabindranath Tagore, the Bengali polymath, who found aspects of Irish nationalism inspiring, especially the use of language, folklore, and mythology.[196] Of particular relevance in India, as it was in Ireland, was the call in 1892 by Douglas Hyde, later the first president of Ireland, for 'de-anglicising' Ireland, for reversing his country's perceived cultural impoverishment by reclaiming Irish language and literature.[197]

Cultural nationalism fed republicanism. On Easter Monday 24 April 1916, roughly 1,200 Irish insurgents seized the General Post Office and other strategic locations across Dublin's city centre. Patrick Pearse proclaimed a free Irish Republic to a rather bewildered group of onlookers. The Easter Rising of 1916 may have been a failure militarily but, to paraphrase W. B. Yeats, it changed utterly the face of Irish history.[198] It also set in train an unstoppable process, which led to the separation of Ireland from Great Britain and accelerated the collapse of the British empire, which by 1914 traversed the globe. In India, the Irish rising of 1916 inspired Bengali nationalists to emulate Sinn Fein and Irish physical force tactics. The Chittagong armoury raid on Good Friday 1930 (18 April) drew inspiration from that of 1916. The Bengali pantheon of heroes included Pearse along with Michael Collins, admired as the master of guerrilla warfare, and Terence McSwiney, the hunger striker, whose example was copied by Jatindranath Das who died in Lahore Jail (1929). Dan Breen's book, *My fight for Irish freedom* (1924), translated into Hindi, Punjabi, and Tamil, became 'one of our Bibles'.[199] In 1933 Subhas Chandra Bose noted that 'in my part of India—Bengal—there is hardly an educated family where books about the Irish heroes are not read and if I may say so, devoured'.[200] Of course, acts of other European revolutionaries also inspired Bengali nationalists but from the 1920s and 1930s the example of Ireland took precedence and the Irish taught the Indians their ABC of freedom fighting. In short, the reverberations of the 1916 rising were felt around the British empire and undoubtedly accelerated its demise.[201]

In addition to rousing Indian nationalists, Ireland provided a model for partition. The Government of Ireland Act (December 1920) partitioned Ireland and established two subordinate parliaments, one in the north (where the Protestants enjoyed a majority) and the other in the south (where the Catholics held sway). Almost exactly a year later the Anglo-Irish Treaty (December 1921) granted dominion status for the 26 counties of the Irish Free State and provided a suitably ambiguous formula 'which would be applied elsewhere in the empire'.[202] Twenty-five years later Mohamed Ali Jinnah, president of the Muslim League, invoked the example of Ireland and pushed for partition just as the Ulster Unionist leader, Sir Edward Carson, who like Jinnah was a lawyer, had done during the 'Home Rule crisis' of 1912–14.[203] M. K. Gandhi, Jawaharlal Nehru, and other members of the National Congress staunchly opposed the creation of Pakistan. The division of Bengal and Punjab along communal lines and the creation in the sub-continent of 'many Ulsters' particularly concerned Nehru, anxieties that De Valera shared.[204] For his part, De Valera had never accepted the legitimacy of Irish partition and Articles 2 and 3 of the 1937 Irish Constitution claimed sovereignty over the six counties that comprise Northern Ireland, a lead that Pakistan, which became a sovereign state in 1947, followed in maintaining a claim to Kashmir.[205]

With the partition in 1920 of Ireland, the British government created in Northern Ireland a Protestant state for a Protestant people. By the 1960s the Catholic population had tired of living as second-class citizens and called for the end to state-sponsored discrimination.[206] What began as a peaceful protest as part of a wider Civil Rights movement quickly degenerated into a bitter war, known as the 'Troubles', that lasted 30 years.[207] The 'Troubles' formed the backdrop for *Making History*, with the play offering a message of reconciliation and inviting audiences to use their history to imagine another future. The significance of where the play was premiered in 1988 cannot be overstated. It took place in the Guildhall, the symbol of imperial power and target of at least two IRA bombs during the 1970s, in the divided and walled city of Derry or Londonderry, as the plantation town developed by the city of London is also known. The opening night of *Making History* passed off without incident unlike the premier in 1981 of Friel's translation of Anton Chekhov's *Three Sisters*, Field Day's second production following the hugely successful staging of *Translations* the previous year. That evening a British army helicopter hovered over the Guildhall for the entire performance in order to drown out the actors' voices. Undaunted, the audience gave them a standing ovation. Such is the power of the arts.[208]

In conclusion, it has been argued here that Ireland served as a laboratory of and for empire from at least the sixteenth until the twentieth centuries. Thanks to the writings especially of Edmund Spenser ethnocentric ideas of cultural superiority fed into the racist ideologies that later characterised English/British imperial rule in the Atlantic, Asia, and Africa. Anglicising policies and practices, developed in Ireland, were also transferred to other colonies, often at the hands of men from Ireland or others who had served there. As the place names or survival of fortified homes and military barracks illustrate, Ireland left distinctive imprints on the physical landscapes of other colonies. Tools of empire—especially relating to the law, knowledge gathering, and mapping—were fine-tuned in Ireland and then deployed in other colonies. That England used Ireland as a colonial laboratory was by no means unique. The Dutch equivalent during the seventeenth century was Formosa (modern-day Taiwan).[209] When it came to developing innovative mapping techniques in the eighteenth century Saint-Domingue (or modern-day Haiti) served as a testing ground for the French.[210] Yet with the Haitian Revolution (1791–1804) the inhabitants of the island, led by a former enslaved African, secured independence. Disrupting colonial rule was what Hugh O'Neill and his allies had done during the Nine Years' War (1603). Securing independence was what the Catholic Confederates achieved during the 1640s. So from the early modern period, Ireland also became a laboratory for resistance to empire, inspiring freedom fighters across the British and other European empires.[211]

6

Empires in Ireland

In *Making History* Hugh O'Neill, earl of Tyrone, insisted that his biographer, Archbishop Lombard, tell the 'truth', particularly about his more controversial relationships with Mabel, the daughter of a Protestant planter, and even Harry Hovenden, his foster brother but 'not a Gael'. Instead, the archbishop hoped 'to tell the best possible narrative', adding 'I'm not sure that "truth" is a primary ingredient—is that a shocking thing to say? Maybe when the time comes, imagination will be as important as information'.[1] Towards the end of the play O'Neill's again instructed Lombard to 'tell them the whole truth'. Lombard replied: 'People think they just want to know the "facts"; they think they believe in some sort of empirical truth, but what they really want is a story'.[2]

We will return to the tensions between 'facts' and 'memory' in Section IV below, which examines how early modern events and experiences of empire were remembered (or not), represented, and misrepresented. The first three sections of this chapter focus on the 'story' of what contemporaries understood about empire in an age when few left their parish and the opportunities to meet people from Asia, Africa, and the Atlantic world were largely limited to those who travelled, served as missionaries, sailors and soldiers, or spent time in cosmopolitan centres like London, Amsterdam, and Lisbon. Thus this chapter explores how empires shaped the lives (Section I), the landscapes (Section II), and the mindsets (Section III) of those living in early modern Ireland. How did imperial commodities, especially food, drink, clothing, furnishings, and representations of empires—in novels, plays, prose, images, travel literature, and maps—form and influence ideas, identities, mindsets, tastes, fashions, and landscapes?

Though initially very small in number peoples from around the world did live in and visit Ireland.[3] A 'blackamoor' was one of 36 people tried and executed in Kilkenny in November 1578.[4] In 1643 John Fortune, 'by birth an Indian Pethagorian but now a Christian' was living in Queen's County (now Laois). According to this own deposition, Fortune had, for 20 years, been a servant to Captain Richard Steele.[5] They probably met in the 1620s during Steele's travels in India and the Middle East. Though unable to sign his name, Fortune prospered in Ireland but with the outbreak of war he had 'Lost his Cattle sheepe cloth howshold goods & other his goodes & chattells of the value of thirtie Powndes'.[6] Like Fortune, others converted to Christianity. In St. Mary's church in Youghal, the baptism was recorded in 1666 of David—formerly known as 'Lampo'—'a negro aged 15 years or thereabout borne in Mountserat one of ye Cariby Islands'.[7] David was probably a servant in the household of a Munster grandee. The funeral entry for Lady Arran included a sketched image of a young black boy holding the train of his mistress at Lady Arran's wake in Dublin in 1669.[8] Other evidence suggests that there was a black servant called 'Scipio' at Kilkenny Castle in the service of Elizabeth, duchess of Ormond. Since the duchess was the chief mourner at her daughter-in-law's funeral, the boy in the drawing may have been Scipio.[9] Aside from these fleeting and tantalising glimpses, 'Scipio' and 'Lampo' were lost from the historical record. Yet Bill Hart has estimated that by the second half of the eighteenth century between 1,000 and 2,000 black people, mostly male domestic servants and probably enslaved Africans, lived scattered throughout the eastern half of Ireland but predominately in Dublin and Munster.[10]

A number of high profile visitors from America and Asia included Ireland on their grand tours of Britain and Europe.[11] For example, in May 1791 leading United Irishmen and other abolitionists welcomed to Belfast Olaudah Equiano, who after purchasing his freedom from slavery wrote a best-selling account of his hellish experiences.[12] David Dickson has suggested that Quaker merchant families hosted him in Dublin and Cork and subscribed to the Irish edition of his *Narrative of the Life of Olaudah Equiano* (1789).[13] In 1799 Abu Talib Isfahani, a relative of the Nawab of Bengal, travelled to Dublin to meet Lord Cornwallis, the lord lieutenant who had suppressed the 1798 rebellion and went on to broker the parliamentary union of 1800/1. Abu Talib had known Cornwallis in India, where, after failing to prevent the American colonies becoming independent, he had served as governor general (1786–92). While he was in Dublin Abu Talib visited the library of Trinity College Dublin. According to his own account, 'there he saw the elegant manuscripts of *Khamsa-i Nizami* and Shahnama and some other Persian books in the language-collection of the library'.[14]

Many of these 'elegant manuscripts' had been donated to the library by Robert Huntington, who served as a chaplain in the British Levant Company and travelled around the Ottoman empire to Egypt, Palestine, Cyprus, Syria, and Istanbul before becoming provost of Trinity in 1681.[15] The library secured further manuscripts from the Mughal empire when in 1806 the directors of the East India Company presented a very fine and magnificently illustrated copy of the tenth-century epic poem 'Shah Namah' from the 'Lib[rary] of Tippoo [Sultan] Sahib'.[16] Tippu Sultan (1750–99), the ruler of Mysore in Southern India, spent much of his life fighting the imperial forces of the East India Company. He died in 1799 following an attack on his fort (at Seringapatam) led by Arthur Wellesley, later duke of Wellington, who was Irish born but found his 'Irishness' a liability. Exquisite works were also taken from the library of the last Mughal emperor, housed in the Red Fort in Delhi, when it was ransacked after an attack in 1857 led by John Nicholson (see Chapter 5).[17] One particularly important volume from the library in the Red Fort is an early seventeenth-century medical textbook (TCD, Ms 1576) by Hakim Hamid. It once formed part of the library of Emperor Shah Jahan (1628–58), the man who oversaw the construction of the Taj Mahal. This exceptionally rare volume allows scholars to track the history of medicine and science in South Asia and to better understand how practitioners of Galenic, Islamic, Ayurvedic, and even Chinese medicine, interacted and influenced each. These manuscripts and books, along with the people from Asia, Africa, and the Americas who visited and lived in early modern Ireland, brought with them knowledge of and artefacts from the empires of the world. These shaped the lives and adorned the homes of at least some people living in early modern Ireland.

I Shaping lives

Ireland's place in the early modern world is well illustrated through an examination of the contents of a wash pit at Rathfarnham castle in Dublin.[18] Archaeological excavations in 2014 unearthed a veritable treasure trove of 17,500 well-preserved artefacts, probably dating from the second half of the seventeenth century. This extraordinary discovery offers a fascinating window into elite material culture but also highlights Ireland's global convergences.[19] Built in the 1580s by Archbishop Adam Loftus, first provost and founder of Trinity College Dublin, Rathfarnham castle was typical of the fortified mansions constructed across early modern Ireland and the English Atlantic.[20] Protestant, well connected, and on the make, members of the Loftus family were amongst thousands of New English settlers who colonised Ireland from the 1530s and made their fortunes, often by dubious means (see Chapter 2 above). The Rathfarnham hoard provides a glimpse into the cosmopolitan material world, both public and private, of a planter dynasty and their household. It highlights the interconnectedness of the early modern world and how the commercial activities of the English, Spanish, Chinese, and Mughal empires extended to the periphery of Western Europe and how the activities of these early modern empires impacted on Ireland.[21] The survival of coins, trade tokens, lead weights, and wax seals tell a story of international commercial engagement. Particularly noteworthy is a jeton, struck at the end of the sixteenth century in Nuremberg, one of Europe's greatest centres of production, along with a silver 'piece of eight', mined and minted at Potosí in Spanish Peru and dated 1655.[22]

Even more exotic is a stunning Colombian emerald, which was excavated along with gold brooches, rings mounted with semi-precious gems, amber beads, and finely engraved sleeve buttons made from silver, gold, and glass.[23] More intimate, is a grooming kit—toothbrush, hair brush, and ear wax spoon—together with a handle for a razor, a fragment of a sponge, and a glass jar apparently containing the remains of red lip or cheek rouge, which was derived from cochineal insects (native to Mexico). Smaller luxury items were recovered from the Rathfarnham wash pit: miniature glass figurines, probably from Nevers in France and the Venetian island of Murano; and exquisite blue and white Chinese porcelain, along with cruder Dutch and English copies. The scale of the Rathfarnham find was exceptional but the recovery of French, Portuguese, Dutch, German, English, and Spanish wares, along with sherds of a Chinese Ming bowl at Dunboy castle in County Cork, once home to the Gaelic lord, O'Sullivan Beare, also testify to wider connections.[24] While hundreds of pottery sherds, excavated between 1987 and 1998 from sites in Galway city, point to close links to Iberia.[25]

Extant fashion items recovered at Rathfarnham included leather and wooden shoe parts (heels, uppers, soles, and buckles). Worn-down heels suggest that these shoes had multiple owners, with mistresses passing on once precious pumps to their daughters and maids, and fathers handing down their shoes to their sons and servants.[26] Though no textiles survived in the damp wash pit, archaeologists recovered wooden and metal buttons, pins, and clasps. These fastened undergarments, dresses, and jackets, no doubt made from locally manufactured woollens and linens or maybe from exquisite silks and satins, tailored in London, or colourful Indian calicoes, which were the height of fashion across Western Europe in the later decades of the seventeenth century. The survival of lace bobbins and bodkins invoke images of intricate lace collars and cuffs worn by members of the elite.[27] Clodagh Tait has shown just how widespread 'English app[ar]ells' had become with people distinguishing in their wills between English and Irish items of clothing.[28] The discovery of clothing—an Irish mantle, an English doublet, and Highland tartan trews—along with leather 'brogue' shoes, all dating from the turn of the seventeenth century, in an Ulster bog on land associated with the O'Cahan lordship has prompted reflection on the relationship between clothing and colonial identities (discussed in Chapter 2).[29]

Unsurprisingly, no bulky household furnishings found their way into the Rathfarnham wash pit, while other highly prized possessions—elaborate wall hangings, damask drapes, and bed covers, or 'Turkey carpets'—so common in the inventories of other grand houses, presumably perished.[30] Men like Gerald Aungier and Richard Hedges brought exquisite Indian textiles to Ireland.[31] For example, in 1675 Aungier sent his brother 'an Indian tent…made of Indian callicoe'. One can only begin to imagine how exotic gifts such as these delighted both the grandees of Dublin and the locals of rural Longford.[32] An inventory of the possessions of Lady Catherine Percival (d. 1679) of Burton in north Cork recorded large and small trunks packed with painted Indian calicoes, 'coarse' calicoes, calico curtains, bedspreads, and quilts, along with Indian silks. Elsewhere Indian textiles provided coverings for windows, walls and floors ('a small painted calico carpet'). According to Marc Caball, 'the frequent arrival of East Indiamen at Kinsale over the course of the seventeenth century' explained 'the presence of such Indian fabrics' throughout Munster, including at the earl of Orrery's grand house at Castle Martyr.[33] Properties belonging to the duke and duchess of Ormond—Dunmore House, Clonmel, Kilkenny Castle, and their apartments in Dublin castle—boasted calico furnishings, 'white Indian Damaske Curtaines' and cushions of 'Indian Stript Silke'.[34] A 1684 inventory recorded the contents of their drawing-room in Kilkenny Castle with its 'ten Japan armed chairs' and squabs (ottomans) with matted bottoms and cushions of green, gold, and white damask; a Japanese chest; a great easy chair 'covered with figured velvet, with a rich gold ground, fringed about with a silver and gold fringe' and matching step; a crystal chandelier, with ten branches and gilt sockets; an Indian screen with six leaves; and two 'Portugal mats under the chairs'; and elaborate firearms for the grate. The curtains were made of, and the furniture upholstered in, the most expensive fabrics (calico, damask, satin, serge, silk brocade, velvet). Turkish carpets and 'Tangier' mats littered the floors and covered the tables and side boards.[35]

Extant ceramics excavated at Rathfarnham and other sites suggests that members of the elite kept up with the latest trends, drinking tea (from Asia) from Chinese porcelain cups and saucers, together with coffee (from Yemen in the Middle East), from fine English-made coffee cups.[36] Though dating from a slightly later period, the armorial china, commissioned in 1722 by Sir Robert Cowan during his time in Bombay, took three years to arrive but is extant in the family home at Mount Stewart in County Down.[37] Sugar, initially reserved for the wealthy, was used to sweeten coffee, tea, and hot drinking chocolate. By the sixteenth century the Atlantic islands of Madeira and Canaries began to replace the Mediterranean as sources for sugar. Over the course of the seventeenth century the production of sugar shifted to the Caribbean, especially Barbados, where the lucrative trade depended on the labour initially of indentured servants and increasingly of enslaved Africans (see Chapter 4). This combined with improved refining techniques, first pioneered by the Dutch, resulted in increased production. Costs fell to the point that by the early eighteenth century the consumption of sugar was commonplace.[38]

Made fashionable first in London, tea came to Ireland later than coffee, and chocolate was the preserve of the elite.[39] After the Restoration, the Irish-born poet laureate Nahum Tate wrote his *Panacea: a poem upon tea* which celebrated urban, civilised life and conspicuous consumption. Here is his account of tea pouring:

> On burning Lamps a silver Vessel plac'd
> A table with surprising Figures grac'd
> And China-Bowls to feast their Sight and Tast:
> The Genial Liquor, decently pour'd out,
> To the admiring Guests is dealt about.
> Scarce had they drunk a first and second Round,
> When the warm Nectar's pleasing Force they found;...
> Thus our Tea-conversation we employ,
> Where with delight, instruction we enjoy;
> Quaffing, without the wast of Time of Wealth,
> The Sov'reign Drink of Pleasure and of Health.[40]

Household inventories of china and other utensils associated with hot beverages show that it was the turn of the eighteenth century before tea consumption really took off and that for much of the later seventeenth century coffee drinking proved more popular, something that the spread of coffee houses underscores (and where tea was increasingly drunk).[41]

Scientific analysis of the food remains in the Rathfarnham wash pit, together with other research led by Susan Flavin as part of the Foodcult project, provides fascinating insights into everyday diet and cultural identities.[42] The range of foodstuffs coming from the New World, often via Iberia and as part of the 'Columbian exchange', was extensive and included marrows, bell peppers, numerous types of beans, turkeys, potatoes, tomatoes, maize, sunflower oil, and a host of other items.[43] Imperialism thus played a significant role in shaping the culinary history of Ireland.[44] The inhabitants of Rathfarnham castle ate locally sourced meat, fowl, game, fish, and foods made from a variety of cereals (especially oats and wheat), along with exotic delicacies like apricots, and peaches, grown under glass, and marrows and courgettes.[45] Elsewhere, on the Clotworthy estate in County Antrim, pineapples were reputedly grown (under glass) for the first time in Ireland in the 1660s. Even more exotic items like coconuts and jars of Indian mangoes also reached Irish shores.[46]

Research has shown that potatoes, indigenous to the Andes and held to have aphrodisiac qualities, probably came to Ireland via Spain (and not with Sir Walter Raleigh as myth has it) during the first decade of the seventeenth century. Within 50 years potato growing, as accounts from the '1641 Depositions' highlight, was reasonably widespread but initially remained a luxury food. There is a wonderful recipe from the 1660s for 'Potato Pie' in the recipe book of Dorothy Parsons from Birr Castle, which involved sugar, dried fruits, rose water, and spices, especially cinnamon, plus eggs, freshly churned butter, and, of course, potatoes. It was the world in a potato pie![47] Towards the end of the seventeenth century potatoes became an important part of the diet of the rural poor. A contemporary noted: 'The meaner people content themselves with little bread, but instead thereof eat potatoes, which with sour milk is the chief part of their diet'.[48] By this period, the use of a variety of Asian spices was ubiquitous, in cooking, for preservation, and for medicinal purposes. In a deposition of July 1645 William Bailie, a merchant from Hacketstown in County Carlow, lamented the loss of spices—cinnamon, cloves, mace, and nutmeg—which he claimed the local insurgents had stolen and then used to flavour their 'mornings draughts'.[49]

The recovery of a large number of clay pipes at Rathfarnham Castle and in other archaeological digs suggests that tobacco smoking proved a particularly popular pastime. Research by Susan Flavin and her team on human remains from this period shows how the teeth were worn down from chewing the pipe.[50] Tobacco was, of course, native to the Americas and by the 1610s and 1620s was widely used in Ireland and elsewhere.[51] Some, including King James VI and I, abhorred the habit, while English and Irish writers alike ridiculed the obsession with tobacco.[52] A New English commentator, Barnaby Rich in *The Irish hubbub* (1617) described the English colonists in Ireland as representing the dregs of England and condemned their addiction to tobacco smoking. Rich's descriptions of smoking were particularly graphic:

> First, it is drawne in at the mouth, then it is snuffled out at the nose, whereby the aire is infected with such a loathsome fume, that those that bee standers by cannot draw their breath, but they must sucke downe some of that filthy vapour, that hath beene blowne out, if not through a pockie nostril, yet (for the most part) through a snotty nose.[53]

A bawdy Irish satire, *Pairlement Chlionne Tomáis*, about rural labourers in Munster, also dating from the early seventeenth century, imagined the arrival of an English trader, Roibín an Tobaca, interrupting a sitting of parliament. In broken and nonsensical English Tomáis haggled with Roibín over the price: 'Is ta for meselfe the mony for fart you all my brothers here'. Having bought the tobacco, each man 'brought out his dirty, broken clay pipe from the bottom of his jerkin or from the ear-piece of his cap, and they set to expelling smoke through their nostrils'.[54] The war of the 1640s did little to dampen the demand for tobacco. An extraordinary vignette from the siege of Cullen Castle in County Waterford revealed how a Mrs Jones 'desiring tobacco' secured it from one of her former servants who had joined the insurgents, by dispatching a seven-year-old boy 'named Rallphit' to collect it for her.[55] As the years passed the love affair with tobacco grew stronger, with consumption doubling between the mid-1660s and mid-1680s. Sir William Petty noted how Irish peasants spent two-sevenths of their food budget on tobacco.[56]

Analysis of prose, poetry, wills, inventories, customs, and legal records illustrate changing consumption patterns.[57] The records of the High Court of Admiralty provide detailed evidence of exotic goods, especially spices, sugar, and tobacco, that Irish merchants lost to pirates and privateers.[58]

Occasionally, wrecks of these early modern vessels, along with their cargoes, are located off the Irish coast. In 1699/1700 a Royal African Company's ship *Amity* was wrecked in Dunworley Bay in Cork en route from London to Africa. The lading list included iron bars, beads, and cloth—to be exchanged for enslaved people—together with one 'negro', probably a personal servant to the captain, who had been saved and sent back to London.[59] The accounts of a Liverpool merchant, Richard Houghton, highlight the extent of his business interests. Of his 140 clients across England, Wales, and Ireland, a Dublin merchant called Thomas Thorne was his largest debtor, owing Richard £1,418-5-0 for supplies, primarily of sugar and tobacco.[60] Of course, exotic imports stood as signifiers of civility, luxury, and wealth and show that Ireland was very much part of the 'consumer revolution' of these years.[61] Excise duties also provided an income stream for the state. By the early eighteenth century ever-increasing customs duties were placed on tobacco, linen, muslin, calicoes, lacquered goods, molasses, treacle, tea, coffee, and cocoa nuts.[62] Hardly surprisingly, then, smuggling was rife and plunder taken by pirates and privateers was easily traded on the black market.[63]

Whether procured legally or not, there were always buyers for the goods of empires. Dublin thrived and went on in 1775 to become the second city of empire with a population of 150,000 (six times that of New York or four times that of Philadelphia).[64] Over the course of the seventeenth century Limerick, Kinsale, Cork, Youghal, and Waterford all prospered on the back of supplying the Caribbean with butter, salt beef, salt pork, and other produce.[65] Early eighteenth-century Irish customs data suggests that over 85 per cent of beef and 80 per cent of butter exported to the Caribbean originated in Ireland.[66] Cork predominated, while Waterford became the centre of Irish provisioning for Newfoundland and Belfast for the linen trade.[67] Irish merchants and mariners with extensive and well-established commercial networks that criss-crossed Europe serviced Flemish, French, and Spanish colonial trade, as well as that of England, providing butter, salt beef and pork. Many prospered. For example, the extended Looby family of Cork Baptists, as Clodagh Tait has shown, sold to the Caribbean shoes and beer, opened their own 'sugar house' in Cork, and in 1703 bought an estate of 200 acres on Antigua, where they quickly became members of the island's assembly and owner of large numbers of enslaved Africans.[68] A vignette in the folklore archive records how 'Blackwater cider was exported to India, the West Indies and other foreign lands' from the mid-seventeenth century.[69] In short, consumption of imperial products within Ireland and the business of provisioning and servicing European colonies, especially in the Atlantic, changed the daily lives of many people living in Ireland, as it did their landscapes.

II Shaping landscapes

A frenzied programme of colonial enterprise in Ireland transformed the landscape. The '1641 Depositions' vividly recapture land transfers and the settlement patterns of the newcomers as they built fortified mansions, villages, schools, and churches; as they nurtured the development of urban settlements and proto-industry; as they cut down woods and drained and enclosed land; as they improved lands by promoting tillage; as they maximised profits from their mills; as they exploited the estate's natural resources; and as they introduced new breeds of cattle.[70] An early seventeenth-century poem recorded the change in the Ulster landscape with 'the mountain all in fenced fields; fairs are held in places of the chase; the green is crossed by girdles of twisted fences'.[71] The urbanisation and proto-industry associated with these years, along with a demand for timber, resulted in extensive deforestation (it is no coincidence that wolves were reduced to extinction in Ireland by the middle of the seventeenth century).[72] The demand for staves for cask making, charcoal for iron-smelting, and timber for the construction of homes and ships grew as the century passed.[73] Security concerns and periods of intense warfare (1590s, 1640s, and 1688–90) also saw the destruction of woodlands. Of course, this took its toll on the environment but Ireland did not experience the same scale of 'environmental degradation' as the Atlantic colonies. For example, between the 1620s and 1670s, colonists, including a significant number of Irish indentured servants, cleared Barbados of most of the native woods and replaced them with sugarcane fields, resulting in soil erosion and climate change.[74]

In Ireland the construction of big houses and towns also transformed the landscape.[75] From one end of the country to the other medieval tower houses and castles were modernised and anglicised: Dunluce and Edenduffcarrick in County Antrim, Maynooth and Kilkea in County Kildare, Barryscourt in County Cork, and Bunratty in County Clare. Grand fortified English-style mansion houses, which retained some defensive features but provided more commodious accommodation, sprang up across Ireland, often boasting walled gardens, orchards, bowling greens, and even tennis courts.[76] Small communities comprised of agricultural workers, traders, and craftsmen, often settled close to these castles and populated villages or towns, where the local lord helped to fund the building of a market square, courthouse, church, and school. In Ulster members of the peerage constructed at least 19 castles during the early decades of the seventeenth century.[77] Elsewhere the earl of Cork built Lismore Castle in County Waterford and Castle Lyons, and grand mansions at Youghal and Bandon in County Cork; the earl of Londonderry built a tower house at Ballinakill, Queen's County; Lords Mountnorris and Wingfield built Castle Annesley at Camolin and Wingfield House at Ballynabowney in County Wexford; and the earl of Meath built a mansion at Kilruddery in Wicklow, with formal gardens that are extant today, and castles at Bray and Kinleston.[78] In 1618 the fourth earl of Clanricarde spent £10,000 he could ill-afford building a grand fortified house with mullioned bay windows and an ornate interior at Portumna, near Galway.[79] These great houses transformed the physical landscape and stood as powerful testaments to the 'civility' of their owners and the privileged position these power brokers enjoyed.[80] It is little wonder then that the insurgents targeted for destruction these fortified mansions and other symbols of the 'improved' and 'civilised' landscape after the outbreak of rebellion on 22 October 1641 (see Chapter 2 above).

Property destroyed or damaged during the 1640s was often rebuilt after the Restoration. Ormond poured a considerable part of his fortune in to remodelling a viceregal lodge at Chapelizod (£3,000) and restoring to splendour Kilkenny Castle and Dunmore House. Viscount Mountjoy rebuilt a fine three-storey mansion at Newtownstewart, which had cost £400 to build in the 1610s and had been damaged during the 1640s.[81] In the mid-1660s the second earl of Clanbrassil modernised Killyleagh Castle and added a second tower.[82] The marquis of Antrim did likewise at Glenarm Castle and in the 1660s there were 73 hearths in the town of Glenarm, many of which would have been in the castle.[83]

During the 1640s insurgents had fired Lord Conway's Lisburn House, which he rebuilt at the Restoration and in the 1660s it boasted 23 hearths.[84] He also invested considerable energies in building a fine mansion with 18 hearths at Portmore, close to Lisburn, which English architects designed under the direction of his gifted wife, Anne, and probably according to the latest classical specifications. In August 1671 the building was 'window high' and the construction was costing £30 per week. Heavy autumn rains delayed progress.[85] Conway imported slate from his Welsh estates and 40 tons of marble out of which Dutch craftsmen carved a marble chimney and other embellishments. A great lover of horses and racing, Conway built an elaborate two-storey stable.[86] Other outbuildings—a brew house and a bake house—were added later. Particular care was given to laying out the 'polite' garden and bowling green and no expense was spared on buying the trees, 'flowers, roots, and seeds' that the gardeners requested. Excavations in 2003 revealed the formal garden with terraces, a perron (or exterior set of steps leading to a main entrance), a gazebo, bowling green, and walled garden.[87] The house was approached along a 'very pleasant and noble' avenue through meadows. Many of the furnishings for the interior came from London.[88] In 1677 Viscount Ranelagh described the Conway estate as 'the best and most absolute Englishlike plantation in this kingdom'.[89] The 2003 excavation also yielded a rich trove of high-quality artefacts dating to the seventeenth century: English, German, and Dutch pottery; decorated delft tiles; clay pipes; goblet, window, and flowerpot glass; brooches, pins, and other fashion-related metal work.[90]

Further south other great houses and developments sprang up. Lord Chancellor Michael Boyle constructed an impressive mansion at Blessington in Wicklow.[91] An early eighteenth-century engraving of Blessington shows a two-storey brick house on an H-plan with a dormered roof and 22 chimneys. A visitor described it 'one of the finest seats in Ireland... The house and furniture are very great and beautiful'.[92] The architect could have been Thomas Lucas, who designed the front of Trinity in 1672, and the mason in charge of the building was Thomas Browne. The mansion and nearby church, which was built in 1683, cost at least £2,300.[93] The earl of Orrery invested in two major developments, one at Castlemartyr and the other at Charleville, so admired by William Penn, which cost him at least £20,000. Formal gardens, many with intricate water features and grand statutes set in landscaped walkways, as well as expensive plantings and delicate fruit trees, adorned these great houses. These dignified gardens served as a symbolic barrier between the 'wild' world—where, as one anonymous critic noted, the Irish farmer 'never buildeth, repaire, or enclosethe the grownde'—and the 'civilised' one they were creating.[94] Well-stocked deer parks, replete with hunting lodges, adjoined many of the great houses.

What then of those who made good on the back of empire, whether in the Atlantic world or in India, and reinvested their wealth back in Ireland? Many who migrated stayed in close touch with their families and, as shown above, sent home exotic gifts and luxurious goods. Others clearly had an ambition to return home, to purchase property, and to invest their profits in securing higher social status. We see this clearly in the case of Gerald Aungier. Shortly after he died in July 1677 the overseers to his will paid the earl of Longford, his brother and executor, 8,664 rupees (or £1,128-12-0 sterling), which was drawn down on two bills, plus his 'encomiendees' worth 5,600 rupees (or roughly £730).[95] Half of Aungier's salary (£500 per annum) was supposed to be paid in India, the remainder accruing in London.[96] It appears, however, that there was rarely sufficient cash to cover this and the Company later paid Longford £2,200 in lieu of his brother's 'salary and gratuity'.[97] In April 1679 Longford reported: 'I have in the East India Company's hands a good sum of money, yet I cannot call upon them for the payment of it till the arrival of their next ships from India, which are expected in June, and by which I have the prospect of a very considerable return from thence of my brother's estate'.[98] What is not clear is how much money Longford inherited nor how much Aungier made during his years in India and remitted annually. The French traveller, Abbé Carré, suggested that he was a very wealthy man, who lost £45,000 worth of goods 'on his private account' in a single voyage in 1673, which represented 'a great blow'.[99] This is probably an exaggeration but it seems likely that Aungier did make a considerable fortune. Over the course of nearly two decades his wealth could well have matched that of his business partner Sir George Oxenden, credited with changing a debt of 50,000 rupees into an estate of 300,000 (roughly £40,000) or that of Elihu Yale, governor of Madras during the 1680s and founder of Yale university, who amassed 200,000 rupees (roughly £26,000) during his 20 years of service.[100] Certainly, Aungier supplied Longford with much-needed capital for his business as a property developer in Restoration Dublin and especially for the development of the city's first suburb around Aungier Street, which today is a bustling thoroughfare.[101] Though in desperate need of restoration, number 9A Aungier Street, with its original staircase and fireplaces, is the only one of these seventeenth-century houses to survive. Aungier may be remembered as the founding father of Bombay—and thus of modern British India—but he was also Ireland's first 'nabob' (a derogatory corruption of the Persian 'nawab'—or official at the Mughal court—used to describe East India Company officials, who amassed large fortunes).

In his recent monograph Andrew MacKillop identified 68 estates in Ireland, mostly in Ulster and Leinster but with a concentration around Cork city, bought with the profits made from service in Asia. He suggests that the figure is low, especially when compared to Scotland (347 estates), but will increase when scholars gain full access to landed records in the Registry of Deeds in Dublin.[102] Drawing on a vast and largely untapped archive in the Public Record Office of Northern Ireland, Edward Teggin's doctoral thesis recovers the career of Sir Robert Cowan (d. 1737) whose Indian fortune (of *c.*£20,000) bought an Ulster estate (Mount Stewart, though originally called Mount Pleasant) for his nephew, the first marquis of Londonderry.[103] The son of a planter and originally from Derry, Cowan spent his early career in Lisbon and this, together with his Presbyterian associations, helped him to secure favour and office in the East India Company, serving as governor of Bombay from 1729 to 1734.[104] Though of a slightly later vintage, one of the wealthiest nabobs was James Alexander, later earl of Caledon, who spent his career in Bengal. Alexander's vast fortune, which MacKillop estimated to be £134,471 in 1775, funded the purchase of a considerable estate at Caledon in north-west Ulster, an Irish title, and great political influence.[105] Another regional dynasty had been founded.[106]

Others made their money in the Caribbean, invariably on the back of slavery. As in the case of those who had prospered in Asia their wealth secured property and underpinned upward social mobility.[107] Some gravitated towards London with a few investing in Ireland.[108] The grandest of all were the Brownes of Westport House in County Mayo. In 1752 Peter Browne married Elizabeth Kelly, heiress of Denis, owner of Jamaican plantations of 20,000 acres and 360 enslaved Africans.[109] Elizabeth's grandfather, Edmund Kelly of Lisaduff County Galway, became attorney general of Jamaica in the 1720s and in the 1740s his son, Denis Kelly or 'Jamaica Kelly', was appointed chief justice. By this point the Kelly family owned an estate that ran from the north to the south of the island. Kelly's daughter and heiress Elizabeth married into the once Catholic, now Protestant, Browne family of Mayo, in 1752. The Brownes became Ireland's premier absentee plantation owners in the Caribbean. Profits made in the New World allowed for the transformation of the Old World family seat at Westport.[110] In a similar vein the tentacles of the banking dynasty of Digges Latouches stretched from Ireland to India to Jamaica, where enslaved peoples worked their sugar plantations. Their mansions—Belfield Dublin and Belfield Jamaica—built on the back of empire, no doubt impressed people at the time, reminding them of the status of their owners, and shaping attitudes about these families.[111]

Of course, the imprint of empire extended further than grand country houses as the example of Sir Hans Sloane (1660–1753) illustrates. The County Down doctor, collector, and naturalist, whose collections served as the founding ones for the British Museum, Natural History Museum, and the British Library, also made his fortune in empire. Closely associated with Scottish planters—the Hamiltons of Clandeboye and Clanbrassil—Sloane was born in Killyleagh in 1660, where he developed a colonial and improving mindset as well as a passion for the local flora and fauna before moving to London, where Robert Boyle mentored him. During the later 1680s Sloane travelled to Jamaica as the personal physician to the second duke of Albermarle and there met his wife, an heiress to a sugar plantation. During his trip Sloane identified over 800 species of plants, treated hundreds of patients, and closely observed the business of sugar production and the misery of slavery. He later published a two-volume account of his time in Jamaica—*A Voyage to the Islands*—in which he described the arrival of a slave ship from the Gold Coast which he wrote was 'very nasty with so many people on board'. He related the punishments meted out to slaves. Those who rebelled were burned by degrees. The punishments for lesser 'crimes' ranged from gelding, chopping off half a foot, placing iron rings on ankles and necks, and vicious beatings. Then the master rubbed into the raw wounds 'pepper and salt to make them smart' or dropped 'melted wax on their skins'.[112] Sloane also collected 'relics of slavery': 'a manati strap for whipping the Negro slaves', 'a noose made from cane split for catching game or hanging runaway negros', 'a bullet used by the runaway Negros in Jamaica made of pewter dishes & lead in a thimble', and the coat made of 'Mahot bark' belonging to 'runaway rebellious negros'.[113] Peter Walmsley has analysed an account of Sloane's treatment of a house slave, called Rose, which was published in *A Voyage*. Walmsley suggests that Sloane was obsessed 'with the traumatic experience of the Jamaican slave'.[114] Though mediated by Sloane, Walmsley carefully reconstructed Rose's trauma, concluding that 'Caribbean chattel slavery is a trauma engine, extraordinary in its violence, and the more so because it is equally inexplicable to both perpetrator and survivor'.[115]

In addition to keeping a close eye on his Jamaican plantations, Sloane invested in the Royal Africa Company and the South Sea Company, both engaged in the slave trade.[116] According to his biographer James Delbourgo: 'It was through this empire that Sloane made his fortune; constructed a vast network for making collections; and established the unique legacy of a free public museum [the British Museum] dedicated to the ideal of universal knowledge'. In short, Delbourgo concludes, 'Sloane's legacy is an artefact of British imperial power'.[117] Though there is no record of how Sloane self-identified, his librarian Thomas Stack boasted in 1728, at the height of Sloane's influence in London: 'What glory...for Ireland to see one of its sons so crowned'.[118] Over the course of his life Sloane also enjoyed deep ties to Ireland, illustrated by his life-long friendship with Sir Arthur Rawdon (1662–95) who lived in Moira, not far from Killyleagh in County Down. As he embarked on his voyage to the Caribbean Sloane wrote to Rawdon thanking him for his support and volunteering to send him anything that he wanted.[119] Like Sloane, Rawdon was a passionate collector. As a result of Sloane's trip, Rawdon asked his gardener James Harlow to bring plants from Jamaica. In May 1692 Harlow arrived in Carrickfergus with 20 cases, each containing over 50 healthy trees, shrubs, and plants. In a hothouse, probably similar to the one in the physic garden in Chelsea in London, Rawdon cultivated his flora, including cacao. He supplied Sloane with plants and exchanged others with botanic gardens and collectors across Britain and Europe (Amsterdam, Leiden, Leipzig, London, Oxford, and Uppsala).[120] On Sir Arthur's premature death, his son, Sir John (1690–1732), and his daughters Brilliana and Dorothy continued to correspond with Sloane and helped Trinity College Dublin to establish its physic garden with gifts of plants.[121] With their passing the remarkable gardens at Moira, a nursery of imperial plants, fell into disrepair.

Sloane and Rawdon were of Protestant planter stock, as were so many of those who made imperial fortunes, but what of Irish Catholics? The profits made by Henry Blake of Galway and Montserrat, where 38 enslaved Africans worked on his sugar plantation, allowed him to purchase in the 1670s two estates, one in County Mayo and another in County Galway.[122] Other Catholic elites, like Sir William Stapleton and his associates in the Leeward Islands, as was shown in Chapter 4, used every opportunity—especially marriage, education, and social interactions—to make themselves English, without compromising their religion nor association with Ireland. Stapleton died in 1686 and in his will he directed that 'all my monies [are] to be invested in land in Ireland'.[123] David Dickson has shown how Irish-born merchants used their imperial fortunes to purchase local property in urban and rural areas.[124]

Penal legislation after 1690 made it more difficult for Catholics to translate their wealth into landed estates in Ireland. Anecdotal evidence suggests that they educated their children in Catholic Europe but then bought property and sought brides in England or France while also retaining strong links to Ireland.[125] Testamentary evidence, for instance, reveals complex Atlantic networks and highlights the importance of money, usually made in the Caribbean, being remitted back in Ireland.[126] For example, in 1787 Anthony French's will included significant legacies for his brother in Dublin and his Aunt Sibela and her children in Galway.[127] His primary heir and nephew, John French Lynch 'of Surrey', died the following year. In his lengthy will John made numerous bequests to his friends in England (London, Surrey, and Bath), France (Nantes), the Caribbean (St. Kitts and Antigua), the 'East Indies' (or India), Madeira, and Ireland (Dublin and especially to family in Galway). His Irish kin also inherited his County Clare property. John's plantation, 'Cabora Terre' in St. Kitts, along with a plantation of 180 acres that belonged to his late uncle Anthony, and 'all my negroes stock and utensils', passed to another nephew.[128] The story of how this wealth—albeit spread over multiple locations and in relatively small amounts that, no doubt, added up over time—impacted Catholic Ireland and especially the merchant communities remains to be told.

III Shaping minds

In an age when most people rarely travelled outside of their locality, how did ideas about empire shape the minds of people living in early modern Ireland? An absence of evidence makes it impossible to determine how the consumption of tobacco, sugar, and spices or the wearing of calicoes invited reflection on the provenance of these foodstuffs or fashion items. However, for members of the elite, maps and travel literature framed their engagement and perceptions of empire, as did prose and plays with imperial themes. Very often one bled into the other. For example, Abraham Cresque's atlas (1375), Mercator's celestial globe (1541), and Ortelius's map of 1572 all show the imaginary island of 'Hy-Brassil' (or Tír na nóg) off the west coast of Ireland, which some suggest gave Brazil its name.[129] 'Hy-Brassil', which was so much a part of Irish legend, later captured the imagination of the popular Irish-born novelist Richard Head who wrote *O-Brazile Or the Inchanted Island* (London, 1675). No doubt it also intrigued his readers.

   Household inventories, along with library and auction catalogues, show that maps, atlases, and globes were prized possessions in the homes of the elite across Ireland.[130] By the turn of the seventeenth century, maps, often illustrated with representations of indigenous peoples—including those by the likes of John Speed which circulated so widely—fired imaginations about the exotic. These captured colonial knowledge by offering visual proof of dominance, the fortifications, and walled towns while also functioning as a tool to shape or manipulate popular perception. Of course, these images also had a significant ideological component that presented subtle messages concerning the 'civility' of colonial subjects: the Americas and Ireland were wild and disordered, while India crumbled, even if it retained hints of a formerly civilised state. Visual representations and maps were often published in travel accounts and through these travellers made 'the foreign familiar to a domestic audience'.[131] Occasionally, these writers and publishers had direct experience of Ireland. For example, John Ogilby, cartographer and publisher of volumes of maps and engravings, began his career during the later 1630s as 'master of the revels' and manager of the Werburgh Theatre in Dublin. One scholar suggests that his engraving of the 'halalchors' or untouchables in India 'bears resemblances to the conception of the uncivilized wild man' depicted by Speed in his maps of Ireland.[132] In other words, Ogilby transferred his ethnographic bias from the Irish to the Indian. More measured was John Ovington, an English clergyman who had been educated at Trinity College Dublin. Ovington later published an account of his voyage to India and his sojourn in Bombay with Gerald Aungier, stressing the perils to the health of Europeans posed by an apparently extreme Indian climate.[133] If India was a land of opportunity and sensual exotic promise for early modern adventurers, it was also a locus of extraordinary danger and the threat of death was always imminent.[134]

Reception of ideas is challenging to document, especially for 'ordinary people'. Recent research, however, has demonstrated how engagement with cartography, ethnography, and natural history shaped the thinking of Irish Franciscans, some of whom also had direct experience of global travel.[135] Others, like Luke Wadding, monitored, from his base in St. Isidores College in Rome, the missions of his confreres, especially in New Spain. Wadding developed a keen interest in the indigenous peoples, flora, and fauna of Latin America, something that the volumes in his library highlight, including two works by his nephew relating to Peru.[136] As Clare Carroll put it, Wadding was the 'epicentre of global Catholicism'.[137] For others, Ireland itself was often used as a simile which, according to Alison Games, was 'proximate and problematic, both familiar and foreign...The exotic were found not only far from home, in India or Jerusalem or America, but right across the Irish sea'.[138] At the turn of the seventeenth century, Fynes Moryson, secretary to Lord Mountjoy, travelled extensively throughout Europe, North Africa, the Middle East, and Turkey but saved his greatest scorn for the 'meere Irish' whom he regarded as filthy, rude, barbaric wild beasts and their women as drunken and subversive sluts. 'The Anatomy of Ireland' (1615) described the Irish as 'more barbarous and more brutish in ther costomes and demeanures then in any other parte of the world that is knowne'.[139] The assiduous gathering of information about native societies also occurred in America. John White's vibrant watercolours of the Algonquins were later published by Thomas Heriot, who accompanied Sir Walter Raleigh on the first voyage to Roanoke in 1585, and with the support of Richard Hakluyt.[140] Direct comparisons, as has been discussed in Chapter 5 above, were made between the distinctive culture, dress, and hair-styles of the indigenous peoples in Ireland and America and of the com-mercial opportunities their natural worlds afforded to enterprising colonists on both sides of the Atlantic.[141]

This 'New World' was a frequent and in many ways omnipresent topic in early modern Irish libraries, and books like Richard Hakluyt's *The Principall Navigations, Voiages and Discoveries Of the English nation* (London, 1589, fur-ther editions, 1599, 1600), along with many others, appear to have circulated widely and 'brought the world into the hands of readers'.[142] Extant cata-logues from Ireland's early modern libraries—Trinity College Dublin, Marsh's Library or the Bolton Library (now in Limerick university)—demonstrate that readers in Ireland had access to the original versions of travel literature, published all over Europe, along with their English translations.[143] It was a truly global body of literature, spanning Africa, the Caribbean, India, the Ottoman Empire, Persia, and Madagascar and connecting readers to the debates and discussions regarding the exploration and exploitation taking place in these regions. The coverage was also diverse and included astronomy, botany, geography, history, linguistics, medicine, topography, and zoology along with particular interest in the practical usage of commodities like spices, tobacco, tea, sugar, and chocolate.

Vivid stories of the lives, customs, and practices of indigenous peoples and accounts of tropical flora and exotic animals—tigers, elephants, rhi-noceroses, colourful birds, and dragon-like reptiles—excited intellects and triggered curiosity. Consider the (almost) random example of William Dampier, the English explorer and pioneer in scientific exploration, who published in 1697 *A new voyage round the world* (extant copies are in Marsh's Library and in Trinity). Dampier gave detailed descriptions of the Cuban flora and fauna and described the major geographic features of the island. His book, which circulated widely, bristled with wonderful anecdotes, including one about an Irish cattle raider called Daniel, and a Cuban alligator. One evening Daniel went to a pond intent on stealing cattle, once a mainstay in Ireland, when an alligator seized him by the knee. Daniel cried for help:

> But poor Daniel not finding any assistance, waited till the Beast opened his Jaw to take better hold, because it is usual for the Alligator to do so; and then snatch'd away his Knee, and slipt the But-end of his Gun in the room of it... [Daniel] cryed out to his Consorts to come and assist him; who... brought him away in their Arms to his Hut; for he was in a deplorable condition, and not able to stand on his Feet, his Knee was so torn with the Alligators Teeth.[144]

Daniel's fate was not recorded but one can only begin to imagine the images conjured in the minds of anyone who listened to or read the story of Irish Daniel and the Cuban alligator.

Theatre proved a particularly effective medium for firing imaginations, and plays like Burnell's *Langartha*, first performed in Dublin in 1640 and discussed in Chapter 3, undoubtedly allowed audiences to imagine worlds beyond Ireland.[145] Another play, *Titus, or the Palme of Christian Courage*, was set in Japan, where the Jesuits had a mission. It contained a strong message about loyalty: first and foremost to Catholicism and then to the Stuarts and the Irish nation. Originally staged by Jesuit students in Kilkenny, the play, comprising five acts, contained a fictional narrative that would have resonated with its audiences.[146] Performed and published in 1644 at the height of peace negotiations between Charles I and the Catholic Confederates, which included concessions for religious toleration, the lessons to be drawn from the play would have been clear.[147]

From the later seventeenth century, empire also informed prose and poetry in English and in Irish. According to Felicity A. Nussbaum: 'These texts address issues of slavery, captivity, commerce and imperial authority... The drama incorporated colonial encounters onto the skins, gestures, and dialogue of white actors at once to fabricate the representation of racial difference, to celebrate and worry it, and finally to grant it a recognizable reality'.[148] One of the most popular writers of the day who tapped into this fascination with the exotic was an Irish-born author Richard Head, author of *Hy-Brassil*, who was best known for his raunchy novel, *The English*

Rogue.[149] First published in 1665, it immediately became a best-seller, which linked Ireland, Virginia, and South Asia. The life story of the hero and narrator, Meriton Latroon, 'the English rouge', mimicked the childhood experiences of Head himself. Latroon was born in an 'Irish bog' in the mid-1630s but fled to England in the wake of the 1641 rebellion having been rescued by his Irish servant ('the faithful infidel'), who pretended he was a Catholic 'and imploring their mercy with his howling *Chram a chrees* [possibly Grá mo chroí or love of my heart], and *St Patricks a gra* [love of St Patrick] procured my mothers, his own, and my safety'.[150] After a debauched career as a petty thief and highwayman in England, Latroon was deported to Virginia before travelling East to India, Ceylon, Siam, and finally Java. There he married 'an Indian-black', settled in Bantam, became a prosperous trader, and embraced God.[151] He also found his 'Englishness' and finally shed his 'Irishness', which was so closely connected to his roguishness.

Early editions of John Dryden's heroic tragedies including the most exotic ones—*Indian Queen* (1664), *Indian Emperor* (1665), *Amboyna* (1673), *Aureng-Zebe* (1675)—are held in the Trinity library and a 1670 edition of the *Indian Emperor* was signed by 'John Worth'.[152] The first Irish novel, *Vertue Rewarded; or, The Irish Princess*, tells the story of strong women and explored marriage, identity, and integration in colonial Ireland and in the Spanish empire. It invited audiences to make comparisons and imagine far-off lands.[153] More provocative still was Aphra Behn's *Oronooko, the royal slave*, published in 1688, the year before she died. It presented an insightful account of slavery and plantation in the early modern world even if her focus was on the individual tragedy of an African prince rather than the practice of slavery. It was the story of Oronooko, and Imoinda, the 'beautiful black Venus' and great love of his life. Oronooko's grandfather, the king of Coramantien (or Angola), sold Imoinda into slavery and shortly afterwards English traders enslaved Oronooko himself. He was shipped to Surinam, then an English (and later a Dutch) colony on the north-east tip of Latin America, where Oronooko met the narrator of the novel, who was the daughter of Surinam's Governor Bynam. There Oronooko serendipitously reunited with Imoinda.[154]

Even though Oronooko was a work of fiction it has been suggested that the novel was based on real events and people, including William Bynam. It was widely believed that the royalist Behn had visited Surinam, a colony of 800 white settlers, 2,500 enslaved Africans, and 500 enslaved Indian Kalinago, and witnessed first-hand the sugar plantations that depended on slave labour.[155] Certainly, it captured trauma that Behn had experienced.[156] Behn also borrowed from a variety of contemporary travel narratives and used to great effect ethnographic descriptions and graphic details, such as the description of pepper being rubbed into Oronooko's wounds after he has been whipped.[157] The novel ended when Oronooko, or Caesar as he became known, led a rebellion of African and Indian slaves. A 'wild Irishman' called Bannister then killed Oronooko by burning him alive, having brutally dismembered him, first his nose and ears, then his arms. This was probably a reference to Major James Bannister, a thuggish figure, who was responsible—after 1667 when the Dutch took over—for evacuating the English colonists and resettling them on Jamaica, where he secured an estate of 3,000 acres and was murdered in 1672.[158] That Behn called Bannister a 'wild Irishman' was interesting since other sources are silent on his background even though we know that the Irish, Catholic and Protestant, settled in the region (see Chapter 4).[159] In a fascinating article, the literary scholar Lee Morrissey seizes on this mention of Bannister to situate Oronooko's life in the context of colonial Ireland and to link his violent death to the execution of Charles I. Morrissey suggests that Bannister was a composite character, both a wild Irishman and a Protestant merchant adventurer. Above all and significantly, Bannister was white, something Oronooko called out with his dying breath. This casual mention of race, along with ethnicity and religion, simply underscores the complexities associated with identity formation.

For the narrator and Aphra Behn herself, Oronooko was not a rebellious slave but a handsome hero of great wit, learning, courage, and honour.[160] Thomas Southerne (1660–1746), the Dublin dramatist and Trinity student, picked up on this when in 1696 he transformed Behn's *Oronooko* into a popular tragedy. The plot was broadly in line with Behn's novel except that Imoinda was white and the play ended when Oronooko—not a wild Irishman—killed his pregnant wife and then himself. The play was a huge hit in London and in Dublin, where there were regular—at times annual performances—of it at one of the Dublin theatres from 1699 until the late 1750s.[161] A playbill for a Smock Alley performance for *Oroonoko* even announced that the singers will perform 'in the Habits of American slaves'.[162] Thus *Oroonoko*'s strong anti-slavery message helped generations to question slavery decades before abolitionism took hold. It also fell to a playwright from Ireland to celebrate the marriage, intimacy, and love between a white woman and a black man. Given how rare these sorts of unions would have been, no doubt Southerne sought to titillate and fire imaginations. That

Southerne conveniently removed the 'wild Irishman'—and thus down-played the aggressive colonialism and ethnocentricity Bannister stood for—is also intriguing in what it had to say about 'Irishness' and 'whiteness'. For as scholars of the later period have noted: 'Whether they like it or not, the Irish are becoming postcolonial white in contradistinction to other postcolonial "others" '.[163]

The language of empires, dominions, provinces, viceroys, conquest, civility, improvement, learning, scientific discovery, and knowledge gathering, together with a curiosity for the exotic, pervaded the writings of Jonathan Swift. Interestingly, Swift did not see himself as 'Irish' but as 'English', yet he spent most of his life in Ireland (64 out of 78 years) and wrote nearly 100 works on Ireland.[164] In *Gulliver's Travels* or *Travels into several remote nations of the world* (1726), Swift wrote: 'Natives are driven out or destroyed, their Princes tortured to discover their Gold; a free Licence given to all Acts of Inhumanity and Lust; the Earth reeking with the Blood of its Inhabitants: And this execrable Crew of Butchers employed in so pious an Expedition, is a *modern Colony* sent to convert an idolatrous and barbarous People'.[165] Swift's depiction of the Yahoos 'includes several elements of the still-prevailing view of the "wild Irish" in racial and behavioural terms'.[166] These fictional texts show, as Daniel Roberts has noted, 'remarkable continuities in their grapplings with the savage implications of empire and its precarious grasp on civility'.[167] Equally, Swift's satirical pamphlet, *A Modest Proposal* (1729), suggested that the only way for the indigent Irish to escape poverty was by fattening up their babies and selling them to the butcher. This makes, as Ian McBride reminds us, for uncomfortable reading and challenges assumptions about Irish barbarity and English civility.[168] It reflected an Ireland where cattle were regarded as being more precious than people and cannibalism was commonplace. Ian Campbell Ross has suggested that Swift drew on published accounts of cannibalism amongst the Tupinambas or Tupi Indians of the Amazon (some of whom Bernardo O'Brien had engaged with); on the history of pre-colonial Peru by Garcilaso de la Vega, the son of an Incan princess and a Spanish conquistador whose work Sir Paul Rycaut translated into English and which also informed *Vertue Rewarded*; and Edmund Spenser, who in *A View of the Present State of Ireland*, recorded how starvation reduced the Irish to cannibalism and underscored their barbarism.[169]

Protestant patriots like Swift may have self-identified as 'English' but he resisted anglicisation at every opportunity, claiming that English imperial policy had reduced the Protestants of Ireland to 'slavery'.[170] Catholic writers made similar arguments, something vividly captured in a collection of three books entitled 'A light to the blind', written at the turn of the eighteenth century. The author wrote that the Irish 'are treated by the ruling powers, not as subjects but in the quality of slaves... That an antient noble nation is this enslaved for to support a mean colony, therin planted by the regicide sword of Cromwell...'Tis a burning shame to an antient, illustrious nation to see themselves like worms trod upon by a mean and regicide colony'.[171] In Book 2 the author called for greater autonomy from England, the abolition of Poynings' Law, the ending of appeals to the English courts and the House of Lords, the freedom to import all goods irrespective of the Navigation Acts, the provision of legal education in Ireland, and the establishment of a mint. Like Patrick Darcy and Sir Phelim O'Neill before him, the author wanted independence from England but within the context of the Stuart multiple monarchy. The authorship of 'A light to the blind' is uncertain though it seems likely it was written by someone very close to Peter Plunkett, fourth earl of Fingal, possibly the earl's uncle.[172] Peter's mother Margaret, a daughter of the earl of Clancarthy, was a lady in waiting to Catherine of Braganza. His grandmother was Mabel Barnewall, daughter of Mary Bagenal and niece of Mabel Bagenal, who had married Hugh O'Neill, earl of Tyrone, in 1591.[173] In *The O'Neill* by Tom Kilroy, O'Neill had justified his decision to marry Mabel, the daughter of an imperial tailor, on the understanding that she would assimilate. O'Neill reminded Mabel that they were both Irish and predicted that 'History will not be able to tell the difference between us'.[174] In this instance, after three generations, history was not able to tell the difference.

IV Memory and early modern empires

This mention of Mabel and Hugh brings us back to Brian Friel's play *Making History* and how early modern empire has been remembered. The contested relationship between 'fact', 'myth/legend' and 'memory', so central in the play, has long exercised historians, including those of Ireland.[175] The publication in 2019 of Guy Beiner's magisterial *Forgetful Remembrance: Social Forgetting and Vernacular Historiography of a Rebellion in Ulster* has put memory studies firmly on the Irish history map.[176] In this and other related publications, Beiner examines how a society 'attempts to obscure problematic

historical episodes'.[177] Beiner's works sit alongside Ian McBride's trailblaz-
ing collection *History and Memory in Modern Ireland* (2001) along with other
works on 1641, Oliver Cromwell, and the siege of Derry.[178] Collectively,
these explore in specific contexts the interfaces between memory, legend,
history, and truth and have much to offer from a methodological perspective on how moments of history are both remembered and forgotten.[179]

Consider the example of Oliver Cromwell. At a 2022 launch of a new
edition of Oliver Cromwell's letters, the British ambassador to Ireland, Paul
Johnston, said that Cromwell's actions in Ireland were 'wholly indefensible'
and that the massacres of civilians by his army, first at Drogheda and then
Wexford (September and October 1649), were among the 'greatest atrocities
in Anglo-Irish history'. The ambassador concluded that Cromwell's brutality 'marked him out as a uniquely despised figure'.[180] In an opinion piece in
the *Irish Times*, Fintan O'Toole concurred, quoting W. B. Yeats: 'You ask
what I have found, and far and wide I go:/ Nothing but Cromwell's house
and Cromwell's murderous crew'. O'Toole noted that in the stories recorded
by the Folklore Commission, Daniel O'Connell is the only historical figure
mentioned more than Oliver Cromwell. He concluded by suggesting that
'Cromwell became one of our curse words and curses linger in the air for
centuries. But perhaps the ability to treat him as history rather than as myth
is a small step towards the lifting of the curse'.[181]

The archive of the Folklore Commission—which chronicled stories
from across the island from the 1930s—vividly illustrates how memories of
what (allegedly) happened during the early modern period have remained
alive in social memory.[182] In her ground-breaking book, *The Devil from Over
the Sea*, Covington reminds us that 'facts' alone cannot explain Cromwell's
legendary status and draws deftly from the rich folklore about him and the
Cromwellians extant in the National Folklore Archive.[183] More generally,
memories of colonisation and the colonial wars caused by imperialism were
recorded by the Folklore Commission. Detailed accounts of military and
commercial affairs are noted, alongside matters relating to land and property,
where the exploits of colonists and colonised were recalled alongside those
who 'grabbed land' and were transplanted.[184] The fundamental importance
of land is playfully illustrated by a story associated with Morette Castle in
Queen's County (now Laois) recorded by a schoolteacher from nearby
Emo. In 1641 insurgents besieged the castle, having first captured its owner,
Mr Fitzgerald, whom they threatened to kill unless his wife surrendered the
castle. Mrs Fitzgerald replied: 'Ah! I can secure a husband any day but not so
a castle'.[185]

Other stories in the Folklore Commission related military action—battles, skirmishes, sieges, massacres—the exploits of individual soldiers, the destruction and burning of homes, farms, and crops, the sufferings of refugees, and the violence, including sexual violence, unleashed on women and children. The name of William Penn, 'founder of Pennsylvania', lived on in the folklore of County Clare. The teller recounted how Penn's father (also William) had married a 'Dutchwoman' and defended Bunratty Castle in 1645 from a parliamentary attack, with his young son at his side.[186] The stories about Sir Frederick Hamilton (c.1590–1647) of Manorhamilton in County Leitrim are particularly numerous and vivid.[187] They recorded his Scottish background, the extent of his plantations, the names of his Scottish tenants ('still common in the district'), and the castle he built, along with the neighbouring village. In 1641 local insurgents burned the castle and Hamilton retaliated by viciously sacking the abbey and town of Sligo 15 miles away.[188] Nearly every account mentioned Hamilton's cruelty, especially towards women and children, nuns and priests.[189] He abducted and held captive a young woman, known as the 'Wild Rose of Lough Gill'.[190] Others he murdered after his spy, a local woman called Shiela Mór, identified them coming from Mass.[191] Being the son of Catholic parents did nothing to prevent him committing, according to one teller, 'some of the most savage atrocities on the local people that had ever been recorded in history'.[192]

The folklore testimonies also attributed considerable agency to women, reinforcing arguments made in Chapter 3 and testifying to the importance of mixed marriages as a means of survival. One from Clooney in County Clare tells the story of the formidable 'Maire Ruadh' O'Brien (1615/16–86) of Leamaneh Castle, whose ghost had, according to the teller, haunted the vicinity for centuries:

> Many strange tales and legends have gathered around this woman's name. One of the last authentic alleges that she had no fewer than twenty-five husbands, all of whom, however she got rid of by various means.... Maire Ruadh used to hang her servants who were unfortunate enough to offend her, the men by the neck, and the women by the hair.... During the troubled year of 1641 she and Connor O'Brien carried out many daring raids on English settlers as is testified in a deposition in Trinity College, Dublin.[193]

While Maire Rua may well have had 25 lovers, it appears that she only married three times. A Cromwellian soldier called John Cooper was her third husband and as a result of this she managed to save most of her estates, even if Cooper insisted that their son be raised a Protestant.[194] It is interesting to note how the teller of the story invoked one of the '1641 Depositions' as evidence of Maire Rua's bravery but omitted to mention her marriage to a Cromwellian, whom he would have regarded as the 'enemy'. Yet this union allowed Maire Rua, or Mary Cooper as she became known, to survive and her portrait to hang in Dromoland Castle where she later died. In a similar vein, marriage to Protestant women—also recorded in the National Folklore Collection—saved their Catholic husbands from being killed during the war of the 1640s.[195] That these stories, which were gathered from across the island, have been transmitted down over the course of 300 years, roughly nine generations, is remarkable even in a country with a strong oral trad-ition.[196] Yet the full potential of this material for the early modern period, as the work of Beiner and Covington shows, remains to be fully unlocked.

This brings us to the role of the historian in shaping narratives, some-thing that Brian Friel interrogated in *Making History* in the exchanges between Lombard and O'Neill. 'I'm not even sure I know what the histo-rian's function is—not to talk of his method', Lombard mused.[197] In *Time's Monster: History, Conscience and Britain's Empire*, Priya Satia suggests: 'Historians are storytellers, custodians of the past, repositories of collective memory, poetic interpreters of what it is to be human. Whether explaining our present or understanding the past on its own terms, their work critically shapes how the past infuses our present'. Her book looks at how accounts of empire mostly by English historians of the nineteenth and twentieth cen-turies, many of whom—like C. S. Mills or Thomas Babington Macaulay—held senior administrative positions, 'guided the consolidation of imperial rule', and shaped public memory.[198] In his powerful account of the role played by the siege of Derry in forming Ulster Protestant mythology, Ian McBride stresses the importance of Macaulay's account of siege in his *History of England* (1848) in the creation of a 'no surrender', beleaguered identity.[199]

In *Imagining Ireland's Pasts*, Nicholas Canny carefully surveyed how the history of early modern Ireland had from the sixteenth century been written and rewritten and how each generation manipulated the past for political purposes and to suit particular sectarian agendas.[200] Canny pays particular attention to how the plantations shaped identity and the imperial concerns of Sir John Temple (1600–77) and Sir Richard Musgrave (1746?–1818). As we have seen in Chapter 3, Temple, in *The Irish Rebellion* (1646), selectively used the '1641 Depositions' to vilify his Catholic opponents and to encour-age English officials to adopt hard-line policies in Ireland.[201] Drawing inspiration from Temple's approach, Musgrave's *Memoirs of Different Rebellions in Ireland* (1801) reproduced eyewitness testimonies of what allegedly occurred as a result of the 1798 rebellion, so brutally repressed by Cornwallis and the British army.[202] In doing so he reminded England that the wider security of the British empire depended on keeping Ireland under control.[203] Both works also fed into established anti-Catholic narratives that helped to sustain a Protestant Unionist identity, especially in Ulster.[204]

Of course, archives are repositories of memory and the fact that propagandists, like Temple, had ransacked and manipulated the '1641 Depositions' for political purposes was one reason behind the decision in 2010 to publish the archive in its entirety. On 22 October 2010, the anniversary of the outbreak of the 1641 rebellion, Dr Mary McAleese, then President of Ireland, launched the 1641 website and an accompanying exhibition on 'Ireland in Turmoil' in the Long Room at Trinity.[205] That evening she acknowledged: 'The events of 1641 have been the subject of considerable dispute and controversy. . . . Facts and truth have been casualties along the way and the distillation of skewed perceptions over generations have contributed to a situation where both sides were confounding mysteries to one another'. The president concluded her perceptive remarks with the recognition that:

> We are, even after the publication of the Depositions, unlikely to agree a common version of history but we can agree that to have a common future, a shared and peaceful future; there is nothing to be gained from ransacking the past for ammunition to justify the furthering of hatred and distrust. There is however everything to be gained from interrogating the past calmly and coherently, in order to understand each other's passions more comprehensively, to make us intelligible to one another, to help us transcend those baleful forces of history so that we can make a new history of good neighbourliness, understanding, and partnership between all the people and traditions on this island.

Building bridges and reconciliation were themes of Mary McAleese's presidency, something that was fully realised during the state visit of Queen Elizabeth II to Ireland in May 2011. The launch of the 1641 exhibition, however, afforded the president an opportunity to make a powerful statement on the importance of acknowledging our shared and contested past without being bound by it.

Ian Paisley, the late Lord Bannside, who during the 'Troubles' had repeatedly invoked 1641 to stir up anti-Catholic sentiment, also attended the launch and responded to the website and exhibition. 'Here are the tragic stories of individuals, and here too is the tragic story of our land. To learn this, I believe, is to know who we are and why we have had to witnesses our own troubles in what became a divided island. A nation that forgets its past commits suicide'. Paisley continued, his voice almost a whisper, and so different to the thundering tones of his prime:

> Before us in these cases is the real hand of history!...And tonight that hand reaches out beyond its page, beyond its century, and touches us. Now, the question is, what will we do? Let us grasp that hand and hold fast to it and introduce its work to our schools. If we learn the lessons of the past we may use them to unlock a stable and promising future for everyone on this island.

The fact that Ireland was at peace allowed public figures to make speeches like these and to embrace with such enthusiasm an historical project that until relatively recently polarised institutions of the state, its subjects, and scholars themselves. In short, with the digitisation and online publication of the '1641 Depositions', memory was finally becoming history.[206]

Other historic events still form part of the DNA of some communities in Northern Ireland. In 1688/1689 a siege occurred in the city of Derry, the memory and commemoration of which have been manipulated over the course of the centuries and invoked by men like Henry Lawrence during the siege of Lucknow in 1857. The siege of Derry, like the Williamite victory at the Battle of the Boyne (1/12 July 1690) or the events surrounding the 1641 rebellion, profoundly shaped Ulster Protestant culture and identity from the seventeenth to the twenty-first centuries.[207] The siege was trigged after a Jacobite force, led by the third earl of Antrim, himself a grandson of Hugh O'Neill, earl of Tyrone, failed in December 1688 to capture the town. Thirteen apprentices shut and locked the gates. The siege began in earnest in April 1689 when the town again refused to surrender to King James II. The siege lasted 105 days, from 18 April until 1 August, and to this day the lifting of the siege is commemorated, a potent reminder that, for some, events of the seventeenth century are still alive. At the time, John Mitchelburne, who revamped the city's fortifications and briefly became governor during the siege, proved key in determining how events would be remembered. On the one hand, he helped to establish in 1718 the original Apprentice Boys club. On the other, he wrote a five-act tragicomedy *Ireland Preserv'd or The Siege of Londonderry* (1705), which sought to justify his conduct but interestingly also challenged cultural expectations by featuring six 'female warriors', including one called 'Amazon', as key martial protagonists during the siege of 1689. It has been suggested that the play paid tribute to his wife who, along with his seven children and a third of the population of the city, died during the siege. Though only a modest success during his lifetime, the play had an enduring legacy. Over 20 editions were printed in Ireland, especially in Ulster, in the eighteenth century, while a new edition appeared in the nineteenth. *Ireland Preserv'd* was also reproduced in locally printed inexpensive chapbook editions and performed widely in schools.[208] The memory and myth of the siege thus passed from generation to generation yielding, as Ian McBride has reminded us, 'different messages at different times'.[209]

Some, particularly in Northern Ireland, continue to celebrate the anniversary of events—especially those associated with the siege of Derry and the Battle of the Boyne—that occurred in the seventeenth century. Others cherish connections with the British empire, which they date back to the plantations, and deny that Ireland was ever a colony at all. In some quarters 'empire' may still be a dirty word. Many in Ireland have, however, either conveniently forgotten our imperial past or are simply oblivious to it. Ignorance of Ireland's engagement with empire has enabled extreme nationalists to manipulate the past. The same holds true for the UK, USA, and, increasingly, other European countries where memory of empire is contested. Yet events of the early twenty-first century—Brexit, 'the culture wars', the campaigns around 'Black Lives Matters' and 'Statues must fall'— along with calls for renaming, reparations and the restitution and repatriation of plundered artefacts have kindled a greater awareness of the importance of revisiting the history of empires.[210] We need to better understand the operation and after lives of empires, how they have shaped the present, and how this might allow us to forge the shared future that Brian Friel imagined in *Making History*.

Endnotes

FM

1. Jane Burbank and Frederick Cooper, *Empires in World History: Power and the Politics of Difference* (Princeton, 2010), pp. 3–4, 8 (quote p. 3).
2. John M. MacKenzie, 'Irish, Scottish, Welsh and English worlds? A Four nation approach to the history of the British Empire', *History Compass, 6/5* (2008), pp. 1244–63. Also see the discussion in Chapter 1, Section I.
3. Ken MacMillan, 'Bound by Our Regal Office: Empire, Sovereignty, and the American Colonies in the Seventeenth Century' in Stephen Foster (ed.), *British North America in the Seventeenth and Eighteenth Centuries* (Oxford, 2013), pp. 67–102 (quote p. 69).
4. Quoted (p. 262) in Thomas Bartlett, ' "This famous island set in a Virginian sea": Ireland in the British Empire, 1690–1801' in P. J. Marshall (ed.), *The Oxford History of the British Empire.* vol. II. *The Eighteenth Century* (Oxford, 1998), pp. 252–75.
5. Quoted in Seamus Deane, Andrew Carpenter, and Jonathan Williams (eds.), *The Field Day Anthology of Irish Writing* (3 vols., Derry, 1991), II, pp. 118–19.
6. For a contemporary Protestant view on identity formation in Ireland see Richard Cox, 'An apparatus or introductory discourse' in *Hibernica Anglicana; or the history of Ireland from the conquest thereof by the English to this present time* (London, 1689); Toby Barnard, 'Identities, Ethnicity and Tradition among Irish Dissenters c.1650–1750' in Kevin Herlihy (ed.), *The Irish Dissenting Tradition 1650–1750* (Dublin, 1995), p. 29.
7. Nicholas Canny, *Imagining Ireland's Pasts: Early Modern Ireland through the Centuries* (Oxford, 2021); Joep Leerson, *Mere Irish and Fíor-Ghael: Studies in the Idea of Irish Nationality, its Development and Literary Expression prior to the Nineteenth Century* (Cork, 1996) offers the best overview of identity formation among the Catholic population in early modern Ireland.
8. Aidan Clarke, 'The policies of the "Old English" in parliament, 1640–1' in J. L. McCracken (ed.), *Historical Studies, V* (London, 1965) and 'Colonial identity in early seventeenth century Ireland' in T. W. Moody (ed.), *Historical Studies. XI. Nationality and the Pursuit of National Independence* (Belfast, 1978).
9. Breandan Ó Buachalla, 'James our true king: The ideology of Irish royalism in the seventeenth century' in D. George Boyce, Robert Eccleshall, and Vincent Geoghegan (eds.), *Political Thought in Ireland since the Seventeenth Century*

(London, 1993). Unfortunately O Buachalla's *tome* on the Stuarts and the intelligensia, 1603–1788, *Ailing ghéar* (Dublin, 1997), is not available in English. Also see Mícheál Mac Craith, 'The Gaelic Reaction to the Reformation' in Steven Ellis and Sarah Barber (eds.) *Conquest and Union. Fashioning a British State, 1485–1725* (Harlow, 1995), pp. 139–61; Bernadette Cunningham, 'Irish language sources for early modern Ireland', *History Ireland*, 4 (1996), pp. 41–8; Marc Caball, 'Bardic poetry and the analysis of Gaelic mentalities', *History Ireland*, 2 (1994), pp. 46–50; and Michelle O Riordan, ' "Political" poems in the mid-seventeenth-century crisis' in Jane Ohlmeyer (ed.), *Ireland from Independence to Occupation* (Cambridge, 1995) and *The Gaelic Mind and the Collapse of the Gaelic World* (Cork, 1990).

10. David Edwards, 'A haven of popery: English Catholic migration to Ireland in the age of plantation' in Alan Ford and John McCafferty (eds.), *The Origins of Sectarianism in Early Modern Ireland* (Cambridge, 2005), pp. 95–126.

11. T. C. Barnard, 'The Protestant interest, 1641–1660' in Ohlmeyer (ed.), *Ireland from Independence to Occupation* and S. J. Connolly, *Religion, Law and Power: The Making of Protestant Ireland* (Oxford, 1992), p. 2.

12. See Chapter 4, Section IV.

13. Discussed in Nuala Zahedieh, 'Trade, plunder and Irishmen in early English Jamaica' in Finola O'Kane and Ciaran O'Neill (eds.), *Ireland, Slavery and the Caribbean: Interdisciplinary Perspectives* (Manchester, 2023), p. 74 and C. Gribben and S. Spurlock (eds.), *Puritans and Catholics in the Trans-Atlantic World 1600–1800* (Philadelphia, 2009).

14. Stephen Howe, *Empire: A Very Short Introduction* (Oxford, 2002), p. 13 and Peter Crooks and Timothy H. Parsons, 'Empires, Bureaucracy and the Paradox of Power' in Peter Crooks and Timothy H. Parsons (eds.), *Empires and Bureaucracy in World History: From Late Antiquity to the Twentieth Century* (Cambridge, 2016), pp. 3–28.

15. Peter Fibiger Bang, C. A. Bayly, and Walter Scheidel (eds.), *The Oxford World History of Empire* (2 vols., Oxford, 2021), I, pp. 12–15.

16. Edward Said, *Culture and Imperialism* (London, 1994), p. 8. Also David Armitage, *The Ideological Origins of the British Empire* (Cambridge, 2000), p. 29.

17. John Darwin, *After Tamerlane: The Rise and Fall of Global Empires, 1400–2000* (London, 2007), p. 416.

18. Jürgen Osterhammel, *Colonialism: A Theoretical Overview* (Munich, 1997), pp. 15–18.

19. *Oxford English Dictionary*, consulted online, 4 July 2022.

20. Osterhammel, *Colonialism*, pp. 15–18.

21. *Oxford English Dictionary* for the meanings of these words.

22. A number of important recent studies have facilitated this including Kenneth J. Andrien, 'Age of exploration, *c.*1500–1650' in Philippa Levine and John Marriott (eds.), *The Ashgate Research Companion to Modern Imperial Histories* (Farnham, 2012), chapter 2; Bang, Bayly, and Scheidel (eds.), *The Oxford World History of Empire*; J. H. Elliott, *Empires of the Atlantic World: Britain and Spain in America 1492–1830* (New Haven, 2006); and Burbank and Cooper, *Empires in World History*.

CHAPTER 01

1. Nicholas Canny, O'Neill, Hugh [Aodh Ó Néill], second earl of Tyrone (*c.*1550–1616), magnate and rebel. *ODNB*. Retrieved 11 Jun. 2022, from https://www.oxforddnb.com/view/10.1093/ref:odnb/9780198614128.001.0001/odnb-9780198614128-e-20775; Hiram Morgan, O'Neill, Hugh (*c.*1550–1616), second earl of Tyrone *DIB*. Retrieved 11 Jun. 2022, from https://www.dib.ie/biography/oneill-hugh-a6962; and Hiram Morgan, *Tyrone's Rebellion. The Outbreak of the Nine Years War in Tudor Ireland* (Suffolk, 1993). Also see Nicholas Canny, 'Hugh O'Neill in Irish historical discourse, *c.*1550–2021', *Irish Historical Studies* 46, (2022), pp. 25–51.

2. R. Morgan, *The Welsh and the Shaping of Early Modern Ireland 1558–1641* (Woodbridge, 2014), pp. 17, 22, 107.

3. Brian Friel, *Making History* (London, 1989), p. 21.

4. Friel, *Making History*, p. 24.

5. Friel, *Making History*, p. 24.

6. Gerard Farrell, *The 'Mere Irish' and the Colonisation of Ulster, 1570–1641* (London, 2017), pp. 31–3.

7. HMC, *Calendar of the manuscripts of the most honourable the marquess of Salisbury ...,* XXI, *1609–1612* (London, 1970), p. 121.

8. Marc Caball, 'Politics and Religion in the Poetry of Fearghal Óg Mac An Bhaird and Eoghan Ruadh Mac An Bhaird' in Pádraig Ó Riain (ed.), *The Life of Red Hugh O'Donnell Historical and Literary Contexts* (Irish Texts Society, Dublin, 2002), p. 81.

9. Morgan, *Tyrone's Rebellion*, p. 124; Hiram Morgan, O'Donnell, 'Red' Hugh (Ó Domhnaill, Aodh Ruadh) *DIB*. Retrieved 11 Jun. 2022, from https://www.dib.ie/biography/odonnell-red-hugh-o-domhnaill-aodh-ruadh-a6343.

10. Angela Bourke et al. (eds.), *The Field Day Anthology of Irish Writing. Irish Women's Writing and Traditions* (2 vols., Cork, 2002; vols. IV and V of the *Field Day Anthology*), V, p. 20.

11. Morgan, O'Donnell, *DIB;* J. Silke, O'Donnell, Hugh [Aodh Ó'Dónaill; known as Red Hugh, Hugh Roe, Aodh Rua], lord of Tyrconnell (1572–1602), chieftain and rebel. *ODNB*. Retrieved 11 Jun. 2022, from https://www.oxforddnb.com/view/10.1093/ref:odnb/9780198614128.001.0001/odnb-9780198614128-e-20554.

12. Morgan, *Tyrone's Rebellion*, pp. 95–6 and Paul Walsh, *Will and Family of H. O'Neill, Earl of Tyrone* (Dublin, 1930).

13. Quoted in Morgan, O'Neill, *DIB*.

14. Audrey Horning, 'Minding the Gaps: Exploring the intersection of political economy, colonial ideologies, and cultural practice in early modern Ireland', *Post-Medieval Archaeology*, 52 (2018), pp. 4–20.

15. Friel, *Making History*, p. 16.

16. Catriona J. McKenzie and Eileen M. Murphy, *Life and Death in Medieval Gaelic Ireland: The Skeletons from Ballyhanna, Co. Donegal* (Dublin, 2018).

17. Allan I. Macinnes, 'Crown, Clan and Fine: The 'Civilising' of Scottish Gaeldom, 1587–1638', *Northern Scotland*, 13 (1993), p. 33; Ciaran Brady, 'The Captains' Games: Army and Society in Elizabethan Ireland' in Thomas Bartlett and Keith Jeffery (eds.), *A Military History of Ireland* (Cambridge, 1996), pp. 144–7.

18. Friel, *Making History*, p. 11.
19. Friel, *Making History*, p. 38.
20. Friel, *Making History*, p. 25. Brendan Kane, 'Masculinity and political geographies in England, Ireland and North America', *European Review of History: Revue européenne d'histoire*, 22, (2015), pp. 595–619.
21. Morgan, O'Neill, *DIB*; Canny, O'Neill, *ODNB*; Hiram Morgan, 'Slán Dé fút go hoíche: Hugh O'Neill's murders' in David Edwards, Pádraig Lenihan, and Clodagh Tait (eds.), *Age of Atrocity. Violence and Political Conflict in Early Modern Ireland* (Dublin, 2007), pp. 95–118; and Thomas Herron, Denna J. Iammarino, and Maryclaire Moroney (eds.), *John Derricke's The Image of Irelande: with a Discoverie of Woodkarne. Essays on text and context* (Manchester, 2021).
22. Friel, *Making History*, pp. 1, 17.
23. Friel, *Making History*, pp. 2, 6; Audrey Horning, 'Clothing and colonialism: The Dungiven costume and the fashioning of early modern identities', *Journal of Social Archaeology*, 14 (2014), pp. 296–318.
24. Quoted in C. P. Meehan, *The Fate and Fortunes of Hugh O'Neill, Earl of Tyrone, and Rory O'Donel, Earl of Tyrconnel* (Dublin, 1868), p. 27.
25. Quoted Meehan, *The Fate and Fortunes of Hugh O'Neill*, p. 419.
26. John McCavitt, *The Flight of the Earls* (Dublin, 2002), pp. 127–33, Morgan, O'Neill, *DIB*, Canny, O'Neill, *ODNB*.
27. Friel, *Making History*, pp. 26–7.
28. Friel, *Making History*, p. 29.
29. Quoted in Canny, O'Neill, *ODNB*.
30. Friel, *Making History*, p. 48.
31. Friel, *Making History*, pp. 49–50.
32. Friel, *Making History*, p. 27.
33. Friel, *Making History*, p. 9.
34. Annaleigh Margey (ed.), *Mapping Ireland c. 1550–1636: A Catalogue of Manuscript Maps of Ireland* (IMC, 2 vols., forthcoming 2023).
35. Friel, *Making History*, p. 6.
36. Friel, *Making History*, p. 6.
37. Friel, *Making History*, p. 25. Also see Brendan Kane and Malcolm Smuts, 'The Politics of Race in England, Scotland and Ireland' in Malcolm Smuts (ed.), *The Oxford Handbook of the Age of Shakespeare* (Oxford, 2016), pp. 346–66.
38. Friel, *Making History*, pp. 3–4.
39. Friel, *Making History*, p. 39.
40. Friel, *Making History*, p. 15.
41. Friel, *Making History*, pp. 14–15.
42. Friel, *Making History*, p. 43. Here Friel evoked Edmund Spenser's descriptions of the Munster wars of the 1570s, Edmund Spenser, *A View of the Present State of Ireland* ed. W. L. Renwick (Oxford, 1970), p. 104.
43. Alison Cathcart, *Plantations by Land and Sea: North Channel Communities of the Atlantic Archipelago c. 1550–1625* (Oxford, 2021), pp. 85–7 and Francis Ludlow and Arlene Crampsie, 'Environmental History of Ireland, 1550–1730' in Jane

Ohlmeyer (ed.), *The Cambridge History of Ireland*. vol. 2. *Early Modern Ireland, 1550–1730* (Cambridge, 2018), pp. 609–11.

44. Farrell, *The 'Mere Irish'*, pp. 73–5.

45. John McGurk, 'The pacification of Ulster, 1600–3' in Edwards, Lenihan, and Tait (eds.), *Age of Atrocity*, pp. 123–4.

46. Friel, *Making History*, p. 9.

47. Tadhg Ó hAnnracháin, Lombard, Peter (*c.*1554–1625) *DIB*. Retrieved 11 Jun. 2022 from https://www.dib.ie/biography/lombard-peter-a4879.

48. In the preface to *The Great O'Neill* Sean O'Faolain noted: 'If anyone wanted to make a study of the manner in which historical myths are created he might well take O'Neill as an example'. More generally see William H. McNeill, 'Mythistory, or Truth, Myth, History, and Historians', *The American Historical Review*, 91 (1986), pp. 1–10.

49. Friel, *Making History*, pp. 8–9.

50. Friel, *Making History*, p. 63.

51. Friel, *Making History*, p. 67.

52. Canny, O'Neill, Morgan, O'Neill, *DIB* and *Tyrone's Rebellion*.

53. Fynes Moryson, *An itinerary written by Fynes Moryson gent., first in the Latine tongue, and then translated by him into English* (London, 1617), part 2, chapter 1, p. 7.

54. Morgan, *Tyrone's Rebellion*, p. 12.

55. Friel, *Making History*, p. 2.

56. Emmett O'Byrne, Aidan Clarke, Judy Barry, Bagenal (O'Neill), Mabel (*c.*1571–95), countess of Tyrone *DIB*. Retrieved 11 Jun. 2022 from https://www.dib.ie/biography/bagenal-oneill-mabel-a6953.

57. Myth and folklore are areas that historians have been loath to engage with until recently, Guy Beiner, *Forgetful Remembrance: Social Forgetting and Vernacular Historiography of a Rebellion in Ulster* (Oxford, 2019) and Sarah Covington, *The Devil from over the Sea: Remembering and Forgetting Oliver Cromwell in Ireland* (Oxford, 2022). Also see Guy Beiner, 'Irish Historical Studies *Avant la Lettre*. The antiquarian genealogy of interdisciplinary scholarship' in R. Allyson, M. Cronin, and B. Ó Conchubhair (eds.), *Routledge International Handbook of Irish Studies* (London, 2021), pp. 47–58 and 'Probing the boundaries of Irish memory: From postmemory to prememory and back', *Irish Historical Studies*, 34 (2014), pp. 296–307; Ian McBride (ed.), *History and Memory in Modern Ireland* (Cambridge, 2001).

58. Thomas Kilroy, *The O'Neill* (Dublin, 1995), pp. 28–9.

59. Kilroy, *The O'Neill*, p. 21.

60. Kilroy, *The O'Neill*, p. 23.

61. In 2007, the 400th anniversary of the 'Flight of the Earls', *Making History* was performed at sites associated with the Nine Years' War in Ireland and Europe.

62. For a good overview of many of these issues see Ian McBride, *Eighteenth Century Ireland: The Isle of Slaves* (Dublin, 2009), introduction.

63. Brendan Bradshaw, *The Irish Constitutional Revolution of the Sixteenth Century* (Cambridge, 1979), pp. 231–57.

64. H. G. Koenigsberger first articulated the 'composite monarchies' or 'multiple kingdoms' model in 'Dominium regale or dominium politicum et regale' reprinted in *Politicians and Virtuosi: Essays on Early Modern History* (London, 1986). Conrad Russell developed it for England, especially in *The Fall of the British Monarchies, 1637–1642* (Oxford, 1990) and *The Causes of the English Civil War* (Oxford 1990); Jane Dawson, 'Two kingdoms or three?: Ireland in Anglo-Scottish relations in the middle of the sixteenth century' in R. A. Mason (ed.), *Scotland and England, 1286–1815* (Edinburgh, 1987), pp. 113–38; Jenny Wormald for Scotland, 'The Creation of Britain: Multiple Kingdoms or Core and Colonies?', *Transactions of the Royal Historical Society*, sixth series, 2 (1992), pp. 175–94; and Michael Perceval-Maxwell for Ireland, 'Ireland and the monarchy in the early Stuart multiple kingdom', *The Historical Journal*, 34 (1991), pp. 279–95.

65. Breandán Ó Buachalla, 'James our true king: The ideology of Irish royalism in the seventeenth century' in D. George Boyce, Robert Eccleshall, and Vincent Geoghegan (eds.), *Political Thought in Ireland Since the Seventeenth Century* (London, 1993), pp. 7–30; Nessa Malone, 'Henry Burnell's *Landgartha*: Family, law and revolution on the Irish stage' in Coleman A. Dennehy (ed.), *Law and Revolution in Seventeenth-Century Ireland* (Dublin, 2020), pp. 65–88; and Aidan Clarke, 'Patrick Darcy and the constitutional relationship between Ireland and Britain' in Jane Ohlmeyer (ed.), *Political Thought in Seventeenth-Century Ireland: Kingdom or Colony?* (Cambridge, 2000), pp. 35–55. For the later period see Éamonn Ó Ciardha, *Ireland and the Jacobite Cause, 1685–1766* (Dublin, 2002) pp. 41–51.

66. Caball, 'Politics and Religion', pp. 85–6; Mícheál Mac Craith, 'Literature in Irish, c.1550–1690: From the Elizabethan Settlement to the Battle of the Boyne' in Margaret Kelleher and Philip O'Leary (eds.), *The Cambridge History of Irish Literature,* vol. 1 to 1890 (2 vols., Cambridge, 2006), p. 216.

67. John Silke, 'Primate Lombard and James I', *Irish Theological Quarterly*, 22 (1955), p. 131.

68. Clarke, 'Patrick Darcy and the constitutional relationship between Ireland and Britain' and Patrick Darcy, *An Argument Delivered by Patrick Darcy, Esquire, By the Express Order of the House of Commons in the Parliament of Ireland, 9 Iunii, 1641* (Waterford, 1643).

69. Quoted in Aidan Clarke, 'Colonial constitutional attitudes in Ireland, 1640–1660', *Proceedings of the Royal Irish Academy,* 90, section c, 11 (1990), p. 359.

70. Patrick Little, 'The English parliament and the Irish constitution, 1641–9' in Mícheál Ó Siochrú (ed.), *Kingdoms in Crisis: Ireland in the 1640s* (Dublin, 2001) and 'Irish Representation in the Protectorate Parliaments', *Parliamentary History,* 23 (2004); Robert Armstrong, 'Ireland at Westminster: the Long Parliament's Irish committees, 1641–1647' in Chris R. Kyle and Jason Peacey (eds.), *Parliament at Work: Parliamentary Committees, Political Power, and Public Access in Early Modern England* (Woodbridge, 2002); Neil Longley York, *Neither Kingdom nor Nation: The Irish Quest for Constitutional Rights, 1698–1800* (Washington, 1994); and Coleman Dennehy, *The Irish Parliament, 1613–89: The Evolution of a Colonial Institution* (Manchester, 2019).

71. Colin Kidd, *British Identities before Nationalism. Ethnicity and Nationhood in the Atlantic World, 1600–1800* (Cambridge, 1999), pp. 146–81. Also see Bartlett, ' "This famous island set in a Virginian sea" ', pp. 253–75.

72. Darcy, *An Argument Delivered by Patrick Darcy*, p. 4.

73. Quoted in Charles Ivar McGrath, *Ireland and Empire 1692–1770* (London, 2012), p. 38.

74. But the act did not silence the debate. In the final quarter of the century, the Protestant ruling elite, known as the 'patriots', presumed that they were entitled to the same rights as Englishmen. They pressed in the 1770s for habeas corpus until the Irish in 1781 secured their own (now rather outdated) version of the English Act of 1679. After the Dublin House of Commons in 1782 voted an Irish Declaration of Independence, Britain repealed the Declaratory Act along with the part of Poynings' law that required the Irish Parliament to first submit its legislation to London for approval. This issue is broadly addressed in James Kelly, ' "Era of Liberty": The Politics of Civil and Political Rights in Eighteenth-Century Ireland' in Jack P. Greene (ed.), *Exclusionary Empire: English Liberty Overseas, 1600–1900* (Cambridge, 2010), pp. 77–111, Kevin Costello, *The Law of Habeas Corpus in Ireland* (Dublin, 2006) and McGrath, *Ireland and Empire*, pp. 39–49, 62–6.

75. Aidan Clarke, 'The History of Poynings' Law, 1615–1641', *Irish Historical Studies*, 18 (1972), pp. 207–22; Micheál Ó Siochrú, 'Catholic Confederates and the constitutional relationship between Ireland and England, 1641–1649' in Ciaran Brady and Jane Ohlmeyer (eds.), *British Interventions in Early Modern Ireland* (Cambridge, 2005), pp. 207–29 and James Kelly, *Poynings' Law and the Making of Law in Ireland, 1660–1800: Monitoring the Constitution* (Dublin, 2007).

76. D. B. Quinn, 'Ireland and Sixteenth Century European Expansion' in T. D. Williams (ed.), *Historical Studies* (London, 1958) and *Ireland and America: Their Early Associations, 1500–1640* (Liverpool, 1991); Nicholas Canny, 'The Ideology of English Colonization: From Ireland to America', *The William and Mary Quarterly*, 30 (1973), pp. 575–98, *The Elizabethan Conquest of Ireland: A Pattern Established 1565–1576* (New York, 1976) and *Kingdom and Colony: Ireland in the Atlantic World, 1560–1800* (Baltimore, 1988). Also see Howard Mumford Jones, 'Origins of the colonial idea in England', *Proceedings of the American Philosophical Society*, 85 (1942), pp. 448–65 and 'The colonial implies: An analysis of the "Promotion" literature of colonization', *Proceedings of the American Philosophical Society*, 90 (1946), pp. 131–61.

77. See for example W. J. Smyth, 'The Western Isle of Ireland and the eastern seaboard of America—England's first frontiers', *Irish Geography*, 11 (1978), pp. 1–23; Rolf Loeber, 'Preliminaries to the Massachusetts Bay Colony: the Irish ventures of Emanuel Downing and John Winthrop Sr' in Toby Barnard, Dáibhí Ó Cróinín, and Katherine Simms (eds.), *'A Miracle of Learning': Studies in Manuscripts and Irish Learning* (Aldershot, 1998), pp. 164–200; Patricia Coughlan, 'Counter-currents in colonial discourse: The political thought of Vincent and Daniel Gookin' in Jane Ohlmeyer (ed.), *Political Thought in Seventeenth Century*

Ireland (Cambridge, 2000), pp. 56–82; William O'Reilly, 'Movements of People in the Atlantic World, 1450–1850' in Nicholas Canny and Philip Morgan (eds.), *The Oxford Handbook of the Atlantic World c. 1450-c. 1850* (Oxford, 2011), p. 316; and Farrell, *The 'Mere Irish'*, especially chapter 2; and Raymond Gillespie, 'Explorers, exploiters and entrepreneurs: early modern Ireland and its context, 1500–1700' in B. J. Graham and L. J. Proudfoot (eds.), *An Historical Geography of Ireland* (London, 1993), pp. 123–57.

78. Éamonn Ó Ciardha and Micheál Ó Siochrú (eds.), *The Plantation of Ulster: Ideology and Practice* (Manchester, 2012), p. 1.

79. Alison Games, *The Web of Empire: English Cosmopolitans in an Age of Expansion, 1560–1660* (Oxford, 2008), p. 256.

80. Steven G. Ellis, 'Writing Irish History: Revisionism, colonialism, and the British Isles', *The Irish Review*, 19 (1996) and *Tudor Frontiers and Noble Power: The Making of the British State* (Oxford, 1995); Hiram Morgan, 'Mid-Atlantic blues', *The Irish Review*, 11 (1991); Stephen Howe, *Ireland and Empire: Colonial Legacies in Irish History and Culture* (Oxford, 2000); Andrew Murphy, 'Ireland and ante/anti-colonial theory', *Irish Studies Review*, 7 (1999) and *But the Irish Sea Betwixt Us: Ireland, Colonialism and Renaissance Literature* (Lexington, Kentucky, 1999). Also see note XX above.

81. See Chapter 5 below where this is discussed in detail.

82. Andrew MacKillop, 'What has the four nations and empire model achieved' in Stephanie Barczewski and Martin Farr (eds.), *The MacKenzie Moment and Imperial History. Essays in Honour of John M. MacKenzie* (London, 2019), pp. 261–83 (quote at p. 275) and *Human Capital and Empire. Scotland, Ireland, Wales and British Imperialism in Asia, c. 1690-c. 1820* (Manchester, 2021), especially the introduction.

83. MacKillop, *Human Capital and Empire*, p. 9.

84. John M. MacKenzie, 'Epilogue: Analysing 'Echoes of Empire' in Contemporary Context: The Personal Odyssey of an Imperial Historian, 1970s–Present' in Kalypso Nicolaïdis, Berry Sèbe, and Gabrielle Maas (eds.), *Echoes of Empire. Memory, Identity and Colonial Legacies* (London, 2015), pp. 189–206 (quote pp. 201–2), and John M. MacKenzie, 'Irish, Scottish, Welsh and English worlds? A Four nation approach to the history of the British Empire', *History Compass*, 6/5 (2008), pp. 1244–63.

85. Robert Bartlett, *The Making of Europe. Conquest, Colonisation and Cultural Change 950–1350* (London, 1993); Robert Bartlett and Angus MacKay (eds.), *Medieval Frontier Societies* (Oxford, 1989); T. Barry, R. Frame, and K. Simms (eds.), *Colony and Frontier in Medieval Ireland. Essays Presented to J. F. Lydon* (Dublin, 1995); James Muldoon, *Identity on the Medieval Irish frontier: Degenerate Englishmen, Wild Irish, Middle Nation* (Gainseville, 2003); John Morrisey, 'Cultural geographies of the contact zone: Gaels, Galls and overlapping territories in late medieval Ireland', *Social and Cultural Geography*, 6 (2005); and Christopher Maginn, *'Civilizing' Gaelic Leinster. The Extension of Tudor Rule in the O'Byrne and O'Toole Lordships* (Dublin, 2005).

86. Michael Hechter, *Internal Colonialism: The Celtic Fringe in British National Development, 1536–1966* (London, 1975). Also see Henry Jones, 'Property, territory, and colonialism: An international legal history of enclosure', *Legal Studies*, 39 (2019), pp. 187–203.

87. Judith Pallot and Denis J. B. Shaw, *Landscape and Settlement in Romanov Russia, 1613–1817* (Oxford, 1990).

88. Allan Greer, *Property and Dispossession: Natives, Empires and Land in Early Modern North Atlantic America* (Cambridge, 2018), p. 8.

89. Pekka Hämäläinen, *The Comanche Empire* (New Haven, 2008).

90. Tony Coult, *About Friel: The Playwright and the Work* (London, 2003) and Martine Pelletier, 'Telling Stories and Making Histories: Brian Friel and Field Day', *Irish University Review*, 24 (1994), pp. 186–97.

91. The Guildhall, the target of at least two IRA bombs during the 1970s, was itself a symbol of empire.

92. John McGurk, *Sir Henry Docwra 1564–1631: Derry's Second Founder* (Dublin, 2006) and David Dickson, *The First Irish Cities: An Eighteenth-Century Transformation* (New Haven and London, 2021), pp. 6–12.

93. Ian McBride, *The Siege of Derry in Ulster Protestant Mythology* (Dublin, 1997), p. 1. Also see Brian Walker, '1641, 1689, 1690 and All That: The Unionist Sense of History', *Irish Review*, 12 (1992), pp. 56–64.

94. Eric Falci and Paige Reynolds (ed.), *Irish Literature in Transition 1980–2020* (Cambridge, 2020), p. 3.

95. Quoted (p. 335) in Ronan McDonald, 'Irish Studies and Its Discontents' in Falci and Reynolds (eds.), *Irish Literature in Transition 1980–2020*, pp. 327–43.

96. McDonald, 'Irish Studies and Its Discontents', p. 335.

97. Edward Said, *Orientalism* (London, 1978) and *Culture and Imperialism* (London, 1994).

98. McDonald, 'Irish Studies and Its Discontents', pp. 330–1. See especially Homi Bhabha, *The Location of Culture* (Abingdon, 1994), Gayatri Spivak, *A Critique of Postcolonial Reason. Toward a History of the Vanishing Present* (Cambridge, Mass., 1999), and Dipesh Chakrabarty, *Provincializing Europe: Postcolonial Thought and Historical Difference* (Princeton, New Jersey, 2000).

99. Clare Carroll, *Circe's Cup: Cultural Transformations in Early Modern Ireland* (Cork, 2001), p. 11.

100. Homi Bhabha, 'Difference, Discrimination, and the Discourse of Colonialism' in Francis Barker et al. (eds.), *The Politics of Theory* (Colchester, 1983), pp. 194–211.

101. Falci and Reynolds (eds.), *Irish Literature in Transition 1980–2020*, p. 15.

102. Donald, 'Irish Studies and Its Discontents', p. 340.

103. Especially Howe, *Ireland and Empire*.

104. I published chapters in both, Jane Ohlmeyer, ' "Civilizinge of those rude partes". The colonization of Ireland and Scotland, 1580s–1640s' in Nicholas Canny (ed.), *The Oxford History of the British Empire*, vol. 1 (Oxford, 1998), pp. 124–47 and 'A Laboratory for Empire?: Early Modern Ireland and

English Imperialism' in Kevin Kenny (ed.), *Ireland and the British Empire* (Oxford, 2004), pp. 26–60.

105. R. R. Davies, *The First English Empire: Power and Identities in the British Isles 1093–1343* (Oxford, 2002). Though later, also see Peter Crooks, 'State of the Union: Perspectives on English Imperialism in the Late Middle Ages', *Past and Present*, 212 (2011), pp. 3–42. Also see John Gillingham, 'Normanizing the English Invaders of Ireland' in Huw Pryce and John Watts (eds.), *Power and Identity in the Middle Ages: Essays in Memory of Rees Davies* (Oxford, 2007), pp. 85–97, Colin Veach, 'Henry II and the ideological foundations of Angevin rule in Ireland'. *Irish Historical Studies*, 42 (2018), pp. 1–25 and 'Ireland in the Angevin Empire'. *History Ireland* (2019), pp. 40–3.

106. In addition to the works noted in note 76 above, see Nicholas Canny (ed.), *Europeans on the Move: Studies on European Migration, 1500–1800* (Oxford, 1994).

107. McGrath, *Ireland and Empire*. Also see K. Jeffrey (ed.), *An Irish Empire? Aspects of Ireland and the British Empire* (Manchester, 1996) and Terence McDonough (ed.), *Was Ireland a colony? Economics, Politics and Culture in Nineteenth-Century Ireland* (Dublin, 2005).

108. A. G. Hopkins, 'Back to the Future: From national history to imperial history', *Past and Present*, 164 (1999), pp. 198–243.

109. Stephen Howe, 'Review Article: When—If Ever—Did Empire End? Recent Studies of Imperialism and Decolonization', *Journal of Contemporary History*, 40 (2005), pp. 585–99 (quote p. 586). See for examples Kathleen Wilson (ed.), *A New Imperial History: Culture, Identity and Modernity in Britain and the Empire 1660–1840* (Cambridge, 2004); Philippa Levine (ed.), *Gender and Empire* (Oxford, 2004); and Catherine Hall and Sonya O. Rose (eds.). *At Home with the Empire: Metropolitan Culture and the Imperial World* (Cambridge, 2006).

110. Peter Cain and Tony Hopkins. *British Imperialism, 1688–2015* (3rd edition, London and New York, 2016). Canny's work is acknowledged in Philippa Levine and John Marriott (eds.), *The Ashgate Research Companion to Modern Imperial Histories* (Farnham, 2012).

111. Joe Cleary, 'Amongst Empires: A Short History of Ireland and Empire Studies in International Context', *Éire-Ireland*, 42 (Spring/Summer, 2007), pp. 11–57 (quote p. 21).

112. Priyamvada Gopal, *Insurgent Empire: Anticolonial Resistance and British Dissent* (London, 2019), p. 36.

113. Martin Thomas and Andrew S. Thompson (eds.), *The Oxford Handbook of The Ends of Empire* (Oxford, 2018). Also see Elizabeth Buettner, *Europe after Empire: Decolonization, Society and Culture* (Cambridge, 2016).

114. Barczewski and Farr (eds.), *The MacKenzie Moment*, p. 7.

115. Stephen Howe, 'Questioning the (Bad) Question: Was Ireland a Colony?'. *Irish Historical Studies*, 37 (2008), pp. 1–15. Also see Ciaran Brady (ed.), *Interpreting Irish History: The Debate on Historical Revisionism* (Dublin, 1994).

116. Audrey Horning, *Ireland in the Virginian Sea. Colonialism in the British Atlantic* (Williamsburg, Virginia, 2013), pp. vii, viii.

117. Audrey Horning, 'Comparative Colonialism: Scales of Analysis and Contemporary Resonances' in Craig N. Cipolla and Katherine Howlett Hayes (eds.), *Rethinking Colonialism: Comparative Archaeological Approaches* (Gainesville, Fl, 2015), pp. 234–46 (quote p. 239).

118. David Armitage, 'Three Concepts of Atlantic History' in David Armitage and Michael J. Braddick (eds.), *The British Atlantic World, 1500–1800* (Basingstoke, 2002), pp. 13–29 and David Brown, *Empire and Enterprise: Money, Power and the Adventurers for Irish Land during the British Civil Wars* (Manchester, 2020), p. 6. Also see David Armitage and Alison Bashford, *Pacific Histories: Ocean, Land, People* ((Basingstoke, 2014).

119. Eliga H. Gould, 'Entangled Histories, Entangled Worlds: The English-Speaking Atlantic as a Spanish Periphery', *American Historical Review*, 12 (2007), pp. 764–86.

120. Sanjay Subrahmanyam, 'Connected Histories: Notes towards a Reconfiguration of Early Modern Eurasia', *Modern Asian Studies*, 31 *Special Issue: The Eurasian Context of the Early Modern History of Mainland South East Asia, 1400–1800* (1997), pp. 735–62 and Simon J. Potter and Jonathan Saha, 'Global History, Imperial History and Connected Histories of Empire'. *Journal of Colonialism and Colonial History*, 16 (2015), retrieved 11 Jun. 2022 from doi:10.1353/cch.2015.0009.

121. Niall Whelehan, 'Playing with Scales: Transnational History and Modern Ireland' in Niall Whelehan (ed.), *Transnational Perspectives on Modern Irish History* (New York, 2015), pp. 7–29.

122. MacKenzie, 'Epilogue', p. 189. For an interesting example of how this might be done see Zoltán Biederman, *(Dis)connected Empires: Imperial Portugal, Sri Lankan Diplomacy, and the Making of a Habsburg Conquest in Asia* (Oxford, 2018) and Christian G. De Vito, 'History without Scale: The Micro-Spatial Perspective', *Past and Present*, 242, issue supplement, 14 (2019), pp. 348–72.

123. Friel, *Making History*, p. 67.

124. Guy Beiner, 'A Short History of Irish Memory in the Long Twentieth Century' in Tom Bartlett (ed.), *The Cambridge History of Ireland*, vol. 4, *1880–2016* (Cambridge, 2018), p. 722.

125. Falci and Reynolds (ed.), *Irish Literature in Transition 1980–2020*, p. 13 and McDonald, 'Irish Studies and Its Discontents', p. 338. Also see Caroline Elkins, *Legacy of Violence: A History of the British Empire* (London, 2022), introduction and Natalie A. Zacek, 'How the Irish became black' in O'Kane and O'Neill (eds.), *Ireland, Slavery and the Caribbean*, pp. 321–36.

126. Liam Hogan, Laura McAtackney, and Matthew C. Reilly, 'The Irish in the Anglo-Caribbean: Servants or Slaves?', *History Ireland*, 24 (2016), pp. 18–22 and Natalie A. Zacek, 'How the Irish became black' in O'Kane and O'Neill (eds.), *Ireland, Slavery and the Caribbean*, pp. 323–9.

127. Christine Kinealy, 'At home with empire: The example of Ireland' in Catherine Hall and Sonya O. Rose (eds.), *At Home with the Empire: Metropolitan Culture and the Imperial World* (Cambridge, 2006), pp. 77–100.

128. For the lectures see https://www.rte.ie/player/series/machnamh-100/SI000000008075?epguid=PL000006154, accessed 24 March 2022.

129. *Guardian*, 11 Feb. 2021. Also see the op eds in *The Irish Times* by Jane Ohlmeyer (29 Dec. 2020) and Seamus Nevin (7 Feb. 2021).

130. Sir Hilary Beckles, 'Irishness is Back from West Britain to West Indies' in Finola O'Kane and Ciaran O'Neill (eds.), *Ireland, Slavery and the Caribbean: Interdisciplinary Perspectives* (Manchester, 2023), pp. xvi–xix (quotes pp. xvii, xviii). I am grateful to the editors for allowing me to read the volume prior to publication.

131. J. Smibert, Berkeley, George (1685–1753). *ODNB*. Retrieved 12 Jun. 2022, from https://www.oxforddnb.com/view/10.1093/ref:odnb/9780198614128. 001.0001/odnb-9780198614128-e-1001941; Tom Jones, *George Berkeley: A Philosophical Life* (Princeton, 2021).

132. https://www.irishtimes.com/culture/what-to-do-about-george-berkeley-trinity-figurehead-and-slave-owner-1.4277555I 18 June 2020 by Joe Humphreys.

133. https://www.irishtimes.com/culture/books/should-irish-slavery-supporter-john-mitchel-s-statue-in-newry-be-taken-down-1.3382077, 7 Feb 2018 by Anthony Russell.

134. Julia Wright, *Ireland, India and Nationalism in Nineteenth-Century Literature* (Cambridge, 2007), p. 7. Also see S. Ryder, 'Ireland, India and popular nationalism in the early nineteenth century' in T. Foley and M. O' Connor (eds.), *Ireland and India: Colonies, Culture and Empire* (Dublin, 2006).

135. P. J. Marshall, *Edmund Burke and the British Empire in the West Indies: Wealth, Power, and Slavery* (Oxford, 2019), pp. 223–33.

136. https://www.irishtimes.com/culture/heritage/sir-michael-o-dwyer-apologist-for-the-amritsar-massacre-was-also-an-irish-nationalist-1.4476044, 7 Feb. 2021 by Seamus Nevin and Kevin Kenny, 'The Irish in the Empire' in Kenny (ed.), *Ireland and the British Empire*, pp. 90–1.

137. Corinne Fowler, *Green Unpleasant Land: Creative Responses to Rural England's Colonial Connections* (Leeds, 2020), pp. 23–6.

138. Priya Satia, *Time's Monster: History, Conscience and Britain's Empire* (London, 2020), p. 274. Also see Robert Aldrich, 'Apologies, Restitutions, and Compensation: Making Reparations for Colonialism' in Thomas and Thompson (eds.), *The Oxford Handbook of The Ends of Empire*, pp. 714–32.

139. See for example https://www.torch.ox.ac.uk/event/decolonising-irish-history-a-panel-discussion and https://www.tcd.ie/trinitylongroomhub/media/news/articles/2021-02-19-Colonial-Legacies.php, both accessed 12 June 2022; Shahmima Akhtar, Dónal Hassett, Kevin Kenny, Laura McAtackney, Ian McBride, Timothy McMahon, Caoimhe Nic Dháibhéid, and Jane Ohlmeyer, 'Decolonising Irish History? Possibilities, Challenges, Practices', *Irish Historical Studies*, 45 (2021), pp. 1–30. Also see Nicholas Draper, 'Ireland and British colonial slave-ownership, 1763–1833' and Sandrine Uwase Ndahiro, ' "Where are you actually from?": Racial issues in the Irish context' in O'Kane and O'Neill (eds.), *Ireland, Slavery and the Caribbean*.

140. John Darwin 'Afterword' in Nicolaïdis, Sèbe, and Maas (eds.), *Echoes of Empire*, pp. 407–10 (quote p. 408). Also see Peter Fibiger Bang, C. A. Bayly, and Walter Scheidel (eds.), *The Oxford World History of Empire* (2 vols., Oxford, 2021).

141. Ann Laura Stoler, *Imperial Debris: On Ruins and Ruination* (Durham, NC, 2013), p. 7. Also see Ann Laura Stoler, *Duress: Imperial Durabilities in Our Times* (Durham, NC, 2016).

142. Hilary Beckles, *Britain's Black Debt: Reparations for Caribbean Slavery and Native Genocide* (Kingston, 2012), p. 211.

143. Jean-Frédéric Schaub, 'The Imperial Question in the History of Ibero-America: The Importance of the Long View' in Nicolaïdis, Sèbe and Maas (ed.), *Echoes of Empire*, pp. 63–80 (quote p. 70).

144. Biederman, *(Dis)connected Empires*, p. 220.

145. Nimmi Gowrinathan and Kate Cronin-Furman, 'The Forever Victims? Tamil Women in Post-War Sri Lanka' (White Paper, 2015), https://www.deviarchy.com/wp/wp-content/uploads/2015/09/The-Forever-Victims-Tamil-Women-in-Post-War-Sri-Lanka.pdf accessed 7 January 2023. I am grateful to Milli Lake for sharing this reference with me.

146. Clare Carroll and Patricia King (eds.), *Ireland and Postcolonial Theory* (Cork, 2003), p. 8.

147. Beiner, *Forgetful Remembrance* and Covington, *The Devil from Over the Sea*. Also see Anne O'Connor, 'Women in Irish Folklore' in M. O'Dowd and M. MacCurtain (eds.), *Women in Early Modern Ireland* (Edinburgh, 1991), pp. 304–17 and Clodagh Tait, 'Worry Work: The Supernatural Labours of Living and Dead Mothers in Irish Folklore', *Past and Present*, 246 (2020), pp. 217–38.

148. Seamus Deane, Andrew Carpenter, and Jonathan Williams (eds.), *The Field Day Anthology of Irish Writing* (3 vols., Derry, 1991) and Bourke et al. (eds.), *The Field Day Anthology of Irish Writing: Irish Women's Writing and Traditions* (2 vols.).

149. Ireland has one of the largest and extensive archives of folklore tradition in the world. Diarmuid Ó Giolláin, *Locating Irish Folklore: Tradition, Modernity, Identity* (Cork, 2000); Micheál Briody, *The Irish Folklore Commission 1935–1970* (Helsinki, 2008); and Mary Daly, '"The State Papers of a forgotten and neglected people"; the National Folklore Collection and the writing of Irish history', *Béaloideas*, 78 (2010), pp. 61–79. I am grateful to Sarah Covington for introducing me to the riches of this archive.

150. Vincent Morely, *The Popular Mind in Eighteenth-Century Ireland* (Cork, 2017) and 'Muting the native voice: The historiography of 18th century Ireland' in Terence Bradley, *Against the Tide: Challenging Revisionism in Irish History* (Belfast, 2022). Also see Breandan Ó Buachalla, *Ailing ghéar* (Dublin, 1997); Bernadette Cunningham, 'Irish language sources for early modern Ireland', *History Ireland*, 4 (1996), pp. 41–8; Marc Caball, 'Bardic poetry and the analysis of Gaelic mentalities', *History Ireland*, 2 (1994), pp. 46–50.

151. An approach called for in Andrien, 'Age of exploration, c.1500–1650', p. 23 and in Susan E. Alcock, Terence N. D'Altroy, Kathleen D. Morrison, and Carla M. Sinopoli (eds.), *Empires: Perspectives from Archaeology and History* (Cambridge, 2001). On the reluctance of historians of Ireland to work across disciplines see Guy Beiner, 'Why Irish History Starved: A Virtual Historiography', *Field Day Review*, 3 (2007), pp. 67–81.

152. See Chapter 4 below.

153. Marisa J. Fuentes, *Dispossessed Lives: Enslaved Women, Violence, and the Archive* (Philadelphia, 2016).

154. Jenny Shaw, 'In the Name of the Mother: The Story of Susannah Mingo, a Woman of Color in the Early English Atlantic', *The William and Mary Quarterly*, 77 (2020), pp. 177–210. Also see Chloe Ireton, 'Margarita de Sossa, Sixteenth-Century Puebla de los Ángeles, New Spain (Mexico)' in Erica L. Ball, Tatiana Seijas, and Terri L. Snyder (eds.), *As If She Were Free: A Collective Biography of Black Women and Emancipation in the Americas* (Cambridge, 2020), pp. 27–42.

155. Ann Laura Stoler, 'Colonial Archives and the Arts of Governance', *Archival Science*, 2 (2002), pp. 87–109 (quote p. 99).

156. Ann Laura Stoler, *Along the Archival Grain: Epistemic Anxieties and Colonial Common Sense* (Princeton, 2008).

157. John Gibney, 'The most controversial documents in Irish history?', *History Ireland*, 19 (2011), pp. 18–19 and Ben Kiernan, 'Afterword—Settler colonies, ethno-religious violence and historical documentation: Comparative reflections on Southeast Asia and Ireland' in Jane Ohlmeyer and Micheál Ó Siochrú (eds.), *Ireland 1641: Contexts and Reactions* (Manchester, 2013), pp. 254–73. The best introduction to the 1641 Depositions remains Aidan Clarke 'The 1641 depositions' in P. Fox (ed.), *Treasures of the Library, Trinity College Dublin* (Dublin, 1986), pp. 111–22.

158. William Smyth, *Map-Making, Landscapes and Memory: A Geography of Colonial and Early Modern Ireland c.1530–1750* (Cork, 2006), p. 115.

159. Dianne Hall, 'Fear, Gender and Violence in Early Modern Ireland' in Michael Champion and Andrew Lynch (eds.), *Understanding Emotions in Early Europe* (Turnhout, Belgium, 2015), pp. 215–32; Dianne Hall, 'Most barbarously and inhumaine maner butchered': Masculinity, Trauma, and Memory in Early Modern Ireland' in Fionnuala Dillane, Naomi McAreavey, and Emilie Price (eds.), *The Body in Pain in Irish Literature and Culture* (London, 2016), pp. 41–7; and Joan Redmond, 'Religion, civility and the "British" of Ireland in the 1641 Irish rebellion', *Irish Historical Studies* (2021), 45 (167), pp. 1–21; Sarah Covington, ' "Those Savage Days of Memory": John Temple and His Narrative of the 1641 Uprising' in Dillane, McAreavey, and Price (eds.), *The Body in Pain in Irish Literature*, pp. 57–76 and ' "Realms so barbarous and cruell": Writing Violence in Early Modern Ireland and England', *History*, 2014, 99 (2014), pp. 487–504; Naomi McAreavey, ' "Paper bullets": Gendering the 1641 rebellion in the writings of Lady Elizabeth Dowdall and Lettice Fitzgerald, baroness of Offaly' in Thomas Herron and Michael Potterton (eds.), *Ireland in the Renaissance, c.1540–1660* (Dublin, 2007), pp. 311–24; Raymond Gillespie, 'Temple's Fate: Reading *The Irish Rebellion* in Late Seventeenth-Century Ireland' in Ciaran Brady and Jane Ohlmeyer (eds.), *British Interventions in Early Modern Ireland* (Cambridge, 2004), chapter 15; Toby Barnard, 'The Uses of 23 October 1641 and Irish Protestant celebrations', *English Historical Review*, 106 (1991), pp. 889–920 and ' "Parlour entertainment in an evening?" Histories of the 1640s' in Micheál Ó Siochrú (ed.), *Kingdoms in Crisis: Ireland in the 1640s* (Dublin, 2001),

pp. 20–43; and John Gibney, *The Shadow of a Year: The 1641 Rebellion in Irish History and Memory* (Madison, Wisconsin, 2013), especially the final chapter.

160. Farrell, *The 'Mere Irish'*, has done this for the native Irish. Also see Eamon Darcy, 'Stories of Trauma in Early Modern Ireland' in Erin Peters and Cynthia Richards (eds.), *Early Modern Trauma: Europe and the Atlantic World* (Lincoln, Nebraska, 2021), pp. 203–26.

161. Frederick Cooper and Ann Laura Stoler, 'Between Metropole and Colony: Rethinking a Research Agenda' in Frederick Cooper and Ann Laura Stoler (eds.), *Tensions of Empire: Colonial Cultures in a Bourgeois World* (Berkeley, 1997), pp. 13, 28–9 and Peter Crooks and Timothy H. Parsons, 'Empires, Bureaucracy and the Paradox of Power' in Peter Crooks and Timothy H. Parsons (eds.), *Empires and Bureaucracy in World History: From Late Antiquity to the Twentieth Century* (Cambridge, 2016), pp. 3–28.

162. Jane Burbank and Frederick Cooper, *Empires in World History: Power and the Politics of Difference* (Princeton, 2010), p. 21.

163. Burbank and Cooper, *Empires in World History*, pp. 10–13.

164. Burbank and Cooper, *Empires in World History*, pp. 13–14.

165. Burbank and Cooper, *Empires in World History*, pp. 14–15.

166. Discussed at length in Chapter 4 below.

167. Burbank and Cooper, *Empires in World History*, pp. 15–16.

168. Burbank and Cooper, *Empires in World History*, pp. 16–17.

169. For example, Bartolomé Yun-Casalilla, *Iberian World Empires and the Globalization of Europe 1415–1668* (London, 2019) and Bartolomé Yun-Casalilla, Ilaria Berti, and Omar Svriz-Wucherer (eds.), *American Globalization, 1492–1850: Trans-Cultural Consumption in Spanish Latin America* (Abingdon, 2022). For other research projects supported under the auspices of the global history network, https://www.globalhistorynetwork.com/projects/index.html, accessed 7 January 2023.

170. Canny and Morgan (eds.), *The Oxford Handbook of the Atlantic World*, especially chapter 9 and Christopher Storrs, 'Magistrates to Administrators, Composite Monarchy to Fiscal-Military Empire: Empire and Bureaucracy in the Spanish Monarchy, c. 1492–1825' in Crooks and Parsons (eds.), *Empires and Bureaucracy in World History*, pp. 291–317.

171. L. H. Roper and Bertrand Van Ruymbeke, 'Introduction' in L. H. Roper and Bertrand Van Ruymbeke (eds). *Constructing Early Modern Empires: Proprietary Ventures in the Atlantic World, 1500–1750* (Leiden, 2007), pp. 14–15 and Leslie Bethell (ed.), *Colonial Brazil* (Cambridge, 1987).

172. My thanks to Glynn Redworth for this.

173. Chiu Hsin-Hui, *The Colonial 'Civilizing Process' in Dutch Formosa: 1624–1662* (Leiden, 2008), p. 9.

174. S. F. Dale, *The Muslim Empires of the Ottomans, Safavids, and Mughals* (Cambridge, 2010). Also see Pratyay Nath, *Climate of Conquest. War, Environment, and Empire in Mughal North India* (Oxford, 2019) and Sanjay Subrahmanyam, 'A Tale of Three Empires: Mughals, Ottomans, and Habsburgs in a Comparative Context', *Common Knowledge*, 12 (2006), pp. 66–92.

175. Michael H. Fisher, 'Mughal Empire' in Levine and Marriott (eds.), *The Ashgate Research Companion*, pp. 161–86.

176. M. Athar Ali, *Mughal India: Studies in Polity, Ideas, Society and Culture* (Oxford, 2006).

177. J. F. Richards, 'Fiscal states in Mughal and British India' in B. Yun-Casalilla and P. O'Brien (eds.), *The Rise of Fiscal States: A Global History, 1500–1914* (Cambridge, 2012), pp. 410–441.

178. Canny (ed.), *The Origins of Empire*, p. 12.

179. Norbert Peabody, 'Knowledge Formation in Colonial India' in Peers and Gooptu (eds.), *India and the British Empire*, pp. 77–83.

CHAPTER 02

1. This chapter draws on Jane Ohlmeyer, 'Conquest, Civilization, Colonization: Ireland, 1540–1660' in Richard Bourke and Ian MacBride (eds.), *The Princeton Guide to Modern Irish History* (Princeton, 2016), pp. 21–47; '"Civilizinge of those rude partes". The colonization of Ireland and Scotland, 1580s–1640s' in Nicholas Canny (ed.), *The Oxford History of the British Empire*, vol. 1 (Oxford, 1998), pp. 124–47; and 'A Laboratory for Empire?: Early Modern Ireland and English Imperialism' in Kevin Kenny (ed.), *Ireland and the British Empire* (Oxford, 2004), pp. 26–60.

2. Douglas Hyde, 'The Necessity of De-Anglicising Ireland' in Seamus Deane, Andrew Carpenter, and Jonathan Williams (eds.), *The Field Day Anthology of Irish Writing* (3 vols., Derry, 1991), II, pp. 527–33.

3. Bernadette Cunningham and Raymond Gillespie, 'The East Ulster bardic family of Ó Gnímh', *Egise*, 20 (1984), p. 108 and Sarah E. McKibben, 'In their "owne countre": Deriding and Defending the Early Modern Irish Nation after Gerald of Wales', *Eolas: The Journal of the American Society of Irish Medieval Studies*, 8 (2015), p. 69, '*Saxa nua dan hainm Éire*' [a new England by the name of Ireland]. Also see Sarah E. McKibben, 'Bardic close reading' in Sarah Covington, Vincent P. Carey, and Valerie McGowan-Doyle (eds.), *Early Modern Ireland: New Sources, Methods and Perspectives* (Abingdon, 2019), chapter 6.

4. Keith Thomas, *In Pursuit of Civility: Manners and Civilization in Early Modern England* (New Haven, 2020); S. G. Ellis, 'Reducing their wilderness...unto civility': England and the 'Celtic fringe'. 1415–1625' in B. Smith (ed.), *Ireland and the English World in the Late Middle Ages: Essays in Honour of Robin Frame* (Basingstoke, 2009), pp. 176–92 and 'Civilising the natives: State formation and the Tudor Monarchy, c.1400–1603' in S. G. Ellis and L. Klusáková (eds.), *Imagining Frontiers: Contesting Identities* (Pisa, 2007), pp. 77–92; and T. C. Barnard, *Improving Ireland? Projectors, Prophets and Profiteers, 1641–1786* (Dublin, 2008).

5. See Chapter 1 above.

6. Clare Carroll and Patricia King (eds.), *Ireland and Postcolonial Theory* (Cork, 2003), p. 7.

7. *CSPI, 1615–1625* (London, 1880), pp. 307–9. For a valuable reading of O'Neill see Brendan Kane, 'Masculinity and political geographies in England, Ireland

and North America', *European Review of History: Revue européenne d'histoire*, 22 (2015), p. 607.

8. Andrew Carpenter, *Verse in English from Tudor and Stuart Ireland* (Cork, 2003), pp. 98–106.

9. Plays like *Captain Thomas Stukeley* (1596–7) and *Sir John Oldcastle* (1599) presented the Gaelic Irish as barbarous, 'naked savages' and cannibals. Christopher Marlowe's *Edward II* (1592) mentioned 'The wild O'Neill, with swarms of Irish kerns,/Lives uncontroll'd within the English Pale' (II.ii.161–5), Stephen O'Neill, *Staging Ireland: Representations in Shakespeare and Renaissance Drama* (Dublin, 2007), pp. 18–19, 73; Joep Leerssen, *Mere Irish and Fíor-Ghael: Studies in the Idea of Irish Nationality, its Development and Literary Expression prior to the Nineteenth Century* (Cork, 1996), especially chapter 3; and Andrew Murphy, *But the Irish Sea Betwixt Us: Ireland, Colonialism and Renaissance Literature* (Lexington, Kentucky, 1999), especially chapter 4.

10. O'Neill, *Staging Ireland*, p. 11; Hiram Morgan, 'Giraldus Cambrensis and the Tudor Conquest of Ireland' in Hiram Morgan (ed.), *Political Ideology in Ireland 1541–1641* (Dublin, 1999), p. 22 and Rory Rapple, 'Shakespeare, the Irish, and Military Culture' in Malcolm Smuts (ed.), *The Oxford Handbook of the Age of Shakespeare* (Oxford, 2016), pp. 103–20.

11. O'Neill, *Staging Ireland*, pp. 42–3 and Hiram Morgan, *Tyrone's Rebellion: The Outbreak of the Nine Years War in Tudor Ireland* (Suffolk, 1993), p. 176.

12. James Muldoon, *Identity on the Medieval Irish Frontier: Degenerate Englishmen, Wild Irish, Middle Nation* (Gainseville, 2003); John Morrisey, 'Cultural geographies of the contact zone: Gaels, Galls and overlapping territories in late medieval Ireland', *Social and Cultural Geography* 6 (2005).

13. Audrey Horning, 'Shapeshifters and mimics: Exploring elite strategies in the early modern British Atlantic' in David Edwards and Colin Rynne (eds.), *The Colonial World of Richard Boyle First Earl of Cork* (Dublin, 2018), pp. 27–42.

14. Andrew Hadfield and Willy Maley, 'Introduction: Irish representations and English alternatives' in Brendan Bradshaw et al. (eds.) *Representing Ireland: Literature and the Origins of Conflict, 1534–1660* (Cambridge, 1993), p. 15; Murphy, *The Irish Sea Betwixt Us*, pp. 7, 58.

15. Homi Bhaba, 'Of mimicry and man: The ambivalence of colonial discourse', *October*, 28, *Discipleship: A Special Issue on Psychoanalysis* (1984), pp. 125–33.

16. Carroll and King (eds.), *Ireland and Postcolonial Theory*, p. 7.

17. R. R. Davies, *The First English Empire: Power and Identities in the British Isles 1093–1343* (Oxford, 2002); and Peter Crooks, 'State of the Union: Perspectives on English Imperialism in the Late Middle Ages', *Past and Present*, No. 212 (2011), pp. 3–42.

18. Crooks, 'State of the Union', p. 5.

19. Crooks, 'State of the Union', p. 41.

20. Jane Ohlmeyer, Richard Ross, and Philip Stern, 'Anglicization of and through Law: British North America, Ireland, and India Compared, *c.*1540–*c.*1800'.

21. For an example of a failed colony see Karen Ordahl Kupperman, 'Errand to the Indies: Puritan Colonization from Providence Island through the Western Design', *The William and Mary Quarterly*, 45 (1988), pp. 70–99.

22. Micheál Ó Siochrú, *God's Executioner: Oliver Cromwell and the Conquest of Ireland* (London, 2008), p. 65 notes that Cromwell asked parliament for £100,000. David Brown, *Empire and Enterprise: Money, Power and the Adventurers for Irish Land during the British Civil Wars* (Manchester, 2020), pp. 166–71 suggests that the amount might have been higher still, roughly £250,000, of which £10,000 was in gold. I am grateful to Dr Brown for sharing insights into how the invasion was financed.

23. Aidan Clarke, 'Patrick Darcy and the Constitutional Relationship between Ireland and Britain' in Jane Ohlmeyer (ed.), *Political Thought in Seventeenth-Century Ireland: Kingdom or Colony?* (Cambridge, 2000), pp. 35–55; and Patrick Darcy, *An Argument Delivered by Patrick Darcy, Esquire, By the Express Order of the House of Commons in the Parliament of Ireland, 9 Iunii, 1641* (Waterford, 1643).

24. See Chapter 1 above.

25. Explored at length in Chapter 5 below.

26. Michael Brown and Seán Patrick Donlan (eds.), *The Laws and Other Legalities of Ireland, 1689–1850* (Farnham, 2011); and J. G. Simms, *The Williamite Confiscation in Ireland, 1690–1703* (London, 1956).

27. See the essays in David Edwards, Pádraig Lenihan, and Clodagh Tait (eds.), *Age of Atrocity: Violence and Political Conflict in Early Modern Ireland* (Dublin, 2007) and Robin Clifton, 'An indiscriminate Blackness? Massacre, counter-massacre and ethnic cleansing in Ireland, 1640–1660' in Mark Levene and Penny Roberts (eds.), *The Massacre in History* (New York and Oxford, 1999), pp. 107–26.

28. Wayne Lee, *Barbarians and Brothers: Anglo-American Warfare, 1500–1865* (Oxford, 2011), chapters 1 and 2.

29. Pádraig Lenihan, 'War and population', *Irish Economic and Social History*, 24 (1997), pp. 1–21. Also see Dianne Hall and Elizabeth Malcolm, 'The Rebels Turkish Tyranny': Understanding Sexual Violence in Ireland during the 1640s', *Gender and History*, 22 (2010), pp. 55–74; Eamon Darcy, *The Irish Rebellion of 1641 and the Wars of the Three Kingdoms* (Woodbridge, 2013), especially chapter 4; Peter Wilson, 'Atrocities in the Thirty Years War' in Jane Ohlmeyer and Micheál Ó Siochrú (eds.), *Ireland 1641: Contexts and Reactions* (Manchester, 2013; paperback 2014), chapter 9; and Erica Charters, Eve Rosenhaft, and Hannah Smith (eds.), *Civilians and War in Europe, 1618–1815* (Liverpool, 2012), especially chapters by Peter Wilson and Barbara Donagan.

30. Mary O'Dowd, 'Women and War in Ireland in the 1640s' in Margaret MacCurtain and Mary O'Dowd (eds.) *Women in Early Modern Ireland* (Dublin, 1991), pp. 91–111; Martyn Bennett, *The Civil Wars Experienced. Britain and Ireland, 1638–1661* (London, 2000); Bernadette Whelan, ' "The weaker vessel"?: The impact of warfare on women in seventeenth-century Ireland' in Christine Meek and Catherine Lawless (eds.), *Studies on Medieval and Early Modern Women: Victims or Viragos* (Dublin, 2005), pp. 120–41 and 'Women and warfare 1641–1691' in

Pádraig Lenihan (ed.), *Conquest and Resistance: War in Seventeenth-Century Ireland* (Leiden, 2001), pp. 317–43; and Alice O'Driscoll, 'Women, gender, and siege during the Wars of the Three Kingdoms, 1639–52' (Unpublished PhD thesis, Cambridge, 2021). For the earlier period see Joan Redmond, 'Memories of violence and New English identities in early modern Ireland', *Historical Research*, 89 (2016), pp. 708–29.

31. There is no grand synthesis of 'anglicisation' in early modern Ireland along the lines of that developed for North America by John Murrin, even though the period has been extensively studied and few will contest the extent to which conquest, colonization, and commercialization effectively anglicised Ireland.

32. Antoinette Burton, *The Trouble with Empire: Challenges to Modern British Imperialism* (Oxford, 2015), p. 6.

33. Stuart Carroll, 'Violence, Civil Society and European Civilisation' in Robert Antony, Stuart Carroll, and Caroline Dodds Pennock (eds.), *The Cambridge World History of Violence*: vol. 3 (Cambridge, 2020), p. 673.

34. Patrick Duffy, David Edwards, and Elizabeth Fitzpatrick (eds.), *Gaelic Ireland: Land Lordship and Settlement c. 1250–c. 1650* (Dublin, 2001), pp. 44–5.

35. Duffy, Edwards, and Fitzpatrick (eds.), *Gaelic Ireland*, p. 44. Also see Chapter 3 below.

36. *The Statutes at Large Passed in the Parliaments held in Ireland (1310–1800)* (20 vols., Dublin, 1786–1801), I, p. 120.

37. Edmund Curtis and R. B. McDowell (eds.), *Irish Historical Documents, 1172–1922* (London, 1943), p. 55; Raymond Gillespie, 'Seventeenth-century Irish music and its cultural context' in Barra Boydell and Kerry Houston (eds.), *Music, Ireland and the Seventeenth Century* (Dublin, 2009), pp. 26–39.

38. Sir John Davies, *A Discoverie of the True Causes why Ireland was never entirely subdued*... (London, 1612), p. 271. Also see Eugene Flanagan, 'The anatomy of Jacobean Ireland: Captain Barnaby Rich, Sir John Davies and the failure of reform, 1609–22' in Hiram Morgan (ed.), *Political Ideology in Ireland 1541–1641* (Dublin, 1999), pp. 158–80. p. 170.

39. Edmund Spenser, *A View of the Present State of Ireland* ed. W. L. Renwick (Oxford, 1970), pp. 51–3. Also see Ann Rosalind Jones and Peter Stallybrass, 'Diamantling Irena: The sexualizing of Ireland in early modern England' in Andrew Parker, Mary Russo, Doris Simmer, and Patricia Yaeger (eds.), *Nationalism and Sexualities* (London, 1992), pp. 157–71.

40. Marie Louise Coolahan, 'Starting points and moving targets: transition and the early modern' in Moyra Haslett (ed.), *Irish Literature in Transition 1700–1780* (Cambridge, 2020), pp. 31–48 (quote p. 34).

41. Gerard Farrell, *The 'Mere Irish' and the Colonisation of Ulster, 1570–1641* (London, 2017), p. 53.

42. Audrey Horning, 'Clothing and colonialism: the Dungiven costume and the fashioning of early modern identities', *Journal of Social Archaeology*, 14 (2014), p. 304.

43. Bernard S. Cohn, *Colonialism and its Forms of Knowledge: The British in India* (Princeton, New Jersey, 1996), p. xvi.

44. Horning, 'Clothing and colonialism', p. 311.
45. https://ids.si.edu/ids/media_view?id=NPG-NPG_65_61Pocahontas_d1&container.fullpage&iframe=true&width=85%25&height=85%25, accessed 5 July 2022.
46. Ulinka Rublack, *Dressing Up: Cultural Identity in Renaissance Europe* (Oxford, 2010).
47. Horning, 'Clothing and colonialism', p. 311.
48. Susan Flavin, 'Consumption and Material Culture in Sixteenth-Century Ireland', *Economic History Review*, 64 (2011), pp. 1073–427 and *Consumption and Culture in Sixteenth-Century Ireland* (Woodbridge, 2014); and Brendan Scott, 'Commodities and the Import Trade in Early Plantation Ulster', *Irish Economic and Social History*, 48 (2021), pp. 92–107.
49. Quoted in S. J. Connolly, *Contested Island: Ireland 1460–1630* (Oxford, 2007), pp. 288–9.
50. Barnabe Rich, *The Irish Hubbub* (London, 1618), G3 47.
51. Quoted in Horning, 'Clothing and colonialism', p. 306. Also see McKibben, 'In their "owne countre"', pp. 66–7.
52. John C. Mac Erlean, S. J. (ed.), *The Poems of David Ó Bruadair* (3 vols., London, 1910–1917), I, pp. 133–8.
53. Leerssen, *Mere Irish and Fíor-Ghael*, pp. 203–4.
54. Amelia Almorza Hidalgo, 'Spanish Women as Agents for a New Material Culture in Colonial Spanish America' in Bartolomé Yun-Casalilla, Ilaria Berti, and Omar Svriz-Wucherer (eds.), *American Globalization, 1492–1850. Trans-Cultural Consumption in Spanish Latin America* (Abingdon, 2022), pp. p. 88 (quote), 89–90.
55. Quoted in Angela Bourke et al. (eds.), *The Field Day Anthology of Irish Writing. Irish Women's Writing and Traditions* (2 vols., Cork, 2002; vols. IV and V of the *Field Day Anthology*), V, p. 468.
56. James Cranford, *The Teares of Ireland* (London, 1642), p. 55.
57. Brian Friel, *Translations* (London, 1981), p. 25.
58. Patricia Palmer, *Language and Conquest in Early Modern Ireland: English Renaissance Literature and Elizabethan Imperial Expansion* (Cambridge, 2001), p. 14.
59. Brian Ó Cuív, 'The Irish Language in the Early Modern Period' in T. W. Moody, F. X. Martin, and F. J. Byrne (eds.), *New History of Ireland*, III, *1534–1691* (Oxford, 1976), p. 529; Marc Caball, 'Culture, Continuity and Change in early seventeenth-century south-west Munster', *Studia Hibernica*, 38 (2012), p. 38 and 'Gaelic and Protestant: A case study in early modern self-fashioning, 1567–1608', *Proceedings of the Royal Irish Academy*, C, 110 (2010), pp. 191–215.
60. Carpenter, *Verse in English*, pp. 11, 210–11, 237.
61. Davies, *Discoverie*, pp. 271–2. Also see Flanagan, 'The anatomy of Jacobean Ireland', pp. 158–80.
62. Daniel Gookin, *Historical Collections of the Indians* (Boston, 1674), p. 81.
63. Gookin, *Historical Collections*, p. 82. Audrey Horning, 'The Irish Worlds of William Penn: Culture, Conflict, and Connections' in Andrew R. Murphy and John Smolenski (eds.), *The Worlds of William Penn* (New Brunswick, 2019), pp. 120–38.
64. Mac Erlean (ed.), *The Poems of David Ó Bruadair*, I, pp. 18–19.

65. Leerssen, *Mere Irish and Fíor-Ghael*, p. 220 and James Kelly and Ciarán MacMurchaidh (eds.), *Irish and English: Essays on the Irish Linguistic and Cultural Frontier, 1600–1900* (Dublin, 2012).

66. Deposition of Ellinor Birne, 16 June 1652, TCD, Ms 811, f. 180v. Palmer, *Language and Conquest in Early Modern Ireland*, pp. 193–204.

67. Marie Louise Coolahan, *Women, Writing, and Language in Early Modern Ireland* (Oxford, 2010), pp. 164–5.

68. Deposition of Katherin Cooke, 24 February 1644, TCD, Ms 836, f. 92v.

69. Deposition of Joan Constable, 6 June 1643, TCD, Ms 836, f. 88v.

70. Palmer, *Language and Conquest in Early Modern Ireland*, p. 204.

71. Quoted in Palmer, *Language and Conquest in Early Modern Ireland*, p. 114.

72. Palmer, *Language and Conquest in Early Modern Ireland*, p. 126 and James Murray, *Enforcing the English Reformation in Ireland: Clerical Resistance and Political Conflict in the Diocese of Dublin, 1534–1590* (Cambridge, 2011).

73. John McCafferty, 'Protestant prelates or godly pastors? The dilemma of the early Stuart episcopate' in Alan Ford and John McCafferty (eds.), *The Origins of Sectarianism in Early Modern Ireland* (Cambridge, 2005), pp. 54–72.

74. Donal Cregan, 'The social and cultural background of a counter-reformation episcopate, 1618–60' in Art Cosgrove and Donal McCartney (eds.), *Studies in Irish History presented to R. Dudley Edwards* (Dublin, 1979), pp. 85–117.

75. Brendan Bradshaw, *The Irish Constitutional Revolution of the Sixteenth Century* (Cambridge, 1979), pp. 193–230 and Christopher Maginn, *'Civilizing' Gaelic Leinster: The Extension of Tudor Rule in the O'Byrne and O'Toole Lordships* (Dublin, 2004), pp. 63–90.

76. Christopher Maginn, 'The Gaelic Peers, the Tudor Sovereigns, and English Multiple Monarchy', *Journal of British Studies,* 50 (2011), pp. 566–86 (quote p. 583).

77. Duffy, Edwards, and Fitzpatrick (eds.), *Gaelic Ireland*, p. 45.

78. David Edwards, 'Collaboration without Anglicisation: The MacGiollapadraig Lordship and Tudor Reform' in Duffy, Edwards, and Fitzpatrick (eds.), *Gaelic Ireland,* pp. 78–96 (quote p. 84).

79. Farrell, *The 'Mere Irish'*, p. 69.

80. Luke McInerney, 'A 1640 register of the Thomond. Papers at Petworth House', *Archivium Hibernicum* 64 (2011), pp. 7–55.

81. Luke McInerney, 'A "most vainglorious man": the writings of Antonius Bruodin', *Archivium Hibernicum*, 70 (2017), pp. 202–83.

82. David Edwards and Keith Sidwell (eds.), *Officina Neolatina: Selected Writings from the Neo-Latin World* (Turnhout, Belgium, 2011), pp. 11–12.

83. Brian Ó Dálaigh (ed.) *Corporation Book of Ennis* (Dublin, 1990), p. 383.

84. *CSPI, 1603–1606* (London, 1872), p. 65.

85. *CSPI, 1603–1606*, p. 470.

86. Jane Ohlmeyer, *Making Ireland English: The Irish Aristocracy in the Seventeenth Century* (New Haven and London, 2012), chapter 4.

87. Michael Hartnett, *Haicéad* (Oldcastle, County Meath, 1993), p. 61.

88. Nicholas Canny, *Imagining Ireland's Pasts: Early Modern Ireland through the Centuries* (Oxford, 2021), p. 115.

89. Bernadette Cunningham, 'Political and Social Change in the Lordships of Clanricard and Thomond, 1596–1641' (unpublished MA thesis, NUI, University of College Galway, 1979), pp. 131–2.

90. Coolahan, 'Starting points and moving targets', pp. 34–5.

91. Coolahan, 'Starting points and moving targets', p. 36. Also see Jane Stevenson and Peter Davidson (eds.), *Early Modern Women Poets: An Anthology* (Oxford, 2001), pp. 175–8 and Bourke et al. (eds.), *The Field Day Anthology of Irish Writing*, IV, pp. 399–402.

92. Brian Ó Dálaigh, 'A Comparative Study of the Wills of the First and Fourth Earls of Thomond', *North Munster Antiquarian Journal*, 34 (1992), p. 61.

93. John Ainsworth (ed.), *Inchiquin Manuscripts* (IMC, Dublin, 1961), p. 512.

94. Marc Caball, 'Local and global: A perspective from early eighteenth-century Gaelic Munster', *Proceedings of the Harvard Celtic Colloquium* 34 (2014), pp. 37, 46.

95. *CSPI, 1647–1660* (London, 1903), p. 311.

96. Wasey Sterry, *The Eton College Register 1441–1698* (London, 1943).

97. Andrew Hadfield, 'Educating the colonial mind: Spenser and the plantation' in Éamonn Ó Ciardha and Micheál Ó Siochrú (eds.), *The Plantation of Ulster: Ideology and Practice* (Manchester, 2012), pp. 158–75 (quote p. 170); David Harris Sacks, 'Love and Fear in the Making of England's Atlantic Empire', *Huntington Library Quarterly*, 83 (2020) special edition 'Ancient Rome in English Political Culture, ca. 1570–1660' edited by Paulina Kewes, pp. 543–65; and Campbell, *Renaissance Humanism and Ethnicity before Race*, pp. 25–6, 33.

98. *CSPI, 1615–1625*, p. 66.

99. Especially Old English and Gaelic boys, *CSPI, 1615–1625*, pp. 83–4, 212–3 (quote).

100. Ian Campbell, *Renaissance Humanism and Ethnicity before Race: The Irish and the English in the Seventeenth Century* (Manchester, 2013), chapter 1.

101. Quoted in Raymond Gillespie, 'Church, State and Education in Early Modern Ireland' in Maurice O'Connell (ed.), *Education, Church and State* (Dublin, 1992), p. 44.

102. Davies, *Discoverie*, p. 272.

103. Timothy Cochran, *Studies in the History of Classical Teaching* (Dublin, 1911), p. 56.

104. *CSPI, 1615–1625*, p. 66.

105. Brown, *Empire and Enterprise*, pp. 33, 124 and Alison Games, *The Web of Empire: English Cosmopolitans in an Age of Expansion, 1560–1660* (Oxford, 2008), pp. 273–5.

106. See Chapter 4.

107. Jane Ohlmeyer, 'Ireland, India and the British Empire', *Studies in People's History*, 2 (2015), pp. 169–88. See Chapter 5.

108. Ohlmeyer, *Making Ireland English*, pp. 433–42.

109. Reginald J. Fletcher (ed.), *The Pension Book of Gray's Inn* I *1569–1669* (London, 1901), p. 295.

110. Jane Ohlmeyer, 'Irish Recusant Lawyers during the Reign of Charles I' in Micheál Ó Siochrú (ed.), *A Kingdom in Crisis: The Confederates and the Irish Civil Wars*

(Dublin, 2000), appendix. For the earlier period see Donal F. Cregan, 'Irish Catholic Admissions to the English Inns of Court, 1558–1625', *Irish Jurist* 5 (1970).

111. Hazel Maynard, 'Irish membership of the English inns of court, 1660–1699: Lawyers, litigation and the legal profession' (Unpublished PhD, University College Dublin, 2006) and Craig Allen Bailey, 'Metropole and Colony: Irish Networks and Patronage in the Eighteenth-Century Empire', *Immigrants and Minorities*, 23 (2005), pp. 161–81.

112. Colm Kenny, 'Not every judge a phoenix: King's Inns under Cromwell' in Coleman A. Dennehy (ed.), *Law and Revolution in Seventeenth-Century Ireland* (Dublin, 2020), pp. 104–27.

113. *CSPI, 1647–60*, p. 311.

114. *CSPI, 1611–1614* (London, 1877), p. 394.

115. Ohlmeyer, *Making Ireland English,* pp. 435–42 and Tadhg Ó hAnnracháin, *Confessionalism and Mobility in Early Modern Ireland* (Oxford, 2021).

116. Spenser, *A View*, p. 162.

117. Tonio Andrade and William Reger (eds.), *The Limits of Empire: European Imperial Formations in Early Modern World History* (Farnham, 2012).

118. Charles Ivar McGrath, *Ireland and Empire 1692–1770* (London, 2012), p. 24.

119. H. F. Kearney, 'The Court of Wards and Liveries in Ireland, 1622–1641', *Proceedings of the Royal Irish Antiquaries*, 57, Section C (1955–6), pp. 29–68.

120. Thomas Carte, *The Life of James Duke of Ormond* (6 vols., Oxford, 1851),VI, p. 214.

121. Public Records Office of Northern Ireland, D.3078/3/1/5, p. 3.

122. Ohlmeyer, *Making Ireland English*, pp. 157–68.

123. Nicholas Canny, *Making Ireland British, 1580–1650* (Oxford, 2001), pp. 428–31.

124. *CSPI, 1625–32* (London, 1900), p. 58; John Cunningham, 'The New English, the past and the law in the 1640s: Sir William Parsons's "Examen Hiberniae"' in Dennehy (ed.), *Law and Revolution*, pp. 89–103.

125. Antony, Carroll, and Dodds Pennock (eds.), *The Cambridge World History of Violence*.

126. Edwards, Lenihan, and Tait (eds.), *Age of Atrocity*.

127. W. Maley, Rich, Barnaby (1542–1617), soldier and author. *ODNB*. Retrieved 13 Jun. 2022, from https://www.oxforddnb.com/view/10.1093/ref:odnb/9780198614128.001.0001/odnb-9780198614128-e-23481

128. Nicholas Canny (ed.), *The Origins of Empire: British Overseas Enterprise to the Close of the Seventeenth Century* (Oxford, 1998), p. 12.

129. See note 22 above.

130. Scott Wheeler, 'The Logistics of Conquest' in P. Lenihan (ed.), *Conquest and Resistance: War in Seventeenth-Century Ireland* (Leiden, 2001), pp. 177–207.

131. Ohlmeyer, *Making Ireland English*, p. 35.

132. McGrath, *Ireland and Empire*, pp. 107, 143, 147, 216.

133. Ciaran Brady, *The Chief Governors: The Rise and Fall of Reform Government in Tudor Ireland* (Cambridge, 1994), pp. 169–208; Vincent Carey, *Surviving the Tudors: The 'Wizard' Earl of Kildare and English Rule in Ireland, 1537–1586* (Dublin, 2002); Maginn, *'Civilizing' Gaelic Leinster* and 'The Gaelic peers, the Tudor Sovereigns, and English Multiple Monarchy', pp. 566–86.

134. A significant minority of whom came from Wales, R. Morgan, *The Welsh and the Shaping of Early Modern Ireland 1558–1641* (Woodbridge, 2014).

135. John McCavitt, *The Flight of the Earls* (Dublin, 2002), p. 180.

136. Jane Burbank and Frederick Cooper, *Empires in World History: Power and the Politics of Difference* (Princeton, 2010), pp. 13–14. For example, see Tolga U. Esmer, 'War, State and the Privatisation of Violence in the Ottoman Empire' in Antony, Carroll, and Dodds Pennock (eds.), *The Cambridge World History of Violence*, p. 213; and Michael H. Fisher, 'Mughal Empire' in Philippa Levine and John Marriott (eds.), *The Ashgate Research Companion to Modern Imperial Histories* (Farnham, 2012), pp. 161–86.

137. Ohlmeyer, *Making Ireland English*; G. R. Mayes, 'The Early Stuarts and the Irish Peerage', *English Historical Review*, 73 (1958), pp. 227–51; and H. M. Scott (ed.), *The European Nobilities in the Seventeenth and Eighteenth Centuries: Northern, Central and Eastern Europe* (2 vols., London, 1995), II, pp. 1–11.

138. Victor Treadwell, *Buckingham and Ireland, 1616–1628: A Study in Anglo-Irish Politics* (Dublin, 1998), pp. 105–6.

139. Ohlmeyer, *Making Ireland English*, p. 136.

140. Ohlmeyer, *Making Ireland English*, pp. 34–50.

141. Roger Manning, *Swordsmen: The Martial Ethos in the Three Kingdoms* (Oxford, 2003), p. 18. See especially David Edwards, 'The escalation of violence in sixteenth-century Ireland' in Edwards, Lenihan, and Tait (eds.), *Age of Atrocity*; Fiona Fitzsimons, 'Cardinal Wolsey, the native affinities, and the failure of reform in Henrician Ireland' in David Edwards (ed.), *Regions and Rulers in Ireland, 1100–1650: Essays for Kenneth Nicholls* (Dublin, 2004), pp. 78–121; David Heffernan, *Debating Tudor Policy in Sixteenth-Century Ireland: 'Reform' Treatises and Political Discourse* (Manchester, 2018).

142. David Edwards, 'Ireland: Security and Conquest' in Susan Doran and Norman Jones (eds.), *The Elizabethan World* (London, 2011), pp. 182–200, 'Two fools and a martial law commissioner: Cultural conflict at the Limerick assize of 1606' in Edwards (ed.), *Regions and rulers in Ireland*, pp. 237–65, 'Political Change and Social Transformation, 1603–1641' in Jane Ohlmeyer (ed.), *The Cambridge History of Ireland. vol. 2. Early Modern Ireland, 1550–1730* (Cambridge, 2018), pp. 48–71 and Edwards, Lenihan, and Tait (eds.), *Age of Atrocity*, pp. 69, 74, 105–6, 120, 127, 207–8.

143. David Edwards, 'Ideology and experience: Spenser's *View* and martial law in Ireland', Morgan (ed.), *Political Ideology in Ireland*, pp. 127–57; Vincent Carey, 'Icons of Atrocity: John Derricke's *Image of Ireland* (1581)' in Allison Kavey (ed.), *World Building and the Early Modern Imagination* (New York, 2010); Patricia Palmer, *The Severed Head and the Grafted Tongue: Literature, Translation and Violence in Early Modern Ireland* (Cambridge, 2014), chapter 1; and Thomas Herron, Denna J. Iammarino, and Maryclaire Moroney (eds.), *John Derricke's The Image of Irelande: With a Discoverie of Woodkarne. Essays on Text and Context* (Manchester, 2021).

144. John M. Collins, *Martial Law and English Laws, c.1500–c.1700* (Cambridge, 2016), pp. 53–6, 65–9, 71 (quote).

145. Davies, *Discoverie*, pp. 113, 266−7 and Stephen Carroll, 'Competing authorities: The clash of martial and common law in early seventeenth-century Ireland' in Dennehy (ed.), *Law and Revolution,* p. 26.

146. Quoted (p. 52) in Aran McArdle, ' "Necessarye to keep order in Ireland", martial law and the 1641 rebellion' in Dennehy (ed.), *Law and Revolution,* pp. 47−64.

147. See the works by Edwards in notes 142 and 143 above, McArdle, ' "Necessarye to keep order in Ireland" ', and Farrell, *The 'Mere Irish',* pp. 47−8.

148. Collins, *Martial Law and English Laws,* pp. 85−6, 97−104, 209−47.

149. Sandra den Otter, 'Law, authority, and Colonial Rule', pp. 168−90 in Douglas M. Peers and Nandini Gooptu (eds.), *India and the British Empire* (Oxford, 2012), chapter 7.

150. Clare Carroll and Vincent Carey (eds.), *Solon his Follie, or A Politique Discourse Touching the Reformation or common-weales conquered, declined or corrupted* by Richard Beacon (Binghamton, NY, 1996), p. xxvii and B4.

151. Quoted in Ted McCormick, *Human Empire: Mobility and Demographic Thought in the British Atlantic World, 1500−1800* (Oxford, 2022), p. 91.

152. Mary O'Dowd, 'Women and the Irish Chancery Court in the Late Sixteenth and Early Seventeenth Centuries', *Irish Historical Studies,* 31 (1999), pp. 470−87. See also Maighréad Ní Mhurchadha, *Fingal, 1603−60: Contending Neighbours in North Dublin* (Dublin, 2005), pp. 36, 142−6; and Jane Ohlmeyer, 'Records of the Irish Court of Chancery: A Preliminary Report for 1627−1634' in Desmond Greer and Norma Dawson (eds.), *Mysteries and Solutions in Irish Legal History* (Dublin, 2001), pp. 15−49.

153. Jon G. Crawford (ed.), *A Star Chamber Court in Ireland: The Court of Castle Chamber, 1571−1641* (Dublin, 2005), pp. 28−58 (quote p. 51); John McCavitt, ' "Good Planets in their Several Spheares": The Establishment of the Assize Circuits in Early Seventeenth Century Ireland', *Irish Jurist,* 14 (1989), pp. 248−78.

154. Margaret Curtis Layton (ed.), *The Council Book for the Province of Munster c.1599−1649* (IMC, Dublin, 2008), p. 240.

155. Layton (ed.), *The Council Book,* p. 240.

156. Brendan Kane, 'Popular politics and the legitimacy of power in early modern Ireland' in Elizabeth FitzPatrick and Audrey Horning (eds.), *Becoming and Belonging in Ireland 1200−1600 AD* (Cork, 2018), pp. 328−43 (quote p. 334).

157. Síle Ní Mhurchú and Brendan Kane, 'Poetic Response to Plantations 1609' in Brían Ó Conchubhair and Samuel Fisher (eds.), *Bone and Marrow/Cnámh agus Smior: An Anthology of Irish Poetry from Medieval to Modern* (Winston-Salem, 2022), p. 377.

158. Brian Mac Cuarta, 'Religious violence against settlers in south Ulster, 1641−2' in Edwards, Lenihan, and Tait (eds.), *Age of Atrocity,* pp. 154−75.

159. Deposition of Thomas Johnson, 14 January 1644, TCD, Ms 831, f. 190v. Also Deposition of Walter Bourke, undated, TCD, Ms 831, f. 169r.

160. Deposition of Walter Bourke, undated, TCD, Ms 831, f. 169r.

161. Keith Pluymers, 'Cow Trials, Climate Causes of Violence', *Environmental History,* 25 (2020), pp. 287−309.

162. Wolfgang Gabbert, 'Human Sacrifice, Ritualised Violence and the Colonial Encounter in the Americas' and Penny Roberts, 'Intercommunal Violence in Europe' in Antony, Carroll, and Dodds Pennock (eds.), *The Cambridge World History of Violence*.

163. Pluymers, 'Cow Trials, Climate Causes of Violence', p. 290; Thomas, *In Pursuit of Civility*, p. 286. Deposition of Andrew Adaire, 9 Jan. 1643, TCD, Ms 831, ff. 174r–178v.

164. Edward Said, *Culture and Imperialism* (London, 1994), p. 78. Also see Allan Greer, *Property and Dispossession: Natives, Empires and Land in Early Modern North Atlantic America* (Cambridge, 2018).

165. Brian Friel, *Making History* (London, 1989), p. 47.

166. John Patrick Montaño, ' "Dycheyng and Hegeying": The Material Culture of the Tudor Plantations in Ireland' in Fiona Bateman and Lionel Pilkington (eds.), *Studies in Settler Colonialism: Politics, Identity and Culture* (Basingstoke, 2011), pp 47–62 (quote p. 51).

167. *CSPI, 1611–1614*, p. 502.

168. Ohlmeyer, *Making Ireland English*, chapter 4.

169. K. W. Nicholls, *Land, Law and Society in Sixteenth-Century Ireland* (O'Donnell Lecture, Dublin, 1976), pp. 4–10.

170. Cunningham, 'Political and Social Change', p. 168 and 'The Composition of Connacht in the Lordships of Clanricarde and Thomond, 1577–1641', *Irish Historical Studies*, 24 (1984), pp. 1–14.

171. Rory Rapple's paper at the 'Ireland and the Wider World' Conference (April 2022) at Huntington Library, San Marino, USA, triggered a fulsome discussion around the precise meaning of the word 'plantation' and how and when it was first used to signify 'colonisation'.

172. Hiram Morgan, 'The colonial venture of Sir Thomas Smith in Ulster, 1571–5', *Historical Journal*, 28 (1987), pp. 261–78; Victor Treadwell (ed.), *The Irish Commission of 1622: An Investigation of the Irish Administration 1615–22 and its Consequences 1623–24* (IMC, Dublin, 2006); and Ted McCormick, *Human Empire: Mobility and Demographic Thought in the British Atlantic World, 1500–1800* (Oxford, 2022), pp. 83–90.

173. David Heffernan, *Walter Devereux First Earl of Essex and the Colonization of North-East Ulster, c.1573–6* (Dublin, 2018), pp. 16, 29.

174. *A letter sent by I. B. Gentleman* (London, [1572]).

175. Edwards and Rynne (eds.), *The Colonial World of Richard Boyle*, p. 16.

176. Michael MacCarthy Morrogh, *The Munster Plantation: English Migration to Southern Ireland, 1583–1641* (Oxford, 1986).

177. Canny, *Making Ireland British*, pp. 318–26 and *The Upstart Earl: A Study of the Social and Mental World of Richard Boyle, First Earl of Cork, 1566–1643* (Cambridge, 1982); Keith Pluymers, *No Wood, No Kingdom. Political Ecology in the English Atlantic* (Philadelphia, 2021).

178. Colin Rynne, 'Colonial entrepreneur and urban developer: the economic and industrial infrastructure of Boyle's Munster estates' in Edwards and Rynne (eds.), *The Colonial World of Richard Boyle*, pp. 89–111.

179. David Dickson, *Old World Colony. Cork and South Munster 1630–1830* (Cork, 2005), pp. 14–15; MacCarthy-Morrogh, *The Munster Plantation*, p. 185.

180. David Heffernan, 'Theory and practice in the Munster Plantation: The estates of Richard Boyle, first earl of Cork, 1602–43' in Edwards and Rynne (eds.), *The Colonial World of Richard Boyle*, pp. 43–63.

181. Audrey Horning, 'Shapeshifters and mimics: Exploring elite strategies in the early modern British Atlantic' in Edwards and Rynne (eds.), *The Colonial World of Richard Boyle*, pp. 27–42.

182. *CSPI, 1606–1608*, p. 268.

183. Ó Ciardha and Ó Siochrú (eds.), *The Plantation of Ulster*, p. 8.

184. John McGurk, *Sir Henry Docwra 1564–1631: Derry's Second Founder* (Dublin, 2006); and Philip Stern, 'Corporate virtue: The languages of empire in early modern British Asia', *Renaissance Studies*, 26 (2012), pp. 510–30.

185. Ian W. Archer, 'The city of London and the Ulster plantation' in Ó Ciardha and Ó Siochrú (eds.), *The Plantation of Ulster*, pp. 78–97.

186. *CSPI, 1608–1610* (London, 1874), p. 520.

187. The Irish population allegedly rose from *c.*1.4 million in 1600 to 2.1 million in 1641 (a growth of one per cent per annum), T. C. Smout, N. C. Landsman, and T. M. Devine, 'Scottish Emigration in the Seventeenth and Eighteenth centuries' in Nicholas Canny (ed.), *Europeans on the Move* (Oxford, 1994), p. 79.

188. Michael Perceval-Maxwell, *The Scottish Migration to Ulster in the Reign of James I* (London, 1973), pp. 217–28, 126; Nicholas Canny, *Making Ireland British, 1580–1650* (Oxford, 2001), pp. 211-2; Tadhg Ó hAnnracháin, *Confessionalism and Mobility in Early Modern Ireland* (Oxford, 2021), p. 115.

189. Susan Migden Socolow, *The Women of Colonial Latin America* (2nd edition, Cambridge, 2015), pp. 57, 62. I owe this reference to Jorge Díaz Ceballos.

190. Jane Ohlmeyer, 'Strafford, the "Londonderry Business" and the "New British History"' in J. F. Merritt (ed.), *The Political World of Thomas Wentworth earl of Strafford 1621–1641* (Cambridge, 1996), pp. 209–29.

191. Spenser, *A View*, p. 165.

192. Dickson, *Old World Colony*, p. 22; Raymond Gillespie, 'The Origins and Development of an Ulster Urban Network, 1600–41', *Irish Historical Studies*, 24 (1984), pp. 15–16; Robert Hunter, 'Ulster Plantation Towns 1609–1641' in David Harkness and Mary O'Dowd (eds.), *The Town in Ireland* (Belfast, 1991), pp. 55–80; and Scott, 'Commodities and the Import Trade in Early Plantation Ulster', pp. 92–107.

193. Phil Withington, 'Plantation and Civil Society' in Ó Ciardha and Ó Siochrú (eds.), *The Plantation of Ulster*, pp. 55–77 (quote p. 69).

194. Raymond Gillespie, *Colonial Ulster: The Settlement of East Ulster, 1600–1641* (Cork, 1985), p. 56; Michael Perceval-Maxwell, *The Scottish Migration to Ulster in the Reign of James I* (London, 1973), pp. 56–60.

195. John H. Andrews, 'The Mapping of Ireland's Cultural Landscape, 1550-1630' in Duffy, Edwards, and Fitzpatrick (eds.), *Gaelic Ireland*, pp. 161, 166.

196. Alison Cathcart, *Plantations by Land and Sea: North Channel Communities of the Atlantic Archipelago c.1550–1625* (London, 2021), p. 267; Karen O. Kupperman, *The Jamestown Project* (Cambridge, Mass., 2007), pp. 1–7.

197. Maurice Lee, Jr., *Great Britain's Solomon: James VI and I in His Three Kingdoms* (Urbana, Illinois, 1990), p. 212. Also Aonghas MacCoinnich, *Plantation and Civility in the North Atlantic World: The Case of the Northern Hebrides, 1570–1639* (Leiden, 2015).

198. Perceval-Maxwell, *Scottish Migration*, pp. 231–2.

199. Colin Breen, 'Randal MacDonnell and early Seventeenth-Century Settlement in Northeast Ulster, 1603–1630' in Ó Siochrú and Ó Ciardha (eds.), *The Plantation of Ulster*, pp. 143–57.

200. BL, Additional Ms 46,188, f. 120.

201. C. Maxwell (ed.), *Irish History from Contemporary Sources (1509–1610)* (London, 1923), p. 301.

202. According to the poet Fearflatha Ó Gnímh the exterior walls were lime-washed and inside embroidered hangings adorned the walls, ornamental carvings decorated the doorways, and the windows had blue and coloured glass in them, Katharine Simms, 'Native Sources of Gaelic Settlement: The House Poems' in Patrick Duffy, David Edwards, and Elizabeth Fitzpatrick (eds.), *Gaelic Ireland: Land Lordship & Settlement c. 1250–c. 1650* (Dublin, 2001), p. 255.

203. Ohlmeyer, *Making Ireland English*, pp. 394–401.

204. Charlene McCoy, 'War and Revolution: County Fermanagh and its Borders, c.1640–c.1666' (Unpublished PhD thesis, Trinity College Dublin, 2007), pp. 128–9.

205. Farrell, *The 'Mere Irish'*, pp. 243–5.

206. Farrell, *The 'Mere Irish'*, pp. 243, 247–8, 271. Depositions of Nicholas Simpson, 6 April 1643, TCD, Ms 834, f. 184 and Ellenor Fullerton, 16 Sept 1642, TCD, Ms 836, f. 50r.

207. Gerard Boate, *Irelands Naturall History* (London, 1652), p. 89.

208. Brian Mac Cuarta, 'Religious violence against settlers in south Ulster, 1641–2' in Edwards, Lenihan, and Tait (eds.), *Age of Atrocity*, pp. 154–75.

209. Deposition of Robert Maxwell, 22 August 1642, TCD, Ms 809, ff. 5r–12v, especially ff. 6v–7r.

210. Priyamvada Gopal, *Insurgent Empire. Anticolonial Resistance and British Dissent* (London, 2019).

211. N. J. A. Williams (ed.), *Pairlement Chlionne Tomáis* (Dublin, 1981), pp. xi–lviii, 74–6, 83, 100–1, 107 (quote).

212. Canny, *Imagining Ireland's Pasts*, chapter 2 and *Making Ireland British*, pp. 426–7; B. O'Buachalla, 'James our True King: The ideology of Irish royalism in the seventeenth century' in D. George Boyce, Robert Eccleshall, and Vincent Geoghegan (eds.), *Political Thought in Ireland since the Seventeenth Century* (London, 1993), p. 10.

213. Quoted in McKibben, 'In their "owne countre"', p. 58.

214. Brian Ó Cuiv, 'The Irish language in the early modern period' in *New History of Ireland*, III, p. 526.

215. Micheál Mac Craith, 'Literature in Irish, c.1550–1690: from the Elizabethan settlement to the Battle of the Boyne' in Margaret Kelleher and Philip O'Leary (eds.), *The Cambridge History of Irish Literature, Volume 1 to 1890* (2 vols., Cambridge, 2006), p. 215.

216. Diarmaid Ó Doibhlin, 'The plantation of Ulster: Aspects of Gaelic letters' in Ó Ciardha and Ó Siochrú (eds.), *The Plantation of Ulster*, pp. 198–217, 202 (quote).

217. John Lynch, *Cambrensis Eversus*, trans. Mathew Kelly (3 vols., Dublin, 1851–2), III, p. 75.

218. David Brown, 'Free, and unfree: Ireland and Barbados, 1620–1660' in Finola O'Kane and Ciaran O'Neill (eds.), *Ireland, Slavery and the Caribbean: Interdisciplinary Perspectives* (Manchester, 2023), pp. 54–73.

219. John Cunningham, 'Transplantation to Connacht, 1641–1680: Theory and Practice' (Unpublished PhD thesis, NUI, Galway, 2009), pp. 344–5, also pp. 212–19. Also see John Cunningham, 'The transplanters' certificates and the historiography of Cromwellian Ireland', *Irish Historical Studies*, 37 (2011), pp. 376–95.

220. Micheál Ó Siochrú and David Brown, 'The Down Survey and the Cromwellian Land Settlement' in Ohlmeyer (ed.), *The Cambridge History of Ireland*, chapter 23. The precise amount of land that Catholics lost is the subject of debate, see *New History of Ireland*, III, p. 428, Kevin McKenny, 'The Restoration Land Settlement in Ireland: A Statistical Interpretation' in Coleman A. Dennehy (ed.), *Restoration Ireland: Always Settling and Never Settled* (Aldershot, Hampshire and Burlington, VT, 2008), pp. 35–52. For the latest statistics, http://downsurvey.tcd.ie/religion.php.

221. Brown, *Empire and Enterprise: Money*.

222. Nicholas Canny, 'The Origins of Empire' in *Oxford History of the British Empire*, pp. 22–3.

223. P. J. Marshall (ed.), *The Oxford History of the British Empire. vol. 2. The Eighteenth Century* (Oxford, 1998), p. 11.

224. Francis G. James, 'Irish Colonial Trade in the Eighteenth Century', *The William and Mary Quarterly*, 20 (1963), pp. 574–84; R. C. Nash, 'Irish Atlantic Trade in the Seventeenth and Eighteenth Centuries', *The William and Mary Quarterly*, 42 (1985), pp. 329–56; David Armitage and Michael J. Braddick (eds.), *The British Atlantic World, 1500–1800* (Basingstoke, Hampshire, 2002; second edition, 2009); Thomas Bartlett, '"This famous island set in a Virginian sea": Ireland in the British Empire, 1690–1801' in Marshall (ed.), *The Oxford History of the British Empire*, pp. 253–75.

225. Quoted (p. 54) in Nuala Zahedieh, 'Economy' in Armitage and Braddick (eds.), *The British Atlantic World*, pp. 53–70.

226. See note 3 above.

227. Jane Fenlon, '"A good painter may get good bread": Thomas Pooley and Garrett Morphey, two gentlemen painters' in Raymond Gillespie and R. F. Foster (eds.), *Irish Provincial Cultures in the Long Eighteenth Century: Making the Middle Sort. Essays for Toby Barnard* (Dublin, 2012), pp. 220–30.

228. Pádraig Lenihan and Keith Sidwell (eds.), *Poema de Hibernia: A Jacobite Latin Epic on the Williamite Wars* (IMC, Dublin, 2018), pp. xxxi, 191 and Éamonn Ó

Ciardha, O'Neill, Sir Neil (Niall) (1657/8–1690), *DIB*, Retrieved 12 Jun. 2022, from https://www.dib.ie/biography/oneill-sir-neil-niall-a6935.

229. Chiu Hsin-Hui, *The Colonial 'Civilizing Process' in Dutch Formosa: 1624–1662* (Leiden, 2008).

230. Susan Kellogg, *Law and the Transformation of Aztec Culture, 1500–1700* (Norman, Oklahoma, 1995); Brian Owensby, *Empire of Law and Indian Justice in Colonial Mexico* (Stanford, 2008); Steve J. Stern, *Peru's Indian Peoples and the Challenge of Spanish Conquest: Huamanga to 1640* (Madison, Wisconsin, 1993). I owe these references to Richard Ross.

CHAPTER 03

1. Daniel Mac Carthy (ed.), ' "Of the takeing awaie of a gentlewoman" as revealed by the documents preserved in her majesty's state paper office', *Journal of the Royal Society of the Antiquaries of Ireland*, 4 (1856–7), pp. 298–311 (quote p. 300).

2. Brian Friel, *Making History* (London, 1989), p. 13.

3. Friel, *Making History*, p. 14.

4. See for example T. W. Moody, F. X. Martin, and F. J. Byrne (eds.), *New History of Ireland*. vol. 3. *Early Modern Ireland, 1534–1691* (Oxford, 1976), where women receive short shrift and do not even merit an index entry.

5. Philippa Levine (ed.). *Gender and Empire* (Oxford, 2004), pp. 1–2 and 'What's British about Gender and Empire? The Problem of Exceptionalism', *Comparative Studies of South Asia, Africa and the Middle East*, 27 (2007), pp. 273–82; Kathleen Wilson, 'Rethinking the Colonial State. Family, Gender, and Governmentality in Eighteenth-Century British Frontiers', *American Historical Review*, 116 (2011), pp. 1295–322.

6. Ann Laura Stoler, 'Colonial Archives and the Arts of Governance', *Archival Science*, 2 (2002), pp. 87–109 (p. 99).

7. Marisa J. Fuentes, *Dispossessed Lives: Enslaved Women, Violence, and the Archive* (Philadelphia, 2016), pp. 5, 7.

8. Michael Roberts, 'Introduction' in Michael Roberts and Simone Clarke (eds.), *Women and Gender in Early Modern Wales* (Cardiff, 2000), pp. 1–13 (quote p. 9).

9. The exceptions are the pioneering works by Margaret MacCurtain and Donncha Ó Corráin (eds.), *Women in Irish Society: The Historical Dimension* (Dublin, 1978) and Margaret MacCurtain and Mary O'Dowd (eds.) *Women in Early Modern Ireland* (Dublin, 1991); Mary O'Dowd, *History of Women in Ireland 1500–1800* (London, 2005), 'Women and the Irish Chancery Court in the Late Sixteenth and Early Seventeenth Centuries', *Irish Historical Studies*, 31 (1999), pp. 470–87, 'Women and the Colonial Experience in Ireland, c.1550–1650' in Terry Brotherstone et al. (eds.), *Gendering Scottish History: An International Approach* (Glasgow, 1999), 'Women and Paid Work in Ireland, 1500–1800' in Bernadette Whelan (ed.), *Women and Paid Work in Ireland* (Dublin, 2000), 'Women and the Law in Early Modern Ireland' in Christine Meek (ed.), *Women in Renaissance and Early Modern Europe* (Dublin, 2000), and 'Men, Women,

Children and the Family, 1550–1730' in Jane Ohlmeyer (ed.), *The Cambridge History of Ireland*. vol. 2. *Early Modern Ireland, 1550–1730* (Cambridge, 2018), chapter 12; Maria Luddy and Mary O'Dowd, *Marriage in Ireland 1660–1925* (Cambridge, 2020) and her contributions to Angela Bourke et al. (eds.), *The Field Day Anthology of Irish Writing: Irish Women's Writing and Traditions* (2 vols., Cork, 2002; vols. IV and V of the *Field Day Anthology*). There are other important works by Dianne Hall, 'Sexual and Family Violence in Europe' in Robert Antony, Stuart Carroll, and Caroline Dodds Pennock (eds.), *The Cambridge World History of Violence*: vol. 3 (Cambridge, 2020), pp. 274–91, 'Fear, Gender and Violence in Early Modern Ireland' in Michael Champion and Andrew Lynch (eds.), *Understanding Emotions in Early Europe* (Turnhout, Belgium, 2015), pp. 215–32 and '"Most barbarously and inhumaine maner butchered": Masculinity, Trauma, and Memory in Early Modern Ireland' in Fionnuala Dillane, Naomi McAreavey, and Emilie Price (eds.), *The Body in Pain in Irish Literature and Culture* (London, 2016), pp. 41–7; and Clodagh Tait, 'Safely delivered: childbirth, wet-nursing, gossip-feasts and churching in Ireland, c. 1530–1690', *Irish Journal of Economic and Social History*, 30 (2003), pp. 1–23, '"Whereat his wife tooke great greef & died": dying of sorrow and killing in anger in seventeenth-century Ireland' in Michael J. Braddick and Phil Withington (eds.), *Popular Culture and Political Agency in Early Modern England and Ireland: Essays in Honour of John Walter* (Woodbridge, 2017), pp. 268–84, and 'Good ladies and ill wives: women on Boyle's estates' in David Edwards and Colin Rynne (eds.), *The Colonial World of Richard Boyle First Earl of Cork* (Dublin, 2018), pp. 205–22.

10. Especially by Marie Louise Coolahan, *Women, Writing, and Language in Early Modern Ireland* (Oxford, 2010) and '"And this deponent further sayeth": orality, print and the 1641 depositions' in Marc Caball and Andrew Carpenter (eds.), *Oral and Print Cultures in Ireland 1600–1900* (Dublin, 2010), pp. 107–26; and Naomi McAreavey, 'Female alliances in Cromwellian Ireland: the social and political network of Elizabeth Butler, marchioness of Ormonde', *Irish Historical Studies* 45 (2021), 22–42, 'Portadown, 1641: Memory and the 1641 Depositions', *Irish University Review*, 47 (2017), pp. 15–31, 'Re(-)Membering Women: Protestant Women's Victim Testimonies during the Irish Rising of 1641', *Journal of the Northern Renaissance*, 2 (2010). http://www.northernrenaissance. org/re-membering-women-protestant-womens-victim-testimonies-during-the-irish-rising-of-1641/ accessed 5 March 2019, '"Paper bullets": gendering the 1641 rebellion in the writings of Lady Elizabeth Dowdall and Lettice Fitzgerald, baroness of Offaly' in Thomas Herron and Michael Potterton (eds.), *Ireland in the Renaissance, c.1540–1660* (Dublin, 2007), pp. 311–24 and Julie A. Eckerle and Naomi McAreavey (eds.), *Women's Life Writing and Early Modern Ireland* (Lincoln Nebraska, 2019).

11. Something that Gerard Farrell has done effectively as he reclaims the stories of the native Irish from official and legal records, *The 'Mere Irish' and the Colonisation of Ulster, 1570–1641* (London, 2017). Also see Clodagh Tait, 'Progress, challenges

and opportunities in early modern gender history, c. 1550–1720', *Irish Historical Studies*, 46 (2022), pp. 244–69.

12. For an important alternative perspective see Brendan Kane, 'Masculinity and political geographies in England, Ireland and North America', *European Review of History: Revue européenne d'histoire*, 22 (2015), pp. 595–619.

13. As occurred in the wake of the American Civil War and conflicts of the twentieth century, when war served as a catalyst 'to shake up the social and political orders', Kaitlyn Webster, Chong Chen, and Kyle Beardsley, 'Conflict, Peace, and the Evolution of Women's Empowerment', *International Organization* 73 (2019), pp. 255–89 examine the period 1900 to 2015 and 'find strong support for arguments positing that, at least in the short and medium term, war shakes up established social and political orders and creates an opportunity for gains in women's empowerment' (p. 256). Also see Helga Hernes, Kathleen Kuehnast, and Chantal de Jonge Oudraat (eds.), *Women and War: Power and Protection in the 21st Century* (Washington DC, 2011). Similarly, for the American Civil War see Stephanie McCurry, *Women's War Fighting and Surviving the American Civil War* (Cambridge, Mass., 2019) and Confederate Reckoning: Power and Politics in the Civil War South (Cambridge, Mass., 2012).

14. Deana Rankin (ed.), *Landgartha. A Tragie-Comedy* by Henry Burnell (Dublin, 2013), p. 44.

15. Alan J. Fletcher, *Drama and the Performing Arts in Pre-Cromwellian Ireland* (Cambridge, 2001), p. 450.

16. Jane Stevenson, *Women Latin Poets: Language, Gender, and Authority, from Antiquity to the Eighteenth Century* (Oxford, 2005).

17. Rankin (ed.), *Landgartha*, p. 12.

18. Christopher Morash, *A History of Irish Theatre 1601–2000* (Cambridge, 2002), pp. 8–9 and Anne Fogarty, 'Literature in English, 1550–1690: from the Elizabethan settlement to the Battle of the Boyne' in Margaret Kelleher and Philip O'Leary (eds.), *The Cambridge History of Irish Literature, Volume 1 to 1890* (2 vols., Cambridge, 2008), pp. 165–6.

19. Quoted in Sabina Sharkey, *Ireland and the Iconography of Rape: Colonisation, Constraint, and Gender* (London, 1994), p. 14. Also see Joyce Lorimer (ed.), *Sir Walter Ralegh's Discoverie of Guiana* (Hakluyt Society, London, 2006); Carolyn Arena, 'Aphra Behn's *Oroonoko*, Indian Slavery, and the Anglo-Dutch Wars' in L. H. Roper, *The Torrid Zone: Caribbean Colonization and Cultural Interaction in the Long Seventeenth Century* (Columbia, South Carolina, 2018), pp. 31–45. Also see Brian Sandberg, ' "Generous Amazons came to the breach": besieged women, agency and subjectivity during the French Wars of Religion', *Gender and History*, 16, 3 (2004), pp. 654–88.

20. Rankin (ed.), *Landgartha*, p. 94.

21. Rankin (ed.), *Landgartha*, p. 97.

22. Rankin (ed.), *Landgartha*, p. 145.

23. Rankin (ed.), *Landgartha*, p. 153.

24. Marie Sophie Hingst, 'One phenomenon, three perspectives. English colonial strategies in Ireland revisited, 1603–1680' (Unpublished PhD, Trinity College

Dublin, 2017), pp. 54–6 and Andrew Murphy, *But the Irish Sea Betwixt Us: Ireland, Colonialism and Renaissance Literature* (Lexington, Kentucky, 1999), p. 127.

25. Bourke et al. (eds.), *The Field Day Anthology of Irish Writing*, IV, p. 400.

26. Anne Fogarty, 'Literature in English, 1550–1690: from the Elizabethan settlement to the Battle of the Boyne' in Kelleher and O'Leary (eds), *The Cambridge History of Irish Literature*, pp. 160–1.

27. Nessa Malone, 'Henry Burnell's *Landgartha*: family, law and revolution on the Irish stage' in Coleman A. Dennehy (ed.), *Law and Revolution in Seventeenth-Century Ireland* (Dublin, 2020), p. 86; Patrick Darcy, *An argument delivered by Patrick Darcy, esquire by the express order of the House of Commons in the Parliament of Ireland, 9 iunii, 1641* (Waterford, 1643), p. 91.

28. Malone, 'Henry Burnell's *Landgartha*', p. 84; Angelina Lynch (ed.), *Cynthia* by Richard Nugent (Dublin, 2010), pp. 25–6, 44; Clare Carroll, *Circe's Cup: Cultural Transformations in Early Modern Ireland* (Cork, 2001); and Sharkey, *Ireland and the Iconography of Rape*.

29. James Kelly, 'A Most Inhuman and Barbarous Piece of Villainy': An Exploration of the Crime of Rape in Eighteenth-Century Ireland', *Eighteenth-Century Ireland / Iris an dá chultúr*, 10 (1995), p. 82.

30. Quoted in Carroll, *Circe's Cup*, p. 3.

31. Éamonn Ó Ciardha, *Ireland and the Jacobite Cause, 1685–1766* (Dublin, 2002).

32. O'Dowd, *A History of Women in Ireland*, p. 252.

33. Quoted in Nigel Everett, *The Woods of Ireland. A History, 700–1800* (Dublin, 2015), p. 111.

34. Ulinka Rublack, 'Wench and maiden: women, war and the pictorial function of the feminine in German cities in the early modern period', *History Workshop Journal*, 44 (1997), pp. 1–21; and Barbara J. Baines, *Representing Rape in the English Early Modern Period* (Lewiston, 2003).

35. James Cranford, *The Teares of Ireland* (London, 1642). Also see Dianne Hall and Elizabeth Malcolm, '"The rebels Turkish tyranny": understanding sexual violence in Ireland during the 1640s', *Gender and History*, 22 (2010), pp. 55–74.

36. Daniel Roberts, '"An example to the whole world": patriotism and imperialism in early Irish fiction' in Moyra Haslett (ed.), *Irish Literature in Transition 1700–1780* (Cambridge, 2020), pp. 214–5.

37. Malone, 'Henry Burnell's *Landgartha*', p. 69.

38. Luddy and O'Dowd, *Marriage in Ireland*, p. 287. Brendan Kane explores what this meant for Irish masculinity, see 'Masculinity and political geographies in England, Ireland and North America', pp. 610–11.

39. Carroll, *Circe's Cup*, p. 3.

40. Carroll, *Circe's Cup*, p. 28.

41. Carroll, *Circe's Cup*, p. 44; Vincent P. Carey, 'Atrocity and history: Grey, Spenser and the slaughter at Smerwick (1580)' in David Edwards, Pádraig Lenihan, and Clodagh Tait (eds.), *Age of Atrocity. Violence and Political Conflict in Early Modern Ireland* (Dublin, 2007), pp. 79–94, p. 80; and Murphy, *But the Irish Sea Betwixt Us*, pp. 80–9.

42. Anthony Pagden, *The Fall of Natural Man: The American Indian and the Origins of Comparative Ethnology* (Cambridge, 1982), p. 26; John Patrick Montaño,

' "Dycheyng and Hegeying": The Material Culture of the Tudor Plantations in Ireland' in Fiona Bateman and Lionel Pilkington (eds.), *Studies in Settler Colonialism: Politics, Identity and Culture* (Basingstoke, 2011), pp. 47–62 and *The Roots of English Colonialism in Ireland* (Cambridge, 2011).

43. Malone, 'Henry Burnell's *Landgartha*', p. 79.

44. Rankin (ed.), *Landgartha*, p. 60; Fogarty, 'Literature in English, 1550–1690', pp. 165–6; and Jane Stevenson and Peter Davidson (eds.), *Early Modern Women Poets. An Anthology* (Oxford, 2001).

45. Vincent Carey, ' "Neither good English nor good Irish": bi-lingualism and identity formation in sixteenth-century Ireland' in Hiram Morgan (ed.), *Political Ideology in Ireland 1541–1641* (Dublin, 1999), pp. 53, 61 (quote).

46. Carey, ' "Neither good English nor good Irish" ', pp. 51–2. The primer forms part of Benjamin Iveagh Library, now in the care of Marsh's Library, Dublin.

47. Mícheál Mac Craith, 'Literature in Irish, *c*.1550–1690: from the Elizabethan settlement to the Battle of the Boyne' in Kelleher and O'Leary (ed.), *The Cambridge History of Irish Literature*, p. 219.

48. Jane Ohlmeyer, *Making Ireland English: The Irish Aristocracy in the Seventeenth Century* (New Haven and London, 2012), pp. 187–9.

49. Gilbert (ed.), *Irish Confederation*, I, p. 2. Sir John Temple, *The Irish Rebellion . . .* (London, 1679) pp. 27–8. Also see Gilbert (ed.), *Irish Confederation*, I, p. 2 and *A Letter from a person of honour . . . written to the earl of Castlehaven* (London, 1681) p. 31.

50. Ted McCormick, ' "A proportionable mixture": William Petty, Political Arithmetic, and the Transmutation of the Irish' in Coleman A. Dennehy (ed.), *Restoration Ireland. Always Settling and Never Settled* (Aldershot, Hampshire and Burlington, VT, 2008), pp. 123–39, (quotes pp. 126–7) and Ted McCormick, *Human Empire. Mobility and Demographic Thought in the British Atlantic World, 1500–1800* (Oxford, 2022), pp. 5, 176–8.

51. Ted McCormick, *William Petty and the Ambitions of Political Arithmetic* (Oxford, 2009), especially chapter 5.

52. Hingst, 'One phenomenon, three perspectives', pp. 24–34.

53. Quoted in Stephen O'Neill, *Staging Ireland: Representations in Shakespeare and Renaissance Drama* (Dublin, 2007), p. 82; Carroll, *Circe's Cup*, p. 50.

54. Edmund Spenser, *A View of the Present State of Ireland* ed. W. L. Renwick (Oxford, 1970), p. 67. Also see Montaño, *The Roots of English Colonialism*, p. 381. Also see Fiona Fitzsimons, 'Fosterage and Gossiprid in Late Medieval Ireland: Some New Evidence' in Patrick Duffy, David Edwards, and Elizabeth Fitzpatrick (eds.), *Gaelic Ireland: Land Lordship and Settlement c. 1250-c. 1650* (Dublin, 2001), pp. 138–42.

55. Spenser, *A View*, p. 61.

56. Spenser, *A View*, pp. 67–8. Also see Vincent Carey, ' "Neither good English nor good Irish": bi-lingualism and identity formation in sixteenth-century Ireland' in Hiram Morgan (ed.), *Political Ideology in Ireland 1541–1641* (Dublin, 1999), p. 49 and Murphy, *But the Irish Sea Betwixt Us*, pp. 73–85.

57. Barnabe Rich, *A New Description of Ireland . . .* (London, 1610), p. 15.

58. Henry Cary, Viscount Falkland, 'To the Well Affected Planters in New Fownde Lande' in Cell (ed.), *Newfoundland Discovered*, pp. 244–5.

59. Amelia Almorza Hidalgo, 'Spanish Women as Agents for a New Material Culture in Colonial Spanish America' in Bartolomé Yun-Casalilla, Ilaria Berti, and Omar Svriz-Wucherer (eds.), *American Globalization, 1492–1850: Trans-Cultural Consumption in Spanish Latin America* (Abingdon, 2022), pp. 78–100.

60. Susan Migden Socolow, *The Women of Colonial Latin America* (2nd edition, Cambridge, 2015), pp. 57, 62 (quote). Also see Sarah E. Owens and Jane E. Mangan (eds.), *Women of the Iberian Atlantic* (Baton Rouge, Louisiana, 2012). I owe these references to Jorge Díaz Ceballos.

61. Ann Marie Plane, *Colonial Intimacies: Indian Marriage in Early New England* (Cornell, 2000), p. 6.

62. Alison Games, *The Web of Empire: English Cosmopolitans in an Age of Expansion, 1560–1660* (Oxford, 2008), pp. 131–2.

63. J. H. Elliott, *Empires of the Atlantic World: Britain and Spain in America 1492–1830* (New Haven, 2006), p. 80.

64. Elliott, *Empires of the Atlantic World,* pp. 81–3, 235 (quote p. 81). Also see Eliga H. Gould, 'Entangled Histories, Entangled Worlds. The English-Speaking Atlantic as a Spanish Periphery', *American Historical Review*, 12 (2007), pp. 764–86 and Ramón A. Gutiérrez, *When Jesus Came, the Corn Mothers Went Away: Marriage, Sexuality, and Power in New Mexico, 1500–1846* (Stanford, 1991).

65. Elliott, *Empires of the Atlantic World*, p. 235.

66. Ann Laura Stoler 'Sexual Affronts and Racial Frontiers: European Identities and the Cultural Politics of Exclusion in Colonial Southeast Asia' in Frederick Cooper and Ann Laura Stoler (eds.), *Tensions of Empire: Colonial Cultures in a Bourgeois World* (Berkeley, 1997), pp. 198–237.

67. Emmett O'Byrne, Aidan Clarke, Judy Barry, Bagenal (O'Neill), Mabel (*c.*1571–95), countess of Tyrone *DIB*. Retrieved 11 Jun. 2022 from https://www.dib.ie/biography/bagenal-oneill-mabel-a6953.

68. *CSPI, 1603–1606* (London, 1872), p. 409.

69. Quoted in Paul Walsh, *Will and Family of H. O'Neill, Earl of Tyrone* (Dublin, 1930), p. 21.

70. Dr Stokes, 'Dudley Loftus: A Dublin Antiquary of the Seventeenth Century', *Proceedings of the Royal Society of the Antiquaries Ireland*, fifth series, 1 (1890–1), pp. 17–30.

71. Ohlmeyer, *Making Ireland English*, pp. 191, 287; John Kingston, 'Catholic Families of the Pale', *Reportum Novum: Dublin Diocesan Historical Record*, 1:2 (1956), pp. 323–50.

72. R. Morgan, *The Welsh and the Shaping of Early Modern Ireland 1558–1641* (Woodbridge, 2014), p. 116.

73. Mabel was still alive in 1686 when she witnessed her son's will, NLI, Fingal Papers 'Report on Private Collections # 6: Fingall papers'. Also see Chapter 6 below.

74. Ohlmeyer, *Making Ireland English*, p. 142 and University of Bangor, Mostyn papers, Ms 5422, deed of 14 March 1650–1.

75. Deposition of Suzanna Stockdale, undated, TCD, Ms 810, ff. 94v–95r.

76. Ohlmeyer, *Making Ireland English*, pp. 197–201.

77. Patrick Little, 'The Earl of Cork and the Fall of the Earl of Strafford', *Historical Journal*, 39 (1996), pp. 619–35 and 'The Geraldine ambitions of the first earl of Cork', *Irish Historical Studies*, 23 (2002).

78. Dorothea Townshend, *The Life and Letters of the Great Earl of Cork* (London, 1904), pp. 478–9.

79. BL, Add. Ms 40,860 Annesley's diary entry for 9 September 1672.

80. Mark Girouard, 'Curraghmore, co. Waterford, Eire', *Country Life* (1963), pp. 257–8.

81. Ohlmeyer, *Making Ireland English*, pp. 184–6.

82. Ohlmeyer, *Making Ireland English*, pp. 187–9 *and* Colm Lennon, 'Religious and social change in early modern Limerick: the testimony of the Sexton family papers' in Liam Irwin and Gearóid Ó Tuathaigh (eds.), *Limerick: History and Society* (Dublin, 2009), pp. 114–18, 121–5.

83. Declan Downey, 'Purity of blood and purity of faith in early modern Ireland' in Alan Ford and John McCafferty (eds.), *The Origins of Sectarianism in Early Modern Ireland* (Cambridge, 2005), pp. 226–8.

84. N. J. A. Williams (ed.), *Pairlement Chlionne Tomáis* (Dublin, 1981); Nicholas Canny, *Imagining Ireland's Pasts: Early Modern Ireland through the Centuries* (Oxford, 2021), pp. 113–14; Mac Craith, 'Literature in Irish, c.1550–1690', pp. 221–2.

85. Clodagh Tait, 'Good ladies and ill wives', pp. 205–22 and 'Writing the social and cultural history of Ireland, 1550–1660: wills as example and inspiration' in Sarah Covington, Vincent P. Carey, and Valerie McGowan-Doyle (eds.), *Early Modern Ireland: New Sources, Methods and Perspectives* (Abingdon, 2019), chapter 2.

86. John Gibney, 'The most controversial documents in Irish history?', *History Ireland*, 19 (2011), pp. 18–19. The best introduction to the 1641 Depositions remains Aidan Clarke 'The 1641 depositions' in P. Fox (ed.), *Treasures of the Library, Trinity College Dublin* (Dublin, 1986), pp. 111–22.

87. Deposition of John Crewes, 1 Sept. 1653, TCD, Ms 829, f. 454r.

88. TCD, Ms 826, ff. 222r–v.

89. Deposition of Ellen Matchett, 3 Sept. 1642, TCD, Ms 836, ff. 58r–59v.

90. Annaleigh Margey and Elaine Murphy, 'Backsliders from the Protestant Religion': Apostasy in the 1641 Depositions', *Archivium Hibernicum*, 65 (2012), pp. 82–188.

91. Deposition of Margery Bellingham, 11 May 1642, TCD, Ms 812, ff. 63r–v.

92. Deposition of Margarett Fagon, 19 Feb. 1642, TCD, Ms 809, f. 303r.

93. Deposition of Jane Smith, 7 Jan. 1644, TCD, Ms 816, f. 232r.

94. Colin Kidd, *British Identities before Nationalism: Ethnicity and Nationhood in the Atlantic World, 1600–1800* (Cambridge, 1999), pp. 146–81.

95. Alison Forrestal, *Catholic Synods in Ireland, 1600–1690* (Dublin, 1998), p. 105.

96. Charles Ivar McGrath, *Ireland and Empire 1692–1770* (London, 2012), pp. 27, 30; and Ian McBride, *Eighteenth Century Ireland: The Isle of Slaves* (Dublin, 2009), p. 146.

97. Dagmar Freist, 'One body, two confessions: Mixed marriages in Germany' in Ulinka Rublack (eds.), *Gender in Early Modern German History* (Cambridge, 2002), pp. 275–303 and 'Crossing Religious Borders: The Experience of Religious

Difference and its Impact on Mixed Marriages in Eighteenth-Century Germany' in C. Scott Dixon, Dagmar Freist, and Mark Greengrass (eds.), *Living with Religious Diversity in Early-Modern Europe* (Farnham, 2009), pp. 203–24.

98. Benjamin Kaplan, *Divided by Faith: Religious Conflict and the Practice of Toleration in Early Modern Europe* (Cambridge, Mass. and London, 2007), pp. 8–11, 263–93 (quote p. 263) and 'Intimate Negotiations: Husbands and Wives of Opposing Faiths in Eighteenth-Century Holland' in Scott Dixon, Freist, and Greengrass (eds.), *Living with Religious Diversity*, pp. 225–48.

99. Though the context was very different, for interesting parallels see Heidi V. Scott, *Contested Territory: Mapping Peru in the Sixteenth and Seventeenth Centuries* (Southbend, Indiana, 2009).

100. Hall, 'Fear, Gender and Violence in Early Modern Ireland', pp. 215–32; and William Palmer, 'Gender, Violence, and Rebellion in Tudor and Early Stuart Ireland', *Sixteenth Century Journal*, 23 (1992), pp. 699–712.

101. Luddy and O'Dowd, *Marriage in Ireland*; Donald Jackson, *Intermarriage in Ireland 1550–1650* (Montreal, 1970); Tait, ' "Good ladies and ill wives" ', pp. 205–22; and Bronagh McShane, 'Clerical Wives in Tudor and Early Stuart Ireland' in Covington, Carey, and McGowan-Doyle (eds.), *Early Modern Ireland*, chapter 4.

102. Jane Ohlmeyer, 'Uncovering Widows in the 1641 Depositions' in Marian Lyons, Terence Dooley, and Salvador Ryan (eds.), *The Historian as Detective: Uncovering Irish Pasts* (Dublin, 2021), pp. 121–4.

103. For some preliminary work on titled female moneylenders see Ohlmeyer, *Making Ireland*, p. 380; and Patricia Stapleton, ' "In Monies and Other Requisites": The 1641 Depositions and the Social Role of Credit in Early Seventeenth-Century Ireland' in Eamon Darcy, Annaleigh Margey, and Elaine Murphy (eds.), *The 1641 Depositions and the Irish Rebellion* (London, 2012), pp. 65–78.

104. Amy Froide, *Never Married: Singlewomen in Early Modern England* (Oxford, 2005), p. 16.

105. Amy Erickson, *Women and Property in Early Modern England* (New York and London 1993). In the absence of pre-war figures for Ireland, one point of comparison is Peter Laslett's sample of 100 rural and urban communities throughout early modern England, which suggest that widows made up 14.9 per cent of the adult female population and single women accounted for 30.2 per cent, J. M. Bennet and Amy Froide (eds.), *Singlewomen in the European Past, 1250–1800* (Philadelphia, 1999), p. 16.

106. Ohlmeyer, 'Uncovering Widows in the 1641 Depositions', pp. 121–4.

107. Deposition of Grace Smith, 25 Feb. 1642[3], TCD, Ms 814, f. 164r.

108. As in England the boundaries between these categories were hierarchal yet fluid and overlapping Keith Wrightson, *English Society 1580–1680* (London, 1982).

109. In the case where a deponent remarried, the profession of the deponent's first husband is only used for statistical purposes. If, however, only the subsequent husband's profession is known then that is the one that is used.

110. The classic work remains Keith Wrightson, *A Social History of England, 1500–1750* (Yale, 2017). On the 'middling sort' see Margaret Hunt, *The Middling*

Sort: Commerce, Gender, and the Family in England, 1680–1780 (Berkeley and LA, 1996) and Tara Hamling and Catherine Richardson, *A Day at Home in Early Modern England: Material Culture and Domestic Life, 1500–1700* (New Haven and London, 2017).

111. Raymond Gillespie, *Reading Ireland: Print, Reading and Social Change in Early Modern Ireland* (Manchester, 2005), *Devoted People. Belief and Religion in Early Modern Ireland* (Manchester, 1997) and 'The Circulation of Print in Seventeenth-Century Ireland', *Studia Hibernica*, 29 (1995–7), pp. 31–58; Jane Ohlmeyer, 'Society: The changing role of print—Ireland (to 1660)' in Joad Raymond (ed.), *The Oxford History of Popular Print Culture, Volume I* (Oxford, 2011), pp. 39–49.

112. Alexandra Shepard, *Accounting for Oneself: Worth, Status and Social Order in Early Modern England* (Oxford, 2015), p. 24.

113. David Cressy, *Literacy and the Social Order: Reading and Writing in Tudor and Stuart England* (Cambridge, 1980), p. 2, chapter 3; Adam Fox, *Oral and Literate Culture in England 1500–1700* (Oxford, 2000), pp. 17–19; Adam Fox and Daniel Woolf (eds.), *The Spoken Word: Oral Culture in Britain* (Manchester, 2003), pp. 22–3.

114. Nicholas Canny, 'The 1641 Depositions as a Source for the Writing of Social History: County Cork as a Case Study' in Patrick O'Flanagan and Cornelius G. Buttimer (eds.), *Cork. History and Society* (Dublin, 1993), pp. 251, 265–67; Susan Flavin, 'Domestic Materiality in Ireland, 1550–1730' in Ohlmeyer (ed.), *The Cambridge History of Ireland*, p. 322; Heidi J. Coburn, 'The built environment and material culture of Ireland in the 1641 Depositions, 1600–1653' (Unpublished PhD thesis, Cambridge, 2017); Farrell, *The 'Mere Irish'*, especially chapter 5. Also see Lorna Weatherill, *Consumer Behaviour and Material Culture in Britain 1660–1760* (London, 1996) which examines the consumption and use of goods among middle ranking households, between the upper gentry and the labourers in England.

115. Jane Fenlon, *Goods and Chattels: A Survey of Early Household Inventories in Ireland* (Dublin, 2003).

116. Hidalgo, 'Spanish Women as Agents for a New Material Culture in Colonial Spanish America' in Yun-Casalilla, Berti, and Svriz-Wucherer (eds.), *American Globalization*, pp. 78–100. In the same volume also see José I. Gasch-Tomás, 'Elites, Women and Chinese Porcelain in New Spain and in Andalusia, Circa 1600: A Global History', pp. 225–44.

117. Deposition of Anne Cappar, 4 Jan. 1642, TCD, Ms 809, ff. 261r–v.

118. Deposition of Jane Mansfeild, 3 Jan. 1642, TCD, Ms 816, ff. 122r–123v.

119. Deposition of Isabell Staples, 3 Jan. 1642, TCD, Ms 833, ff. 60rv.

120. Deposition of Dame Jane Forbes, 3 Sept. 1642, TCD, Ms 817, ff. 187r–v.

121. Amanda Capern, Briony McDonagh, and Jennifer Aston (eds.), *Women and the Land, 1500–1900* (Woodbridge, 2019), especially Amanda Flather, 'Women, work and land: The spatial dynamics of gender relations in early modern England, 1550–1750', pp. 29–50.

122. http://downsurvey.tcd.ie/ accessed 8 March 2019. The Down Survey Maps website, published online in 2013, provides digital images of all the surviving

Down Survey maps at parish, barony, and county level, together with the written descriptions of each barony and parish that accompanied the original maps. There are *c.*2,000 maps covering over 60,000 townlands. Taken in the years 1656–8, under the direction of Sir William Petty, the Down Survey is the first ever detailed land survey on a national scale anywhere in the world.

123. At least five per cent (*c.*295 out of *c.*9,200) of the people mentioned as land-holders in 1641 were women, although the final figure may be much higher. There are inconsistencies, for example, around the recording of marriage settlements. I owe this figure to Peter Crooks, who is leading the 'Beyond 2022' project, https://beyond2022.ie, accessed 28 July 2022.

124. Deposition of Mary Ward, 2 April 1642, TCD, Ms 834, f. 176r.

125. Deposition of Agnes Windsor, 4 Jan. 1642, TCD, Ms 835, f. 188r.

126. Deposition of Jane Stewart, 23 April 1644, TCD, Ms 831, ff. 73r–74r.

127. Deposition of Ann Baker, 5 Oct. 1642, TCD, Ms 822, f. 103r.

128. Deposition of Sarah Roades, 24 Feb. 1645, TCD, Ms 810, f. 299r.

129. Maria Ågren and Amy Louise Erickson (eds.), *The Marital Economy in Scandinavia and Britain, 1400–1900* (Aldershot, 2005); Maria Ågren (ed.), *Making a Living, Making a Difference: Gender and Work in Early Modern European Society* (Oxford, 2017); Julie Hardwick, *Family Business: Litigation and the Political Economies of Daily Life in Early Modern France* (Oxford, 2009) and *Practice of Patriarchy: Gender and the Politics of Household Authority in Early Modern France* (Pennsylvania, 1998); Janine M. Lanza, 'Women and work' in Jane Couchman and Allyson M. Poska (eds.), *The Ashgate Research Companion to Women and Gender in Early Modern Europe* (Farnham, 2013), pp. 279–98.

130. Jane Whittle, 'Enterprising widows and active wives: Women's unpaid work in the household economy of early modern England', *The History of the Family*, 19 (2014), pp. 283–300 (quote p. 297).

131. Whittle, 'Enterprising widows and active wives', p. 286.

132. Historians emphasise the links between credit and credit networks, family formation, financial stability/instability, and commercialisation of land both among urban and village dwellers in early modern England, Scotland, Sweden, France, and Germany, Susan Dyer Amussen, *An Ordered Society: Gender and Class in Early Modern England* (New York, 1988) and ' "Being stirred to much unquietness": Violence and domestic violence in early modern England', *Journal of Women's History*, 6 (1994), pp. 70–89; Joanne Bailey, *Unquiet Lives: Marriage and Marriage Breakdown in England, 1660–1800* (Cambridge, 2003); Maria Ågren, 'Providing security for others: Swedish women in early modern credit networks' in Elise M. Dermineur (ed.), *Women and Credit in Pre-industrial Europe* (Turnhout, 2018), pp. 121–42; Govind P. Sreenivasan, *The Peasants of Ottobeuren, 1487–1726: A Rural Society in Early Modern Europe* (Cambridge, 2004); and Cathryn Spence, *Women, Credit, and Debt in Early Modern Scotland* (Manchester, 2016).

133. For examples see deposition of Lindsey Ellin, 29 April 1642, TCD, Ms 810, ff. 163r–164v and deposition of Elizabeth Stevens, 17 Oct. 1642, TCD, Ms 829, ff. 163r–164v.

134. For example, the losses of a pre-war widow from Youghal, Frances Kerrine, recorded on 9 Nov. 1642, were £899 of which £493 (55 per cent) was in debts, deposition of ffrannces Kerrine, 9 November 1642, TCD, Ms 823, f. 216r. For Grace Carter, a pre-war widow from Tipperary, 'good debts' (totalling £21-13-0) due from 11 men, all named, deposition of Grace Carter, 7 August 1642, TCD, Ms 821, ff. 98r–v.

135. Anne Laurence, *Women in England 1500–1760: A Social History* (London, 1994), p. 131.

136. Whittle, 'Enterprising widows and active wives', p. 289; Craig Muldrew, ' "A Mutual Assent of her Mind"? Women, Debt, Litigation and Contract in Early Modern England', *History Workshop Journal*, 55 (2003), pp. 47–71; and Spence, *Women, Credit, and Debt in Early Modern Scotland*.

137. Deposition of Katherin Allard, 20 July 1642, TCD, Ms 823, f. 33r.

138. Kenneth Nicholls, 'The other massacre: English killings of Irish, 1641–3' in Edwards, Lenihan, and Tait (eds.), *Age of Atrocity*, pp. 176–19; and Joan Redmond, 'Memories of violence and New English identities in early modern Ireland', *Historical Research*, 89 (2016), pp. 708–29.

139. Ken Wiggins, *A Place of Great Consequence: Archaeological Excavations at King John's Castle, Limerick, 1990–8* (Dublin, 2016); Mark Clinton, Linda Fibiger, and Damian Shiels, 'Archaeology of massacre: The Carrickmines mass grave and the siege of March 1642' in Edwards, Lenihan, and Tait (eds.), *Age of Atrocity*, pp. 192–203; and Emmett O'Byrne, 'The Walshes and the massacre at Carrickmines', *Archaeology Ireland*, 17, 3 (2003), pp 8–11. Also see Barra Ó Donnabhain and Maria-Cecilia Lozada (eds.), *Archaeological Human Remains: Legacies of Imperialism, Communism and Colonialism* (New York, 2018); Damian Shiels, 'Siege and slaughter', *Archaeology Ireland*, 33, 4 (2019), pp. 35–8 and 'Identifying and interpreting Ireland's post-medieval conflict', *Journal of Irish Archaeology*, 17 (2008), pp. 137–52; Paul O'Keefe and Damian Shiels, ' "A more miserable siege hath not been seen" ', *Archaeology Ireland*, 22 (2008), pp. 10–13; William O. Frazer, 'Field of Fire: Evidence for Wartime Conflict in a 17th-Century Cottier Settlement in County Meath, Ireland', *Journal of Conflict Archaeology*, 3 (2007), pp. 173–95.

140. TCD, Ms 837, ff. 4, 11.

141. Deposition of Joseph Wheeler, Elizabeth Gilbert, Rebecca Hill, Thomas Lewis, Jonas Wheeler, Patrick Maxwell, John Kevan, 5 July 1643, TCD, Ms 812, ff. 202r–208v. Also see Patricia Palmer, *Language and Conquest in Early Modern Ireland: English Renaissance Literature and Elizabethan Imperial Expansion* (Cambridge, 2001), chapter 4, 'Missing Bodies, Absent Bards: Spenser, Shakespeare and a Crisis in Criticism', *English Literary Renaissance* 36.3 (2006), pp. 376–95, ' "A headlesse Ladie" and "a horses loade of heads": Writing the Beheading', *Renaissance Quarterly* 60 (2007), pp. 25–57, *The Severed Head and the Grafted Tongue: Translating Violence in Early Modern Ireland.* (Cambridge,

2014) and 'Gender, Violence, and Rebellion', pp. 699–712; and Nicci MacLeod and Barbara Fennell, 'Lexico-grammatical portraits of vulnerable women in war: The 1641 Depositions', *Journal of Historical Pragmatics*, 13 (2012), pp. 259–90.

142. Tait, '"Whereat his wife tooke great greef & died"', pp. 268–84; and Hall, 'Fear, Gender and Violence in Early Modern Ireland', pp. 215–32.

143. Hall, '"Most barbarously and inhumaine maner butchered"', pp. 41–7; Joan Redmond, 'Religion, civility and the "British" of Ireland in the 1641 Irish rebellion', *Irish Historical Studies*, 45 (2021), pp. 1–21.

144. Charles Zika, 'Visualising Violence in Reformation Europe' in Antony, Carroll, and Dodds Pennock (eds.). *The Cambridge World History of Violence*, pp. 634–59.

145. Judith Pollman, *Memory in Early Modern Europe 1500–1800* (Oxford, 2017); Ethan Shagan, 'Constructing discord: ideology, propaganda, and English response to the Irish Rebellion of 1641', *Journal of British Studies*, 36 (1997), pp. 4–34; Igor Pérez Tostado, 'An Irish Black Legend? 1641 and the Iberian Atlantic' in Jane Ohlmeyer and Micheál Ó Siochrú (eds.), *Ireland 1641: Contexts and Reactions* (Manchester, 2013), chapter 13.

146. Clodagh Tait, 'Whereat his wife tooke great greef & died', pp. 268–84. More generally, Penny Roberts, 'Intercommunal Violence in Europe' in Antony, Carroll, and Dodds Pennock (eds.), *The Cambridge World History of Violence*, pp. 531–52.

147. McAreavey, 'Paper bullets', pp. 311–24.

148. Palmer, 'Gender, Violence', pp. 699–712 and MacLeod and Fennell, 'Lexico-grammatical portraits of vulnerable women in war', pp. 259–90.

149. Sarah Covington, 'Those Savage Days of Memory': John Temple and His Narrative of the 1641 Uprising' in Fionnuala Dillane, Naomi McAreavey, and Emilie Price (eds.), *The Body in Pain in Irish Literature and Culture* (London, 2016), pp. 57–76 (quote pp. 59–60).

150. Jane Ohlmeyer, *Civil War and Restoration in the Three Stuart Kingdoms: The Political Career of Randal MacDonnell First Marquis of Antrim (1609–83)* (Cambridge, 1993).

151. Examination of Alice Countess Dowager of Antrim, 9 Feb. 1652[3], TCD, Ms 383, ff. 22r–23r.

152. Examination of Jane Roberts, 17 Aug. 1652, TCD, Ms, 834, f. 188r.

153. Deposition of Robert Maxwell, 22 Aug. 1642, TCD, Ms 809, ff. 5r–12v (quote f. 9r).

154. Farrell, *The 'Mere Irish'*, p. 243.

155. Kaplan, *Divided by Faith*. Also see the various essays in Ole Peter Grell and Bob Scribner (eds.), *Tolerance and Intolerance in the European Reformation* (Cambridge, 1996); Scott Dixon, Freist, and Greengrass (eds.), *Living with Religious Diversity*; Alexandra Walsham, *Charitable Hatred: Tolerance and Intolerance in England, 1500–1700* (Manchester, 2006); Ethan Shagan, *The Rule of Moderation: Violence, Religion and the Politics of Restraint in Early Modern England* (Cambridge, 2011); Laura Lisy-Wagner and Graeme Murdock, 'Tolerance and Intolerance' in Howard Louthan and Graeme Murdock (eds.), *A Companion to the Reformation in Central Europe* (Leiden: Brill, 2015); and Roberts, 'Intercommunal Violence in Europe', pp. 531–52.

156. Kaplan, *Divided by Faith*, p. 263.
157. [Anonymous] *Vertue Rewarded; or, The Irish Princess* eds. Ian Campbell Ross and Anne Markey (Dublin, 2010).
158. *Vertue Rewarded*, pp. 21, 73.
159. See Chapter 6 below for a discussion of Aphra Behn's *Oroonoko*.
160. Games, *The Web of Empire*, pp. 131–2.
161. Ian Campbell Ross, ' "A very knowing American": The Inca Garcilaso de la Vega and Swift's Modest Proposal', *Modern Language Quarterly*, 68 (2007), pp. 493–516.
162. Also his *The Present state of the Ottoman Empire* (1666), *Vertue Rewarded*, pp. 156–7.
163. Roberts, "An example to the whole world", p. 214.
164. Kidd, *British Identities before Nationalism*, pp. 146–81.
165. Carroll, *Circe's Cup*, p. 3.

CHAPTER 04

1. Brian Friel, *Making History* (London, 1989), p. 27.
2. Joep Leerson, *Mere Irish and Fíor-Ghael: Studies in the Idea of Irish Nationality, its Development and Literary Expression prior to the Nineteenth Century* (Cork, 1996) offers the best overview of identity formation among the catholic population in early modern Ireland.
3. David Edwards, 'A haven of popery: English Catholic migration to Ireland in the age of plantation' in Alan Ford and John McCafferty (eds.), *The Origins of Sectarianism in Early Modern Ireland* (Cambridge, 2005), pp. 95–126.
4. Friel, *Making History*, p. 47.
5. Sonia Tycko, 'Bound and Filed: A Seventeenth-Century Service Indenture from a Scattered Archive', *Early American Studies: An Interdisciplinary Journal*, 19 (2021), pp. 166–90 and 'The Legality of Prisoner of War Labour In England, 1648–1655', *Past and Present*, 246 (2020), pp. 35–68.
6. David Brown, 'Free, and unfree: Ireland and Barbados, 1620–1660' in Finola O'Kane and Ciaran O'Neill (eds.), *Ireland, Slavery and the Caribbean: Interdisciplinary Perspectives* (Manchester, 2023), p. 63.
7. David Brown, *Empire and Enterprise: Money, Power and the Adventurers for Irish Land during the British Civil Wars* (Manchester, 2020), pp. 24, 28–30, 64.
8. Brown, 'Free, and unfree', p. 58.
9. BL, Egerton Ms 80, f. 33.
10. *A certificate From the Lord Moor and Sir Henry Titchborne* (London, 1642).
11. John Cunningham, *Conquest and land in Ireland: The Transplantation to Connacht, 1649–1680* (Woodbridge, 2011) and 'The transplanters' certificates and the historiography of Cromwellian Ireland', *Irish Historical Studies*, 37 (2011), pp. 376–95.
12. Micheál Ó Siochrú and David Brown, 'The Down Survey and the Cromwellian Land Settlement' in Jane Ohlmeyer (ed.), *The Cambridge History of Ireland. vol. 2. Early Modern Ireland, 1550–1730* (Cambridge, 2018), chapter 23. Also see Chapter 2 above.

13. P. J. Marshall, 'The English in Asia to 1700' in Canny (ed.), *Oxford History*, I, p. 276; Karl S. Bottigheimer, *English Money and Irish Land: The 'Adventurers' in the Cromwellian Settlement of Ireland* (Oxford, 1971), p. 192.

14. Brown, *Empire and Enterprise*, p. 212.

15. John Lynch, *Cambrensis Eversus*, trans. Matthew Kelly (3 vols., Dublin, 1851–2), III, pp. xxvii, 75.

16. Brown, *Empire and Enterprise*, pp. 169, 181, 205.

17. Richard B. Sheridan, *Sugar and Slavery: An Economic History of the British West Indies, 1623–1775* (Kingston, 1974), pp. 88–90.

18. Sheridan, *Sugar and Slavery*, p. 90.

19. Louis M. Cullen, 'Merchant Communities, the navigation acts and the Irish and Scottish responses' in L. M. Cullen and T. C. Smout (eds.), *Comparative Aspects of Scottish and Irish Social History* (Edinburgh, 1977), pp. 165–76; Brown, *Empire and Enterprise*, p. 216.

20. Brown, *Empire and Enterprise*, p. 179.

21. Clare Carroll, *Circe's Cup: Cultural Transformations in Early Modern Ireland* (Cork, 2001), p. 27; Marie Sophie Hingst, 'One phenomenon, three perspectives. English colonial strategies in Ireland revisited, 1603–1680' (Unpublished PhD thesis, Trinity College Dublin, 2017), pp. 211, 246; and William Petty, *Political Arithmetick, or, A Discourse concerning the Extent and Value of Lands, People, Buildings* (London, 1691).

22. David O'Shaughnessy, 'Introduction: "Tolerably Numerous": Recovering the London Irish of the Eighteenth Century', *Eighteenth-Century Life*, 39 (2015), pp. 1–13. Also see Chapter 2 above.

23. Bethany Marsh, '"Distressed Protestants or Irish vagrants?" Charity and the organisation of relief to "Irish" refugees in England, 1641–1651' (Unpublished PhD thesis, Nottingham, 2019) and '"Lodging the Irish": An examination of parochial charity dispensed in Nottinghamshire to refugees from Ireland, 1641–1651', *Midland History* (2017), pp. 1–23; and Joseph Cope, *England and the 1641 Irish Rebellion* (Woodbridge, 2009).

24. Alison Games, *The Web of Empire: English Cosmopolitans in an Age of Expansion, 1560–1660* (Oxford, 2008), pp. 10–11.

25. Ian Whyte, *Migration and Society in Britain 1550–1830* (NY, 2000), pp. 76, 99.

26. Donal Cregan, 'Irish Recusant Lawyers in Politics in the Reign of James I', *The Irish Jurist*, 5 (1970), pp. 306–20 and 'Catholic Admissions to the English Inns of Court', *The Irish Jurist*, 5 (1970), pp. 95–114; Jane Ohlmeyer, 'Irish Recusant Lawyers during the Reign of Charles I' in Micheál Ó Siochrú (ed.), *Kingdoms in Crisis: Ireland in the 1640s* (Dublin, 2001), pp. 63–89; and John Bergin, 'The Irish Catholic Interest at the London Inns of Court, 1674–1800', *Eighteenth Century Ireland*, 24 (2009), pp. 36–61.

27. Thomas M. Truxes, 'London's Irish Merchant Community and North Atlantic Commerce in the Mid-Eighteenth Century' in David Dickson, Jan Parmentier, and Jane Ohlmeyer (eds.), *Irish and Scottish Mercantile Networks in Europe and Overseas in the Seventeenth and Eighteenth Centuries* (Ghent, 2007), pp. 271–309.

28. Craig Bailey, *Irish London: Middle-Class Migration in the Global Eighteenth-Century* (Liverpool, 2013) and 'Metropole and Colony: Irish Networks and Patronage in the Eighteenth-Century Empire', *Immigrants and Minorities*, 23 (2005), pp. 161–81.

29. Bergin, 'Irish Catholics', pp. 66–102 and L. M. Cullen, 'The Two George Fitzgeralds of London, 1718–1759' in Dickson, Parmentier, and Ohlmeyer (eds.), *Irish and Scottish Mercantile Networks*, chapter 11.

30. Craig Bailey, 'The Nesbitts of London and their networks' in Dickson, Parmentier, and Ohlmeyer (eds.), *Irish and Scottish Mercantile Networks*, pp. 231–50.

31. For example, see the special issue of *Eighteenth-Century Life*, 39 (2015), Bailey, *Irish London* and Roy Foster, *Paddy and Mr Punch: Connections in Irish and English History* (London, 2011).

32. BL, Additional Ms 18,730, Annesley's Diary 1675–1684.

33. Jane Ohlmeyer, *Making Ireland English: The Irish Aristocracy in the Seventeenth Century* (New Haven and London, 2012), chapter 11.

34. BL, Additional Ms 40,860, Annesley's Diary 1671–1675, and Additional Ms 18,730, Annesley's Diary 1675–1684.

35. G. T. Cell (ed.), *Newfoundland Discovered: English Attempts at Colonisation, 1610–1630* (London: Hakluyt Society, 1982) and John Mannion, 'Irish Migration and Settlement in Newfoundland: The Formative Phase, 1697–1732', *Newfoundland Studies*, 17 (2001), pp. 257–93.

36. Victor Treadwell, *Buckingham and Ireland, 1616–1628: A Study in Anglo-Irish Politics* (Dublin, 1998), p. 305.

37. Cell (ed.), *Newfoundland Discovered*, pp. 45–59 (quote p. 54).

38. Debra A. Meyers, 'Calvert's Catholic Colony' in Louis Roper and Bertrand Van Ruymbeke (eds.), *Constructing Early Modern Empires: Proprietary Ventures in the Atlantic World, 1500–1750* (Leiden, 2007), pp. 357–88. She does not mention the close Irish links and associations.

39. John D. Krugler, *English and Catholic: The Lords Baltimore in the Seventeenth Century* (Baltimore and London, 2004), especially chapter 3.

40. BL, Additional Ms 18,730, Annesley's Diary 1675–1684 and Daniel D. Jordan, *Thomas Butler, Earl of Ossory, 1634–80: A Privileged Witness* (Dublin, 2022).

41. Linda Colley, *Captives: Britain, Empire and the World, 1600–1850* (London, 2002), p. 30.

42. E. S. de Beer (ed.), *The Diary of John Evelyn* (6 vols., Oxford, 1955), IV, pp. 208–11; E. M. G. Routh, *Tangier: England's Lost Atlantic Outpost, 1661–1684* (1912), pp. 146–87, 310.

43. HL, Ellesmere papers, Box 212, EL 8467 'The present state...of Tangier', 19 April 1679 and BL, Sloane Ms 1952, ff. 19–33, A letter from Lord Inchiquin giving a Narrative of the state of Tangier from April 1678 to 1680.

44. David Appleby, 'God forbid it should come to that': The feud between Colonel Molesworth and Major-General O'Brien in Portugal, 1663', *The Seventeenth Century*, 26 (2011), pp. 346–67; Robert Latham and William Matthews (eds.), *The Diary of Samuel Pepys* (11 vols., Berkeley and LA, 1979–83), V, 302.

45. HL, Ellesmere papers, Box 212, EL 8467 'The present state...of Tangier', 19 April 1679. Also see Colley, *Captives*, pp. 26–39; William J. Bulman, *Anglican*

Enlightenment: Orientalism, Religion and Politics in England and its Empire, 1648–1715 (Cambridge, 2015), pp. 45–64, 210–14.

46. Alistair Malcolm, 'Serving the King at Home and Abroad: The Tangier Garrison under Charles II, 1662–1684' in Anthony McElligott, Liam Chambers, Ciara Brethnach, and Catherine Lawless (eds.), *Power in History from Medieval Ireland to the Post-Modern World* (Historical Studies XXVII, Dublin, 2011), pp. 109–24 and HL, Ellesmere papers, Box 212, EL 8467 'The present state . . . of Tangier', 19 April 1679.

47. Colley, *Captives*, p. 39.

48. T. Stein, 'Tangier in the Restoration Empire', *Historical Journal*, 54 (2011), pp. 985–1011.

49. TNA, PROB 11/414/66, will undated but enrolled 13 January 1691/2. Thomas M. Truxes, *Irish-American Trade, 1660–1783* (Cambridge, 1988), p. 14. James died shortly after his father and bequeathed all of his estate to his elder brother, William, John Ainsworth (ed.), *Inchiquin Manuscripts* (IMC, Dublin, 1961), p. 517.

50. *CSP Colonial, 1689–1692* (London, 1901), pp. 295–6.

51. Stein, 'Tangier in the Restoration Empire', p. 991.

52. Jane Ohlmeyer, 'Eastward Enterprises: Colonial Ireland, Colonial India', *Past and Present*, 240 (2018), pp. 83–118.

53. Southwell served as ambassador between 1665 and 1670, Joana Pinheiro de Almeida Troni, 'Irishmen at the Portuguese Court in the seventeenth century' in Igor Pérez Tostado and Enrique García Hernán (eds.), *Irlanda y el Atlántico Ibérico: Movilidad, participación e intercambio cultural (1580–1823)/Ireland and the Iberian Atlantic: Mobility, Involvement and Cross-Cultural Exchange (1580–1823)* (Valencia, 2010), pp. 155–63.

54. Lance A. Betros, 'A Glimpse of Empire: New York Governor Thomas Dongan and the Evolution of English Imperial Policy, 1683–1688' (Unpublished PhD thesis, Chapel Hill, 1988). Thanks to Marion Casey for drawing this and other references to Dongan to my attention.

55. Robert C. Ritchie, Coote, Richard, first earl of Bellamont (1636–1701), politician and colonial governor. *ODNB*. Retrieved 14 Jun. 2022, from https://www.oxforddnb.com/view/10.1093/ref:odnb/9780198614128.001.0001/odnb-9780198614128-e-6247.

56. Evan Haefeli, 'Toleration and Empire: The Origins of American Religious Pluralism' in Stephen Foster (ed.), *British North America in the Seventeenth and Eighteenth Centuries* (Oxford, 2013), pp. 114–15, 121–3, Maura Jane Farrelly, 'American Identity and English Catholicism in the Atlantic World' in D'Maris Coffman, Adrian Leonard, and William O'Reilly (eds.), *The Atlantic World: 1400–1850* (London, 2015), pp. 393–412; Handler and Reilly, 'Father Antoine Biet's Account Revisited: Irish Catholics in Mid-Seventeenth-Century Barbados', pp. 33–46.

57. Meyers, 'Calvert's Catholic Colony', pp. 357–88 and Krugler, *English and Catholic*. Maryland would not always remain so tolerant of Catholics; in 1704 laws were enacted to discourage the immigration and importation of Catholics.

58. Farrelly, 'American Identity and English Catholicism', pp. 393–412.

59. Zahedieh, 'Trade, plunder and Irishmen', pp. 74, 76; BL, Additional Ms 12,429, f. 166v, King William's instructions to Inchiquin dated 5 Dec 1689. In 1687 the Catholics on the Island petitioned the king for the liberty of conscience.

60. Andrew R. Murphy, "The Roads to and from Cork: The Irish Origins of William Penn's Theory of Religious Toleration' in Andrew R. Murphy and John Smolenski (eds.), *The Worlds of William Penn* (New Brunswick, New Jersey, 2019), pp. 139–54.

61. Fawcett (ed.), *The Western Presidency, 1670–1677*, p. 214. Catherine B. Asher and Cynthia Talbot, *India before Europe* (Cambridge, 2006), p. 225, Stephen Frederic Dale, *The Muslim Empires of the Ottomans, Safavids, and Mughals* (Cambridge, 2010), G. J. Ames, 'The role of religion in the transfer and rise of Bombay, c.1661–1687', *The Historical Journal*, 77 (2003), pp. 317–40.

62. Ohlmeyer, *Making Ireland English*, chapters 5 and 6.

63. Finola O'Kane and Ciaran O'Neill, 'Introduction' in O'Kane and O'Neill (eds.), *Ireland, Slavery and the Caribbean*, p. 10.

64. Ken MacMillan, 'Imperial constitutions: Sovereignty and law in the British Atlantic' in H. V. Bowen, Elizabeth Mancke, and John G. Reid (eds.), *Britain's Oceanic Empire: Atlantic and Indian Ocean Worlds, c.1550–1850* (Cambridge, 2012), pp. 69–97 and Christopher Tomlins, 'Legal Cartography of Colonization, the Legal Polyphony of Settlement: English Intrusions on the American Mainland in the Seventeenth Century', The Symposium: Colonialism, Culture, and the Law, 26 *Law & Soc. Inquiry* 315 (2001), pp. 315–65.

65. Ken MacMillan, 'Bound by Our Regal Office: Empire, Sovereignty, and the American Colonies in the Seventeenth Century' in Stephen Foster (ed.), *British North America in the Seventeenth and Eighteenth Centuries* (Oxford, 2013), pp. 80–90, 100–1 (quote p. 100).

66. T. Bartlett, '"This famous island set in a Virginian sea": Ireland in the British Empire, 1690–1801' in P. J. Marshall (ed.), *The Oxford History of the British Empire. vol. 2. The Eighteenth Century* (Oxford, 1998), p. 254.

67. Nini Rodgers, 'A Changing Presence: The Irish in the Caribbean in the seventeenth and eighteenth centuries' in Alison Donnell, Maria McGarrity, and Evelyn O'Callaghan (eds.), *Caribbean Irish Connections: Interdisciplinary Perspectives* (Kingston, Jamaica, 2015), pp. 17–32 (quote pp. 27–8).

68. K. Block and J. Shaw, 'Subjects without an Empire: The Irish in the Early Modern Caribbean', *Past and Present*, 210 (2011), pp. 33–60.

69. For a useful overview see Hiram Morgan, 'On the Pig's Back: Subaltern Imperialism, Anti-colonialism and the Irish Rise to Globalism' in Jürgen Elvert and Martina Elvert (eds.), *Agenten, Akteure, Abenteurer: Beiträge zur Ausstellung »Europa und das Meer* (Berlin, 2018), pp. 375–96.

70. William O'Reilly, 'Ireland in the Atlantic World: Migration and Cultural Transfer' in Ohlmeyer (ed.), *The Cambridge History of Ireland*, pp. 390–2.

71. Arturo Griffin, 'Conquistadores, Soldiers and Entrepreneurs: Early Irish Presence in Chile', *Irish Migration Studies in Latin America*, 4 (2006), pp. 216–20.

72. Thomas O'Connor, *Irish Voices from the Spanish Inquisition: Migrants, Converts and Brokers in Early Modern Iberia* (Basingstoke, 2016), p. 90.

73. Connie Kelleher, *The Alliance of Pirates: Ireland and Atlantic Piracy in the Early Seventeenth Century* (Cork, 2020).

74. David Edwards, 'Virginian connections: The wider Atlantic setting of Boyle's Munster estate and clientele' in David Edwards and Colin Rynne (eds.), *The Colonial World of Richard Boyle First Earl of Cork* (Dublin, 2018), pp. 74–88.

75. O'Connor, *Irish Voices from the Spanish Inquisition*, pp. 83–6; Linda Colley, 'Going Native, Telling Tales: Captivity, Collaborations and Empire', *Past and Present*, 168 (2000), pp. 170–93; Colley, *Captives*, pp. 44–59; and Nabil Matar, *Islam in Britain, 1558–1685* (Cambridge, 1998), pp. 7, 16, 37.

76. Colley, *Captives*, p. 50.

77. Jane Ohlmeyer, 'Irish privateers during the civil war, 1642–50' in *The Mariner's Mirror*, 76 (1990), pp. 119–34 and ' "The Dunkirk of Ireland": Wexford privateers during the 1640s' in *Journal of the Wexford Historical Society*, 12 (1988–9), pp. 23–49.

78. Nina Rodgers, 'The Irish and the Atlantic Slave Trade', *History Ireland* 15 (2007), pp. 17–23.

79. Joyce Lorimer (ed.), *English and Irish Settlement on the River Amazon 1550–1646* (Hakluyt Society, London, 1989), pp. 45, xv.

80. Lorimer (ed.), *English and Irish Settlement*, pp. 303, 428.

81. Lorimer (ed.), *English and Irish Settlement*, pp. 73, 263–4 (quotes).

82. L. H. Roper, *Advancing Empire: English Interests and Overseas Expansion, 1613–1688* (Cambridge, 2017), pp. 16, 29 and Brown, *Empire and Enterprise*, pp. 28, 114, 123, 145.

83. Lorimer (ed.), *English and Irish Settlement*, pp. 416, 423. Also see Hal Langfur, 'Race and Violence in Portuguese America' in Robert Antony, Stuart Carroll, and Caroline Dodds Pennock (eds.), *The Cambridge World History of Violence: vol. 3* (Cambridge, 2020), pp. 55–76.

84. Mark Meuwese, 'Fear, uncertainty, and violence in the Dutch colonization of Brazil (1624–1662)' in Lauric Henneton and Louis Roper (eds.), *Fear and the Shaping of Early American Societies* (Leiden, 2016), pp. 93–114.

85. Lorimer (ed.), *English and Irish Settlement*, pp. 74, 265–6.

86. See Chapter 3, Section I.

87. Lorimer (ed.), *English and Irish Settlement*, pp. 112, 408.

88. Lorimer (ed.), *English and Irish Settlement*, pp. 120–4 and Nicholas Bomba, 'The Hibernian Amazon: A struggle for sovereignty in the Portuguese court, 1643–1648', *Journal of Early Modern History*, 11 (2007), pp. 447–74.

89. Bomba, 'The Hibernian Amazon', p. 473.

90. *CSP Colonial, 1669–1674* (London, 1889), pp. 487–8.

91. *CSP Colonial, 1661–1668* (London, 1880), p. 320.

92. Irish migration to the Netherlands and engagement with the Dutch global empire has been little studied despite the richness of the Dutch archives.

93. Lorimer (ed.), *English and Irish Settlement*, pp. 74, 265–6.

94. Ben Hazard, ' "*In Novi Orbis Amplitudine*": Irish Franciscan Views of the Americas in the Seventeenth Century, 1601–83' in Tostado and Hernán (eds.), *Irlanda y el Atlántico Ibérico*, p. 193.

95. Richard Hakluyt, *The Principal Navigations, Voyages and Discoveries of the English Nation* (2 vols., Hakluyt Society, Cambridge, 1965), II, p. 795.

96. Patricia Palmer, *Language and Conquest in Early Modern Ireland: English Renaissance Literature and Elizabethan Imperial Expansion* (Cambridge, 2001), p. 134; Patrick F. McDevitt, 'Ireland, Latin America, and an Atlantic Liberation Theology' in Jorge Cañizares-Esguerra and Erik R. Seeman (eds.), *The Atlantic in Global History, 1500–2000* (2nd edition, London and New York, 2018), p. 294.

97. Dáibhí Ó Cróinín (ed.), *A New History of Ireland*. vol. 1. *Prehistoric and Early Ireland* (Oxford, 2005), p. 981. I owe this reference to Bríona Nic Dhiarmada.

98. Hazard, "*In Novi Orbis Amplitudine*", pp. 193–209.

99. O'Connor, *Irish Voices from the Spanish Inquisition*, pp. 98–9.

100. J. J. Silke, 'Irish Scholarship and the Renaissance, 1580–1673', *Studies in the Renaissance*, 20 (1973), pp. 169–206 and Matteo Binasco (ed.), *Luke Wadding, the Irish Franciscans, and Global Catholicism* (Abingdon, 2020).

101. L. M. Cullen, 'The Irish Diaspora of the Seventeenth and Eighteenth Centuries' in Nicholas Canny (ed.), *Europeans on the Move: Studies on European Migration, 1500–1800* (Oxford, 1994), pp. 124, 139.

102. For example, see Harman Murtagh, 'Irish soldiers abroad, 1600–1800' in Thomas Bartlett and Keith Jeffery (eds.), *A Military History of Ireland* (Cambridge, 1996), pp. 294–314; Steve Murdoch, 'Northern Exposure: Irishmen and Scandinavia in the Seventeenth Century', *History Ireland*, 6 (1998), pp. 5–6; and Declan M. Downey, 'Wild geese and the double-headed eagle: Irish integration in Austria c.1630–c.1918' in Paul Leifer and Eda Sagarra (eds.), *Austro-Irish Links Through the Centuries* (Vienna, 2002), pp. 41–57.

103. Thomas Bartlett, ' "Rishti": Irish Soldiers in India 1750–1920' in Jyoti Atwal and Eunan O'Halpin (eds.), *India, Ireland and Anti-Imperial Struggle: Remembering the Connaught Rangers Mutiny, 1920* (New Delhi, 2021), p. 25 and Kevin Kenny, 'The Irish in the Empire' in Kevin Kenny (ed.), *Oxford History of the British Empire: Ireland and the British Empire* (Oxford, 2004), p. 104.

104. Tadhg Ó hAnnracháin, *Confessionalism and Mobility in Early Modern Ireland* (Oxford, 2021), chapter 1.

105. Phillip Williams, 'The Irish in the Spanish Royal Armada, 1650–1670: Community and Solidarity in the Irish Tercio' in Oscar Recio Morales (ed.), *Redes de nación y espacios de poder: la comunidad irlandesa en España y la América española, 1600–1825 / Power Strategies: Spain and Ireland, 1600–1825* (Valencia, 2012), pp. 171–82.

106. Jan Parmentier, 'The Irish Connection: The Irish Merchant Community in Ostend and Bruges during the late Seventeenth and Eighteenth Centuries', *Eighteenth-Century Ireland / Iris an dá chultúr*, 2005, 20 (2005), pp. 31–54.

107. Jimmy McCrohan, 'An Irish Merchant in Late Seventeenth Century Malaga' in Tostado and Hernán (eds.), *Irlanda y el Atlántico Ibérico*, pp. 23–33.

108. Karin Schüller, 'Irish-Iberian Trade from the Mid-Sixteenth to the Mid-Seventeenth Centuries' and Óscar Recio Morales, 'Identity and Loyalty: Irish Traders in Seventeenth-Century Iberia' in Dickson, Parmentier, and Ohlmeyer (eds.), *Irish and Scottish Mercantile Networks*, pp. 175–95 and 197–210.

109. Pedro O'Neill Teixeira, 'The Lisbon Irish in the eighteenth century' in Tostado and Hernán (eds.), *Irlanda y el Atlántico Ibérico*, pp. 253–66; Patricia O'Connell, *The Irish College at Lisbon* (Dublin, 2001).

110. Nicholas Canny, 'Ireland and Continental Europe' in Alvin Jackson (ed.), *The Oxford Handbook of Modern Irish History* (Oxford, 2014), pp. 333–55 and Jane Ohlmeyer, 'Seventeenth-century Ireland and Scotland and their Wider Worlds' in T. O'Connor and M. Lyons (eds.), *Irish Communities in Early Modern Europe* (Dublin, 2006), pp. 457–84.

111. O'Connor, *Irish Voices from the Spanish Inquisition*, p. 104.

112. O'Connor, *Irish Voices from the Spanish Inquisition*, 105–16.

113. R. D. Crewe, 'Brave New Spain: An Irishman's Independence Plot in Seventeenth Century Mexico', *Past and Present*, 207 (2010), pp. 53–87 and S. Kline, 'William Lamport/Guillén de Lombardo (1611–1659)' in Karen Racine and Beatriz G. Mamigonian (eds.), *The Human Tradition in the Atlantic World, 1500–1850* (Plymouth, 2010), pp. 43–56.

114. Morgan, 'On the Pig's Back', pp. 375–96 and Tim Fanning, *Paisanos. The Forgotten Irish who Changed the Face of Latin America* (Dublin, 2016).

115. O'Connor, *Irish Voices from the Spanish Inquisition*, pp. 94, 95.

116. O'Connor, *Irish Voices from the Spanish Inquisition*, pp. 94–5.

117. Nicole von Germeten, 'Who was Captain Cornelio Cornelius? Dying for Honour on the Old Spanish Main' in Morales, *Redes de nación y espacios de poder*, pp. 277–90.

118. Block and Shaw, 'Subjects without an Empire', pp. 38–48 (quote p. 42).

119. Oscar Recio Morales, *Ireland and the Spanish Empire 1600–1825* (Dublin, 2010), pp. 235–57, 275 (quote).

120. Jorge L. Chinea, 'Irish Indentured Servants, Papists and Colonists in Spanish Colonial Puerto Rico, ca. 1650–1800', *Irish Migration Studies in Latin America*, 5 (2007), pp. 171–81.

121. Fernández Moya Rafael, 'The Irish Presence in the History and Place Names of Cuba', *Irish Migration Studies in Latin America*, 3 (2007), pp. 189–97 and Nini Rodgers, *Ireland, Slavery and Anti-Slavery, 1612–1685* (London, 2007), pp. 272–77.

122. Carmen Lario de Oñate, 'Irish Integration in eighteenth-century maritime mercantile city of Cadiz' in Tostado and Hernán (eds.), *Irlanda y el Atlántico Ibérico*, pp. 183–90 and 'The Irish Traders of Eighteenth-Century Cádiz' in Dickson, Parmentier, and Ohlmeyer (eds.), *Irish and Scottish Mercantile Networks*, pp. 211–30.

123. Guy Saupin, 'Les Réseaux Commerciaux des Irlandais de Nantes sous le Règne de Louis XIV' in Dickson, Parmentier, and Ohlmeyer (eds.), *Irish and Scottish Mercantile Networks*, pp. 115–46.

124. David Dickson, 'Setting out the terrain: Ireland and the Caribbean in the eighteenth century' in O'Kane and O'Neill (eds.), *Ireland, Slavery and the Caribbean*, pp. 25–6.

125. Rodgers, *Ireland, Slavery and Anti-Slavery*, p. 106.

126. Dickson, 'Setting out the terrain', p. 26.

127. Robert Louis Stein, *The French Sugar Business in the Eighteenth Century* (Baton Rouge, 1988).

128. Stein, *The French Slave Trade in the Eighteenth Century*, pp. 28–9, 59, 153–8.

129. Finola O'Kane, 'Comparing imperial design strategies: The Franco-Irish plantations of Saint-Domingue' in O'Kane and O'Neill (eds.), *Ireland, Slavery and the Caribbean*, pp. 156–78.

130. Dickson, 'Setting out the terrain', p. 27.

131. Matteo Binasco, 'Few, Uncooperative, and endangered: The activity of the Irish Catholic Priests in the West Indies of the Seventeenth Century, 1638–1668' in Tostado and Hernán (eds.), *Irlanda y el Atlántico Ibérico*, pp. 211–23.

132. Account of the present state of the Leeward Islands delivered to the Committee of the Council for Plantations by Sir Charles Wheeler, TNA, CO 1/29, ff. 161–6.

133. Rodgers, *Ireland, Slavery and Anti-Slavery*, pp. 57–8.

134. Orla Power, 'The "Quadripartite Concern" of St. Croix: An Irish Catholic Experiment in the Danish West Indies' in David T. Gleeson (ed.), *The Irish in the Atlantic World* (Columbia, South Carolina, 2010), pp. 213–28, 'The 18th century Irish sugar and slave trade at St. Croix, Danish West Indies' in Tostado and Hernán (eds.), *Irlanda y el Atlántico Ibérico*, pp. 51–68, and 'Friends, Foe, or Family? Catholic Creoles, French Huguenots, Scottish Dissenters: Aspects of the Irish Diaspora at St. Croix, Danish West Indies, 1760' in Niall Whelehan (ed.), *Transnational Perspectives on Modern Irish History* (New York, 2015), pp. 30–44.

135. Clare Carroll, 'Irish Protestants in the Theatre of the World: The Apostolic Hospice for the Converting, Rome, 1677–1745' in Matteo Binasco (ed.), *Rome and Irish Catholicism in the Atlantic World, 1622–1908* (Basingstoke, 2019), pp. 167–91.

136. See for example, Block and Shaw, 'Subjects without an Empire', pp. 33–60; O'Connor, *Irish Voices from the Spanish Inquisition*; and Tostado and Hernán (eds.), *Irlanda y el Atlántico Ibérico*.

137. Jenny Shaw, 'From perfidious papists to prosperous planters: Making Irish elites in the early modern English Caribbean' in O'Kane and O'Neill (eds.), *Ireland, Slavery and the Caribbean*, pp. 43–5.

138. Cullen, 'The Irish Diaspora, p. 113 and Jenny Shaw, *Everyday Life in the Early English Caribbean: Irish, Africans, and the Construction of Difference* (London, 2013), p. 16.

139. See for example L. H. Roper, *The Torrid Zone: Caribbean Colonization and Cultural Interaction in the Long Seventeenth Century* (Columbia, South Carolina, 2018).

140. Natalie A. Zacek, *Settler Society in the English Leeward Islands, 1670–1776* (Cambridge, 2010).

141. For an excellent introduction see Hilary McD. Beckles, 'The "Hub of Empire": the Caribbean and Britain in the Seventeenth Century' in Nicholas Canny (ed.), *The Oxford History of the British Empire*, vol. 1 (Oxford, 1998), pp. 218–40. Of particular value, even though they date from the 1930s, are Aubrey Gwynn's various publications: 'Early Irish Emigration to the West Indies (1612–43)', *Studies: An Irish Quarterly*, 18 (1929), pp. 377–93; Part 2 (1929), pp. 648–63; 'Indentured Servants and Negro Slaves in Barbados, 1642–1650', *Studies: An*

Irish Quarterly Review, 19 (1930), pp. 279–94; 'Cromwell's Policy of Transportation – Part 1', *Studies*, 19 (1930), pp. 607–23; Part 2, 20 (1931), pp. 291–305; 'The first Irish priests in the New World', *Studies*, 21 (1932), pp. 213–28; 'Documents Relating to the Irish in the West Indies', *Analecta Hibernica*, 4 (1932), pp. 139–286; and 'An Irish settlement on the Amazon 1612–29', *Proceedings of the Royal Irish Academy*, 41 (1932), pp. 1–54.

142. Kerby Miller, *Emigrants and Exiles: Ireland and the Irish Exodus to North America* (Oxford, 1985), p. 137.

143. Brown, *Empire and Enterprise*, p. 206.

144. See for examples Gwynn, 'Documents Relating to the Irish in the West Indies', p. 278 and London Metropolitan Archive, MR/E/616, for the indenture of July 1684 of 'Richard Swann from Dublin, aged 16 years, son of Richard Swann (deceased), agrees to go with Francis Parties of London, merchant, to Maryland aboard the ship Benedict Leonard'. I am grateful to Sonia Tycko for drawing this indenture to my attention. No doubt a deep trawl of the extant indentures in the London Metropolitan Archive will yield further people from Ireland or with Irish connections.

145. For careful analysis of the important legal distinctions between chattel slavery and indentured service see Liam Hogan, Laura McAtackney, and Matthew C. Reilly, 'The Irish in the Anglo-Caribbean: Servants or Slaves?', *History Ireland*, 24 (2016), pp. 18–22. Also see Liam Hogan's website, https://limerick1914.medium.com/all-of-my-work-on-the-irish-slaves-meme-2015-16-4965e445802a, accessed 1 Sept. 2022.

146. Richard Ligon, *A True and Exact History of the Island of Barbados* (London, 1673), pp. 44 (quote), 46, 107.

147. Richard S. Dunn, *Sugar and Slaves: The Rise of the Planter Class* (Chapel Hill, North Carolina, 1972), p. 247.

148. Dunn, *Sugar and Slaves*, p. 127 and Hilary McD. Beckles, 'A "riotous and unruly lot": Irish Indentured Servants and Freemen in the English West Indies, 1644–1713', *The William and Mary Quarterly*, 47 (1990), p. 510; *CSP, Colonial 1677–1680* (London, 1896), pp. 262–68. Figures for Montserrat differ slightly from those presented by Dunn, see Akenson, *If the Irish Ran the World*, p. 106 and have been used for black people on Montserrat.

149. The figure in Dunn, *Sugar and Slaves*, is 992.

150. The figure in Dunn, *Sugar and Slaves*, is 8,449.

151. Clodagh Tait, 'Progress, challenges and opportunities in early modern gender history, c.1550–1720', *Irish Historical Studies*, 46 (2022), pp. 244–5.

152. Sheridan, *Sugar and Slavery*, pp. 164–7; A. Burns, *History of the British West Indies* (New York, 1965), p. 342; and J. R. V. Johnston, 'The Stapleton Sugar Plantations in the Leeward Islands', *Bulletin of the John Rylands Library*, 48 (1965), pp. 175–206.

153. Dunn, *Sugar and Slaves*, p. 127

154. Petition of Major Edward Hamilton to the king, TNA, CO 1/33, no. 106, f. 277; Vere Langford Oliver, *Caribbeana: Being Miscellaneous Papers Relating to*

History . . . of the British West Indies (4 vols., London, 1912–14), III, pp. 27–35, 70–81, 178.

155. Matteo Binasco, 'The Activity of Irish Priests in the West Indies: 1638–1669', *Irish Migration Studies in Latin America*, 7 (2011), pp. 97–107 (quote p. 98) and Brown, *Empire and Enterprise*, pp. 24, 27.

156. Oliver, *Caribbeana*, II, pp. 68–77.

157. Oliver, *Caribbeana*, III, pp. 132–9.

158. *CSP, Colonial 1669–1674* (London, 1889), pp. 444–7 (quote p. 445).

159. Block and Shaw, 'Subjects without an Empire', p. 35.

160. Anon., *A brief and true remonstrance of the illegall proceedings of Roger Osburn* ([c.1654]) in Carla Pestana and Sharon V. Salinger (eds.), *The Early English Caribbean, 1570–1700* (4 vols., London, 2014), III, p. 285 and *CSP, Colonial 1574–1660* (London, 1860), p. 420. Also see Akenson, *If the Irish Ran the World*, pp. 58–61.

161. Anon., *A brief and true remonstrance* in Pestana and Salinger (eds.), *The Early English Caribbean*, III, pp. 283–4.

162. Binasco, 'The Activity of Irish Priests in the West Indies', pp. 97–107 (quote p. 98).

163. Matteo Binasco, *Making, Breaking and Remaking the Irish Missionary Network: Ireland, Rome and the West Indies in the Seventeenth Century* (Basingstoke, 2020) and 'Few, Uncooperative, and endangered: The activity of the Irish Catholic Priests in the West Indies of the Seventeenth Century, 1638–1668' in Donnell, McGarrity, O'Callaghan (eds.), *Caribbean Irish Connections*, pp. 211–23.

164. Scott Spurlock, 'Catholics in a Puritan Atlantic: The Liminality of Empire's Edge' in C Gribben and S. Spurlock (eds.), *Puritans and Catholics in the Trans-Atlantic World 1600–1800* (Philadelphia, 2009), pp. 21–46 (quote p. 27).

165. Rodgers, 'A Changing Presence', p. 20.

166. Oliver, *Caribbeana*, II, pp. 316–20 and 342–47.

167. Rodgers, *Ireland, Slavery and Anti-Slavery*, p. 51 and Martin J. Blake (ed.), *Blake Family Records 1600 to 1700* (London, 1905), pp. 106–13 and Gwynn, 'Documents Relating to the Irish in the West Indies', pp. 273–7.

168. Lydia M. Pulsipher and Conrad M. Goodwin, 'A sugar-boiling house at Galways: An Irish sugar plantation in Montserrat, West Indies', *Post-Medieval Archaeology*, 16 (1982), pp. 21–7.

169. *CSP, Colonial 1689–1692* (London, 1901), p. 112.

170. *CSP, Colonial 1701* (London, 1910), p. 349.

171. *CSP, Colonial 1701* (London, 1910), p. 349.

172. Oliver *Caribbeana*, IV (London, 1916), pp. 302–21.

173. Akenson, *If the Irish Ran the World*, p. 7.

174. Elena Perekhvalskaya, 'Irish in the West Indies: Irish Influence on the Formation of English-based Creoles', *Studia Celto-Slavica*, 7 (2015), p. 195.

175. Survey and Landscape on Montserrat https://blogs.brown.edu/archaeology/fieldwork/montserrat/, accessed 14 June 2022 and John F. Cherry and Krysta Ryzewski, *An Archaeological History of Montserrat in the West Indies* (Oxford, 2020) and Perekhvalskaya, 'Irish in the West Indies', p. 195.

176. John C. Messenger, 'The Influence of the Irish in Montserrat', *Caribbean Quarterly*, 13 (1967), pp. 3–26 and Kate Spanos, 'Locating Montserrat between the black and green', *Irish Migration Studies in Latin America*, 9 (2019), pp. 1–15.

177. Brown, 'Free, and unfree', p. 60.

178. Dunn, *Sugar and Slaves*, pp. 141, 155 and Beckles, 'A "riotous and unruly lot"', p. 505.

179. Dunn, *Sugar and Slaves*, p. 57 and Beckles, 'A "riotous and unruly lot"', p. 506.

180. Trevor Burnard, 'European Migration to Jamaica, 1655–1780', *The William and Mary Quarterly*, 53 (1996), pp. 769–96 and Spurlock, 'Catholics in a Puritan Atlantic', pp. 21–46.

181. Brown, 'Free, and unfree', p. 65.

182. 'The humble overtures of divers persons nearly concerned in the present posture and condition of the island of Barbados', TNA, CO 1/69, no. 2.

183. Brown, 'Free, and unfree', p. 68.

184. Binasco, 'Few, Uncooperative, and Endangered', p. 222.

185. Beckles, 'A "riotous and unruly lot"', p. 510 and *Black Rebellion in Barbados: The Struggle against Slavery, 1627–1838* (Bridgetown, 1984). Also see Hilary McD. Beckles, *The First Black Slave Society: Britain's 'Barbarity Time' in Barbados, 1636–1876* (Kingston, 2016).

186. Gwynn, 'Documents Relating to the Irish in the West Indies', p. 250.

187. *CSP, Colonial 1675–1676* (London, 1893), p. 445.

188. Beckles, 'A "riotous and unruly lot"', pp. 510–11.

189. Rodgers, *Ireland*, pp. 43–4; Jerome S. Handler and Matthew C. Reilly, 'Father Antoine Biet's Account Revisited: Irish Catholics in Mid-Seventeenth-Century Barbados' in Donnell, McGarrity, O'Callaghan (eds.), *Caribbean Irish Connections*, pp. 33–46.

190. Jill Sheppard, *The 'Redlegs' of Barbados, their Origins and History* (Millwood, New York, 1977); Matthew Reilly, 'The Irish in Barbados: Labour, landscape and legacy' in Donnell, McGarrity, O'Callaghan (eds.), *Caribbean Irish Connections*, pp. 47–63 and *Archaeology below the Cliff: Race, Class, and Redlegs in Barbadian Sugar Society* (Tuscaloosa, 2019).

191. Rodgers, *Ireland, Slavery and Anti-Slavery*, p. 42.

192. Natalie A. Zacek, 'How the Irish became black' in O'Kane and O'Neill (eds.), *Ireland, Slavery and the Caribbean* pp. 321–36.

193. For example, Barnewall, Blake, Burke, Butler, Bryan, Fitzgerald, Fitzjames, Fitzpatrick, French, Ireland, Kelly, Murphy, McCarthy, Nugent, Roach, Sinott, and Skerrett, Oliver *Caribbeana*, IV, pp. 25, 54, 114, 154, 217, 243, 318, 350; V, pp. 9, 62, 116, 143, 177, 235, 269, 293.

194. Shaw, *Everyday Life in the Early English Caribbean*, pp. 1–3 and Block and Shaw, 'Subjects without an Empire', pp. 33–4.

195. Spurlock, 'Catholics in a Puritan Atlantic', pp. 39–40.

196. Perekhvalskaya, 'Irish in the West Indies', p. 194.

197. Quoted (p. 145) in Éamonn ó Ciardha, 'Tories and Moss-troopers in Scotland and Ireland in the Interregnum: A political dimension' in John R. Young (ed.), *Celtic Dimensions of the British Civil Wars* (Edinburgh, 1997), pp. 141–63.

198. Nuala Zahedieh, 'Trade, plunder and Irishmen in early English Jamaica' in O'Kane and O'Neill (eds.), *Ireland, Slavery and the Caribbean*, pp. 74–86.

199. Beckles, 'A "riotous and unruly lot"', pp. 520–1.

200. *CSP, Colonial 1689–1692* (London, 1901), p. 295.

201. *CSP, Colonial 1689–1692* (London, 1901), p. 316.

202. BL, Additional Ms 12,429, f. 168v, King William's instructions to Inchiquin dated 5 Dec. 1689.

203. BL, Additional Ms 12,429, f. 169v, King William's instructions to Inchiquin dated 5 Dec. 1689.

204. BL, Additional Ms 12,429, f. 174v–177r, Inchiquin's speeches to the Assembly in Jamaica, 9 June and 30 July 1691.

205. *CSP, Colonial 1689–1692* (London, 1901), p. 597.

206. Zahedieh, 'Trade, plunder and Irishmen', p. 78 and Alejandro García Montón, *Genoese Entrepreneurship and the Asiento Slave Trade, 1650–1700* (London, 2022).

207. *CSP Colonial, 1689–1692* (London, 1901), pp. 295–6.

208. Ainsworth (ed.), *Inchiquin Manuscripts*, p. 517.

209. Karst de Jong, 'The Irish in Jamaica during the long eighteenth century (1698–1836)' (Unpublished PhD thesis, Queens University Belfast, 2017), pp. 30–1 and David A. Fleming, 'Sir Eyre Coote and the governorship of Jamaica, 1805–1808' in O'Kane and O'Neill (eds.), *Ireland, Slavery and the Caribbean*, p. 179.

210. O'Connor, *Irish Voices from the Spanish Inquisition,* pp. 93, 96.

211. Zahedieh, 'Trade, plunder and Irishmen', pp. 76–7.

212. Michael Pawson and David Buisseret, *Port Royal, Jamaica* (Oxford, 1975), pp. 65, 67 and Thomas M. Truxes, 'Doing business in the wartime Caribbean: John Byrn, Irish merchant of Kingston, Jamaica (September–October 1756)' in O'Kane and O'Neill (eds.), *Ireland, Slavery and the Caribbean*, pp. 87–102.

213. Gwynn, 'Documents Relating to the Irish in the West Indies', p. 282.

214. Burnard, 'European Migration to Jamaica', pp. 769–96 and James Robertson, 'Making Jamaica English' in Roper, *The Torrid Zone*, pp. 105–17.

215. Hazard, '"In Novi Orbis Amplitudine"', pp. 197–8.

216. J. Horn, 'Tobacco Colonies: The Shaping of English Society in the Seventeenth-Century Chesapeake' in Canny (ed.), *The Oxford History of the British Empire*, pp. 176–7.

217. Elodie Peyrol-Kleiber, *Les premiers Irlandais du Nouveau Monde: une migration atlantique (1618–1705)* (Rennes, 2016) and '"Ffourty thousand to cut the Protestants throats": The Irish threat in the Chesapeake and the West Indies (1620–1700)' in Lauric Henneton and Louis Roper (eds.), *Fear and the Shaping of Early American Societies* (Leiden, 2016), pp. 160–81; Nicholas Canny, 'English migration into and across the Atlantic during the seventeenth and eighteenth centuries' in Canny (ed.), *Europeans on the Move*, pp. 64–75.

218. Brown, *Empire and Enterprise,* pp. 24, 27.

219. *CSP, Colonial 1574–1660* (London, 1860), p. 401.

220. *CSP, Colonial 1574–1660* (London, 1860), p. 407.

221. *CSP, Colonial 1574–1660* (London, 1860), p. 409.

222. Quoted in Leslie Herman, 'Building Narratives: Ireland and the "Colonial Period" in American Architectural History' (Unpublished PhD thesis, Columbia University, 2019), p. 280.

223. Peyrol-Kleiber, ' "Ffourty thousand to cut the Protestants throats" ', p. 169.

224. J. Horn, *Adapting to a New World: English Society in the Seventeenth-Century Chesapeake* (Chapel Hill, North Carolina, 1994), pp. 23–6; Dunn, *Sugar and Slaves*.

225. Quoted in Peyrol-Kleiber, ' "Ffourty thousand to cut the Protestants throats" ', p. 177.

226. Robert Weir, ' "Shaftesbury's Darling": British Settlement in the Carolinas at the Close of the Seventeenth Century' in Canny (ed.), *The Origins of Empire*, pp. 375–97.

227. Rodgers, *Ireland, Slavery and Anti-Slavery*, p. 211.

228. Spurlock, 'Catholics in a Puritan Atlantic', pp. 24–5.

229. For a detailed case study of one Irish Catholic, Charles Carroll, who travelled to Maryland in 1688 as the attorney general, see Ronald Hoffman, *Princes of Ireland, Planters of Maryland: A Carroll Saga, 1500–1782* (Chapel Hill, North Carolina, 2000).

230. Rodgers, *Ireland, Slavery and Anti-Slavery*, pp. 197–200.

231. Cullen, 'The Irish diaspora', pp. 126–7, 139.

232. Gwynn, 'Documents Relating to the Irish in the West Indies', p. 286.

233. Patrick Griffin, *The People with No Name: Ireland's Ulster Scots, America's Scots Irish, and the Creation of a British Atlantic World, 1689–1764* (Princeton, 2002).

234. Herman, 'Building Narratives', pp. 288, 291.

235. Thanks to Marion Casey for confirming this.

236. John H. Kennedy, *Thomas Dongan Governor of New York (1682–1688)* (Washington, DC, 1930).

237. David William Voorhees, ' "Imprisoning Persons at their Pleasure": The Anti-Catholic Hysteria of 1689 in the Middle Colonies' in Henneton and Roper (eds.), *Fear and the Shaping of Early American Societies*, pp. 182–204 (quote p. 184).

238. Ritchie, Coote. *ODNB*.

239. *CSP, Colonial 1700* (London, 1910), p. 622.

240. Spurlock, 'Catholics in a Puritan Atlantic', pp. 21–46; Igor Pérez Tostado, 'The Irish in the Iberian Atlantic and Rome: Globalized Individuals and the Rise of Transatlantic Networks of Information' in Binasco (ed.), *Rome and Irish Catholicism*, pp. 23–45; Colin Barr, ' "Imperium in Imperio": Irish Episcopal Imperialism in the Nineteenth', *The English Historical Review*, 123 (2008), pp. 611–50; Nicholas Canny, 'How the Local Can be Global and the Global Local: Ireland, Irish Catholics, and European Overseas Empires, 1500–1900' in Patrick Griffin and Francis D. Cogliano (eds.), *Ireland and America: Empire, Revolution and Sovereignty* (Virginia, 2021), pp. 23–52.

241. For a discussion of this 'Protestant International' see J. F. Boscher, 'Huguenot Merchants and the Protestant International in the Seventeenth Century', *The William and Mary Quarterly*, third series, 52 (1995), pp. 77–102.

242. Quoted (p. 368) in Gabriel Glickman, 'Protestantism, Colonization and the New England Company in Restoration Politics', *Historical Journal*, 59 (2016), pp. 365–91.

243. R. E. W. Maddison, 'Robert Boyle and the Irish Bible', *Bulletin of the John Rylands Library*, 41 (1958), pp. 81–101; Mícheál Mac Craith, 'Literature in Irish, *c.* 1550–1690: From the Elizabethan Settlement to the Battle of the Boyne' in Margaret Kelleher and Philip O'Leary (eds.), *The Cambridge History of Irish Literature, Volume 1 to 1890* (2 vols., Cambridge: Cambridge University Press, 2006), p. 196.

244. Glickman, 'Protestantism, Colonization and the New England Company in Restoration Politics', pp. 375–6.

245. Barry Crosbie, 'Irish Religious Networks in Colonial South Asia, ca. 1788–1858' in Colin Barr and Hilary Carey (eds.), *Religion and Greater Ireland: Christianity and Irish Global Networks* (Montreal and Kingston, 2015), pp. 209–28; Hilary Carey, *God's Empire: Religion and Colonialism in the British World, c.1801–1908* (Cambridge, 2011); Hilary Carey (ed.), *Empires of Religion* (Basingstoke, 2008).

246. Quoted in Canny (ed.), *The Origins of Empire*, p. 6.

247. Brown, *Empire and Enterprise*, pp. 33, 124 and Games, *The Web of Empire*, pp. 273–5.

248. Keith Pluymers, *No Wood, No Kingdom. Political Ecology in the English Atlantic* (Philadelphia, 2021), p. 229.

249. J. Smibert, Berkeley, George (1685–1753). *ODNB*. Retrieved 12 Jun. 2022, from https://www.oxforddnb.com/view/10.1093/ref:odnb/9780198614128.001.0001/odnb-9780198614128-e-1001941.

250. Quoted in Herman, 'Building Narratives', p. 382.

251. https://www.irishtimes.com/culture/what-to-do-about-george-berkeley-trinity-figurehead-and-slave-owner-1.4277555l 18 June 2020 by Joe Humphreys.

252. Parmentier, 'The Irish Connection', pp. 31–54. More generally see Andrew Philips and J. C. Sharman, *Outsourcing Empire: How Company-States Made the Modern World* (Princeton, 2020).

253. Philip J. Stern, *The Company-State: Corporate Sovereignty and the Early Modern Foundations of the British Empire in India* (Oxford, 2011), 'British Asia and British Atlantic: Comparisons and Connections', *The William and Mary Quarterly*, 63 (2006), pp. 693–712 and 'From the Fringes of History: Tracing the Roots of the English East India Company-State', in Sameetah Agha and Elizabeth Kolsky (eds.), *Fringes of Empire: People, Places, and Spaces in Colonial India* (New Delhi, 2009), pp. 19–44.

254. H. V. Bowen, Elizabeth Mancke, and John G. Reid (eds.), *Britain's Oceanic Empire: Atlantic and Indian Ocean Worlds, c.1550–1850* (Cambridge, 2012), p. 4.

255. Stern, 'British Asia and British Atlantic', p. 705; Bartlett, ' "This famous island set in a Virginian sea" ', p. 254.

256. Marshall, 'The English in Asia to 1700', p. 276; Bottigheimer, *English Money and Irish Land*, p. 192.

257. They were Joseph Ashe, Samuel Barnardston, Robert Boyle, Thomas Chamberlain, James Edwards, Arthur Ingram, Martin Noel, Maurice and William Thomson, and Robert Titchborne.

258. Ethel Bruce Sainsbury (ed.), *A Calendar of the Court Minutes etc. of the East India Company, 1660–1663*, with an introduction and notes by Sir William Foster (Oxford, 1922), p. 147; http://www.historyofparliamentonline.org/volume/1660-1690/member/ashe-sir-joseph-1617-86. Aungier quickly became an integral and trusted part of Ashe's global commercial empire and enjoyed access to his closest business associates.

259. TNA, PROB/11/357/273. Also see Bailey, *Irish London*, pp. 202–3; John Burke, *A Genealogical and Heraldic History of the Commoners of Great Britain and Ireland* (4 vols., London, 1833–38), II, 578–81 and TCD, Ms 816, Deposition of Thomas Ashe of St. John's, Co. Meath, 19 Feb. 1641[2], ff. 90r–v.

260. Bottigheimer, *English Money and Irish Land*, p. 198; downsurvey.tcd.ie returns Elizabeth Ash against 7 townlands in Clanwilliam and Jonathan Ash against 5 townlands; NLI, Genealogical Office, MS 93, pp. 64–5; TNA, PROB 11/293/280; and Arthur Vicars, *Index to the Prerogative Wills of Ireland, 1536–1810* (Dublin, 1897) p. 13. Brown, 'Free, and unfree', p. 65.

261. Robert Boyle, 'The Correspondence of Robert Boyle' edited by Michael Hunter, Antonio Clericuzio, and Lawrence Principe (7 vols., London, 2001), IV, p. 436; S/tern, The Company-State, pp. 113–5; Paddy O'Sullivan, 'The English East India Company at Dunaniel', *Bandon Historical Journal*, 4 (1988), pp. 3–14.

262. *Charters granted to the East-India Company from 1601...* (NS, 1774), 84.

263. BL, IOR/E/3/87, Company to President and Council in Surat, 10 Mar. 1668[9], f. 115v.

264. BL, IOR/E/3/87, Company to President and Council in Surat, 10 Mar. 1668[9], f. 114.

265. Pius Malekandathil, *Portuguese Cochin and the Maritime Trade of India 1500–1663* (New Delhi, 2001) and *The Mughals, the Portuguese and the Indian Ocean. Changing Imageries of Maritime India* (New Delhi, 2013), 58–70; Saumya Varghese, 'Urbanization and trade in Goa (1510–1660)' (Unpublished PhD thesis, Jawaharlal Nehru University, 2010).

266. Raymond Gillespie, 'The Origins and Development of an Ulster Urban Network, 1600–41', *Irish Historical Studies*, 24 (1984), pp. 15–16. See also Robert Hunter, 'Ulster Plantation Towns 1609–1641' in David Harkness and Mary O'Dowd (eds.), *The Town in Ireland* (Belfast, 1991), pp. 55–80.

267. http://www.historyofparliamentonline.org/volume/1660-1690/member/biddulph-sir-theophilus-1612-83, accessed 14 June 2022.

268. http://www.british-history.ac.uk/no-series/london-aldermen/hen3-1912/pp75-119, accessed 14 June 2022.

269. http://www.historyofparliamentonline.org/volume/1690-1715/member/turner-sir-william-1615-93, accessed 14 June 2022.

270. Ian W. Archer, 'The city of London and the Ulster plantation' in Éamonn Ó Ciardha and Micheál Ó Siochrú (eds.), *The Plantation of Ulster: Ideology and Practice* (Manchester, 2012), pp. 78–97.

271. T. W. Moody, *The Londonderry Plantation, 1609–41: The City of London and the Plantation in Ulster* (Belfast, 1939).

272. P. J. Marshall, 'The British in Asia: Trade to Dominion, 1700–1765' in P. J. Marshall (ed.), *The Oxford History of the British Empire*. vol. II. *The Eighteenth Century* (Oxford, 1998), pp. 487–507.

273. According to K. N. Chaudhuri 250,000 pieces of calico were imported in 1664, which accounted for 73 per cent of the entire trade of the East India Company. Over the next two decades the amount increased to 1.5 million pieces and the overall share of textiles stood at 83 per cent, with roughly half coming via Surat, K. N. Chaudhuri, *The Trading World of Asia and the English East India Company, 1660–1760* (Cambridge, 1978), p. 282.

274. Holden Furber, *Rival Empires of Trade in the Orient, 1600–1800* (Minneapolis, 1976), p. 92.

275. Beverly Lemire, *Fashion's Favourite: The Cotton Trade and the Consumer in Britain, 1660–1800* (Oxford, 1991); and Giorgio Riello, 'The Indian Apprenticeship: The trade of Indian textiles as the making of European cottons' in Giorgio Riello and Tirthankar Roy (eds.), *How India Clothed the World: The World of South Asian Textiles, 1500–1850* (Leiden, 2009), pp. 332–4 and *Cotton: The Fabric that Made the Modern World* (Cambridge, 2013).

276. William Robert Scott (ed.), *The Constitution and Finance of English, Scottish and Irish Joint-Stock Companies to 1720* (3 vols., Cambridge, 1910–12), I, pp. 302–4.

277. *CSPI, 1625–32* (London, 1900), p. 484 and R. Barlow and H. Yule (eds.), *The Diary of William Hedges 1681–1687* (3 vols., London, 1887–9), II, p. 316.

278. Fryer's eulogy cited in Sir Charles Fawcett (ed.), *The English Factories in India*, n[ew] s[eries], vol. 1 *The Western Presidency, 1670–1677* (Oxford, 1936), p. 279, R. Barlow and H. Yule (eds.), *The Diary of William Hedges 1681–1687* (3 vols., London, 1887–9), II, p. 316, and Robert Batchelor, *The Selden Map and the Making of a Global City, 1549–1689* (Chicago, 2014), 182–4. For an example see BL, Oriental Ms/reg 16.b.14, 'A Chronicle of the Kings of Persees'.

279. Richard J. Ross, 'Puritan Godly Discipline in Comparative Perspective: Legal Pluralism and the Sources of 'Intensity', *American Historical Review*, 113 (2008), pp. 975–1002 and Karen Ordahl Kupperman, 'Errand to the Indies: Puritan Colonization from Providence Island through the Western Design', *The William and Mary Quarterly*, 45, (1988), pp. 70–99.

280. BL, IOR/E/3/35, Aungier and Council at Bombay to the Company in London, 16 Dec. 1674, f. 177. The library in Surat held multiple copies of Bibles 'in languages', albeit some of which had 'bin damnified by ye worme' during the monsoon, BL, IOR/E/3/34, 'Acco[un]tt of Bookes Remayning in the Library of Surratt July 31st Anno Domini 1673', f. 86.

281. HL, Ellesmere papers, Box 212, EL 8467, 'The present state... of Tangier', 19 April 1679.

282. Canny, 'How the Local Can be Global and the Global Local', pp. 197–200, 202; Gwynn, 'Documents Relating to the Irish in the West Indies', p. 277.

283. Vincent Gookin, *The Great Case of Transplantation in Ireland Discussed* (London, 1655), p. 20.

284. Block and Shaw, 'Subjects without an Empire', p. 60.

285. Block and Shaw, 'Subjects without an Empire', p. 34 and Zacek, 'How the Irish became black'. Also see Andrew Murphy, *But the Irish Sea Betwixt Us: Ireland, Colonialism and Renaissance Literature* (Lexington, Kentucky, 1999), p. 15.

286. O'Reilly, 'Ireland in the Atlantic World', p. 387. Also see N. Canny and A. Pagden (eds.), *Colonial Identity in the Atlantic World, 1500–1800* (Princeton, 1987) and Charles Ivar McGrath, *Ireland and Empire 1692–1770* (London, 2012), pp. 4–15.

287. See Chapter 2 above and Shaw, 'From perfidious papists to prosperous planters', pp. 44–9.

288. *CSP, Colonial 1669–1674* (London, 1889), p. 442.

289. Bergin, 'Irish Catholics and Their Networks in Eighteenth-Century London', p. 82.

290. Will of Nicholas Tuite of London, PROB 11/983/95, dated 27 Nov. 1772.

291. Quoted (p. 65) in Rodgers, *Ireland, Slavery and Anti-Slavery*.

292. Sheppard, *The 'Redlegs' of Barbados* and John F Cherry and Krysta Ryzewski, *An Archaeological History of Montserrat in the West Indies* (Oxford, 2020).

293. Will of Anthony French of Mitcham, Surrey, PROB 11/1158/208, will dated 16 May 1787 and probate granted 31 Oct 1787.

294. Marisa J. Fuentes, *Dispossessed Lives: Enslaved Women, Violence, and the Archive* (Philadelphia, 2016).

295. Jenny Shaw, 'In the Name of the Mother: The Story of Susannah Mingo, a Woman of Color in the Early English Atlantic', *The William and Mary Quarterly*, 77 (2020), pp. 177–210.

296. Herman, 'Building Narratives', p. 283.

297. Lucius R. Paige, *History of Cambridge, Massachusetts, 1630–1877, with a genealogical register* (Boston, 1877), p. 394.

298. BL, Additional Ms 40,708, ff. 1–2, Gerald Aungier to Sir George Oxenden, 7 Oct. 1662.

299. BL, Additional Ms 40,701, f. 13v, Sir George Oxenden to Gerald Aungier, Surat, 26 Feb. 1666[7].

300. Ohlmeyer, 'Eastward Enterprises', pp. 117–18.

301. Marc Caball, 'Munster and India: The local and global in early modern Ireland' in Sarah Covington, Vincent P. Carey, and Valerie McGowan-Doyle (eds.), *Early Modern Ireland: New Sources, Methods and Perspectives* (Abingdon, 2019), pp. 139–41 (quote p. 140).

302. James Delbourgo, *Collecting the World: The Life and Curiosity of Hans Sloane* (London, 2017), p. 200.

303. Kidd, *British Identities before Nationalism. Ethnicity and Nationhood in the Atlantic World, 1600–1800* (Cambridge, 1999), pp. 146–81 (quotes p. 180, 179).

304. Andrew MacKillop, 'What has the four nations and empire model achieved' in Stephanie Barczewski and Martin Farr (eds.), *The MacKenzie Moment and Imperial History: Essays in Honour of John M. MacKenzie* (London, 2019), pp. 261–83 (quote at p. 275) and *Human Capital and Empire: Scotland, Ireland, Wales and British Imperialism in Asia, c.1690–c.1820* (Manchester, 2021), especially the introduction.

305. Zahedieh, 'Trade, plunder and Irishmen', p. 74.
306. Shona Helen Johnston, 'Papists in a Protestant World: The Catholic Anglo-Atlantic in the Seventeenth-Century' (Unpublished PhD, Georgetown University, 2011).
307. D. Greene and F. Kelly (eds.), *Irish Bardic Poetry: Texts and Translations, Together with an Introductory Lecture by Osborn Bergin* (Dublin Institute for Advanced Studies, 1970, repr. 1984), pp. 49–50, 231–2.
308. See Chapter 3, Section II. Also see Nicholas Canny, *Imagining Ireland's Pasts. Early Modern Ireland through the Centuries* (Oxford, 2021).
309. John M. MacKenzie, 'Epilogue: Analysing "Echoes of Empire" in Contemporary Context: The Personal Odyssey of an Imperial Historian, 1970s–Present' in Kalypso Nicolaïdis, Berry Sèbe, and Gabrielle Maas (eds.), *Echoes of Empire: Memory, Identity and Colonial Legacies* (London, 2015) pp. 189–206 (quote pp. 201–2), and 'Irish, Scottish, Welsh and English worlds? A Four nation approach to the history of the British Empire', *History Compass*, 6/5 (2008), pp. 1244–63.
310. Friel, *Making History*, p. 27.

CHAPTER 05

1. Brian Friel, *Translations* (London, 1981), p. 90.
2. Julia C. Obert, 'Troubles Literature and the End of the Troubles' in Eric Falci and Paige Reynolds (eds.), *Irish Literature in Transition 1980–2020* (Cambridge, 2020), pp. 65–80.
3. Finola O'Kane, 'Comparing imperial design strategies: The Franco-Irish plantations of Saint-Domingue' in Finola O'Kane and Ciaran O'Neill (eds.), *Ireland, Slavery and the Caribbean: Interdisciplinary Perspectives* (Manchester, 2023), pp. 156–78.
4. Falci and Reynolds (eds.), *Irish Literature in Transition 1980–2020*, p. 3.
5. D. B. Quinn, 'Ireland and Sixteenth Century European Expansion' in T. D. Williams (ed.), *Historical Studies* (London, 1958) and Nicholas Canny, 'The Ideology of English Colonization: From Ireland to America', *The William and Mary Quarterly*, 30 (1973), pp. 575–98 and again in *The Elizabethan Conquest of Ireland: A Pattern Established 1565–1576* (New York, 1976).
6. Discussed in Chapter 1 above. Also see James Bell *Empire, Religion and Revolution in Early Virginia, 1607–1786* (Basingstoke, 2013).
7. Karen O. Kupperman, *The Jamestown Project* (Cambridge, Mass. and London, 2007).
8. Audrey J. Horning, *Ireland in the Virginian Sea: Colonialism in the British Atlantic* (Chapel Hill, 2013), pp. 1–16 (quote p. 13).
9. Alison Games, *The Web of Empire: English Cosmopolitans in an Age of Expansion, 1560–1660* (Oxford, 2008), pp. 123–4, 256.
10. Horning, *Ireland in the Virginian Sea*, pp. 13, 76, 84 and Rory Rapple, ' "Not Falstaff alone, but also Iago": Sir Ralph Lane's approach to officeholding in both Ireland and Virginia', *Journal of British Studies* (forthcoming, 2023). I am grateful to Professor Rapple for sharing this with me in advance of publication.
11. Games, *The Web of Empire*, chapter 8.

12. Chaim M. Rosenberg, *Losing America, Conquering India: Lord Cornwallis and the Remaking of the British Empire* (Jefferson, North Carolina, 2017); Barry Crosbie, *Irish Imperial Networks: Migration, Social Communication and Exchange in Nineteenth-Century India* (Cambridge, 2012), chapter 3.

13. Jane Ohlmeyer, 'Eastward Enterprises: Colonial Ireland, Colonial India', *Past and Present*, 240 (2018), pp. 83–118.

14. I. Bruce Watson, 'Fortifications and the "idea" of force in early English India Company relations with India' in Patrick Tuck (ed.), *The East India Company: 1600–1858*. vol. IV. *Trade Finance and Power* (London, 1998), p. vii and H. V. Bowen, 'British India, 1756–1813: The Metropolitan Context' in P. J. Marshall (ed.), *The Oxford History of the British Empire*. vol. 2. *The Eighteenth Century* (Oxford, 1998), p. 530.

15. Philip J. Stern, *The Company-State: Corporate Sovereignty and the Early Modern Foundations of the British Empire in India* (Oxford, 2011), 'British Asia and British Atlantic: Comparisons and Connections', *The William and Mary Quarterly*, 63 (2006), pp. 693–712 and 'From the Fringes of History: Tracing the Roots of the English East India Company-State' in Sameetah Agha and Elizabeth Kolsky (eds.), *Fringes of Empire: People, Places, and Spaces in Colonial India* (New Delhi, 2009), pp. 19–44.

16. P. J. Marshall, 'The First British Empire' in Robin Winks (ed.), *The Oxford History of the British Empire*. vol. 5. *Historiography* (Oxford, 1999), pp. 43–53. A new generation of scholars is challenging these assumptions and calling for fresh frameworks, Philip Stern, '"A Politie of Civill & Military Power": Political Thought and the Late Seventeenth-Century Foundations of the East India Company-State', *Journal of British Studies*, 47 (2008), pp. 253–83. Also see D. Washbrook, 'Progress and Problems: South Asian Economic and Social story, c.1720–1860', *Modern Asian Studies*, 22 (1988), pp. 57–96 and Jon E. Wilson, 'Early Colonial India beyond Empire', *The Historical Journal*, 50 (2007), pp. 951–70.

17. Kathleen Wilson, 'Rethinking the Colonial State. Family, Gender, and Governmentality in Eighteenth-Century British Frontiers', *American Historical Review*, 116 (2011), pp. 1295–322, especially p. 1296.

18. Bernard S. Cohn, *Colonialism and its Forms of Knowledge: The British in India* (Princeton, New Jersey, 1996).

19. Hiram Morgan (ed.), *Political Ideology in Ireland 1541–1641* (Dublin, 1999), p. 9.

20. Phil Withington, 'Plantation and civil society' in Éamonn Ó Ciardha and Micheál Ó Siochrú (eds.), *The Plantation of Ulster: Ideology and Practice* (Manchester, 2012) pp. 55–77 and David Harris Sacks, 'Love and Fear in the Making of England's Atlantic Empire', *Huntington Library Quarterly*, 83 (2020) special edition 'Ancient Rome in English Political Culture, ca. 1570–1660' edited by Paulina Kewes, pp. 543–65. I owe this reference to David Harris Sacks.

21. Thomas Smith, *A letter sent by I.B. Gentleman vnto his very frende Maystet [sic]...* (London, 1572) and Samantha Watson, 'To plant and improve: Justifying the consolidation of Tudor and Stuart imperial rule in Ireland, 1509 to 1625' (Unpublished PhD thesis, University of New South Wales, 2014).

22. Ted McCormick, *Human Empire: Mobility and Demographic Thought in the British Atlantic World, 1500–1800* (Oxford, 2022), pp. 83–90. See Chapter 2 above.

23. Ian Campbell, *Renaissance Humanism and Ethnicity before Race: The Irish and the English in the Seventeenth Century* (Manchester, 2013). Also see Chapter 2 above. Clare Carroll and Vincent Carey (eds.), *Solon his Follie, or A Politique Discourse Touching the Reformation or common-weales conquered, declined or corrupted* by Richard Beacon (Binghamton, NY, 1996).

24. E. M. Hinton, 'Rych's anatomy of Ireland (1615)', *Publications of the Modern Language Association of America*, 55 (1940), pp. 73–101, p. 83 (quote). Also see C. L. Falkiner (ed.), 'Barnaby Rich's "Remembrances of the state of Ireland, 1612"', *Proceedings, Royal Irish Academy*, 26, C (1906–7), pp. 125–42, Eugene Flanagan, 'The anatomy of Jacobean Ireland: Captain Barnaby Rich, Sir John Davies and the failure of reform, 1609-22' in Morgan (ed.), *Political Ideology in Ireland*, p. 176; Anne Fogarty, 'Literature in English, 1550–1690: From the Elizabethan settlement to the Battle of the Boyne' in Margaret Kelleher and Philip O'Leary (eds.), *The Cambridge History of Irish Literature, Volume 1 to 1890* (2 vols., Cambridge, 2008), p. 157.

25. BL, IOR/E/3/33, Aungier and Council at Bombay to the Company in London, 21 Dec. 1672, ff. 281r–281v.

26. Rebecca Bushnell, *A Culture of Teaching. Early Modern Humanism in Theory and Practice* (Ithaca, 1996). Also see Michael Braddick, 'Civility and Authority' in David Armitage and Michael J. Braddick (eds.), *The British Atlantic World, 1500–1800* (Basingstoke, 2002), 93–112, Andrew Fitzmaurice, 'The civic solution to the crisis of English colonization, 1609–1625', *The Historical Journal*, 42 (1999), pp. 25–51 and 'The Commercial Ideology of Colonization in Jacobean England: Robert Johnson, Giovanni Botero, and the Pursuit of Greatness', *The William and Mary Quarterly*, third series, 64 (2007), pp. 791–820.

27. Watson, 'To plant and improve', p. 282 and John Patrick Montaño, *The Roots of English Colonialism in Ireland* (Cambridge, 2011), p. 23. Also see Rebecca Bushnell, 'Experience, truth, and natural history in early English gardening books' in Donald R. Kelly and David Harris Sacks (eds.), *The Historical Imagination in Early Modern Britain: History, Rhetoric, and Fiction, 1500–1800* (Cambridge, 1997), pp. 179–209. I owe this reference to David Harris Sacks.

28. *CSPI, 1608–1610* (London, 1874), p. 17; Clare Carroll, *Circe's Cup: Cultural Transformations in Early Modern Ireland* (Cork, 2001), p. 13.

29. BL, IOR/E/3/34, Aungier at Bombay to Matthew Gray and Council at Surat, 27 Oct. 1673, f. 204v.

30. BL, IOR/E/3/34, Aungier at Bombay to the Company in London, 15 Jan. 1673[4], f. 339v.

31. Montaño, *The Roots of English Colonialism*, p. 23 and Patricia Seed, *Ceremonies of Possession in Europe's Conquest of the New World 1492–1640* (Cambridge, 1995), chapter 1.

32. Ohlmeyer, 'Eastward Enterprises', pp. 98, 110–11.

33. Joep Leerssen, 'Wildness, wilderness, and Ireland: Medieval and early-modern patterns in the demarcation of civility', *Journal of the History of Ideas* 56 (1995), pp. 25–39, especially pp. 32–4.

34. Andrew Hadfield and John McVeagh (eds.), *Strangers to that Land: British Perceptions of Ireland from the Reformation to the Famine* (Gerrards Cross, Buckinghamshire, 1994), p. 27.

35. Hadfield and McVeagh (eds.), *Strangers to that Land*, p. 28.

36. Sarah E. McKibben, 'In their "owne countre": Deriding and Defending the Early Modern Irish Nation after Gerald of Wales', *Eolas: The Journal of the American Society of Irish Medieval Studies*, 8 (2015), pp. 39–70 (p. 43).

37. Hiram Morgan, 'Giraldus Cambrensis and the Tudor Conquest of Ireland' in Morgan (ed.), *Political Ideology in Ireland*, pp. 22–44; Montaño, *The Roots of English Colonialism*, pp. 6–10; and Andrew Murphy, *But the Irish Sea Betwixt Us: Ireland, Colonialism and Renaissance Literature* (Lexington, Kentucky, 1999), chapter 2.

38. Stuart Carroll, 'Violence, Civil Society and European Civilisation' in Robert Antony, Stuart Carroll, and Caroline Dodds Pennock (eds.), *The Cambridge World History of Violence:* vol. 3 (Cambridge, 2020), p. 673.

39. Campbell, *Renaissance Humanism and Ethnicity before Race*, pp. 3–7, 190–1.

40. Keith Thomas, *In Pursuit of Civility: Manners and Civilization in Early Modern England* (New Haven, 2020), p. 236. Also see Ronald Raminelli, 'The meaning of color and race in Portuguese America, 1640–1750' in *Oxford Research Encyclopaedia: Latin American History* (Oxford, 2020), pp. 1–21.

41. Nicholas Canny, *Imagining Ireland's Pasts: Early Modern Ireland through the Centuries* (Oxford, 2021), p. 28.

42. Stephen O'Neill, *Staging Ireland: Representations in Shakespeare and Renaissance Drama* (Dublin, 2007), pp. 17, 32; Carroll, *Circe's Cup*, p. 18; and John Soderberg, 'Animals make the man: Violence, masculinity, and the colonial project in Derricke's *Image of* Ireland' in Thomas Herron, Denna J. Iammarino, and Maryclaire Moroney (eds.), *John Derricke's The Image of Irelande: with a Discoverie of Woodkarne. Essays on Text and Context* (Manchester, 2021), pp. 49–64.

43. Andrew Carpenter, *Verse in English from Tudor and Stuart Ireland* (Cork, 2003), p. 109.

44. Carpenter, *Verse*, pp. 111–12.

45. Hadfield and McVeagh (eds.), *Strangers to that Land*, p. 47. Also see Annaleigh Margey, 'Cannibalism at Knocknamase Castle, 1641' in Terence Dooley, Mary Ann Lyons, and Salvador Ryan (eds.), *The Historian as Detective: Uncovering Irish Pasts. Essays in Honour of Raymond Gillespie* (Dublin, 2021), pp. 117–20.

46. Wolfgang Gabbert, 'Human Sacrifice, Ritualised Violence and the Colonial Encounter in the Americas' in Robert Antony, Stuart Carroll, and Caroline Dodds Pennock (eds.), *The Cambridge World History of Violence:* vol. 3 (Cambridge, 2020), p. 96 and Catherine Armstrong, '"Boiled and stewed with roots and herbs": Everyday tales of cannibalism in early modern Virginia' in Angela McShane and Garthine Walker (eds.), *The Extraordinary and the Everyday in Early Modern England: Essays in Celebration of the Work of Bernard Capp* (Basingstoke, 2010), pp 161–76.

47. John McGurk, *The Elizabethan Conquest of Ireland* (Manchester, 1997), p. 18.
48. David Edwards, 'Ideology and experience: Spenser's *View* and martial law in Ireland' in Morgan (ed.), *Political Ideology in Ireland*, pp. 127–57 (quote p. 128).
49. Edwards, 'Ideology and experience: Spenser's *View* and martial law in Ireland', p. 156; Montaño, *The Roots of English Colonialism*, p. 344; Andrew Hadfield, 'Educating the colonial mind: Spenser and the plantation' and Willy Maley, 'Angling for Ulster: Ireland and plantation in Jacobean literature' in Ó Ciardha and Ó Siochrú (eds.), *The Plantation of Ulster*, pp. 158–75; O'Neill, *Staging Ireland*, pp. 68, 81, 86, 218, 221, 228, 247.
50. Quoted in Thomas, *In Pursuit of Civility*, pp. 212–13.
51. Stuart Carroll, 'Violence, Civil Society and European Civilisation' in Antony, Carroll, and Dodds Pennock (eds.), *The Cambridge World History of Violence*, p. 673.
52. Canny, *The Elizabethan Conquest of Ireland*, p. 160 and 'The Ideology of English Colonization: From Ireland to America', pp. 575–98; D. B. Quinn, 'Ireland and Sixteenth Century European Expansion', pp. 20–32; J. H. Elliott, *Empires of the Atlantic World: Britain and Spain in America 1492–1830* (New Haven, 2006), p. 24. See also Rolf Loeber, 'Preliminaries to the Massachusetts Bay Colony: The Irish ventures of Emanuel Downing and John Winthrop Sr' in Toby Barnard, Dáibhí Ó Cróinín, and Katherine Simms (eds.), *'A Miracle of Learning': Studies in Manuscripts and Irish Learning* (Aldershot, 1998), pp. 164–200; Patricia Coughlan, 'Counter-currents in colonial discourse: The political thought of Vincent and Daniel Gookin' in Jane Ohlmeyer (ed.), *Political Thought in Seventeenth Century Ireland* (Cambridge, 2000), pp. 56–82.
53. Wayne Lee, *Barbarians and Brothers: Anglo-American Warfare, 1500–1865* (Oxford, 2011), pp. 57, 60, 123–5, 242.
54. Sacks, 'Love and Fear in the Making of England's Atlantic Empire', pp. 552–4, 563.
55. Eliga H. Gould, 'Entangled Histories, Entangled Worlds: The English-Speaking Atlantic as a Spanish Periphery', *American Historical Review*, 12 (2007), pp. 764–86 (quote p. 769).
56. John Smith, *The Generall Historie of Virginia...* (London, 1624), p. 147.
57. David Harris Sacks, 'The true temper of empire: dominion, friendship and exchange in the English Atlantic, c. 1575–1625', *Renaissance Studies*, 26 (2012), pp. 554–8 (quote p. 555).
58. Alison Games, 'Violence on the Fringes: The Virginia (1622) and Amboya (1623) Massacres', *History*, 99 (2014), pp. 505–29.
59. Gerard Farrell, *The 'Mere Irish' and the Colonisation of Ulster, 1570–1641* (London, 2017), pp. 280–3; Micheál Ó Siochrú, 'Extirpation and Annihilation in Cromwellian Ireland' in Ben Kiernan, *The Cambridge World History of Genocide*, vol. 2, *Genocide in the Indigenous, Early Modern, and Imperial Worlds, from c.1535 to World War One* (Cambridge, 2022), chapter 7.
60. Quoted (p. 80) in J. H. Elliott, *Empires of the Atlantic World: Britain and Spain in America 1492–1830* (New Haven, 2006).
61. *The English Empire in America: Or a Prospect of His Majesties Dominions in the West-Indies...* (London, 1685), p. 85.
62. *The English Empire in America*, pp. 88, 131. Italics in the original.

63. Brendan Kane, 'Masculinity and political geographies in England, Ireland and North America', *European Review of History: Revue européenne d'histoire*, 22 (2015), pp. 595–619 (quote p. 599).

64. Carla Pestana and Sharon V. Salinger (eds.), *The Early English Caribbean, 1570–1700* (4 vols., London, 2014), III, pp. 283–4.

65. Quoted in Hilary McD. Beckles, 'A "riotous and unruly lot": Irish Indentured Servants and Freemen in the English West Indies, 1644–1713', *The William and Mary Quarterly*, 47 (1990), p. 517.

66. Morgan Godwyn, *The Negro's and Indians Advocate* (London, 1680), p. 35.

67. Godwyn, *The Negro's and Indians Advocate* (London, 1680), p. 36.

68. Quoted in Kevin Whelan, 'The Green Atlantic: Radical reciprocities between Ireland and America in the long eighteenth century' in Kathleen Wilson (ed.), *A New Imperial History: Culture, Identity and Modernity in Britain and the Empire 1660–1840* (Cambridge, 2004), p. 233.

69. Catherine Hall and Sonya O. Rose (eds.), *At Home with the Empire: Metropolitan Culture and the Imperial World* (Cambridge, 2006), pp. 19–20.

70. Ann L. Stoler, 'Intimidations of Empire: Predicaments of the Tactile and Unseen' in Ann L. Stoler (ed.), *Haunted by Empire* (Durham, NC, 2006), p. 2.

71. William Petty, *Political Arithmetick, or, A Discourse concerning the Extent and Value of Lands, People, Buildings* (London, 1691), p. 22.

72. Carroll, *Circe's Cup*, pp. 31, 39, 40 (quote).

73. Raymond Gillespie, 'Temple's Fate: Reading *The Irish Rebellion* in Late Seventeenth-Century Ireland' in Ciaran Brady and Jane Ohlmeyer (eds.), *British Interventions in Early Modern Ireland* (Cambridge, 2004), pp. 315–33; Toby Barnard, 'The Uses of 23 October 1641 and Irish Protestant Celebrations', *English Historical Review*, 106 (1991), pp. 889–920 and ' "Parlour entertainment in an evening?" Histories of the 1640s' in Micheál Ó Siochrú (ed.), *Kingdoms in Crisis: Ireland in the 1640s* (Dublin, 2001), pp. 20–43; John Gibney, *The Shadow of a Year: The 1641 Rebellion in Irish History and Memory* (Madison, Wisconsin, 2013), especially the final chapter.

74. John Ogilby, *Asia, The First Part. Being an Accurate Description of Persia and the several Provinces thereof* (London, 1673), p. 115.

75. Rita Banerjee, *India in Early Modern English Travel Writings: Protestantism, Enlightenment, and Toleration* (Leiden, 2021), pp. 170–1, 234.

76. Perry Curtis, *Apes and Angels: The Irishman in Victorian Caricature* (Washington DC, 1997). Also see Tom Bartlett, 'Ireland, Empire, and Union, 1690–1801' in Kevin Kenny (ed.), *Ireland and the British Empire* (Oxford, 2004), p. 86.

77. Quoted in Michael Silvestri, *Ireland and India: Nationalism, Empire and Memory* (London, 2009), p. 37. Roger Casement made similar arguments, Margaret O'Callaghan, 'Ireland, Empire, and British Foreign Policy: Roger Casement and the First World War, *Breac: A Digital Journal of Irish Studies* (2016), https://breac.nd.edu, accessed 15 June 2022.

78. TNA, Colonial Office 1/31, ff. 4–5. I am grateful to Mark Goldie for sharing his transcript of the memorandum with me.

79. *CSP, Colonial 1677–1680* (London, 1896), p. 82.

80. Aidan Clarke, 'The history of Poynings' Law, 1615–1641', *Irish Historical Studies*, 18 (1972), pp. 207–22; Micheál Ó Siochrú, 'Catholic Confederates and the constitutional relationship between Ireland and England, 1641–1649' in Ciaran Brady and Jane Ohlmeyer (eds.), *British Interventions in Early Modern Ireland* (Cambridge, 2005), pp. 207–29; and James Kelly, *Poynings' Law and the Making of Law in Ireland, 1660–1800: Monitoring the Constitution* (Dublin, 2007).

81. *CSP, Colonial 1677–1680* (London, 1896), pp. 158, 178.

82. *CSP, Colonial 1677–1680* (London, 1896), p. 310.

83. Aaron Graham, 'Searching for sovereignties: The formation of the penal laws and slave codes in Ireland and the British Caribbean, *c.*1680–*c.*1720' in O'Kane and O'Neill (eds.), *Ireland, Slavery and the Caribbean*, pp. 146–7.

84. David Fitzpatrick, 'Ireland and Empire' in Andrew Porter (ed.), *The Oxford History of the British Empire*. vol. 3. *The Nineteenth Century* (Oxford, 1999), p. 520.

85. Jerry Bannister, 'The oriental Atlantic: Governance and regulatory frameworks in the British Atlantic world' in H. V. Bowen, Elizabeth Mancke, and John G. Reid (eds.), *Britain's Oceanic Empire: Atlantic and Indian Ocean Worlds, c.1550–1850* (Cambridge, 2012), pp. 151–78 (quote p. 155).

86. See Chapter 4 above. Christopher Tomlins, 'Legal Cartography of Colonization, the Legal Polyphony of Settlement: English Intrusions on the American Mainland in the Seventeenth Century', The Symposium: Colonialism, Culture, and the Law, 26 *Law & Soc. Inquiry*, 315 (2001), pp. 315–65.

87. E. M. Rose, 'Viscounts in Virginia: A Proposal to Create American Noblemen (1619)', *Huntington Library Quarterly*, 83 (2020), pp. 184–95 and Jane Ohlmeyer, *Making Ireland English: The Irish Aristocracy in the Seventeenth Century* (New Haven and London, 2012), chapter 2.

88. John M. Collins, *Martial Law and English Laws, c.1500–c.1700* (Cambridge, 2016), p. 98.

89. Ó Ciardha and Ó Siochrú (eds.), *The Plantation of Ulster*, p. 1 and Finola O'Kane and Ciaran O'Neill, 'Introduction' in O'Kane and O'Neill (eds.), *Ireland, Slavery and the Caribbean*, p. 2.

90. James Walvin, *Fruits of Empire: Exotic Produce and British Taste, 1660–1800* (London, 1997), pp. 132–3, 146 (quote), 154. Also see Sacks, 'Love and Fear in the Making of England's Atlantic Empire', pp. 543–65.

91. Leslie Herman, 'Building Narratives: Ireland and the "Colonial Period" in American Architectural History' (Unpublished PhD, Columbia University, 2019), pp. 95, 114.

92. Emily Mann, 'Two islands, many forts: Ireland and Bermuda in 1624' in O'Kane and O'Neill (eds.), *Ireland, Slavery and the Caribbean*, pp. 215–39.

93. Charles Ivar McGrath, 'Imperial barrack-building in eighteenth-century Ireland and Jamaica' in O'Kane and O'Neill (eds.), *Ireland, Slavery and the Caribbean*, pp. 240–55 (quote p. 242).

94. Nicholas Canny (ed.), *The Origins of Empire: British Overseas Enterprise to the Close of the Seventeenth Century* (Oxford, 1998), pp. 9–10.

95. Louis P. Nelson, 'The architectures of empire in Jamaica: The Irish connection' in Finola O'Kane and Ciaran O'Neill (eds.), *Ireland, Slavery and the Caribbean: Interdisciplinary Perspectives* (Manchester, 2023), pp. 256–81 and Herman, 'Building Narratives', pp. 138, 144.

96. Luke Joseph Pecoraro, ' "Mr. Gookin Out of Ireland, Wholly Upon his Owne Adventure": An Archaeological Study of Intercolonial and Transatlantic Connections in the Seventeenth Century' (Unpublished PhD, Boston University, 2015).

97. Herman, 'Building Narratives', pp. 136, 151.

98. Quoted in Herman, 'Building Narratives', p. 384.

99. Ó Ciardha and Ó Siochrú (eds.), *The Plantation of Ulster*, p. 9; Robert Home, *Of Planting and Planning* (London, 1997), pp. 16–17.

100. Isabel Grubb (ed.), *My Irish Journal 1669–1670 by* William Penn (London, 1952).

101. Herman, 'Building Narratives', pp. 190–4; David Dickson, *Old World Colony. Cork and South Munster 1630–1830* (Cork, 2005), pp. 48, 50, 173; Ohlmeyer, *Making* pp. 317–19, 409.

102. Ted McCormick, *William Petty and the Ambitions of Political Arithmetic* (Oxford, 2009), especially chapters 5 and 6.

103. McCormick, *William Petty*, p. 238.

104. McCormick, *William Petty*, pp. 235–38; Herman, 'Building Narratives', pp. 215–33, 246, 254, 298. Marcus Gallo, 'William Penn, William Petty, and Surveying: The Irish Connection' in Andrew R. Murphy and John Smolenski (eds.), *The Worlds of William Penn* (New Brunswick, New Jersey, 2019), pp. 101–19.

105. Herman, 'Building Narratives', pp. 260–77.

106. Herman, 'Building Narratives', p. 3.

107. Sir Charles Fawcett (ed.), *The English Factories in India*, new series, vol. 1 *The Western Presidency, 1670–1677* (Oxford, 1936), p. 44.

108. Many of the directors had colonial interests in Ireland, see Chapter 4 above.

109. BL, IOR/E/3/33, Aungier and Council at Bombay to the Company in London, 21 Dec. 1672, f. 284.

110. See Chapter 2, Section I.

111. IOR/G/36/105 ff.24–6 [1]: John Goodier and Henry Young at Bombay, 19–30 Oct. 1668, f. 24.

112. IOR/E/3/33, Aungier and Council at Bombay to the Company in London, 21 Dec. 1672, f. 284v.

113. S. Ahmed Khan, *Anglo-Portuguese Negotiations Relating to Bombay, 1660–1677* (Oxford, 1922), pp. 490–4.

114. He demonstrated a familiarity with civil, canon, and common law and did not hesitate to cite legal texts like Henry Swinburne, *A briefe treatise of Testaments and last Wills*, first published in 1590 and a standard book on family law, John Cowell's *Institutes of the Laws of England,* or other works 'which I have studied', BL, IOR, Mss Eur Photo Eur 149/11 Correspondence, Original—Secretary of State (1668–70), f. 32.

115. BL, IOR/E/3/34, 'Acco[un]tt of Bookes Remayning in the Library of Surratt July 31st Anno Domini 1673', f. 86.
116. Richard Bolton, *The Statutes of Ireland*... (Dublin, 1621) and *A justice of peace for Ireland, consisting of two bookes; whereunto are added many presidents of indictments of treasons, felonies*... (Dublin, 1638 and London, 1683).
117. Aungier has been credited as being the 'architect of the judicial system' in Bombay, http://bombayhighcourt.nic.in/history.php; accessed 15 June 2022.
118. BL, IOR/E/3/33, Aungier and Council at Bombay to the Company in London, 11 Jan. 1672[3], f. 330v.
119. George W. Forrest (ed.), *Selections from the letters, despatches, and other state papers preserved in the Bombay Secretariat Home Series* (2 vols., Bombay, 1887), I, p. 55.
120. BL, IOR/E/3/32, Aungier and Council at Swally to the Company in London, 7 Nov. 1671, f. 96.
121. Ohlmeyer, *Making Ireland English* and Ted McCormick, '"A proportionable mixture": William Petty, Political Arithmetic, and the Transmutation of the Irish' in Coleman A. Dennehy (ed.), *Restoration Ireland: Always Settling and Never Settled*. (Aldershot, Hampshire and Burlington, VT, 2008), pp. 123–39. For this strong sense of Englishness in the Atlantic world see Joyce Chaplain, 'The British Atlantic' in Nicholas Canny and Philip Morgan (eds.), *The Oxford Handbook of the Atlantic World c.1450–c.1850* (Oxford, 2011), pp. 219–34.
122. Quoted in Crosbie, *Irish Imperial Networks*, p. 135. Also see E. Stokes, *English Utilitarians and India* (Oxford, 1959) and Caroline Elkins, *Legacy of Violence: A History of the British Empire* (London, 2022), p. 12.
123. See Chapter 2.
124. Seed, *Ceremonies of Possession*; Richard L. Kagan, 'People and Places in the Americas: A comparative approach' in Canny and Morgan (eds.), *The Oxford Handbook of the Atlantic World*, pp. 341–61; Sandra den Otter, 'Law, authority, and Colonial Rule' in Douglas M. Peers and Nandini Gooptu (eds.), *India and the British Empire* (Oxford, 2012), pp. 168–90.
125. *CSP, Colonial 1689–1692* (London, 1901), p. 295.
126. Alix Chartrand, 'The evolution of British Imperial perceptions in Ireland and India c.1650–1800' (Unpublished PhD thesis, Cambridge University, 2018) and Éamonn ó Ciardha, 'Tories and Moss-troopers in Scotland and Ireland in the Interregnum: A political dimension' in John R. Young (ed.), *Celtic Dimensions of the British Civil Wars* (Edinburgh, 1997), pp. 141–63.
127. Collins, *Martial Law and English Laws*, pp. 97–104, 210–11, 276–80.
128. Jennifer Wells, 'Anglicizing Social Control and Punishment, from Irish Servants to East Indian Slaves', paper presented at conference on 'Anglicization of Law and through Law: Early Modern British North America, India, and Ireland Compared', Newberry Library (April 2016) (cited with permission of author); Stern, *The Company State*, pp. 22, 75.
129. Graham, 'Searching for sovereignties', pp. 142, 145.
130. Ohlmeyer, 'Eastward Enterprises', pp. 96–102.

131. BL, IOR/E/3/33, Gerald Aungier and Council at Bombay to the East India Company in London, 21 Dec. 1672, ff. 275r–275v.

132. Forrest (ed.), *Selections from the letters,* p. 386.

133. BL, IOR/E/3/34, Aungier and Council at Bombay to the East India Company in London, 15 Dec. 1673–19 Jan. 1673[4], f. 280 and BL, IOR/E/3/34, Aungier and Council at Bombay to the East India Company in London, 19 Jan. 1673[4], f. 290. On Ireland see J. H. Andrews, *Shapes of Ireland: Maps and their Makers, 1564–1839* (Dublin, 1997) and http://downsurvey.tcd.ie, accessed 15 June 2022.

134. BL, IOR/E/3/38, 'Description of the East India Company's houses on Bombay island', [1677], ff. 200–3.

135. Kane, 'Masculinity and political geographies', pp. 595–619 and Annaleigh Margey, 'Plantations, 1550–1641' in Jane Ohlmeyer (ed.), *The Cambridge History of Ireland. vol. 2. Early Modern Ireland, 1550–1730* (Cambridge, 2018), chapter 22.

136. Montaño, *The Roots of English Colonialism,* pp. 178–83.

137. Marie Sophie Hingst, 'One phenomenon, three perspectives: English colonial strategies in Ireland revisited, 1603–1680' (Unpublished PhD, Trinity College Dublin, 2017), pp. 54–6, 76.

138. Of particular importance are the various maps and surveys associated with the plantations of Munster and Ulster, the Strafford Survey of Connacht (1636–40), Sir William Petty's 'Down Survey' (1654–9) comprising *c.*2,000 maps covering over 60,000 townlands, and the 'Civil Survey' (1654–6). McCormick, *William Petty,* chapter 3. The Books of Survey and Distribution 'being abstracts of various surveys and instruments of title, 1636–1703' are especially noteworthy. See the introduction to R. C. Simington (ed.), *Books of Survey and Distribution. Being abstracts of various surveys and instruments of title, 1636–1703* vol. 1 *County of Roscommon* (IMC, Dublin, 1949); Robert C. Simington, 'Annesley collection photographic acquisition by the National Library', *Analecta Hibernica,* 16 (1946), pp. 350–4; Geraldine Talon, 'Books of survey and distribution, County Westmeath: A comparative survey, with reference to their administrative context and chronological sequence', *Analecta Hibernica,* 28 (1978), pp. 105–15.

139. http://downsurvey.tcd.ie/index.html, accessed 12 April 2022. The Down Survey Maps website, published online in 2013, provides digital images of all the surviving Down Survey maps at parish, barony, and county level, together with the written descriptions of each barony and parish that accompanied the original maps.

140. Hingst, 'One phenomenon, three perspectives', pp. 193–207.

141. Allan Greer, *Property and Dispossession: Natives, Empires and Land in Early Modern North Atlantic America* (Cambridge, 2018), p. 282.

142. Herman, 'Building Narratives', p. 300; Gallo, 'William Penn, William Petty, and Surveying', pp. 101–19.

143. Herman, 'Building Narratives', pp. 232–3 and Timothy Earl Miller, 'Gold for Secrets: The Hartlib Circle and The Early English Empire, 1630–1660' (Unpublished DPhil thesis, Oxford, 2020).

144. McCormick, *Human Empire*, p. 5.

145. Herman, 'Building Narratives', pp. 232–3.

146. McCormick, *William Petty and the Ambitions of Political Arithmetic*; Wilson, 'Rethinking the Colonial State', pp. 1295–322.

147. John Ovington, *A voyage to Suratt in the year 1689 giving a large account of that city and its inhabitations and of the English factory there: likewise a description of Madiera, St. Jago, Annobon, Cabenda, and Malemba* (London, 1696), p. 142; BL, IOR/E/3/36: ff. 45–6 List of the English, men and women, on Bombay, together with a list of those who died over past 3 years, taken 30 August 1675.

148. BL, IOR/E/3/36: ff. 45–6.

149. For examples from the Caribbean see Vere Langford Oliver (ed.), *Caribbeana: Being Miscellaneous Papers Relating to History ... of the British West Indies* (4 vols., London, 1912–1914), II, pp. 316–20 and 342–47; III, pp. 27–35, 70–81, 132–39, 173–79.

150. BL, IOR/E/3/34, Aungier and Council at Bombay to the Company in London, 15 Dec. 1673–19 Jan 1673[4], f. 280, BL, IOR/E/3/34, Aungier and Council at Bombay to the Company in London, 19 Jan. 1673[4], f. 290, and BL, IOR/E/3/88, Company to President and Council in Surat, 8 Mar. 1675[6], f. 132v.

151. Fawcett (ed.), *The Western Presidency, 1670–1677*, p. 106; M. D. David, 'The Beginning of Bombay's Economic Development, 1661–1708', *Journal of Indian History*, 55 (1977), pp. 217–18, 197–240.

152. Bernard S. Cohn, *Colonialism and its Forms of Knowledge: The British in India* (Princeton, New Jersey, 1996).

153. Crosbie, *Irish Imperial Networks*, pp. 100–1, 106, 110–11. Also see Ciara Boylan, 'Victorian ideologies of improvement: Sir Charles Trevelyan in India and Ireland' in T. Foley and M. O'Connor (eds.), *Ireland and India: Colonies, Culture and Empire* (Dublin, 2006), pp. 167–78 and Christopher Bayly, *Empire and Information: Intelligence Gathering and Social Communication in India, 1780–1870* (Cambridge, 1996).

154. Richard Drayton, *Nature's Government: Science, Imperial Britain and the 'Improvement' of the World* (New Delhi, 2005), pp. 10, 52, 55–8 and David Arnold, 'Agriculture and "Improvement" in Early Colonial India: A Pre-History of Development', *Journal of Agrarian Change*, 5 (2005), pp. 505–25.

155. For the latter period, Chris Bayly, 'Ireland, India and the Empire: 1780–1914', *Transactions of the Royal Historical Society*, 6th Series, 10 (2000), pp. 377–97.

156. S. B. Cook, *Imperial Affinities: Nineteenth-Century Analogies and Exchanges Between India and Ireland* (New Delhi, 1993), p. 7.

157. Cook, *Imperial Affinities*, p. 17.

158. Chartrand, 'The evolution of British Imperial perceptions'.

159. Jane Ohlmeyer, 'Ireland, India and the British Empire', *Studies in People's History*, 2 (2015), pp. 169–88.

160. Alvin Jackson, 'Ireland, the Union, and the Empire, 1800–1960' in Kenny (ed.), *Ireland and the British Empire*, p. 125; and Virginia Crossman, 'Local Government in Nineteenth-Century Ireland' in Terence McDonough (ed.), *Was Ireland a Colony? Economics, Politics and Culture in Nineteenth-Century Ireland* (Dublin, 2005), pp. 102–16.

161. R. C. Hawkins, 'The "Irish Model" and the empire: A case for reassessment' in D. M. Anderson and D. Killingray (eds.), *Policing the Empire: Government, Authority and Control, 1830–1940* (Manchester, 1991), pp. 18–32; and Keith Jeffrey (ed.), *An Irish Empire? Aspects of Ireland and the British Empire* (Manchester 1996), p. 10.

162. Michael Silvestri, '"The Sinn Fein of India": Irish Nationalism and the Policing of Revolutionary Terrorism in Bengal', *Journal of British Studies*, 39 (2000), pp. 478–85 and ' "An Irishman Is Specially Suited to Be a Policeman": Sir Charles Tegart & Revolutionary Terrorism in Bengal', *History Ireland*, 8 (2000), pp. 40–4. More generally see Shasi Tharoor, *Inglorious Empire: What the British Did to India* (London, 2016).

163. BL, IOR/E/3/36, ff. 45–6. Thomas Bartlett, ' "Rishti": Irish Soldiers in India 1750–1920' in Jyoti Atwal and Eunan O'Halpin (eds.), *India, Ireland and Anti-Imperial Struggle: Remembering the Connaught Rangers Mutiny, 1920* (New Delhi, 2021), pp. 21–31.

164. Thomas Bartlett, 'The Irish soldier in India, 1750–1947' in Michael Holmes and Denis Holmes (eds.), *Ireland and India: Connections, Comparisons, Contrasts* (Dublin, 1997), pp. 12–28; and Fitzpatrick, 'Ireland and Empire' in Porter (ed.), *The Nineteenth Century*, pp. 498, 511.

165. Andrew MacKillop, *Human Capital and Empire: Scotland, Ireland, Wales and British Imperialism in Asia, c.1690–c.1820* (Manchester, 2021), p. 269; and Kevin Kenny, 'The Irish in the Empire' in Kenny (ed.), *Ireland and the British Empire*, pp. 104–8.

166. T. G. Fraser, 'Ireland and India' in Jeffrey (ed.), *An Irish Empire?*, p. 81.

167. Silvestri, *Ireland and India*, chapter 3; quoting (p. 107) William Dalrymple.

168. 'Notes for examinations in various Oriental languages, Indian Civil Service Commission papers and some Trinity College Dublin papers' (TCD, Ms 2723).

169. Christopher Shepard, 'Cramming, instrumentality and the education of Irish imperial elites' in David Dickson, Justyna Pyz, and Christopher Shepard (eds.), *Irish Classrooms and British Empire: Imperial Contexts in the Origins of Modern Education* (Dublin, 2012), pp. 172–83.

170. S. B. Cook, 'The Irish Raj: Social origins and careers of Irishmen in the Indian Civil Service. 1855–1911', *Journal of Social History*, 20 (1987), pp. 507–29; and Kenny (ed.), *Ireland and the British Empire*, pp. 102–3.

171. Antoinette Burton, *The Trouble with Empire: Challenges to Modern British Imperialism* (Oxford, 2015), p. 1.

172. Priyamvada Gopal, *Insurgent Empire: Anticolonial Resistance and British Dissent* (London, 2019), pp. 29–35.

173. Burton, *The Trouble with Empire*, p. 10 and Gopal, *Insurgent Empire*, p. 35.

174. Jack P. Greene, 'Britain's Overseas Empire before 1780: Overwhelmingly Successful and Bureaucratically Challenged' in Peter Crooks and Timothy H. Parsons (eds.), *Empires and Bureaucracy in World History: From Late Antiquity to the Twentieth Century* (Cambridge, 2016), pp. 318–43.

175. *CSP, Colonial 1677–1680* (London, 1896), pp. 347, 367, 457.

176. *CSP, Colonial 1677–1680* (London, 1896), p. 371.

177. Jack P. Greene, *Peripheries and Center: Constitutional Development in the Extended Polities of the British Empire and the United States, 1607–1788* (Athens, Georgia, 1987), p. 33, 40; Collins, *Martial Law and English Laws*, pp. 238–9; and Robert Weir, 'Shaftesbury's Darling': British Settlement in the Carolinas at the Close of the Seventeenth Century' in Canny (ed.), *The Origins of Empire*, pp. 375–97.

178. See Chapter 4 above.

179. Jack P. Greene, *The Intellectual Heritage of the Constitutional Era* (Philadelphia, 1986), pp. 16, 19, 23.

180. Charles Ivar McGrath, *Ireland and Empire 1692–1770* (London, 2012), p. 38.

181. Whelan, 'The Green Atlantic', pp. 216–38.

182. The focus here is India but it is important to acknowledge the humanitarian work of Roger Casement in the Belgian Congo and on behalf of the Putumayo peoples of the Amazon, Angus Mitchel, *Casement* (London, 2005); and Margaret O'Callaghan, 'With the eyes of another race, of a people once hunted themselves': Casement, colonialism and a remembered past' in D. George Boyce and Alan O'Day (eds.), *Ireland in Transition, 1867–1921* (London, 2004).

183. Fraser, 'Ireland and India' in Jeffrey (ed.), *An Irish Empire*, p. 85.

184. Jill Bender, 'The Imperial Politics of Famine: The 1873–74 Bengal Famine and Irish Parliamentary Nationalism', *Eire-Ireland*, special issue 42 (2007), pp. 145–6; and Peter Gray, 'Famine and Land in Ireland and India 1845–1880: James Caird and the Political Economy of Hunger', *The Historical Journal*, 49 (2006), pp. 193–215.

185. Deidre McMahon, 'Ireland, the Empire and the Commonwealth', Kenny (ed.), *Ireland and the British Empire*, pp. 188–9.

186. Cook, *Imperial Affinities*, p. 130. Also see Jackson, 'Ireland, the Union, and the Empire, 1800–1960' in Kenny, (ed.), *Ireland and the British Empire*, pp. 132–3.

187. Fitzpatrick, 'Ireland and Empire' in Porter (ed.), *The Nineteenth Century*, pp. 497, 517.

188. Cook, *Imperial Affinities*; and Tony Ballantyne, 'The Sinews of Empire: Ireland, India and the Construction of British Colonial Knowledge' in McDonough (ed.), *Was Ireland a Colony?*, p. 157.

189. Cook, 'The Irish Raj', pp. 507–29; and Crosbie, *Irish Imperial Networks*, pp. 96, 208.

190. Andrew Gailey, *The Lost Imperialist: Lord Dufferin, Memory and Mythmaking in an Age of Celebrity* (London, 2015) enjoyed unprecedented access to Dufferin's archive much of which is still in private hands at Clandeboy in County Antrim. Also 'Lord Dufferin and the character of the Indian nationalist leadership' in Bipan Chandra, *Nationalism and Colonialism in Modern India* (New Delhi, 1981), pp. 275–96.

191. Quoted in Fraser, 'Ireland and India' in Jeffrey (ed.), *An Irish Empire?*, p. 87.

192. Quoted in Kaori Nagai, *Empire of Analogies: Kipling, India and Ireland* (Cork, 2006), p. 113.

193. Quoted in McMahon, 'Ireland, the Empire and the Commonwealth' in Kenny (ed.), *Ireland and the British Empire*, p. 187.

194. H. V. Brasted, 'Indian Nationalist development and the influence of Irish home rule, 1870–86', *Modern Asia Studies* 12 (1980), 37–63.

195. Crosbie, *Irish Imperial Networks*, pp. 224, 233; and Brasted, 'Indian Nationalist development', pp. 37–63.

196. Gauri Viswanathan, 'Ireland, India and the Poetics of Internationalism', *Journal of World History*, 15 (2004), pp. 7–30.

197. Douglas Hyde, 'The Necessity of De-Anglicising Ireland' in Seamus Deane, Andrew Carpenter, and Jonathan Williams (eds.), *The Field Day Anthology of Irish Writing* (3 vols., Derry, 1991), II, pp. 527–33.

198. William Butler Yeats, 'Easter 1916' in *The Collected Poems of W. B. Yeats* (Ware, Hartfordshire, 2008), p. 152.

199. Silvestri, *Ireland and India*, pp. 47–74 (quote p. 62).

200. Silvestri, ' "The Sinn Fein of India" ', p. 466.

201. Kate O'Malley, *Ireland, India and Empire: Indo-Irish Radical Connections, 1919–64* (Manchester, 2009).

202. Jackson, 'Ireland, the Union, and the Empire, 1800–1960' in Kenny (ed.), *Ireland and the British Empire*, p. 144.

203. Nicholas Mansergh, *The Prelude to Partition: Concepts and Aims in Ireland and India* (Cambridge, 1978), pp. 5–58.

204. T. G. Fraser, *Partition in Ireland, India and Palestine: Theory and Practice* (London, 1984), pp. 120–8; and Fraser, 'Ireland and India' in Jeffrey (ed.), *An Irish Empire?*, pp. 90–1.

205. Brian Girvan, 'Political Independence and democratic consolidation' in Holmes and Holmes (eds.), *Ireland and India*, p. 130.

206. Marianne Ellliott, *The Catholics of Ulster: A History* (London, 2000).

207. Paul Bew and Gordon Gillespie, *Northern Ireland: A Chronology of the Troubles 1968–1999* (London, 1999); and Paul Bew, Peter Gibbon, and Henry Patterson, *Northern Ireland 1921–2001* (London, 2002).

208. I am grateful to Stephen Rea for sharing this story with me.

209. Chiu Hsin-Hui, *The Colonial 'Civilizing Process' in Dutch Formosa: 1624–1662* (Leiden, 2008).

210. O'Kane, 'Comparing imperial design strategies', pp. 156–78.

211. See, for examples, French-controlled Algeria, Patrick Anderson, *Rewriting the Troubles: War and Propaganda. Ireland and Algeria* (Belfast, 2022) and Latin America, Tim Fanning, *Paisanos: The Forgotten Irish who Changed the Face of Latin America* (Dublin, 2016).

CHAPTER 06

1. Brian Friel, *Making History* (London, 1989), pp. 8–9

2. Friel, *Making History*, p. 66. Also see Chapter 1 above.

3. Tom Earle and Kate Lowe (eds.), *Black Africans in Renaissance Europe* (Cambridge, 2005).

4. J. S. Brewer and William Bullen (eds.), *Calendar of Carew Manuscripts* (2 vols., London, 1868), II, p. 144. I am grateful to Coleman Dennehy for sharing this reference with me.

5. Deposition of John Fortune, 21 June 1643, TCD, Ms 815, ff. 322r–322v.

6. Jonathan Jeffrey Wright, 'The Indian and the spy: A story of empire from 1640s Ireland' in Terence Dooley, Mary Ann Lyons, and Salvador Ryan (eds.), *The Historian as Detective: Uncovering Irish Pasts. Essays in Honour of Raymond Gillespie* (Dublin, 2021), pp. 125–7.

7. Representative Church Body Library, Dublin, 'The old registry book Youghal from 1665 to 1720' (P608/1/1). For adult baptism of Africans see Miranda Kaufmann, *Black Tudors: the Untold Story* (London, 2017), 159–63; and Connie Kelleher, *The Alliance of Pirates: Ireland and Atlantic Piracy in the Early Seventeenth Century* (Cork, 2020), p. 214.

8. NLI, Genealogical Office, Ms 67 pp. 137–8, 143; *An account of the solemn funeral and interrment of the right honourable the Countess of Arran, as it was lately sent in a letter or narrative from Dublin. Bearing date, Aug. 21. 1668* ([London], 1668), pp. 2–3. Also in *CSPI, 1666–1669* (London, 1908), pp. 637–41.

9. I am grateful to Bill Hart for this reference.

10. W. A. Hart, 'Africans in Eighteenth-Century Ireland', *Irish Historical Studies*, 33 (2002), pp. 19–32.

11. Coll Thrush, *Indigenous London: Native Travelers at the Heart of Empire* (New Haven and London, 2016).

12. Nini Rodgers, 'Equiano in Belfast: A study of the anti-slavery ethos in a Northern Town', *Slavery & Abolition. A journal of Slave and Post-Slave Studies*, 18 (1997), pp. 73–89 and Olaudah Equiano, *The Interesting Narrative of the Life of Olaudah Equiano* with a foreword by David Olusoga (London, 2021).

13. David Dickson, 'Setting out the terrain: Ireland and the Caribbean in the eighteenth century' in Finola O'Kane and Ciaran O'Neill (eds.), *Ireland, Slavery and the Caribbean: Interdisciplinary Perspectives* (Manchester, 2023), p. 32.

14. Gulfishan Khan, *Indian Muslim Perceptions of the West during the Eighteenth Century* (Karachi, 1998), pp. 95, 98, 219. I am grateful to Gulfishan Khan for bringing this to my attention.

15. Wollina, Torsten, 'Arabic Manuscripts in Trinity: The Huntingdon Collection (part 1)', in *Damascus Anecdotes*, March 8, 2020, https://thecamel.hypotheses. org/1661, accessed 16 June 2022.

16. TCD, MUN/LIB/1/53, p. 259.

17. Also see poem by Vasfi, taken after the siege of Delhi 1857, by George Roe Boyce MA (TCD, Ms 1611) and a Persian translation of an Arabic work by Kazvíní, 'taken after the seige of Khota [1858]' (TCD, Ms 2170). I am grateful to Jane Maxwell for sharing these references with me.

18. Jacqueline Hill and Colm Lennon (eds.), *Luxury and Austerity: Historical Studies XXI* (Dublin, 1999); and Toby Barnard, *Making the Grand Figure: Lives and Possessions in Ireland, 1641–1770* (New Haven, 2004) and *A Guide to Sources for the History of Material Culture in Ireland, 1500–2000* (Dublin, 2005).

19. Jane Ohlmeyer, 'Introduction: Ireland in the Early Modern World' in Jane Ohlmeyer (ed.), *The Cambridge History of Ireland.* vol. 2. *Early Modern Ireland, 1550–1730* (Cambridge, 2018), pp. 1–4; and Audrey Horning and Eric Schweickart, 'Globalization and the spread of capitalism: Material resonances', *Post-Medieval Archaeology*, 50 (2016), pp. 34–52.

20. Louis P. Nelson, 'The architectures of empire in Jamaica: The Irish connection' in O'Kane and O'Neill (eds.), *Ireland, Slavery and the Caribbean*, pp. 256–81.

21. For material culture in New Spain see Amelia Almorza Hidalgo, 'Spanish Women as Agents for a New Material Culture in Colonial Spanish America' and José l. Gasch-Tomás, 'Elites, Women and Chinese Porcelain in New Spain and in Andalusia, Circa 1600: A Global History' in Bartolomé Yun-Casalilla, Ilaria Berti, and Omar Svriz-Wucherer (eds.), *American Globalization, 1492–1850: Trans-Cultural Consumption in Spanish Latin America* (Abingdon, 2022), pp. 78–100 and pp. 225–44.

22. A. Giacometti and A. MacGowan, *Rathfarnham Castle Excavations, 2014* (Dublin, 2015), especially chapter 7.

23. Kelleher, *The Alliance of Pirates*, pp. 284–5 and Hazel Forsyth, *The Cheapside Hoard: London's Lost Jewels* (London, 2013).

24. Colin Breen, 'The maritime cultural landscape in medieval Gaelic Ireland' in Patrick Duffy, David Edwards, and Elizabeth Fitzpatrick (eds.), *Gaelic Ireland: Land Lordship and Settlement c. 1250–c. 1650* (Dublin, 2001), p. 427.

25. Audrey Horning, *Ireland in the Virginian Sea: Colonialism in the British Atlantic* (Williamsburg, Virginia, 2013), pp. 20–2.

26. John Nicholl, 'The leather finds from Rathfarnam Castle', *Archaeology Ireland*, 30 (2016), pp. 26–9.

27. Discussed in Chapter 2 above.

28. Clodagh Tait, 'Writing the social and cultural history of Ireland, 1550–1660: Wills as example and inspiration' in Sarah Covington, Vincent P. Carey, and Valerie McGowan-Doyle (eds.), *Early Modern Ireland: New Sources, Methods and Perspectives* (Abingdon, 2019), chapter 2.

29. Audrey Horning, 'Clothing and colonialism: The Dungiven costume and the fashioning of early modern identities', *Journal of Social Archaeology*, 14 (2014), pp. 296–318.

30. Brian Ó Dálaigh, 'An Inventory of the Contents of Bunratty Castle and the Will of Henry, Fifth Earl of Thomond, 1639', *North Munster Antiquarian Journal*, 36 (1995), pp. 139–65; Hector MacDonnell, 'A Seventeenth Century Inventory from Dunluce Castle, County Antrim', *Journal of the Royal Society of Antiquaries*, 122 (1992), pp. 109–27; BL, Additional Charter 13,340; and Edward MacLysaght (ed.), *Calendar of the Orrery Papers* (IMC, Dublin, 1941).

31. Marc Caball, 'Munster and India: The local and global in early modern Ireland' in Covington, Carey and McGowan-Doyle (eds.), *Early Modern Ireland*, chapter 8.

32. BL, IOR/E/3/35, Aungier and Council at Bombay to the Company in London, 18 Jan. 1674[5], f. 220, BL, IOR/B/33, f. 266, Court minutes, 14 July 1675 and BL, IOR/E/3/88, Company to President and Council in Surat, 8 Mar. 1675[6], f. 139v.

33. Caball, 'Munster and India', p. 131. For examples of Indian textiles generally in seventeenth-century Ireland see Jane Fenlon, *Goods and Chattels: A Survey of Early Household Inventories in Ireland* (Dublin, 2003), pp. 113, 115, 117, 119; and MacLysaght (ed.), *Calendar of the Orrery Papers*, pp. 168–79, 358–9.

34. Fenlon, *Goods and Chattels*, pp. 105–20.

35. HMC, *Calendar of the Manuscripts of the Marquess of Ormonde, Preserved at Kilkenny Castle* (Old and New Series, 11 vols., London, 1895–1920), NS, VII, pp. 502–7.

36. Lorna Weatherall, *Consumer Behaviour and Material Culture in Britain 1660–1760* (London, 1996), pp. 31, 86.

37. Edward Owen Teggin, 'The East India Company Career of Sir Robert Cowan in Bombay and the Western Indian Ocean, c. 1719–35' (Unpublished PhD thesis, Trinity College Dublin, 2020), p. 305 and Robert Cowan to John Scattergood, Bombay, 13 April 1722, Public Records Office of Northern Ireland, D654/B/1/1AA, f. 137v. I am grateful to Dr Teggin for sharing this with me.

38. James Walvin, *Fruits of Empire: Exotic Produce and British Taste, 1660–1800* (London, 1997), pp. 117–27.

39. J. Amelang, 'The New World in the Old? The absence of empire in early modern Madrid', *Cuadernos de Historia de España*, 82 (2008), pp. 147–64.

40. Andrew Carpenter, *Verse in English from Eighteenth-Century Ireland* (Cork, 1998), pp. 54–5.

41. Weatherall, *Consumer Behaviour*.

42. Madeline Shanahan, *Manuscript Recipe Books as Archaeological Objects: Text and Food in the Early Modern World* (Lanham, Maryland, 2015) and Susan Flavin, 'Domestic Materiality in Ireland, 1550–1730' in Ohlmeyer (ed.), *The Cambridge History of Ireland*, chapter 13.

43. Amelang, 'The New World in the Old?', pp. 147–64; Bethany Aram and Bartolomé Yun-Casalilla (eds.), *Global Goods and the Spanish Empire, 1492–1824: Circulation, Resistance and Diversity* (Basingstoke, 2014); and Walvin, *Fruits of Empire*, pp. 92, 105.

44. Lizzie Collingham, *The Taste of Empire: How Britain's Quest for Food Shaped the Modern World* (New York, 2017).

45. Alfred Cosby, *The Columbian Exchange: Biological and Cultural Consequences of 1492* (Westport, Connecticut, 1972).

46. BL, IOR/E/3/35, Aungier and Council at Bombay to the Company in London, 18 Jan. 1674[5], f. 220, BL, IOR/B/33, f. 266, Court minutes, 14 July 1675; BL, IOR/E/3/88, Company to President and Council in Surat, 8 Mar. 1675[6], f. 139v; Kelleher, *The Alliance of Pirates*, p. 149.

47. Danielle Clarke (ed.), *Receipt Books from Birr Castle, County Offaly, 1640–1920* (IMC, Dublin, forthcoming, 2023).

48. William O. Frazer, 'Field of Fire: Evidence for Wartime Conflict in a 17th-Century Cottier Settlement in County Meath, Ireland', *Journal of Conflict Archaeology*, 3 (2007), pp. 173–95 (quote p. 186). Also N. J. A. Williams (ed.), *Pairlement Chloinne Tómais* (Dublin, 1981), p. xvii.

49. Deposition of William Bailie, 16 July 1645, TCD, Ms 812, ff. 45r–v.

50. https://foodcult.eu, accessed 16 June 2022.

51. Walvin, *Fruits of Empire*, pp. 117–19; and Brendan Scott, 'Commodities and the Import Trade in Early Plantation Ulster', *Irish Economic and Social History*, 48 (2021), pp. 101–2.

52. Jon Stobart, *Sugar and Spice: Grocers and Groceries in Provincial England, 1650–1830* (Oxford, 2013), pp. 33–4.

53. Barnaby Rich, *The Irish hubbub, or, The English hue and crie briefly pursuing the base conditions, and most notorious offences of the vile, vaine, and wicked age, no lesse smarting*

then tickling: a merriment whereby to make the wise to laugh, and fooles to be angry (London, 1618), p. 44.

54. Williams (ed.), *Pairlement Chlionne Tómáis*, pp. xvii, 97 and Gerard Farrell, *The 'Mere Irish' and the Colonisation of Ulster, 1570–1641* (London, 2017), p. 122.

55. Examination of Joane Greete and Phillice Blake, 25 Aug. 1652, TCD, Ms 821, f. 272v.

56. Thomas Truxes, *Irish American Trade, 1660–1783* (Cambridge, 1988), p. 21.

57. Tait, 'Writing the social and cultural history of Ireland' and Susan Flavin, 'Domestic Materiality'.

58. John Appleby (ed.), *A Calendar of Material relating to Ireland from the High Court of Admiralty Examinations, 1536–1641* (IMC, Dublin, 1992) and Elaine Murphy (ed.), *A Calendar of Material Relating to Ireland from the High Court of Admiralty, 1641–1660* (IMC, Dublin, 2011).

59. http://www.courtmacsherrybarryroehistory.com/wrecks-in-dunworley, accessed 16 June 2022. I am grateful to Connie Kelleher for sharing this with me.

60. Stobart, *Sugar and Spice,* p. 69.

61. Maxine Berg, *Luxury and Pleasure in Eighteenth-Century Britain* (Oxford and New York, 2005).

62. McGrath, *Ireland and Empire*, pp. 173, 176.

63. Kelleher, *The Alliance of Pirates,* pp. 95, 152, 156–7, 160, 162; Jane Ohlmeyer, 'Irish privateers during the civil war, 1642–50', *The Mariner's Mirror*, 76 (1990), pp 119–34 and ' "The Dunkirk of Ireland": Wexford privateers during the 1640s', *Journal of the Wexford Historical Society*, 12 (1988–9), pp. 23–49; Murphy (ed.), *A Calendar of Material*, entries 107, 185, 323, 425, 506, 512, 616, 736, 769, 788, 795, 911, 1011, 1147.

64. Thomas Truxes, *Irish American Trade, 1660–1783* (Cambridge, 1988), p. 73.

65. Nini Rodgers, 'Ireland and the Black Atlantic in the Eighteenth Century', *Irish Historical Studies*, 32 (2000), pp. 174–92 and David Dickson, *The First Irish Cities: An Eighteenth-Century Transformation* (New Haven and London, 2021), chapters 3, 4, and 5.

66. Dickson, 'Setting out the terrain', p. 23.

67. David Dickson, *Old World Colony: Cork and South Munster 1630–1830* (Cork, 2005), especially chapters 4 and 10; Stephen J. Hornsby, 'Geographies of the British Atlantic World' in H. V. Bowen, Elizabeth Mancke, and John G. Reid (eds.), *Britain's Oceanic Empire: Atlantic and Indian Ocean worlds, c.1550–1850* (Cambridge, 2012), pp. 15–44.

68. Clodagh Tait, 'From beer and shoes to sugar and slaves: Five Baptist Loobys in Cork and Antigua' in Dooley, Lyons, and Ryan (eds.), *The Historian as Detective*, pp. 131–4.

69. National Folklore Collection, The Schools' Collection, Volume 0647, Page 12, https://www.duchas.ie/en/cbes/4428133/4380926/4459370, accessed 16 June 2022.

70. Nicholas Canny, *Making Ireland British 1580–1650* (Oxford, 2001); William Smyth, *Map-making, Landscapes and Memory: A Geography of Colonial and Early*

Modern Ireland c1530–1750 (Cork, 2006); and Keith Pluymers, 'Cow Trials, Climate Causes of Violence', *Environmental History*, 25: 2 (2020), pp. 287–309.

71. Quoted in C. Maxwell (ed.), *Irish History from Contemporary Sources (1509–1610)* (London, 1923), p. 291.

72. Francis Ludlow and Arlene Crampsie, 'Environmental History of Ireland, 1550–1730' in Ohlmeyer (ed.), *The Cambridge History of Ireland*, chapter 24; Keith Pluymers, *No Wood, No Kingdom: Political Ecology in the English Atlantic* (Philadelphia, 2021), especially chapter 1, and 'Taming the wilderness in sixteenth and seventeenth century Ireland and Virginia', *Environmental History* 16 (2011), pp. 610–32.

73. Kenneth Nicholls, 'Woodland Cover in pre-Modern Ireland' in Patrick Duffy, David Edwards, and Elizabeth Fitzpatrick (eds.), *Gaelic Ireland: Land Lordship and Settlement c. 1250–c. 1650* (Dublin, 2001), chapter 6; Joseph Nunan, 'Boyle and the East India Company in Co. Cork: A case study in colonial competition' in Edwards and Rynne (eds.), *The Colonial World of Richard Boyle*, pp. 64–73; and Nigel Everett, *The Woods of Ireland: A History, 700–1800* (Dublin, 2015).

74. Keith Pluymers, *No Wood, No Kingdom: Political Ecology in the English Atlantic* (Philadelphia, 2021), especially chapter 5, and 'Taming the wilderness in sixteenth and seventeenth century Ireland and Virginia', *Environmental History* 16 (2011), pp. 610–32.

75. Sharon Weadick, 'How popular were fortified houses in Irish castle building history? A look at their numbers in the archaeological record and distribution patterns' in Colin Rynne and James Lyttleton (eds.), *Plantation Ireland: Settlement and Material Culture, c. 1550–c.1700* (Dublin, 2009), p. 62; James Lyttleton, 'Gaelic classicism in the Irish midland plantations: An archaeological reflection' and Tadhg O'Keeffe, 'Plantation-era great houses in Munster: A note on Sir Walter Raleigh's house and its context' in Thomas Herron and Michael Potterton (ed.), *Ireland in the Renaissance, c.1540–1660* (Dublin, 2007), pp. 231–54 and 274–88.

76. David Sweetman, *The Medieval Castles in Ireland* (Cork, 1999), p. 175.

77. The earl of Antrim built castles at Ballycastle, Ballygalley, Glenarm, and Kilwaughter; Viscount Chichester built a mansion, Joymount, at Carrickfergus, and castles at Belfast and Dungannon in County Tyrone; and Lord Conway built a grand house at Lisburn. In County Down Lord Cromwell constructed a castle at Lecale, Viscount Claneboye built one at Bangor, and Viscount Montgomery one at Newtown. Lord Blayney built Castle Blayney and another in Monaghan. In County Tyrone the earl of Castlehaven oversaw the erection of Ballynahatty near Omagh, Lord Hamilton built a castle at Strabane, and Lord Castle Stewart one near Stewartstown. Lord Balfour of Glenawley built Castle Balfour in County Fermanagh and Lord Charlemont a mansion at Castlecaulfeild and an impressive house at Charlemount, Jane Ohlmeyer, *Making Ireland English: The Irish Aristocracy in the Seventeenth Century* (New Haven and London, 2012), chapter 14.

78. Sheila Pim, 'The history of gardening in Ireland' in E. Charles Nelson and A. Brady (eds.), *Irish Gardening and Horticulture* (Dublin, 1979), pp. 45–69 and

Pluymers, 'Taming the wilderness in sixteenth and seventeenth century Ireland and Virginia', pp. 610–32.

79. Jane Fenlon (ed.), *Clanricard's Castle: Portumna House, Co. Galway* (Dublin, 2012); Hanneke Ronnes, 'Continental traces at Carrick-on-Suir and contemporary Irish castles: A preliminary study of date-and-initial stones' in Herron and Potterton (ed.), *Ireland in the Renaissance*, pp. 260–1.

80. Smyth, *Map-making, Landscapes and Memory*, p. 383; and John Patrick Montaño, ' "Dycheyng and Hegeying": The Material Culture of the Tudor Plantations in Ireland' in Fiona Bateman and Lionel Pilkington (eds.), *Studies in Settler Colonialism: Politics, Identity and Culture* (Basingstoke, 2011), p. 57.

81. William Roulston, 'Seventeenth century manors in the barony of Strabane' in James Lyttleton and Tadhg O'Keefe (eds.), *The Manor in Medieval and Early Modern Ireland* (Dublin, 2005), p. 169.

82. William Roulston, 'Domestic architecture in Ireland, 1640–1740' in Audrey J. Horning et al. (eds.), *The Post-Medieval Archaeology of Ireland 1550–1850* (Bray, County Wicklow, 2007), pp. 330–1.

83. Carleton, *Heads and Hearths*, p. 117.

84. S. J. Carleton, *Heads and Hearths: The Hearth Money Rolls and Poll Tax Returns for County Antrim, 1660–69* (Belfast, 1991), p. 142.

85. *CSPD, Jan. to Nov. 1671* (London, 1895), pp. 410, 427, 474, 501, 513; *CSPI, 1669–1670* (London, 1910), p. 246; Carleton, *Heads and Hearths*, p. 139.

86. Rolf Loeber, 'Irish Country Houses and Castles of the Late Caroline Period: An Unremembered Past Recaptured', *Quarterly Bulletin of the Irish Georgian Society*, 14 (1973), pp. 33, 40; *CSPD, Jan.–Nov. 1671* (London, 1895), pp. 112, 221.

87. https://ipmag.ie/projects/post-medieval-ireland-excavations-database.html, Line 23: 2003:0019, Antrim, Lisburn Castle Gardens, Lisburn, accessed 16 June 2022.

88. *CSPD, 1673–1675* (London, 1904), p. 135; Edward Berwick (ed.), *The Rawdon Papers...* (London, 1819), p. 232; *CSPD, Jan. to Nov. 1671* (London, 1895), pp. 54–5, 324.

89. *CSPD, March 1677 to Feb. 1678* (London, 1911), p. 445.

90. https://ipmag.ie/projects/post-medieval-ireland-excavations-database.html, Line 23: 2003:0019, Antrim, Lisburn Castle Gardens, Lisburn, accessed 16 June 2022.

91. Rolf Loeber, *A Biographical Dictionary of Architects in Ireland 1600–1720* (London, 1981), pp. 107–8.

92. Quoted in Brian de Breffney, 'The Building of the Mansion at Blessington, 1672', *Irish Artists Review Yearbook* (1988), p. 73.

93. de Breffney, 'The Building of the Mansion at Blessington', pp. 73–7.

94. Andrew Hadfield and John McVeagh (eds.), *Strangers to that Land: British Perceptions of Ireland from the Reformation to the Famine* (Gerrards Cross, Buckinghamshire, 1994), p. 64.

95. Thomas Rolt and Council at Surat to the East India Company in London, IOR/E/3/39, 17 Feb. 1679, ff. 227–v.

96. Gerald Aungier and Council at Bombay to Matthew Gray and Council at Surat, 23 Oct. 1673, IOR/E/3/34, f. 191.

97. Ethel Bruce Sainsbury (ed.), *A Calendar of the Court Minutes etc. of the East India Company, 1677–1679* (Oxford, 1938), p. 290.

98. Longford to Arran, London, 29 Aug. 1679, Bodl., Carte Ms 243, f. 387. Also see *Calendar of the Manuscripts of the Marquess of Ormonde. K.P. Preserved at Kilkenny Castle*, New Series, vol. V. (London, 1908), pp. 51, 165, 193, 351–2.

99. Lady Fawcett, Charles Fawcett, Richard Burn (eds.), *The Travels of the Abbé Carré in India and the Near East, 1672 to 1674* (2 vols., London, 1947), II, p. 721.

100. Ian Bruce Watson, *Foundation for Empire: English Private Trade in India 1659–1760* (New Delhi, 1980), pp. 106–7.

101. Nuala T. Burke, 'An Early Modern Dublin Suburb: The Estate of Francis Aungier, Earl of Longford', *Irish Geography*, 6 (1972), pp. 365–85.

102. Andrew MacKillop, *Human Capital and Empire: Scotland, Ireland, Wales and British Imperialism in Asia, c.1690–c.1820* (Manchester, 2021), p. 235.

103. Stephanie Barczewski, *Country Houses and the British Empire 1700–1930* (Manchester, 2014), p. 107. Also see Corinne Fowler, *Green Unpleasant Land: Creative Responses to Rural England's Colonial Connections* (Leeds, 2020).

104. Teggin, 'The East India Company Career of Sir Robert Cowan'.

105. MacKillop, *Human Capital and Empire*, p. 233; his vast archive is also in the Public Records Office of Northern Ireland.

106. Peter H. Reid, 'The Decline and Fall of the British Country House Library', *Libraries and Culture*, 36 (2001), pp. 345–66.

107. Nicholas Draper, 'Ireland and British colonial slave-ownership, 1763–1833' in O'Kane and O'Neill (eds.), *Ireland, Slavery and the Caribbean: Interdisciplinary Perspectives* (Manchester, 2023), pp. 103–24.

108. Dickson, 'Setting out the terrain', p. 28.

109. Finola O'Kane, 'The Irish-Jamaican Plantation of Kelly's Pen, Jamaica: The Rare 1749 Inventory of Its Slaves, Stock and Household Goods', *Caribbean Quarterly* (2018), pp. 452–66.

110. Nini Rodgers, 'A Changing Presence: The Irish in the Caribbean in the Seventeenth and Eighteenth Centuries' in Alison Donnell, Maria McGarrity, and Evelyn O'Callaghan (eds.), *Caribbean Irish Connections: Interdisciplinary Perspectives* (Kingston, Jamaica, 2015), p. 24; Finola O'Kane, 'Designed in Parallel or in Translation? The linked Jamaican and Irish landscapes of the Browne family, Marquises of Sligo' in O'Kane and O'Neill (eds.), *Ireland, Slavery and the Caribbean*, pp. 282–301 and Stephanie Barczewski, *Country Houses and the British Empire 1700–1930* (Manchester, 2014), p. 106. Also see Margot Finn and Kate Smith (eds.), *The East India Company at Home 1757–1857* (London, 2018).

111. Finola O'Kane, 'What's in a name? The Connected Histories of Belfield, Co. Dublin and Belfield St Mary's, Jamaica' in Finola O'Kane and Ellen Rowley (eds.), *Making Belfield* (Dublin, 2020), pp. 150–64; Dickson, 'Setting out the terrain', p. 30; and Rodgers, *Ireland, Slavery and Anti-Slavery*, p. 164; Barczewski, *Country Houses*, p. 72.

112. Hans Sloane, *A Voyage to the Islands Madera, Barbados, Nieves, S Christophers and Jamaica* (2 vols., London 1707, 1725), I, [pp. 3–4].

113. Peter Walmsley, 'Hans Sloane and the Melancholy Slave' in Erin Peters and Cynthia Richards (eds.), *Early Modern Trauma: Europe and the Atlantic World* (Lincoln, Nebraska, 2021), pp. 151–76 (quote p. 151).

114. Walmsley, 'Hans Sloane and the Melancholy Slave', p. 152.

115. Walmsley, 'Hans Sloane and the Melancholy Slave', p. 168.

116. Barczewski, *Country Houses*, pp. 228–9.

117. James Delbourgo, *Collecting the World: The Life and Curiosity of Hans Sloane* (London, 2017), pp. xxi, 341.

118. Delbourgo, *Collecting the World,* p. 200.

119. HL, HA 15790 Sir Hans Sloane to Sir Arthur Rawdon, 10 Sept. 1687, Portsmouth.

120. Sloane, *A Voyage to the Islands*, I, [pp. 3–4]; Jill H. Casid, *Sowing Empire: Landscape and Colonization* (Minneapolis, 2005).

121. D. W. Hayton, 'Thomas Prior, Sir John Rawdon, third baronet, and the mentality and ideology of "improvement": A question of upbringing' in Raymond Gillespie and R. F. Foster (eds.), *Irish Provincial Cultures in the Long Eighteenth Century: Making the Middle Sort. Essays for Toby Barnard* (Dublin, 2012) pp. 106–32.

122. Rodgers, *Ireland, Slavery and Anti-Slavery*, p. 51 and Martin J. Blake (ed.), *Blake Family Records 1600 to 1700* (London, 1905), pp. 106–13 and Gwynn, 'Documents Relating to the Irish in the West Indies', pp. 273–7.

123. Dickson, 'Setting out the terrain', p. 27.

124. Dickson, 'Setting out the terrain', p. 24.

125. Nicholas Canny, 'How the Local Can be Global and the Global Local: Ireland, Irish Catholics, and European Overseas Empires, 1500–1900' in Patrick Griffin and Francis D. Cogliano (eds.), *Ireland and America: Empire, Revolution and Sovereignty* (Virginia, 2021), pp. 23–52.

126. Will of John French Lynch formerly called John French of Mitcham, Surrey, TNA, PROB 11/1168/241, 30 July 1788 and will of Anthony Lynch of Hampton, Middlesex, 18 April 1757, TNA, PROB 11/829/321. See Craig Bailey, *Irish London: Middle-Class Migration in the Global Eighteenth-Century* (Liverpool, 2013), pp. 157, 159, 174.

127. Will of Anthony French of Mitcham, Surrey, TNA, PROB 11/1158/208, will dated 16 May 1787 and probate granted 31 Oct 1787.

128. Will of John French Lynch formerly called John French of Mitcham, Surrey, TNA, PROB 11/1168/241, 30 July 1788.

129. Angus Mitchell (ed.), 'Hy-Brassil: Irish origins of Brazil' by Roger Casement, *Irish Migration Studies in Latin America*, 4 (2006), pp. 157–65.

130. HMC, *Ormonde MSS*, NS, VII, pp. 512–27; *Bibliotheca Angleseiana* (London, 1686); Diarmuid Ó Catháin, 'John Fergus MD: Eighteenth-Century Doctor, Book Collector and Irish Scholar', *Journal, Royal Society of Antiquaries of Ireland*, 118 (1988), pp. 139–62; and Caball, 'Munster and India', pp. 130–2.

131. Alison Games, *The Web of Empire: English Cosmopolitans in an Age of Expansion, 1560–1660* (Oxford, 2008), p. 12.

132. John Ogilby, *Asia, The First Part. Being an Accurate Description of Persia and the several Provinces thereof* (London, 1673), p. 115; Rita Banerjee, *India in Early*

Modern English Travel Writings: Protestantism, Enlightenment, and Toleration (Leiden, 2021), pp. 170–1, 234 (quote p. 171).

133. John Ovington, *A voyage to Surat, in the year, 1689* (London, 1696), 139. Also see Banerjee, *India in Early Modern English Travel Writings*, pp. 47, 236–7.

134. P. J. Marshall, 'Taming the exotic: The British and India in the seventeenth and eighteenth centuries' in G. S. Rousseau and Roy Porter (eds.), *Exoticism in the Enlightenment* (Manchester, 1990), pp. 46–65.

135. See Chapter 4.

136. Ben Hazard, '"*In Novi Orbis Amplitudine*": Irish Franciscan Views of the Americas in the Seventeenth Century, 1601–83' in Igor Pérez Tostado and Enrique García Hernán (eds.), *Irlanda y el Atlántico Ibérico. Movilidad, participación e intercambio cultural (1580–1823)/Ireland and the Iberian Atlantic: Mobility, Involvement and Cross-Cultural Exchange (1580–1823)* (Valencia, 2010), pp. 193–209.

137. Matteo Binasco (ed.), *Luke Wadding, the Irish Franciscans, and Global Catholicism* (Abingdon, 2020), especially essays by Igor Perez Tostado, John McCafferty, and Clare Lois Carroll.

138. Games, *The Web of Empire*, p. 41.

139. Hadfield and McVeagh (eds.), *Strangers to that Land*, p. 47.

140. Thomas Harriot, *Brief And True Report Of The New Found Land Of Virginia* (London, 1590). I am grateful to David Harris Sacks for sharing with me his insights on this tract.

141. See Chapter 5 above.

142. Games, *The Web of Empire*, p. 21.

143. Máire Kennedy, 'Nations of the mind: French culture in Ireland and the international booktrade' in Michael O'Dea and Kevin Whelan (eds.), *Nations and Nationalisms: France, Britain, Ireland and the Eighteenth-Century Context* (Oxford, 1995), pp. 147–58.

144. William Dampier, *A new voyage round the world describing particularly the isthmus of America, several coasts and islands in the West Indies...*(London, 1697).

145. Patricia Coughlan, '"Enter Revenge": Henry Birkhead and *Cola's Furie*', *Theatre Research International*, 15 (1990), pp. 1–17; Alan Fletcher, *Drama, Performance, and Polity in Pre-Cromwellian Ireland* (Toronto, 2000); and Christopher Morash, *A History of Irish Theatre 1601–2000* (Cambridge, 2002). For the importance of civic processions see Alan Fletcher, 'Select Document: Ormond's Civic Entry into Kilkenny, 29/31 August 1646', *Irish Historical Studies*, 35 (2007), pp. 365–78.

146. *Titus, or the Palme of Christian courage...*(Waterford, 1644).

147. *Titus, or the Palme of Christian courage*, p. 1. Raymond Gillespie, 'Political Ideas and their Social Contexts in Seventeenth-Century Ireland' in Jane Ohlmeyer (ed.), *Political Thought in Seventeenth-Century Ireland: Kingdom or Colony?* (Cambridge, 2000), p. 119, and Morash, *A History of Irish Theatre*, pp. 302–3.

148. Felicity A. Nussbaum, 'The Theatre of empire: Racial counterfeit, racial realism', Kathleen Wilson (ed.), *A New Imperial History: Culture, Identity and Modernity in Britain and the Empire 1660–1840* (Cambridge, 2004), pp. 71–90 (quote p. 71).

149. Richard Head, *The English Rogue: Described in the life of Meriton Latroon, a witty extravagant comprehending the most eminent cheats of both sexes* (London, 1666). Also see Anne Fogarty, 'Literature in English, 1550–1690: From the Elizabethan settlement to the Battle of the Boyne' in Margaret Kelleher and Philip O'Leary (eds.), *The Cambridge History of Irish Literature, Volume 1 to 1890* (2 vols., Cambridge, 2008), pp. 140–90.

150. Head, *The English Rogue*, chapter 1, p. 5 (the pagination is erratic). I am grateful to John Cunningham for this translation and for identifying another example of the use of 'Cramacrees', http://www.earlystuartlibels.net/htdocs/misc_section/R8.html, accessed 27 July 2016.

151. Carmen Nocentelli, 'Made in India: How Meriton Latroon Became an Englishman' in Jonathan Gil Harris (ed.), *Indography: Writing the 'Indian' in Early Modern England* (New York, 2012), pp. 223–48.

152. TCD, DD.nn.13.

153. [Anonymous] *Vertue Rewarded; or, The Irish Princess*, eds. Ian Campbell Ross and Anne Markey (Dublin, 2010). See Chapter 3.

154. Alison Games, 'Cohabitation, Suriname-style: English Inhabitants in Dutch Suriname after 1667', *The William and Mary Quarterly*, 72 (2015), pp. 195–242.

155. Richard S. Dunn, *Sugar and Slaves: The Rise of the Planter Class* (Chapel Hill, NC, 1972), pp. 257–8.

156. Cynthia Richard, 'Imperfect Enjoyments and Female Disappointments. Understanding Trauma in Aphra Behn's 'The Disappointment' and *Oroonoko*' in Peters and Richards (eds.), *Early Modern Trauma*, pp. 249–71. Also see Natalie Zemon Davis (ed.), *Women on the Margins: Three Seventeenth-Century Lives* (Cambridge, Mass., 1995), pp. 191–95.

157. Carolyn Arena, 'Aphra Behn's *Oroonoko*, Indian Slavery, and the Anglo-Dutch Wars' in L. H. Roper (ed.), *The Torrid Zone: Caribbean Colonization and Cultural Interaction in the Long Seventeenth Century* (Columbia, South Carolina, 2018), pp. 31–45.

158. Suze Zijlstra and Tom Weterings, 'Colonial Life in Times of War: The Impact of European Wars on Suriname' and James Robertson, 'Making Jamaica English' in Roper (ed.), *The Torrid Zone*, pp. 76–104 and 105–17.

159. For example, Henry Blennerhassett (c.1594–1632), the son of Ulster planters, drowned in the Amazon while settling Guiana.

160. Lee Morrissey, 'Transplanting English Plantations in Aphra Behn's Oroonoko', *The Global South*, 10 (2016), pp. 11–26.

161. John C. Greene and Gladys L. H. Clark, *The Dublin Stage, 1720–1745: A Calendar of Plays, Entertainments and Afterpieces* (London, 1993) and John Greene, *Theatre in Dublin 1745–1820: A History* (2 vols., Bethlehem, Pennsylvania, 2011), La Tourette Stockwell, *Dublin Theatre and Theatre Customs (1637–1820)* (Kingsport, Tennessee, 1937) and Esther K. Sheldon, *Thomas Sheridan of Smock Alley* (Princeton, 1967). I owe these references to Chris Morash and David O'Shaughnessy.

162. Greene, *Theatre in Dublin 1745–1820,* I, p. 397. Thanks to Chris Morash for drawing this to my attention.

163. Antoinette Burton, *The Trouble with Empire: Challenges to Modern British Imperialism* (Oxford, 2015) p. 266. Also see David Roediger and James Barrett, 'Inbetween Peoples: Race, Nationality and the "New Immigrant" Working Class', *Journal of American Ethnic History,* 16 (1997), pp. 3–44.

164. Moyra Haslett (ed.), *Irish Literature in Transition 1700–1780* (Cambridge, 2020), p. 14.

165. *The Cambridge Edition of the Works of Jonathan Swift* xvi: *Gulliver's Travels,* ed. David Womersley (2012), p. 441.

166. Daniel Roberts, '"An example to the whole world": Patriotism and imperialism in early Irish fiction' in Haslett (ed.), *Irish Literature in Transition 1700–1780,* pp. 214–15.

167. Roberts, '"An example to the whole world"', p. 222.

168. Ian McBride, 'The Politics of *A Modest Proposal:* Swift and the Irish Crisis of the Late 1720s', *Past and Present,* 244 (2019), pp. 89–122.

169. Ian Campbell Ross, '"A very knowing American": The Inca Garcilaso de la Vega and Swift's Modest Proposal', *Modern Language Quarterly,* 68 (2007), pp. 493–516. Also see Chapter 3 above and [anon] *Vertue Rewarded; or, The Irish Princess,* eds. Ian Campbell Ross and Anne Markey (Dublin, 2010).

170. Ian McBride, *Eighteenth Century Ireland: The Isle of Slaves* (Dublin, 2009), pp. 274–5; Rodgers, *Ireland, Slavery and Anti-Slavery,* p. 187.

171. Quoted in Clare Carroll, *Circe's Cup: Cultural Transformations in Early Modern Ireland* (Cork, 2001), p. 27.

172. Patrick Kelly, '"A Light to the Blind": The Voice of the Dispossessed Elite in the Generation after the Defeat at Limerick', *Irish Historical Studies,* 24 (1985), pp. 431–62.

173. John Bergin, 'Irish Catholics and Their Networks in Eighteenth-Century London', *Eighteenth-Century Life,* 39 (2015), pp. 68–71, 84–5. Mabel was still alive in 1686 when she witnessed her son's will, will of Lucas, earl of Fingal, NLI Fingal Papers 'Report on Private Collections #6: Fingall papers'.

174. Thomas Kilroy, *The O'Neill* (Dublin, 1995), p. 23.

175. For an excellent recent contribution see Sarah Covington, *The Devil from Over the Sea: Remembering and Forgetting Oliver Cromwell in Ireland* (Oxford, 2022), pp. 9–16.

176. Guy Beiner, *Forgetful Remembrance: Social Forgetting and Vernacular Historiography of a Rebellion in Ulster* (Oxford, 2019).

177. Guy Beiner, 'Why Irish History Starved: A Virtual Historiography', *Field Day Review,* 3 (2007), pp. 67–81, 'Between Trauma and Triumphalism: The Easter Rising, the Somme, and the Crux of Deep Memory in Modern Ireland', *Journal of British Studies* 46 (2007), pp. 366–89, 'Irish Studies and the Dynamics of Disremembering' in M. Corporaal, C. Cusack, and R. van den Beuken (eds.), *Irish Studies and the Dynamics of Memory: Transitions and Transformations* (Oxford and Bern, 2017), pp. 297–313, 'Irish Historical Studies *Avant la Lettre.* The antiquarian genealogy of interdisciplinary scholarship' in R. Allyson,

M. Cronin and B. Ó Conchubhair (eds.), *Routledge International Handbook of Irish Studies* (London, 2021), pp. 47–58, and 'Probing the boundaries of Irish memory: From postmemory to prememory and back', *Irish Historical Studies*, 34 (2014), pp. 296–307.

178. Ian McBride (ed.), *History and Memory in Modern Ireland* (Cambridge, 2001).

179. John Gibney, *The Shadow of a Year: The 1641 Rebellion in Irish History and Memory* (2013), Sarah Covington, *The Devil from Over the Sea: Remembering and Forgetting Oliver Cromwell in Ireland* (2022), and Ian McBride, *The Siege of Derry in Ulster Protestant Mythology* (1997), which each address the 'social memory' of deeply traumatic moments in Ireland's past. It is also important to note works on history and memory by historians of the English civil wars, especially Erin Peters, *Commemoration and Oblivion in Royalist Print Culture, 1658–1667* (London, 2017).

180. https://www.irishtimes.com/history/2022/11/28/cromwell-did-more-to-stain-anglo-irish-relations-than-any-other-figure-says-british-ambassador/, accessed 8 January 2023. The volume being launched was Elaine Murphy, Micheál Ó Siochrú, and Jason Peacey (eds.), *The letters, writings and speeches of Oliver Cromwell. vol. 2. 1 February 1649 to 12 December 1653* (3 vols., Oxford, 2022).

181. Fintan O'Toole, 'Treating Cromwell as History may help towards lifting his curse', *Irish Times*, 3 December 2022, https://www.irishtimes.com/opinion/2022/12/03/fintan-otoole-impossible-to-think-of-cromwell-in-ireland-without-acknowledging-catastrophe/, accessed 8 January 2023.

182. Ireland has one of the largest archives of folklore tradition in the world. Diarmuid Ó Giolláin, *Locating Irish Folklore: Tradition, Modernity, Identity* (Cork, 2000); Micheál Briody, *The Irish Folklore Commission 1935–1970* (Helsinki, 2008); and Mary Daly, '"The State Papers of a forgotten and neglected people": The National Folklore Collection and the writing of Irish history', *Béaloideas*, 78 (2010), pp. 61–79.

183. Covington, *The Devil from Over the Sea*, chapter 6, and 'Dung Beetles and the "Vulgar Traditions": Applying Folkloric Sources and Methods to Early Modern Ireland' in Covington, Carey and McGowan-Doyle (eds.), *Early Modern Ireland*, chapter 13.

184. For examples, National Folklore Collection, The Schools' Collection, Volume 0563, Page 048–51, https://www.duchas.ie/en/cbes/4922243/4863764/5020381 and The Schools' Collection, Volume 0901, Page 077, https://www.duchas.ie/en/cbes/5009337/5008371/5134675.

185. National Folklore Collection, The Schools' Collection, Volume 0836, Page 001g–001i, https://www.duchas.ie/en/cbes/4770043/4768749/4818126.

186. National Folklore Collection, The Schools' Collection, Volume 0599, Page 405, https://www.duchas.ie/en/cbes/5177654/5177409/5191767.

187. National Folklore Collection, The Schools' Collection, Volume 0195, Page 004, https://www.dib.ie/biography/hamilton-sir-frederick-a3737 and https://www.duchas.ie/en/cbes/4602739/4599931/4632477.

188. National Folklore Collection, The Schools' Collection, Volume 0193, Page 087–089, https://www.duchas.ie/en/cbes/4602734/4599564/4632494, The Schools' Collection, Volume 0194, Page 131–3 offers a particularly detailed account of his holdings and castle, https://www.duchas.ie/en/cbes/4649683/4646390/4650813, and The Schools' Collection, Volume 0160, Page 319, https://www.duchas.ie/en/cbes/4701681/4692380/4726960.

189. National Folklore Collection, The Schools' Collection, Volume 0197, Page 080–081, https://www.duchas.ie/en/cbes/4602748/4600742/4632974, and The Schools' Collection, Volume 0197, Page 086https://www.duchas.ie/en/cbes/4602748/4600747.

190. National Folklore Collection, The Schools' Collection, Volume 0194, Page 131–3 https://www.duchas.ie/en/cbes/4649683/4646390/4650813.

191. National Folklore Collection, The Schools' Collection, Volume 0197, Page 085–086 https://www.duchas.ie/en/cbes/4602748/4600746/4632984. Also The Schools' Collection, Volume 0197, Page 088–089, https://www.duchas.ie/en/cbes/4602748/4600749/4632990, The Schools' Collection, Volume 0197, Page 083. https://www.duchas.ie/en/cbes/4602748/4600744/4632979, and The Schools' Collection, Volume 0197, Page 092, https://www.duchas.ie/en/cbes/4602748/4600753/4632997.

192. National Folklore Collection, The Schools' Collection, Volume 0190, Page 011–013 https://www.duchas.ie/en/cbes/4602723/4598445/4626432.

193. National Folklore Collection, The Schools' Collection, Volume 0593, Page 415–17, https://www.duchas.ie/en/cbes/5177635/5174823/5189127.

194. John Ainsworth (ed.), *Inchiquin Manuscripts* (IMC, Dublin, 1961), p. 5; National Folklore Collection, https://www.dib.ie/biography/obrien-maire-maire-rua-a6484.

195. National Folklore Collection, The Schools' Collection, Volume 1015, Page 432–3, https://www.duchas.ie/en/cbes/5162181/5161746/5193122.

196. Scholars have suggested that cultural memories become institutionalised after 100 years or three generations, which is clearly not the case in Ireland, Aleida Assman and Linda Shortt (eds.), *Memory and Political Change* (Basingstoke, 2012).

197. Friel, *Making History*, pp. 8–9.

198. Priya Satia, *Time's Monster: History, Conscience and Britain's Empire* (London, 2020), pp. 1, 5.

199. Ian McBride, *The Siege of Derry in Ulster Protestant Mythology* (Dublin, 1997), pp. 59–60.

200. Nicholas Canny, *Imagining Ireland's Pasts: Early Modern Ireland through the Centuries* (Oxford, 2021).

201. Sarah Covington, '"Realms so barbarous and cruell": Writing Violence in Early Modern Ireland and England', *History*, 99 (2014), pp. 487–504.

202. Clare O'Halloran, *Golden Ages and Barbarous Nations: Antiquarian Debate and Cultural Politics in Ireland, c.1750–1800* (Cork, 2004), pp. 141–57; Canny, *Imagining Ireland's Pasts*, pp. 214–17.

203. Canny, *Imagining Ireland's Pasts*, pp. 95–100, 214–17.

204. Raymond Gillespie, 'Temple's Fate: Reading *The Irish Rebellion* in Late Seventeenth-Century Ireland' in Ciaran Brady and Jane Ohlmeyer (eds.), *British Interventions in Early Modern Ireland* (Cambridge, 2004), pp. 315–33; Toby Barnard, 'The Uses of 23 October 1641 and Irish Protestant Celebrations', *English Historical Review*, 106 (1991), pp. 889–920 and '"Parlour entertainment in an evening?" Histories of the 1640s' in Micheál Ó Siochrú (ed.), *Kingdoms in Crisis: Ireland in the 1640s* (Dublin, 2001), pp. 20–43; Gibney, *The Shadow of a Year*, especially the final chapter.

205. An exhibition, entitled 'Ireland in Turmoil', which featured the depositions and related material on display in the Long Room, ran between October 2010 and April 2011. For a virtual tour of the exhibition see http://www.tcd.ie/Library/assets/swf/Exhibitions/1641/TCD/.

206. Jane Ohlmeyer and Micheál Ó Siochrú (eds.), *Ireland 1641: Contexts and Reactions* (Manchester, 2013).

207. McBride, *The Siege of Derry* and John Gibney's *The Shadow of a Year: The 1641 Rebellion in Irish History and Memory* (Dublin, 2013).

208. John Mitchelburne, *Ireland Preserv'd; or, the Siege of London-Derry. A Tragi-Comedy* (Belfast, 1744); Karen A. Holland, 'Disputed Heroes: Early Accounts of the Siege of Londonderry', *New Hibernia Review*, 18 (2014), p. 21; and Alice O'Driscoll, 'Women, gender, and siege during the Wars of the Three Kingdoms, 1639–52' (Unpublished PhD thesis, Cambridge, 2021).

209. McBride, *The Siege of Derry*, p. 79.

210. Caroline Elkins, *Legacy of Violence: A History of the British Empire* (London, 2022), introduction.

Bibliography

MANUSCRIPT

ARCHIVES IN IRELAND

Public Records Office of Northern Ireland, Belfast:
D654/B/1/1AA
D3078/3/1/5
National Library of Ireland, Dublin:
Genealogical Office, Ms 67
National Folklore Collection, Dublin:
The Schools' Collection, Volumes 0160, 0190, 0193, 0194, 0195, 0197, 0563, 0593, 0599, 0647, 0836, 0901 and 1015—consulted online https://www.duchas.ie/en/info/cbe
Representative Church Body Library, Dublin, Ireland
P608/1/1, 'The old registry book Youghal from 1665 to 1720'
Trinity College, Dublin, Ireland:
Ms 809–841 1641 Depositions—consulted online https://1641.tcd.ie
Ms 1,576
Ms 1,611
Ms 2,170
Ms 2,723
MUN/LIB/1/53

ARCHIVES IN LONDON

British Library:
Additional Ms 12,429
Additional Ms 18,730
Additional Ms 40,701
Additional Ms 40,708
Additional Ms 40,860
Additional Ms 46,188
Additional Charter 13,340
Egerton Ms 80
Sloane Ms 1,952

Oriental Ms/reg 16.b.14, 'A Chronicle of the Kings of Persees'
IOR/E/3/32
IOR/E/3/33
IOR/E/3/34
IOR/E/3/35
IOR/E/3/36
IOR/E/3/38
IOR/E/3/87
IOR/E/3/88
The National Archives:
CO 1/29
CO 1/31
CO 1/33
CO 1/69
PROB 11/414/66
PROB 11/829/321
PROB 11/983/95
PROB 11/1158/208
PROB 11/1168/241
London Metropolitan Archive:
MR/E/616, indenture of July 1684

ARCHIVES IN THE USA

Huntington Library, San Marino, California:
Ellesmere papers, Box 212, EL 8,467
Hastings Ms, HA 840
Hastings Ms, HA 15,790

PRIMARY PRINTED

[anonymous] *A certificate From the Lord Moor and Sir Henry Titchborne* (London, 1642)
[anonymous] *The English Empire in America: Or a Prospect of His Majesties Dominions in the West-Indies . . .* (London, 1685)
[anonymous] *Vertue Rewarded; or, The Irish Princess*, eds. Ian Campbell Ross and Anne Markey (Dublin, 2010)
John Ainsworth (ed.), *Inchiquin Manuscripts* (IMC, Dublin, 1961)
John Appleby (ed.), *A Calendar of Material relating to Ireland from the High Court of Admiralty Examinations, 1536–1641* (IMC, Dublin, 1992)
R. Barlow and H. Yule (eds.), *The diary of William Hedges 1681–1687* (3 vols., London, 1887–9)
E. S. de Beer (ed.), *The Diary of John Evelyn* (6 vols., Oxford, 1955)
Gerard Boate, *Irelands Naturall History* (London, 1652)

Angela Bourke et al. (eds.), *The Field Day Anthology of Irish Writing: Irish Women's Writing and Traditions* (2 vols., Cork, 2002; vols. IV and V of the *Field Day Anthology*)

Robert Boyle, *The Correspondence of Robert Boyle*, eds. Michael Hunter, Antonio Clericuzio, and Lawrence Principe (7 vols., London, 2001)

Andrew Carpenter, *Verse in English from Eighteenth-Century Ireland* (Cork, 1998)

Andrew Carpenter, *Verse in English from Tudor and Stuart Ireland* (Cork, 2003)

Clare Carroll and Vincent Carey (eds.), *Solon his Follie, or A Politique Discourse Touching the Reformation or common-weales conquered, declined or corrupted* by Richard Beacon (Binghamton, NY, 1996)

Thomas Carte, *The life of James duke of Ormond* (6 vols., Oxford, 1851)

G. T. Cell (ed.), *Newfoundland Discovered: English Attempts at Colonisation, 1610–1630* (London: Hakluyt Society, 1982)

James Cranford, *The Teares of Ireland* (London, 1642)

Jon G. Crawford (ed.), *A Star Chamber Court in Ireland. The court of castle chamber, 1571–1641* (Dublin, 2005)

Edmund Curtis and R. B. McDowell (eds.), *Irish Historical Documents, 1172–1922* (London, 1943)

William Dampier, *A new voyage round the world describing particularly the isthmus of America, several coasts and islands in the West Indies . . .* (London, 1697)

Patrick Darcy, *An Argument Delivered by Patrick Darcy, Esquire, By the Express Order of the House of Commons in the Parliament of Ireland, 9 Iunii, 1641* (Waterford, 1643)

Sir John Davies, *A Discoverie of the True Causes why Ireland was never entirely subdued . . .* (London, 1612)

Seamus Deane, Andrew Carpenter, and Jonathan Williams (eds.), *The Field Day Anthology of Irish Writing* (3 vols., Derry, 1991)

Olaudah Equiano, *The Interesting Narrative of the Life of Olaudah Equiano* with a foreword by David Olusoga (London, 2021)

C. L. Falkiner (ed.), 'Barnaby Rich's "Remembrances of the state of Ireland, 1612"', *Proceedings, Royal Irish Academy*, 26, C (1906–7), pp. 125–42

Sir Charles Fawcett (ed.), *The English Factories in India*, n[ew] s[eries], vol. 1 *The Western Presidency, 1670–1677* (Oxford, 1936)

George W. Forrest (ed.), *Selections from the letters, despatches, and other state papers preserved in the Bombay Secretariat Home Series* (2 vols., Bombay, 1887)

Morgan Godwyn, *The Negro's and Indians Advocate* (London, 1680)

Daniel Gookin, *Historical Collections of the Indians* (Boston, 1674)

D. Greene and F. Kelly (eds.), *Irish Bardic Poetry: Texts and Translations, Together with an Introductory Lecture by Osborn Bergin* (Dublin Institute for Advanced Studies, 1970, repr. 1984)

Isabel Grubb (ed.), *My Irish Journal 1669–1670 by* William Penn (London, 1952)

Aubrey Gwynn, 'Documents Relating to the Irish in the West Indies', *Analecta Hibernica*, 4 (1932), pp. 139–286

Andrew Hadfield and John McVeagh (eds.), *Strangers to that Land: British Perceptions of Ireland from the Reformation to the Famine* (Gerrards Cross, Buckinghamshire, 1994)

Richard Hakluyt, *The Principal Navigations, Voyages and Discoveries of the English Nation* (2 vols., Hakluyt Society, Cambridge, 1965)

Thomas Harriot, *Brief And True Report Of The New Found Land Of Virginia* (London, 1590)

Richard Head, *The English Rogue: Described in the life of Meriton Latroon, a witty extravagant comprehending the most eminent cheats of both sexes* (London, 1666)

E. M. Hinton, 'Rych's anatomy of Ireland (1615)', *Publications of the Modern Language Association of America*, 55 (1940), pp. 73–101

Robert Latham and William Matthews (eds.), *The Diary of Samuel Pepys* (11 vols., Berkeley and Los Angeles, 1979–83)

Margaret Curtis Layton (ed.), *The Council Book for the Province of Munster c. 1599–1649* (IMC, Dublin, 2008)

Richard Ligon, *A true and exact history of the island of Barbados* (London, 1673)

Joyce Lorimer (ed.), *English and Irish Settlement on the River Amazon 1550–1646* (Hakluyt Society, London, 1989)

John Lynch, *Cambrensis Eversus*, trans. Mathew Kelly (3 vols., Dublin, 1851–2)

John C. Mac Erlean, S. J., *The Poems of David Ó Bruadair* (3 vols., London, 1910–17)

Edward MacLysaght (ed.), *Calendar of the Orrery Papers* (IMC, Dublin, 1941)

C. Maxwell (ed.), *Irish History from Contemporary Sources (1509–1610)* (London, 1923)

John Mitchelburne, *Ireland Preserv'd; or, the Siege of London-Derry. A Tragi-Comedy.* (Belfast, 1744)

Fynes Moryson, *An itinerary written by Fynes Moryson gent., first in the Latine tongue, and then translated by him into English* (London, 1617)

Elaine Murphy (ed.), *A Calendar of Material Relating to Ireland from the High Court of Admiralty, 1641–1660* (IMC, Dublin, 2011)

John Ogilby, *Asia, The First Part. Being an Accurate Description of Persia and the several Provinces thereof* (London, 1673)

Vere Langford Oliver, *Caribbeana. Being Miscellaneous Papers Relating to History . . . of the British West Indies* (4 vols., London, 1912–14)

John Ovington, *A voyage to Suratt in the year 1689 giving a large account of that city and its inhabitations and of the English factory there: likewise a description of Madiera, St. Jago, Annobon, Cabenda, and Malemba* (London, 1696)

Carla Pestana and Sharon V. Salinger (eds.), *The Early English Caribbean, 1570–1700* (4 vols., London, 2014)

William Petty, *Political Arithmetick, or, A Discourse concerning the Extent and Value of Lands, People, Buildings* (London, 1691)

Barnaby Rich, *The Irish hubbub, or, The English hue and crie briefly pursuing the base conditions, and most notorious offences of the vile, vaine, and wicked age, no lesse smarting then tickling: a merriment whereby to make the wise to laugh, and fooles to be angry* (London, 1618)

Ethel Bruce Sainsbury (ed.), *A Calendar of the Court Minutes etc. of the East India Company, 1660–1663*, with an introduction and notes by Sir William Foster (Oxford, 1922)

Hans Sloane, *A Voyage to the Islands Madera, Barbados, Nieves, S Christophers and Jamaica* (2 vols., London 1707, 1725)

John Smith, *The Generall Historie of Virginia* ... (London, 1624)

Thomas Smith, *A letter sent by I.B. Gentleman vnto his very frende Maystet [sic]* ... (London, 1572)

Edmund Spenser, *A View of the Present State of Ireland*, ed. W. L. Renwick (Oxford, 1970)

The Statutes at Large Passed in the Parliaments held in Ireland (1310–1800) (20 vols., Dublin, 1786–1801)

Victor Treadwell (ed.), *The Irish Commission of 1622. An investigation of the Irish administration 1615–22 and its consequences 1623–24* (IMC, Dublin, 2006)

N. J. A. Williams (ed.), *Pairlement Chlionne Tómáis* (Dublin, 1981)

SECONDARY

S. Ahmed Khan, *Anglo-Portuguese negotiations relating to Bombay, 1660–1677* (Oxford, 1922)

D. H. Akenson, *If the Irish Ran the World: Montserrat, 1630–1730* (Montreal and Kingston, 1997)

Shahmima Akhtar, Dónal Hassett, Kevin Kenny, Laura McAtackney, Ian McBride, Timothy McMahon, Caoimhe Nic Dháibhéid, and Jane Ohlmeyer, 'Decolonising Irish History? Possibilities, Challenges, Practices', *Irish Historical Studies*, 45 (2021), pp. 1–30

J. Amelang, 'The New World in the Old? The absence of empire in early modern Madrid', *Cuadernos de Historia de España*, 82 (2008), pp. 147–64

Tonio Andrade and William Reger (eds.), *The Limits of Empire: European Imperial Formations in Early Modern World History* (Farnham, 2012)

J. H. Andrews, *Shapes of Ireland: Maps and their Makers, 1564–1839* (Dublin, 1997)

Kenneth J. Andrien, 'Age of exploration, c. 1500–1650' in Philippa Levine and John Marriott (eds.), *The Ashgate Research Companion to Modern Imperial Histories* (Farnham, 2012)

Robert Antony, Stuart Carroll, and Caroline Dodds Pennock (eds.), *The Cambridge World History of Violence*: vol. 3 (Cambridge, 2020)

David Appleby, 'God forbid it should come to that': The feud between Colonel Molesworth and Major-General O'Brien in Portugal, 1663', *The Seventeenth Century*, 26 (2011), pp. 346–67

Bethany Aram and Bartolomé Yun-Casalilla (eds.), *Global Goods and the Spanish Empire, 1492–1824: Circulation, Resistance and Diversity* (Basingstoke, 2014)

Carolyn Arena, 'Aphra Behn's *Oroonoko*, Indian Slavery, and the Anglo-Dutch Wars' in L. H. Roper (ed.), *The Torrid Zone: Caribbean Colonization and Cultural Interaction in the Long Seventeenth Century* (Columbia, South Carolina, 2018), pp. 31–45

David Armitage, *The Ideological Origins of the British Empire* (Cambridge, 2000)

David Armitage and Alison Bashford, *Pacific Histories: Ocean, Land, People* ((Basingstoke, 2014)

David Armitage and Michael J. Braddick (eds.), *The British Atlantic World, 1500–1800* (Basingstoke, 2002)

Catherine Armstrong,' "Boiled and stewed with roots and herbs": Everyday tales of cannibalism in early modern Virginia' in Angela McShane and Garthine Walker (eds.), *The Extraordinary and the Everyday in Early Modern England: Essays in Celebration of the Work of Bernard Capp* (Basingstoke, 2010)

Robert Armstrong,'Ireland at Westminster:The Long Parliament's Irish committees, 1641–1647' in Chris R. Kyle and Jason Peacey (eds.), *Parliament at Work: Parliamentary Committees, Political Power, and Public Access in Early Modern England* (Woodbridge, 2002)

David Arnold, 'Agriculture and "Improvement" in Early Colonial India: A Pre-History of Development', *Journal of Agrarian Change*, 5 (2005), pp. 505–25

Catherine B. Asher and Cynthia Talbot, *India before Europe* (Cambridge, 2006)

Aleida Assman and Linda Shortt (eds.), *Memory and Political Change* (Basingstoke, 2012)

M. Athar Ali, *Mughal India. Studies in Polity, Ideas, Society and Culture* (Oxford, 2006)

Craig Bailey, *Irish London: Middle-Class Migration in the Global Eighteenth-Century* (Liverpool, 2013)

Craig Bailey, 'Metropole and Colony: Irish Networks and Patronage in the Eighteenth-Century Empire', *Immigrants and Minorities,* 23 (2005)

Craig Bailey, 'The Nesbitts of London and their networks' in David Dickson, Jan Parmentier, and Jane Ohlmeyer (eds.), *Irish and Scottish Mercantile Networks in Europe and Overseas in the Seventeenth and Eighteenth Centuries* (Ghent, 2007)

Rita Banerjee, *India in Early Modern English Travel Writings: Protestantism, Enlightenment, and Toleration* (Leiden, 2021)

Stephanie Barczewski, *Country Houses and the British Empire 1700–1930* (Manchester, 2014)

Stephanie Barczewski and Martin Farr (eds.), *The MacKenzie Moment and Imperial History: Essays in Honour of John M. MacKenzie* (London, 2019)

Toby Barnard, 'The Uses of 23 October 1641 and Irish Protestant Celebrations', *English Historical Review*, 106 (1991)

Toby Barnard, ' "Parlour entertainment in an evening?" Histories of the 1640s' in Micheál Ó Siochrú (ed.), *Kingdoms in Crisis: Ireland in the 1640s* (Dublin, 2001), pp. 20–43

Toby Barnard, *Making the Grand Figure: Lives and Possessions in Ireland, 1641–1770* (New Haven, 2004)

Toby Barnard, *A Guide to Sources for the History of Material Culture in Ireland, 1500–2000* (Dublin, 2005)

Colin Barr,' "Imperium in Imperio": Irish Episcopal Imperialism in the Nineteenth', *The English Historical Review*, 123 (2008), pp. 611–50

T. B. Barry, R. Frame, and K. Simms (eds.), *Colony and Frontier in Medieval Ireland: Essays Presented to J. F. Lydon* (Dublin, 1995)

Robert Bartlett, *The Making of Europe: Conquest, Colonisation and Cultural Change 950–1350* (London, 1993)

Robert Bartlett and Angus MacKay (eds.), *Medieval Frontier Societies* (Oxford, 1989)

Thomas Bartlett, '"Rishti": Irish Soldiers in India 1750–1920' in Jyoti Atwal and Eunan O'Halpin (eds.), *India, Ireland and Anti-Imperial Struggle: Remembering the Connaught Rangers Mutiny, 1920* (New Delhi, 2021), pp. 21–31

Thomas Bartlett, 'The Irish soldier in India, 1750–1947' in Michael Holmes and Denis Holmes (eds.), *Ireland and India: Connections, Comparisons, Contrasts* (Dublin, 1997)

Thomas Bartlett, '"This famous island set in a Virginian sea": Ireland in the British Empire, 1690–1801' in P. J. Marshall (ed.), *The Oxford History of the British Empire*, vol. 2. *The Eighteenth Century* (Oxford, 1998)

Thomas Bartlett and Keith Jeffery (eds.), *A Military History of Ireland* (Cambridge, 1996)

Chris Bayly, 'Ireland, India and the Empire: 1780–1914', *Transactions of the Royal Historical Society*, 6th Series, 10 (2000)

Hilary McD. Beckles, *Black Rebellion in Barbados: The Struggle against Slavery, 1627–1838* (Bridgetown, 1984)

Hilary McD. Beckles, 'A "riotous and unruly lot": Irish Indentured Servants and Freemen in the English West Indies, 1644–1713', *The William and Mary Quarterly*, 47 (1990), pp. 503–22

Hilary McD. Beckles, 'The "Hub of Empire": The Caribbean and Britain in the Seventeenth Century' in Nicholas Canny (ed.), *The Oxford History of the British Empire*, vol. 1 (Oxford, 1998)

Hilary McD. Beckles, *The First Black Slave Society: Britain's 'Barbarity Time' in Barbados, 1636–1876* (Kingston, 2016)

Guy Beiner, 'Why Irish History Starved: A Virtual Historiography', *Field Day Review*, 3 (2007), pp. 67–81

Guy Beiner, 'Between Trauma and Triumphalism: The Easter Rising, the Somme, and the Crux of Deep Memory in Modern Ireland', *Journal of British Studies* 46 (2007), pp. 366–89

Guy Beiner, 'Probing the boundaries of Irish memory: From postmemory to pre-memory and back', *Irish Historical Studies*, 34 (2014), pp. 296–307

Guy Beiner, 'Irish Studies and the Dynamics of Disremembering' in M. Corporaal, C. Cusack, and R. van den Beuken (eds.), *Irish Studies and the Dynamics of Memory: Transitions and Transformations* (Oxford and Bern, 2017)

Guy Beiner, *Forgetful Remembrance: Social Forgetting and Vernacular Historiography of a Rebellion in Ulster* (Oxford, 2019)

Guy Beiner, 'Irish Historical Studies *Avant la Lettre*: The antiquarian genealogy of interdisciplinary scholarship' in R. Allyson, M. Cronin, and B. Ó Conchubhair (eds.), *Routledge International Handbook of Irish Studies* (London, 2021), pp. 47–58

James Bell, *Empire, Religion and Revolution in Early Virginia, 1607–1786* (Basingstoke, 2013)

Jill Bender, 'The Imperial Politics of Famine: The 1873–74 Bengal Famine and Irish Parliamentary Nationalism', *Eire-Ireland*, special issue 42 (2007)

John Bergin, 'The Irish Catholic Interest at the London Inns of court, 1674–1800', *Eighteenth Century Ireland*, 24 (2009), pp. 36–61

Homi Bhabha, 'Difference, Discrimination, and the Discourse of Colonialism' in Francis Barker et al. (eds.), *The Politics of Theory* (Colchester, 1983)

Homi Bhabha, 'Of mimicry and man: The ambivalence of colonial discourse', *October*, 28, Discipleship: A Special Issue on Psychoanalysis (1984), pp. 125–33

Homi Bhabha, *The Location of Culture* (Abingdon, 1994)

Matteo Binasco, 'The Activity of Irish Priests in the West Indies: 1638–1669', *Irish Migration Studies in Latin America*, 7 (2011), pp. 97–107

Matteo Binasco (ed.), *Rome and Irish Catholicism in the Atlantic World, 1622–1908* (Basingstoke, 2019)

Matteo Binasco (ed.), *Luke Wadding, the Irish Franciscans, and Global Catholicism* (Abingdon, 2020)

Matteo Binasco, *Making, Breaking and Remaking the Irish Missionary Network. Ireland, Rome and the West Indies in the Seventeenth Century* (Basingstoke, 2020)

K. Block and J. Shaw, 'Subjects without an Empire: The Irish in the Early Modern Caribbean', *Past and Present*, 210 (2011), pp. 33–60

Nicholas Bomba, 'The Hibernian Amazon: A struggle for sovereignty in the Portuguese court, 1643–1648', *Journal of Early Modern History*, 11 (2007), pp. 447–74

J. F. Boscher, 'Huguenot Merchants and the Protestant International in the Seventeenth Century', *The William and Mary Quarterly*, third series, 52 (1995), pp. 77–102

Karl S. Bottigheimer, *English Money and Irish Land: The 'Adventurers' in the Cromwellian Settlement of Ireland* (Oxford, 1971)

H. V. Bowen, Elizabeth Mancke, and John G. Reid (eds.), *Britain's Oceanic Empire: Atlantic and Indian Ocean Worlds, c.1550–1850* (Cambridge, 2012)

Brendan Bradshaw, *The Irish Constitutional Revolution of the Sixteenth Century* (Cambridge, 1979)

Brendan Bradshaw et al. (eds.) *Representing Ireland: Literature and the Origins of Conflict, 1534–1660* (Cambridge, 1993)

Ciaran Brady, *The Chief Governors: The Rise and Fall of Reform Government in Tudor Ireland* (Cambridge, 1994)

Ciaran Brady (ed.), *Interpreting Irish History: The Debate on Historical Revisionism* (Dublin, 1994)

Ciaran Brady, 'The Captains' Games: Army and Society in Elizabethan Ireland' in Thomas Bartlett and Keith Jeffery (eds.), *A Military History of Ireland* (Cambridge, 1996)

H. V. Brasted, 'Indian Nationalist development and the influence of Irish home rule, 1870–86', *Modern Asia Studies* 12 (1980), 37–63

Micheál Briody, *The Irish Folklore Commission 1935–1970* (Helsinki, 2008)

David Brown, *Empire and Enterprise. Money, Power and the Adventurers for Irish Land during the British Civil Wars* (Manchester, 2020)

Elizabeth Buettner, *Europe after Empire: Decolonization, Society and Culture* (Cambridge, 2016)

William J. Bulman, *Anglican Enlightenment: Orientalism, Religion and Politics in England and its Empire, 1648–1715* (Cambridge, 2015)

Jane Burbank and Frederick Cooper, *Empires in World History: Power and the Politics of Difference* (Princeton, 2010)

Nuala T. Burke, 'An Early Modern Dublin Suburb: The Estate of Francis Aungier, Earl of Longford', *Irish Geography*, 6 (1972), pp. 365–85

Trevor Burnard, 'European Migration to Jamaica, 1655–1780', *The William and Mary Quarterly*, 53 (1996), pp. 769–96

Antoinette Burton, *The Trouble with Empire: Challenges to Modern British Imperialism* (Oxford, 2015)

Rebecca Bushnell, *A Culture of Teaching: Early Modern Humanism in Theory and Practice* (Ithaca, 1996)

Rebecca Bushnell, 'Experience, truth, and natural history in early English gardening books' in Donald R. Kelly and David Harris Sacks (eds.), *The Historical Imagination in Early Modern Britain: History, Rhetoric, and Fiction, 1500–1800* (Cambridge, 1997)

Marc Caball, 'Politics and Religion in the Poetry of Fearghal Óg Mac An Bhaird and Eoghan Ruadh Mac An Bhaird' in Pádraig Ó Riain (ed.), *The Life of Red Hugh O'Donnell Historical and Literary Contexts* (Irish Texts Society, Dublin, 2002)

Marc Caball, 'Gaelic and Protestant: A case study in early modern self-fashioning, 1567–1608', *Proceedings of the Royal Irish Academy*, C, 110 (2010), pp. 191–215

Marc Caball, 'Culture, Continuity and Change in early seventeenth-century south-west Munster', *Studia Hibernica*, 38 (2012)

Marc Caball, 'Local and global: A perspective from early eighteenth-century Gaelic Munster', *Proceedings of the Harvard Celtic Colloquium* 34 (2014)

Marc Caball, 'Munster and India: The local and global in early modern Ireland' in Sarah Covington, Vincent P. Carey, and Valerie McGowan-Doyle (eds.), *Early Modern Ireland: New Sources, Methods and Perspectives* (Abingdon, 2019), pp. 139–41

Ian Campbell, *Renaissance Humanism and Ethnicity before Race: The Irish and the English in the Seventeenth Century* (Manchester, 2013)

Ian Campbell Ross, ' "A very knowing American": The Inca Garcilaso de la Vega and Swift's Modest Proposal', *Modern Language Quarterly*, 68 (2007), pp. 493–516

Nicholas Canny, 'The Ideology of English Colonization: From Ireland to America', *The William and Mary Quarterly*, 30 (1973), pp. 575–98

Nicholas Canny, 'Hugh O'Neill in Irish historical discourse, c.1550–2021', *Irish Historical Studies* 46, (2022), pp. 25–51

Nicholas Canny, *The Elizabethan Conquest of Ireland: A Pattern Established 1565–1576* (New York, 1976)

Nicholas Canny, *Kingdom and Colony: Ireland in the Atlantic World, 1560–1800* (Baltimore, 1988)

Nicholas Canny (ed.), *Europeans on the Move: Studies on European Migration, 1500–1800* (Oxford, 1994)

Nicholas Canny, *Making Ireland British, 1580–1650* (Oxford, 2001)

Nicholas Canny, 'Ireland and Continental Europe' in Alvin Jackson (ed.), *The Oxford Handbook of Modern Irish History* (Oxford, 2014)

Nicholas Canny, *Imagining Ireland's Pasts: Early Modern Ireland through the Centuries* (Oxford, 2021)

Nicholas Canny, 'How the Local Can be Global and the Global Local: Ireland, Irish Catholics, and European Overseas Empires, 1500–1900' in Patrick Griffin and Francis D. Cogliano (eds.), *Ireland and America: Empire, Revolution and Sovereignty* (Virginia, 2021)

Nicholas Canny and Philip Morgan (eds.), *The Oxford Handbook of the Atlantic World c.1450–c.1850* (Oxford, 2011)

Nicholas Canny and A. Pagden (eds.), *Colonial Identity in the Atlantic World, 1500–1800* (Princeton, 1987)

Hilary Carey, *God's Empire: Religion and Colonialism in the British World, c.1801–1908* (Cambridge, 2011)

Hilary Carey (ed.), *Empires of Religion* (Basingstoke, 2008)

Vincent Carey, *Surviving the Tudors: The 'Wizard' Earl of Kildare and English Rule in Ireland, 1537–1586* (Dublin, 2002)

Vincent Carey, 'Icons of Atrocity: John Derricke's *Image of Ireland* (1581)' in Allison Kavey (ed.), *World Building and the Early Modern Imagination* (New York, 2010)

Clare Carroll, *Circe's Cup: Cultural Transformations in Early Modern Ireland* (Cork, 2001)

Clare Carroll and Patricia King (eds.), *Ireland and Postcolonial Theory* (Cork, 2003)

Jill H. Casid, *Sowing Empire: Landscape and Colonization* (Minneapolis, 2005)

Alison Cathcart, *Plantations by Land and Sea: North Channel Communities of the Atlantic Archipelago c.1550–1625* (Oxford, 2021)

Bipan Chandra, *Nationalism and Colonialism in Modern India* (New Delhi, 1981)

K. N. Chaudhuri, *The Trading World of Asia and the English East India Company, 1660–1760* (Cambridge, 1978)

John F. Cherry and Krysta Ryzewski, *An Archaeological History of Montserrat in the West Indies* (Oxford, 2020)

Aidan Clarke, 'The History of Poynings' Law, 1615–1641', *Irish Historical Studies*, 18 (1972), pp. 207–22

Aidan Clarke 'The 1641 depositions' in P. Fox (ed.), *Treasures of the Library: Trinity College Dublin* (Dublin, 1986)

Aidan Clarke, 'Colonial constitutional attitudes in Ireland, 1640–1660', *Proceedings of the Royal Irish Academy*, 90, section c, 11 (1990)

Aidan Clarke, 'Patrick Darcy and the constitutional relationship between Ireland and Britain' in Jane Ohlmeyer (ed.), *Political Thought in Seventeenth-Century Ireland: Kingdom or Colony?* (Cambridge, 2000)

Joe Cleary, 'Amongst Empires: A Short History of Ireland and Empire Studies in International Context', *Éire-Ireland*, 42 (Spring/Summer, 2007), pp. 11–57

Bernard S. Cohn, *Colonialism and its Forms of Knowledge: The British in India* (Princeton, New Jersey, 1996)

John M. Collins, *Martial Law and English Laws, c.1500–c.1700* (Cambridge, 2016)

Linda Colley, 'Going Native, Telling Tales: Captivity, Collaborations and Empire', *Past and Present*, 168 (2000), pp. 170–93

Linda Colley, *Captives. Britain, Empire and the World, 1600–1850* (London, 2002)

S. B. Cook, 'The Irish Raj: Social origins and careers of Irishmen in the Indian Civil Service. 1855–1911', *Journal of Social History*, 20 (1987), pp. 507–29

S. B. Cook, *Imperial Affinities: Nineteenth-Century Analogies and Exchanges between India and Ireland* (New Delhi, 1993)

Frederick Cooper and Ann Laura Stoler (eds.), *Tensions of Empire: Colonial Cultures in a Bourgeois World* (Berkeley, 1997)

Joseph Cope, *England and the 1641 Irish Rebellion* (Woodbridge, 2009)

Alfred Cosby, *The Columbian Exchange: Biological and Cultural Consequences of 1492* (Westport, Connecticut, 1972)

Patricia Coughlan, 'Counter-currents in colonial discourse: The political thought of Vincent and Daniel Gookin' in Jane Ohlmeyer (ed.), *Political Thought in Seventeenth Century Ireland* (Cambridge, 2000)

Tony Coult, *About Friel: The Playwright and the Work* (London, 2003)

Sarah Covington, '"Realms so barbarous and cruell": Writing Violence in Early Modern Ireland and England', *History*, 2014, 99 (2014), pp. 487–504

Sarah Covington, '"Those Savage Days of Memory": John Temple and His Narrative of the 1641 Uprising' in Fionnuala Dillane, Naomi McAreavey, and Emilie Price (eds.), *The Body in Pain in Irish Literature and Culture* (London, 2016)

Sarah Covington, 'Dung Beetles and the "Vulgar Traditions": Applying folkloric Sources and Methods to Early Modern Ireland' in Sarah Covington, Vincent P. Carey, and Valerie McGowan-Doyle (eds.), *Early Modern Ireland: New Sources, Methods and Perspectives* (Abingdon, 2019)

Sarah Covington, Vincent P. Carey, and Valerie McGowan-Doyle (eds.), *Early Modern Ireland: New Sources, Methods and Perspectives* (Abingdon, 2019)

Sarah Covington, *The Devil from over the Sea: Remembering and Forgetting Oliver Cromwell in Ireland* (Oxford, 2022)

Donal Cregan, 'Catholic Admissions to the English Inns of Court', *The Irish Jurist*, 5 (1970), pp. 95–114

Donal Cregan, 'Irish Recusant Lawyers in Politics in the Reign of James I', *The Irish Jurist*, 5 (1970), pp. 306–20

R. D. Crewe, 'Brave New Spain: An Irishman's Independence Plot in Seventeenth Century Mexico', *Past and Present*, 207 (2010), pp. 53–87

Peter Crooks, 'Representation and Dissent: "Parliamentarianism" and the Structure of Politics in Colonial Ireland, c. 1370–1420', *English Historical Review*, 512 (2010), pp. 1–34

Peter Crooks, 'State of the Union: Perspectives on English Imperialism in the Late Middle Ages', *Past and Present*, 212 (2011), pp. 3–42

Peter Crooks and Timothy H. Parsons (eds.), *Empires and Bureaucracy in World History: From Late Antiquity to the Twentieth Century* (Cambridge, 2016)

Barry Crosbie, *Irish Imperial Networks: Migration, Social Communication and Exchange in Nineteenth-Century India* (Cambridge, 2012)

Barry Crosbie, 'Irish Religious Networks in Colonial South Asia, ca. 1788–1858' in Colin Barr and Hilary Carey (eds.), *Religion and Greater Ireland: Christianity and Irish Global Networks* (Montreal and Kingston, 2015)

Louis M. Cullen, 'Merchant Communities, the navigation acts and the Irish and Scottish responses' in L. M. Cullen and T. C. Smout (eds.), *Comparative Aspects of Scottish and Irish Social History* (Edinburgh, 1977)

Louis M. Cullen, 'The Irish Diaspora of the Seventeenth and Eighteenth Centuries' in Nicholas Canny (ed.), *Europeans on the Move: Studies on European Migration, 1500–1800* (Oxford, 1994)

Louis M. Cullen, 'The Two George Fitzgeralds of London, 1718–1759' in David Dickson, Jan Parmentier, and Jane Ohlmeyer (eds.), *Irish and Scottish Mercantile Networks in Europe and Overseas in the Seventeenth and Eighteenth Centuries* (Ghent, 2007)

Bernadette Cunningham and Raymond Gillespie, 'The East Ulster bardic family of Ó Gnímh', *Egise*, 20 (1984)

John Cunningham, 'The transplanters' certificates and the historiography of Cromwellian Ireland', *Irish Historical Studies,* 37 (2011), pp. 376–95

Perry Curtis, *Apes and Angels: The Irishman in Victorian Caricature* (Washington DC, 1997)

S. F. Dale, *The Muslim Empires of the Ottomans, Safavids, and Mughals* (Cambridge, 2010)

Mary Daly, ' "The State Papers of a forgotten and neglected people": The National Folklore Collection and the writing of Irish history', *Béaloideas,* 78 (2010), pp. 61–79

John Darwin, *After Tamerlane: The Rise and Fall of Global Empires, 1400–2000* (London, 2007)

M. D. David, 'The Beginning of Bombay's Economic Development, 1661–1708', *Journal of Indian History,* 55 (1977), pp. 217–18, 197–240

R. R. Davies, *The First English Empire: Power and Identities in the British Isles 1093–1343* (Oxford, 2002)

Jane Dawson, 'Two kingdoms or three?: Ireland in Anglo-Scottish relations in the middle of the sixteenth century' in R. A. Mason (ed.), *Scotland and England, 1286–1815* (Edinburgh, 1987), pp. 113–38

James Delbourgo, *Collecting the World: The Life and Curiosity of Hans Sloane* (London, 2017)

Coleman Dennehy, *The Irish Parliament, 1613–89: The Evolution of a Colonial Institution* (Manchester, 2019)

Coleman Dennehy (ed.), *Law and Revolution in Seventeenth-Century Ireland* (Dublin, 2020)

David Dickson, *The First Irish Cities: An Eighteenth-Century Transformation* (New Haven and London, 2021)

David Dickson, *Old World Colony: Cork and South Munster 1630–1830* (Cork, 2005)

Alison Donnell, Maria McGarrity, and Evelyn O'Callaghan (eds.), *Caribbean Irish Connections: Interdisciplinary Perspectives* (Kingston, Jamaica, 2015)

Terence Dooley, Mary Ann Lyons, and Salvador Ryan (eds.), *The Historian as Detective. Uncovering Irish Pasts: Essays in Honour of Raymond Gillespie* (Dublin, 2021)

Richard S. Dunn, *Sugar and Slaves: The Rise of the Planter Class* (Chapel Hill, North Carolina, 1972)

Declan M. Downey, 'Wild geese and the double-headed eagle: Irish integration in Austria c.1630–c.1918' in Paul Leifer and Eda Sagarra (eds.), *Austro-Irish Links through the Centuries* (Vienna, 2002)

Richard Drayton, *Nature's Government: Science, Imperial Britain and the 'Improvement' of the World* (New Delhi, 2005)

Patrick Duffy, David Edwards, and Elizabeth Fitzpatrick (eds.), *Gaelic Ireland: Land Lordship and Settlement c.1250–c.1650* (Dublin, 2001)

Tom Earle and Kate Lowe (eds.), *Black Africans in Renaissance Europe* (Cambridge, 2005)

David Edwards, Pádraig Lenihan, and Clodagh Tait (eds.), *Age of Atrocity: Violence and Political Conflict in Early Modern Ireland* (Dublin, 2007)

David Edwards (ed.), *Regions and Rulers in Ireland, 1100–1650: Essays for Kenneth Nicholls* (Dublin, 2004)

David Edwards, 'Ireland: Security and Conquest' in Susan Doran and Norman Jones (eds.), *The Elizabethan World* (London, 2011)

David Edwards, 'Virginian connections: The wider Atlantic setting of Boyle's Munster estate and clientele' in David Edwards and Colin Rynne (eds.), *The Colonial World of Richard Boyle First Earl of Cork* (Dublin, 2018)

David Edwards and Colin Rynne (eds.), *The Colonial World of Richard Boyle First Earl of Cork* (Dublin, 2018)

Caroline Elkins, *Legacy of Violence: A History of the British Empire* (London, 2022)

J. H. Elliott, *Empires of the Atlantic World: Britain and Spain in America 1492–1830* (New Haven, 2006)

Steven G. Ellis, *Tudor Frontiers and Noble Power: The Making of the British State* (Oxford, 1995)

Steven G. Ellis, 'Writing Irish History: Revisionism, colonialism, and the British Isles', *The Irish Review*, 19 (1996), pp. 1–21

Steven G. Ellis, 'Civilising the natives: State formation and the Tudor Monarchy, c.1400–1603' in S. G. Ellis and L. Klusaková (eds.), *Imagining Frontiers: Contesting Identities* (Pisa, 2007)

Steven G. Ellis, 'Reducing their wilderness ... unto civility': England and the "Celtic fringe" 1415–1625' in B. Smith (ed.), *Ireland and the English World in the Late Middle Ages: Essays in Honour of Robin Frame* (Basingstoke, 2009), pp. 176–92

Nigel Everett, *The Woods of Ireland: A History, 700–1800* (Dublin, 2015)

Eric Falci and Paige Reynolds (ed.), *Irish Literature in Transition 1980–2020* (Cambridge, 2020)

Tim Fanning, *Paisanos: The Forgotten Irish who Changed the Face of Latin America* (Dublin, 2016)

Gerard Farrell, *The 'Mere Irish' and the Colonisation of Ulster, 1570–1641* (London, 2017)

Maura Jane Farrelly, 'American Identity and English Catholicism in the Atlantic World' in D'Maris Coffman, Adrian Leonard, and William O'Reilly (eds.), *The Atlantic World: 1400–1850* (London, 2015)

Jane Fenlon, *Goods and Chattels: A Survey of Early Household Inventories in Ireland* (Dublin, 2003)

Jane Fenlon (ed.), *Clanricard's Castle: Portumna House, Co. Galway* (Dublin, 2012)

Jane Fenlon, 'A good painter may get good bread': Thomas Pooley and Garrett Morphey, two gentlemen painters' in Raymond Gillespie and R. F. Foster (eds.), *Irish Provincial Cultures in the Long Eighteenth Century: Making the Middle Sort: Essays for Toby Barnard* (Dublin, 2012)

Peter Fibiger Bang, C. A. Bayly, and Walter Scheidel (eds.), *The Oxford World History of Empire* (2 vols., Oxford, 2021)

Margot Finn and Kate Smith (eds.), *The East India Company at Home 1757–1857* (London, 2018)

Andrew Fitzmaurice, 'The civic solution to the crisis of English colonization, 1609–1625', *The Historical Journal*, 42 (1999), pp. 25–51

Andrew Fitzmaurice, 'The Commercial Ideology of Colonization in Jacobean England: Robert Johnson, Giovanni Botero, and the Pursuit of Greatness', *The William and Mary Quarterly*, third series, 64 (2007), pp. 791–820

Susan Flavin, 'Consumption and Material Culture in Sixteenth-Century Ireland', *Economic History Review*, 64 (2011), pp. 1073–427

Susan Flavin, *Consumption and Culture in Sixteenth-Century Ireland* (Woodbridge, 2014)

T. Foley and M. O'Connor (eds.), *Ireland and India: Colonies, Culture and Empire* (Dublin, 2006)

Alan Fletcher, *Drama, Performance, and Polity in Pre-Cromwellian Ireland* (Toronto, 2000)

Roy Foster, *Paddy and Mr Punch: Connections in Irish and English History* (London, 2011)

Corinne Fowler, *Green Unpleasant Land: Creative Responses to Rural England's Colonial Connections* (Leeds, 2020)

William O. Frazer, 'Field of Fire: Evidence for Wartime Conflict in a 17th- Century Cottier Settlement in County Meath, Ireland', *Journal of Conflict Archaeology*, 3 (2007), pp. 173–95

Brian Friel, *Making History* (London, 1989)

Marisa J. Fuentes, *Dispossessed Lives: Enslaved Women, Violence, and the Archive* (Philadelphia, 2016)

Holden Furber, *Rival Empires of Trade in the Orient, 1600–1800* (Minneapolis, 1976)

Andrew Gailey, *The Lost Imperialist: Lord Dufferin, Memory and Mythmaking in an Age of Celebrity* (London, 2015)

Marcus Gallo, 'William Penn, William Petty, and Surveying: The Irish Connection' in Andrew R. Murphy and John Smolenski (eds.), *The Worlds of William Penn* (New Brunswick, New Jersey, 2019)

Alison Games, *The Web of Empire: English Cosmopolitans in an Age of Expansion, 1560–1660* (Oxford, 2008)

Alison Games, 'Violence on the Fringes: The Virginia (1622) and Amboya (1623) Massacres', *History*, 99 (2014), pp. 505–29

Alison Games, 'Cohabitation, Suriname-style: English Inhabitants in Dutch Suriname after 1667', *The William and Mary Quarterly*, 72 (2015), pp. 195–242

John Gibney, 'The most controversial documents in Irish history?', *History Ireland*, 19 (2011), pp. 18–19

John Gibney, *The Shadow of a Year: The 1641 Rebellion in Irish History and Memory* (Madison, 2013)

Raymond Gillespie, 'The Origins and Development of an Ulster Urban Network, 1600–41', *Irish Historical Studies*, 24 (1984)

Raymond Gillespie, *Colonial Ulster: The Settlement of East Ulster, 1600–1641* (Cork, 1985)

Raymond Gillespie, 'Explorers, exploiters and entrepreneurs: early modern Ireland and its context, 1500–1700' in B. J. Graham and L. J. Proudfoot (eds.), *An Historical Geography of Ireland* (London, 1993)

Raymond Gillespie, 'Political Ideas and their Social Contexts in Seventeenth-Century Ireland' in Jane Ohlmeyer (ed.), *Political Thought in Seventeenth-Century Ireland: Kingdom or Colony?* (Cambridge, 2000)

Raymond Gillespie, 'Temple's Fate: Reading *The Irish Rebellion* in Late Seventeenth-Century Ireland' in Ciaran Brady and Jane Ohlmeyer (eds.), *British Interventions in Early Modern Ireland* (Cambridge, 2004)

Raymond Gillespie, 'Seventeenth-century Irish music and its cultural context' in Barra Boydell and Kerry Houston (eds.), *Music, Ireland and the Seventeenth Century* (Dublin, 2009)

Gabriel Glickman, 'Protestantism, Colonization and the New England Company in Restoration Politics', *Historical Journal*, 59 (2016), pp. 365–91

Priyamvada Gopal, *Insurgent Empire: Anticolonial Resistance and British Dissent* (London, 2019)

Eliga H. Gould, 'Entangled Histories, Entangled Worlds: The English-Speaking Atlantic as a Spanish Periphery', *American Historical Review*, 12 (2007), pp. 764–86

Peter Gray, 'Famine and Land in Ireland and India 1845–1880: James Caird and the Political Economy of Hunger', *The Historical Journal*, 49 (2006), pp. 193–215

Jack P. Greene, *The Intellectual Heritage of the Constitutional Era* (Philadelphia, 1986)

Jack P. Greene, *Peripheries and Center: Constitutional Development in the Extended Polities of the British Empire and the United States, 1607–1788* (Athens, Georgia, 1987)

John C. Greene and Gladys L. H. Clark, *The Dublin Stage, 1720–1745: A Calendar of Plays, Entertainments and Afterpieces* (London, 1993)

John Greene, *Theatre in Dublin 1745–1820: A History*, 2 vols. (Bethlehem, Pennsylvania, 2011)

Allan Greer, *Property and Dispossession: Natives, Empires and Land in Early Modern North Atlantic America* (Cambridge, 2018)

Arturo Griffin, 'Conquistadores, Soldiers and Entrepreneurs: Early Irish Presence in Chile', *Irish Migration Studies in Latin America*, 4 (2006), pp. 216–20

Patrick Griffin, *The People with No Name: Ireland's Ulster Scots, America's Scots Irish, and the Creation of a British Atlantic World, 1689–1764* (Princeton, 2002)

Aubrey Gwynn, 'Early Irish Emigration to the West Indies (1612–43)', *Studies: An Irish Quarterly*, 18 (1929), pp. 377–93; Part 2 (1929), pp. 648–63

Aubrey Gwynn, 'Indentured Servants and Negro Slaves in Barbados, 1642–1650', *Studies: An Irish Quarterly Review*, 19 (1930), pp. 279–94

Aubrey Gwynn, 'Cromwell's Policy of Transportation – Part 1', *Studies*, 19 (1930), pp. 607–23; Part 2, 20 (1931), pp. 291–305

Aubrey Gwynn, 'The first Irish priests in the New World', *Studies*, 21 (1932), pp. 213–28

Aubrey Gwynn, 'An Irish settlement on the Amazon 1612–29', *Proceedings of the Royal Irish Academy*, 41 (1932), pp. 1–54

Evan Haefeli, 'Toleration and Empire: The Origins of American Religious Pluralism' in Stephen Foster (ed.), *British North America in the Seventeenth and Eighteenth Centuries* (Oxford, 2013), pp. 114–15, 121–3

Catherine Hall and Sonya O. Rose (eds.). *At Home with the Empire: Metropolitan Culture and the Imperial World* (Cambridge, 2006)

Dianne Hall, 'Fear, Gender and Violence in Early Modern Ireland' in Michael Champion and Andrew Lynch (eds.), *Understanding Emotions in Early Europe* (Turnhout, Belgium, 2015), pp. 215–32

Dianne Hall, '"Most barbarously and inhumaine maner butchered": Masculinity, Trauma, and Memory in Early Modern Ireland' in Fionnuala Dillane, Naomi McAreavey, and Emilie Price (eds.), *The Body in Pain in Irish Literature and Culture* (London, 2016), pp. 41–7

Pekka Hämäläinen, *The Comanche Empire* (New Haven, 2008)

David Harris Sacks, 'The true temper of empire: dominion, friendship and exchange in the English Atlantic, c. 1575–1625', *Renaissance Studies*, 26 (2012), pp. 531–58

David Harris Sacks, 'Love and Fear in the Making of England's Atlantic Empire', *Huntington Library Quarterly*, 83 (2020) special edition 'Ancient Rome in English Political Culture, ca. 1570–1660', ed. Paulina Kewes, pp. 543–65

W. A. Hart, 'Africans in Eighteenth-Century Ireland', *Irish Historical Studies*, 33 (2002), pp. 19–32

Moyra Haslett (ed.), *Irish Literature in Transition 1700–1780* (Cambridge, 2020)

R. C. Hawkins, 'The "Irish Model" and the empire: A case for reassessment' in D. M. Anderson and D. Killingray (eds.), *Policing the Empire: Government, Authority and Control, 1830–1940* (Manchester, 1991)

Michael Hechter, *Internal Colonialism: The Celtic Fringe in British National Development, 1536–1966* (London, 1975)

David Heffernan, *Walter Devereux First Earl of Essex and the Colonization of North-East Ulster, c. 1573–6* (Dublin, 2018)

David Heffernan, *Debating Tudor Policy in Sixteenth-Century Ireland: 'Reform' Treatises and Political Discourse* (Manchester, 2018)

Thomas Herron and Michael Potterton (ed.), *Ireland in the Renaissance, c. 1540–1660* (Dublin, 2007)

Thomas Herron, Denna J. Iammarino, and Maryclaire Moroney (eds.), *John Derricke's The Image of Irelande: with a Discoverie of Woodkarne. Essays on text and context* (Manchester, 2021)

Jacqueline Hill and Colm Lennon (eds.), *Luxury and Austerity: Historical Studies XXI* (Dublin, 1999)

Ronald Hoffman, *Princes of Ireland, Planters of Maryland: A Carroll Saga, 1500–1782* (Chapel Hill, North Carolina, 2000)

Liam Hogan, Laura McAtackney, and Matthew C. Reilly, 'The Irish in the Anglo-Caribbean: Servants or Slaves?', *History Ireland*, 24 (2016), pp. 18–22

Karen A. Holland, 'Disputed Heroes: Early Accounts of the Siege of Londonderry', *New Hibernia Review*, 18 (2014)

Robert Home, *Of Planting and Planning* (London, 1997)

A. G. Hopkins, 'Back to the Future: From national history to imperial history', *Past and Present*, 164 (1999), pp. 198–243

Audrey Horning, *Ireland in the Virginian Sea: Colonialism in the British Atlantic* (Williamsburg, Virginia, 2013)

Audrey Horning, 'Clothing and colonialism: The Dungiven costume and the fashioning of early modern identities', *Journal of Social Archaeology*, 14 (2014), pp. 296–318

Audrey Horning, 'Comparative Colonialism: Scales of Analysis and Contemporary Resonances' in Craig N. Cipolla and Katherine Howlett Hayes (eds.), *Rethinking Colonialism: Comparative Archaeological Approaches* (Gainesville, Fl, 2015)

Audrey Horning, 'Minding the Gaps: Exploring the intersection of political economy, colonial ideologies, and cultural practice in early modern Ireland', *Post-Medieval Archaeology*, 52 (2018), pp. 4–20

Audrey Horning, 'Shapeshifters and mimics: Exploring elite strategies in the early modern British Atlantic' in David Edwards and Colin Rynne (eds.), *The Colonial World of Richard Boyle First Earl of Cork* (Dublin, 2018)

Audrey Horning, 'The Irish Worlds of William Penn: Culture, Conflict, and Connections' in Andrew R. Murphy and John Smolenski (eds.), *The Worlds of William Penn* (New Brunswick, 2019)

Audrey Horning and Eric Schweickart, 'Globalization and the spread of capitalism: Material resonances', *Post-Medieval Archaeology*, 50 (2016), pp. 34–52

Stephen Howe, *Ireland and Empire: Colonial Legacies in Irish History and Culture* (Oxford, 2000)

Stephen Howe, *Empire: A Very Short Introduction* (Oxford, 2002)

Stephen Howe, 'Review Article: When—If Ever—Did Empire End? Recent Studies of Imperialism and Decolonization', *Journal of Contemporary History*, 40 (2005), pp. 585–99

Stephen Howe, 'Questioning the (Bad) Question: Was Ireland a Colony?'. *Irish Historical Studies*, 37 (2008), pp. 1–15

Chiu Hsin-Hui, *The Colonial 'Civilizing Process' in Dutch Formosa: 1624–1662* (Leiden: Brill, 2008)

Robert Hunter, 'Ulster Plantation Towns 1609–1641' in David Harkness and Mary O'Dowd (eds.), *The Town in Ireland* (Belfast, 1991)

Chloe Ireton, 'Black Africans' Freedom Litigation Suits to Define Just War and Just Slavery in the Early Spanish Empire', *Renaissance Quarterly*, 73 (2020), pp. 1277–319

Chloe Ireton, 'Margarita de Sossa, Sixteenth-Century Puebla de los Ángeles, New Spain (Mexico)' in Erica L. Ball, Tatiana Seijas, and Terri L. Snyder (eds.), *As If She Were Free: A Collective Biography of Black Women and Emancipation in the Americas* (Cambridge, 2020)

Keith Jeffrey (ed.), *An Irish Empire? Aspects of Ireland and the British Empire* (Manchester 1996)

J. R. V. Johnston, 'The Stapleton Sugar Plantations in the Leeward Islands', *Bulletin of the John Rylands Library*, 48 (1965), pp. 175–206

Brendan Kane, 'Masculinity and political geographies in England, Ireland and North America', *European Review of History: Revue européenne d'histoire*, 22, (2015), pp. 595–619

Brendan Kane, 'Popular politics and the legitimacy of power in early modern Ireland' in Elizabeth FitzPatrick and Audrey Horning (eds.), *Becoming and Belonging in Ireland 1200–1600 AD* (Cork, 2018)

Brendan Kane and Malcolm Smuts, 'The Politics of Race in England, Scotland and Ireland' in Malcolm Smuts (ed.), *The Oxford Handbook of the Age of Shakespeare* (Oxford, 2016)

Miranda Kaufmann, *Black Tudors: The Untold Story* (London, 2017)

Connie Kelleher, *The Alliance of Pirates: Ireland and Atlantic Piracy in the Early Seventeenth Century* (Cork, 2020)

Margaret Kelleher and Philip O'Leary (eds.), *The Cambridge History of Irish Literature, Volume 1 to 1890*, 2 vols. (Cambridge, 2006)

James Kelly, *Poynings' Law and the Making of Law in Ireland, 1660–1800: Monitoring the Constitution* (Dublin, 2007)

James Kelly, ' "Era of Liberty": The Politics of Civil and Political Rights in Eighteenth-Century Ireland' in Jack P. Greene (ed.), *Exclusionary Empire: English Liberty Overseas, 1600–1900* (Cambridge, 2010)

Patrick Kelly, ' "A Light to the Blind": The Voice of the Dispossessed Elite in the Generation after the Defeat at Limerick', *Irish Historical Studies*, 24 (1985), pp. 431–62

John H. Kennedy, *Thomas Dongan Governor of New York (1682–1688)* (Washington, DC, 1930)

Gulfishan Khan, *Indian Muslim Perceptions of the West during the Eighteenth Century* (Karachi, 1998)

Colin Kidd, *British Identities before Nationalism: Ethnicity and Nationhood in the Atlantic World, 1600–1800* (Cambridge, 1999)

Thomas Kilroy, *The O'Neill* (Dublin, 1995)

S. Kline, 'William Lamport/Guillén de Lombardo (1611–1659)' in Karen Racine and Beatriz G. Mamigonian (eds.), *The Human Tradition in the Atlantic World, 1500–1850* (Plymouth, 2010)

H. G. Koenigsberger, 'Dominium regale or dominium politicum et regale' reprinted in *Politicians and Virtuosi: Essays on Early Modern History* (London, 1986)

John D. Krugler, *English and Catholic: The Lords Baltimore in the Seventeenth Century* (Baltimore and London, 2004)

Karen Ordahl Kupperman, 'Errand to the Indies: Puritan Colonization from Providence Island through the Western Design', *The William and Mary Quarterly*, 45 (1988), pp. 70–99

Karen O. Kupperman, *The Jamestown Project* (Cambridge, Mass., 2007)

Hal Langfur, 'Race and Violence in Portuguese America' in Robert Antony, Stuart Carroll, and Caroline Dodds Pennock (eds.), *The Cambridge World History of Violence*: vol. 3 (Cambridge, 2020)

Maurice Lee, Jr., *Great Britain's Solomon: James VI and I in His Three Kingdoms* (Urbana, Illinois, 1990)

Wayne Lee, *Barbarians and Brothers: Anglo-American Warfare, 1500–1865* (Oxford, 2011)

Joep Leerssen, 'Wildness, wilderness, and Ireland: Medieval and early-modern patterns in the demarcation of civility', *Journal of the History of Ideas* 56 (1995), pp. 25–39

Joep Leerssen, *Mere Irish and Fíor-Ghael: Studies in the Idea of Irish Nationality, its Development and Literary Expression prior to the Nineteenth Century* (Cork, 1996)

Beverly Lemire, *Fashion's Favourite: The Cotton Trade and the Consumer in Britain, 1660–1800* (Oxford, 1991)

P. Lenihan (ed.), *Conquest and Resistance: War in Seventeenth-Century Ireland* (Leiden, 2001)

Patrick Little, 'The English parliament and the Irish constitution, 1641–9' in Micheál Ó Siochrú (ed.), *Kingdoms in Crisis: Ireland in the 1640s* (Dublin, 2001)

Rolf Loeber, *A Biographical Dictionary of Architects in Ireland 1600–1720* (London, 1981)

Rolf Loeber, 'Preliminaries to the Massachusetts Bay Colony: The Irish ventures of Emanuel Downing and John Winthrop Sr' in Toby Barnard, Dáibhí Ó Cróinín, and Katherine Simms (eds.), *'A Miracle of Learning': Studies in Manuscripts and Irish Learning* (Aldershot, 1998)

Neil Longley York, *Neither Kingdom nor Nation: The Irish Quest for Constitutional Rights, 1698–1800* (Washington, 1994)

Francis Ludlow and Arlene Crampsie, 'Environmental History of Ireland, 1550–1730' in Jane Ohlmeyer (ed.), *The Cambridge History of Ireland*, vol. 2. *Early Modern Ireland, 1550–1730* (Cambridge, 2018)

James Lyttleton and Tadhg O'Keefe (eds.), *The Manor in Medieval and Early Modern Ireland* (Dublin, 2005)

Naomi McAreavey, ' "Paper bullets": Gendering the 1641 rebellion in the writings of Lady Elizabeth Dowdall and Lettice Fitzgerald, baroness of Offaly' in Thomas Herron and Michael Potterton (eds.), *Ireland in the Renaissance, c.1540–1660* (Dublin, 2007)

Ian McBride, *The Siege of Derry in Ulster Protestant Mythology* (Dublin, 1997)

Ian McBride (ed.), *History and Memory in Modern Ireland* (Cambridge, 2001)

Ian McBride, *Eighteenth Century Ireland: The Isle of Slaves* (Dublin, 2009)

Ian McBride, 'The Politics of *A Modest Proposal*: Swift and the Irish Crisis of the Late 1720s', *Past and Present*, 244 (2019), pp. 89–122

John McCafferty, 'Protestant prelates or godly pastors? The dilemma of the early Stuart episcopate' in Alan Ford and John McCafferty (eds.), *The Origins of Sectarianism in Early Modern Ireland* (Cambridge, 2005), pp. 54–72

Michael MacCarthy Morrogh, *The Munster Plantation: English Migration to Southern Ireland, 1583–1641* (Oxford, 1986)

John McCavitt, ' "Good Planets in their Several Spheares": The Establishment of the Assize Circuits in Early Seventeenth Century Ireland', *Irish Jurist*, 14 (1989), pp. 248–78

John McCavitt, *The Flight of the Earls* (Dublin, 2002)

Aonghas MacCoinnich, *Plantation and Civility in the North Atlantic World: The Case of the Northern Hebrides, 1570–1639* (Leiden, 2015)

Ted McCormick, ' "A proportionable mixture": William Petty, Political Arithmetic, and the Transmutation of the Irish' in Coleman A. Dennehy (ed.), *Restoration Ireland: Always Settling and Never Settled*. (Aldershot, Hampshire and Burlington, VT, 2008)

Ted McCormick, *William Petty and the Ambitions of Political Arithmetic* (Oxford, 2009)

Ted McCormick, *Human Empire: Mobility and Demographic Thought in the British Atlantic World, 1500–1800* (Oxford, 2022)

Mícheál Mac Craith, 'Literature in Irish, *c.*1550–1690: From the Elizabethan settlement to the Battle of the Boyne' in Margaret Kelleher and Philip O'Leary (eds.), *The Cambridge History of Irish Literature*, vol. 1 to 1890 (2 vols., Cambridge, 2006)

Patrick F. McDevitt, 'Ireland, Latin America, and an Atlantic Liberation Theology' in Jorge Cañizares-Esguerra and Erik R. Seeman (eds.), *The Atlantic in Global History, 1500–2000* (2nd edition, London and New York, 2018)

Hector MacDonnell, 'A Seventeenth Century Inventory from Dunluce Castle, County Antrim', *Journal of the Royal Society of Antiquaries*, 122 (1992), pp. 109–27

Terence McDonough (ed.), *Was Ireland a Colony? Economics, Politics and Culture in Nineteenth-Century Ireland* (Dublin, 2005)

Charles Ivar McGrath, *Ireland and Empire 1692–1770* (London, 2012)

John McGurk, *Sir Henry Docwra 1564–1631: Derry's Second Founder* (Dublin, 2006)

Luke McInerney, 'A 1640 register of the Thomond: Papers at Petworth House', *Archivium Hibernicum* 64 (2011), pp. 7–55

Luke McInerney, 'A "most vainglorious man": The writings of Antonius Bruodin', *Archivium Hibernicum*, 70 (2017), pp. 202–83

Kevin McKenny, 'The Restoration Land Settlement in Ireland: A Statistical Interpretation' in Coleman A. Dennehy (ed.), *Restoration Ireland: Always Settling and Never Settled* (Aldershot, Hampshire and Burlington, VT, 2008)

Catriona J. McKenzie and Eileen M. Murphy, *Life and Death in Medieval Gaelic Ireland. The Skeletons from Ballyhanna, Co. Donegal* (Dublin, 2018)

John M. MacKenzie, 'Epilogue: Analysing 'Echoes of Empire' in Contemporary Context: The Personal Odyssey of an Imperial Historian, 1970s–Present' in Kalypso Nicolaïdis, Berry Sèbe, and Gabrielle Maas (eds.), *Echoes of Empire: Memory, Identity and Colonial Legacies* (London, 2015)

John M. MacKenzie, 'Irish, Scottish, Welsh and English worlds? A Four nation approach to the history of the British Empire', *History Compass, 6/5* (2008), pp. 1244–63

Sarah E. McKibben, 'In their "owne countre": Deriding and Defending the Early Modern Irish Nation after Gerald of Wales', *Eolas: The Journal of the American Society of Irish Medieval Studies*, 8 (2015)

Andrew MacKillop, 'What has the four nations and empire model achieved' in Stephanie Barczewski and Martin Farr (eds.), *The MacKenzie Moment and Imperial History. Essays in Honour of John M. MacKenzie* (London, 2019)

Andrew MacKillop, *Human Capital and Empire: Scotland, Ireland, Wales and British Imperialism in Asia, c.1690–c.1820* (Manchester, 2021)

Ken MacMillan, 'Imperial constitutions: sovereignty and law in the British Atlantic' in H. V. Bowen, Elizabeth Mancke, and John G. Reid (eds.), *Britain's Oceanic Empire: Atlantic and Indian Ocean Worlds, c.1550–1850* (Cambridge, 2012)

Ken MacMillan, 'Bound by Our Regal Office: Empire, Sovereignty, and the American Colonies in the Seventeenth Century' in Stephen Foster (ed.), *British North America in the Seventeenth and Eighteenth Centuries* (Oxford, 2013)

R. E. W. Maddison, 'Robert Boyle and the Irish Bible', *Bulletin of the John Rylands Library*, 41 (1958), pp. 81–101

Christopher Maginn, *'Civilizing' Gaelic Leinster: The Extension of Tudor Rule in the O'Byrne and O'Toole Lordships* (Dublin, 2005)

Alistair Malcolm, 'Serving the King at Home and Abroad: The Tangier Garrison under Charles II, 1662–1684' in Anthony McElligott, Liam Chambers, Ciara Brethnach, and Catherine Lawless (eds.), *Power in History from Medieval Ireland to the Post-Modern World.* (Historical Studies XXVII, Dublin, 2011)

Pius Malekandathil, *Portuguese Cochin and the Maritime Trade of India 1500–1663* (New Delhi, 2001)

Pius Malekandathil, *The Mughals, the Portuguese and the Indian Ocean: Changing Imageries of Maritime India* (New Delhi, 2013)

Nessa Malone, 'Henry Burnell's *Landgartha:* Family, law and revolution on the Irish stage' in Coleman A. Dennehy (ed.), *Law and Revolution in Seventeenth-Century Ireland* (Dublin, 2020), pp. 65–88

Roger Manning, *Swordsmen: The Martial Ethos in the Three Kingdoms* (Oxford, 2003)

John Mannion, 'Irish Migration and Settlement in Newfoundland: The Formative Phase, 1697–1732', *Newfoundland Studies*, 17 (2001), pp. 257–93

Annaleigh Margey (ed.), *Mapping Ireland c. 1550–1636: A Catalogue of Manuscript Maps of Ireland* (IMC, 2 vols., forthcoming 2023)

Bethany Marsh, ' "Lodging the Irish": An examination of parochial charity dispensed in Nottinghamshire to refugees from Ireland, 1641–1651', *Midland History* (2017), pp. 1–23, doi: 10.1080/0047729X.2017.1376375

P. J. Marshall, 'Taming the exotic: The British and India in the seventeenth and eighteenth centuries' in G. S. Rousseau and Roy Porter (eds.), *Exoticism in the Enlightenment* (Manchester, 1990)

P. J. Marshall, 'The British in Asia: Trade to Dominion, 1700–1765' in P. J. Marshall (ed.), *The Oxford History of the British Empire*, vol. 1. *The Eighteenth Century* (Oxford, 1998)

P. J. Marshall, 'The First British Empire' in Robin Winks (ed.), *The Oxford History of the British Empire*, vol. 5. *Historiography* (Oxford, 1999)

P. J. Marshall, *Edmund Burke and the British Empire in the West Indies: Wealth, Power, and Slavery* (Oxford, 2019)

Nabil Matar, *Islam in Britain, 1558–1685* (Cambridge, 1998)

G. R. Mayes, 'The Early Stuarts and the Irish Peerage', *English Historical Review*, 73 (1958), pp. 227–51

C. P. Meehan, *The Fate and Fortunes of Hugh O'Neill, Earl of Tyrone, and Rory O'Donel, Earl of Tyrconnel* (Dublin, 1868)

John C. Messenger, 'The Influence of the Irish in Montserrat', *Caribbean Quarterly*, 13 (1967), pp. 3–26

Mark Meuwese, 'Fear, uncertainty, and violence in the Dutch colonization of Brazil (1624–1662)' in Lauric Henneton and Louis Roper (eds.), *Fear and the Shaping of Early American Societies* (Leiden, 2016)

Debra A. Meyers, 'Calvert's Catholic Colony' in Louis Roper and Bertrand Van Ruymbeke (eds.), *Constructing Early Modern Empires: Proprietary Ventures in the Atlantic World, 1500–1750* (Leiden, 2007)

Kerby Miller, *Emigrants and Exiles: Ireland and the Irish Exodus to North America* (Oxford, 1985)

Angus Mitchell (ed.), 'Hy-Brassil: Irish origins of Brazil' by Roger Casement, *Irish Migration Studies in Latin America*, 4 (2006), pp. 157–65

John Patrick Montaño, *The Roots of English Colonialism in Ireland* (Cambridge, 2011)

John Patrick Montaño, '"Dycheyng and Hegeying": The Material Culture of the Tudor Plantations in Ireland' in Fiona Bateman and Lionel Pilkington (eds.), *Studies in Settler Colonialism: Politics, Identity and Culture* (Basingstoke, 2011)

Alejandro García Montón, *Genoese Entrepreneurship and the Asiento Slave Trade, 1650–1700* (London, 2022)

T. W. Moody, *The Londonderry Plantation, 1609–41: The City of London and the Plantation in Ulster* (Belfast, 1939)

Oscar Recio Morales, *Ireland and the Spanish Empire 1600–1825* (Dublin, 2010)

Oscar Recio Morales (ed.), *Redes de nación y espacios de poder: la comunidad irlandesa en España y la América Española, 1600–1825/Power Strategies: Spain and Ireland, 1600–1825* (Valencia, 2012)

Christopher Morash, *A History of Irish Theatre 1601–2000* (Cambridge, 2002)

Hiram Morgan, 'The colonial venture of Sir Thomas Smith in Ulster, 1571–5', *Historical Journal*, 28 (1987), pp. 261–78

Hiram Morgan, 'Mid-Atlantic blues', *The Irish Review*, 11 (1991), pp. 50–5

Hiram Morgan, *Tyrone's Rebellion: The Outbreak of the Nine Years War in Tudor Ireland* (Suffolk, 1993)

Hiram Morgan (ed.), *Political Ideology in Ireland 1541–1641* (Dublin, 1999)

Hiram Morgan, 'On the Pig's Back: Subaltern Imperialism, Anti-colonialism and the Irish rise to Globalism' in Jürgen Elvert and Martina Elvert (eds.), *Agenten, Akteure, Abenteurer: Beiträge zur Ausstellung »Europa und das Meer«* (Berlin, 2018)

R. Morgan, *The Welsh and the Shaping of Early Modern Ireland 1558–1641* (Woodbridge, 2014)

John Morrisey, 'Cultural geographies of the contact zone: Gaels, Galls and overlapping territories in late medieval Ireland', *Social and Cultural Geography*, 6 (2005)

Lee Morrissey, 'Transplanting English Plantations in Aphra Behn's Oroonoko', *The Global South*, 10 (2016), pp. 11–26

James Muldoon, *Identity on the Medieval Irish Frontier: Degenerate Englishmen, Wild Irish, Middle Nation* (Gainseville, 2003)

Howard Mumford Jones, 'Origins of the colonial idea in England', *Proceedings of the American Philosophical Society*, 85 (1942), pp. 448–65

Howard Mumford Jones, 'The colonial implies: An analysis of the "Promotion" literature of colonization', *Proceedings of the American Philosophical Society*, 90 (1946), pp. 131–61

Steve Murdoch, 'Northern Exposure: Irishmen and Scandinavia in the Seventeenth Century', *History Ireland*, 6 (1998), pp. 5–6

Andrew R. Murphy, 'Ireland and ante/anti-colonial theory', *Irish Studies Review*, 7 (1999), pp. 153–61

Andrew R. Murphy, *But the Irish Sea betwixt us: Ireland, Colonialism and Renaissance Literature* (Lexington, Kentucky, 1999)

Andrew R. Murphy, 'The Roads to and from Cork: The Irish Origins of William Penn's Theory of Religious Toleration' in Andrew R. Murphy and John Smolenski (eds.), *The Worlds of William Penn* (New Brunswick, New Jersey, 2019)

James Murray, *Enforcing the English Reformation in Ireland: Clerical Resistance and Political Conflict in the Diocese of Dublin, 1534–1590* (Cambridge, 2011)

Kaori Nagai, *Empire of Analogies: Kipling, India and Ireland* (Cork, 2006)

Pratyay Nath, *Climate of Conquest: War, Environment, and Empire in Mughal North India* (Oxford, 2019)

K. W. Nicholls, *Land, Law and Society in Sixteenth-Century Ireland* (O'Donnell Lecture, Dublin, 1976)

Kenneth Nicholls, 'Woodland Cover in pre-Modern Ireland' in Patrick Duffy, David Edwards, and Elizabeth Fitzpatrick (eds.), *Gaelic Ireland: Land Lordship and Settlement c. 1250–c. 1650* (Dublin, 2001)

Maighréad Ní Mhurchadha, *Fingal, 1603–60: Contending Neighbours in North Dublin* (Dublin, 2005)

Sile Ni Mhurchú and Brendan Kane, 'Poetic Response to Plantations 1609' in Brían Ó Conchubhair and Samuel Fisher (eds.), *Bone and Marrow/Cnámh agus Smior: An Anthology of Irish Poetry from Medieval to Modern* (Winston-Salem, 2022)

Carmen Nocentelli, 'Made in India: How Meriton Latroon became an Englishman' in Jonathan Gil Harris (ed.), *Indography: Writing the 'Indian' in Early Modern England* (New York, 2012)

Breandán Ó Buachalla, 'James our true king: The ideology of Irish royalism in the seventeenth century' in D. George Boyce, Robert Eccleshall, and Vincent Geoghegan (eds.), *Political Thought in Ireland since the Seventeenth Century* (London, 1993)

Margaret O'Callaghan, 'With the eyes of another race, of a people once hunted themselves': Casement, colonialism and a remembered past' in D. George Boyce and Alan O'Day (eds.), *Ireland in Transition, 1867–1921* (London, 2004)

Éamonn Ó Ciardha, 'Tories and Moss-troopers in Scotland and Ireland in the Interregnum: A political dimension' in John R. Young (ed.), *Celtic Dimensions of the British Civil Wars* (Edinburgh, 1997)

Éamonn Ó Ciardha, *Ireland and the Jacobite Cause, 1685–1766* (Dublin, 2002)

Éamonn Ó Ciardha and Micheál Ó Siochrú (eds.), *The Plantation of Ulster: Ideology and Practice* (Manchester, 2012)

Patricia O'Connell, *The Irish College at Lisbon* (Dublin, 2001)

Thomas O'Connor, *Irish Voices from the Spanish Inquisition: Migrants, Converts and Brokers in Early Modern Iberia* (Basingstoke, 2016)

Brian Ó Dálaigh, 'A Comparative Study of the Wills of the First and Fourth Earls of Thomond', *North Munster Antiquarian Journal*, 34 (1992), pp. 48–63

Brian Ó Dálaigh, 'An Inventory of the Contents of Bunratty Castle and the Will of Henry, Fifth Earl of Thomond, 1639', *North Munster Antiquarian Journal*, 36 (1995), pp. 139–65

Mary O'Dowd, 'Women and the Irish Chancery Court in the Late Sixteenth and Early Seventeenth Centuries', *Irish Historical Studies*, 31 (1999), pp. 470–87

Diarmuid Ó Giolláin, *Locating Irish Folklore: Tradition, Modernity, Identity* (Cork, 2000)

Clare O'Halloran, *Golden Ages and Barbarous Nations: Antiquarian Debate and Cultural Politics in Ireland, c.1750–1800* (Cork, 2004)

Tadhg Ó hAnnracháin, *Confessionalism and Mobility in Early Modern Ireland* (Oxford, 2021)

Jane Ohlmeyer, ' "The Dunkirk of Ireland": Wexford privateers during the 1640s', *Journal of the Wexford Historical Society*, 12 (1988–9), pp. 23–49

Jane Ohlmeyer, 'Irish privateers during the civil war, 1642–50', *The Mariner's Mirror*, 76 (1990), pp. 119–34

Jane Ohlmeyer, 'Strafford, the "Londonderry Business" and the "New British History" ' in J. F. Merritt (ed.), *The Political World of Thomas Wentworth Earl of Strafford 1621–1641* (Cambridge, 1996)

Jane Ohlmeyer, ' "Civilizinge of those rude partes": The colonization of Ireland and Scotland, 1580s–1640s' in Nicholas Canny (ed.), *The Oxford History of the British Empire*, vol. 1 (Oxford, 1998)

Jane Ohlmeyer, 'Records of the Irish Court of Chancery: A Preliminary Report for 1627–1634' in Desmond Greer and Norma Dawson (eds.), *Mysteries and Solutions in Irish Legal History* (Dublin, 2001)

Jane Ohlmeyer, 'Irish Recusant Lawyers during the Reign of Charles I' in Micheál Ó Siochrú (ed.), *Kingdoms in Crisis: Ireland in the 1640s* (Dublin, 2001)

Jane Ohlmeyer, 'A Laboratory for Empire?: Early Modern Ireland and English Imperialism' in Kevin Kenny (ed.), *Ireland and the British Empire* (Oxford, 2004)

Jane Ohlmeyer, 'Seventeenth-century Ireland and Scotland and their Wider Worlds' in T. O'Connor and M. Lyons (eds.), *Irish Communities in Early Modern Europe* (Dublin, 2006)

Jane Ohlmeyer, *Making Ireland English: The Irish Aristocracy in the Seventeenth Century* (New Haven and London, 2012)

Jane Ohlmeyer, 'Ireland, India and the British Empire', *Studies in People's History*, 2 (2015), pp. 169–88

Jane Ohlmeyer, 'Conquest, Civilization, Colonization: Ireland, 1540–1660' in Richard Bourke and Ian MacBride (eds.), *The Princeton Guide to Modern Irish History* (Princeton, 2016)

Jane Ohlmeyer (ed.), *The Cambridge History of Ireland*, vol. 2. *Early Modern Ireland, 1550–1730* (Cambridge, 2018)

Jane Ohlmeyer, 'Eastward Enterprises: Colonial Ireland, Colonial India', *Past and Present*, 240 (2018), pp. 83–118

Jane Ohlmeyer and Micheál Ó Siochrú (eds.), *Ireland 1641: Contexts and Reactions* (Manchester, 2013)

Finola O'Kane, 'The Irish-Jamaican Plantation of Kelly's Pen, Jamaica: The Rare 1749 Inventory of Its Slaves, Stock and Household Goods', *Caribbean Quarterly* (2018), pp. 452–66,doi: 10.1080/00086495.2018.1531557

Finola O'Kane, 'What's in a name? The Connected Histories of Belfield, Co. Dublin and Belfield St Mary's, Jamaica' in Finola O'Kane and Ellen Rowley (eds.), *Making Belfield* (Dublin, 2020)

Finola O'Kane and Ciaran O'Neill (eds.), *Ireland, Slavery and the Caribbean; Interdisciplinary Perspectives 1620–1830* (Manchester, 2023)

Kate O'Malley, *Ireland, India and Empire: Indo-Irish Radical Connections, 1919–64* (Manchester, 2009)

Stephen O'Neill, *Staging Ireland: Representations in Shakespeare and Renaissance Drama* (Dublin, 2007)

William O'Reilly, 'Movements of People in the Atlantic World, 1450–1850' in Nicholas Canny and Philip Morgan (eds.), *The Oxford Handbook of the Atlantic World c.1450–c.1850* (Oxford, 2011)

William O'Reilly, 'Ireland in the Atlantic World: Migration and Cultural Transfer' in Jane Ohlmeyer (ed.), *The Cambridge History of Ireland*, vol. 2. *Early Modern Ireland, 1550–1730* (Cambridge, 2018)

David O'Shaughnessy, 'Introduction: "Tolerably Numerous": Recovering the London Irish of the Eighteenth Century', *Eighteenth-Century Life*, 39 (2015), pp. 1–13

Micheál Ó Siochrú, 'Catholic Confederates and the constitutional relationship between Ireland and England, 1641–1649' in Ciaran Brady and Jane Ohlmeyer (eds.), *British Interventions in Early Modern Ireland* (Cambridge, 2005)

Micheál Ó Siochrú, *God's Executioner: Oliver Cromwell and the Conquest of Ireland* (London, 2008)

Micheál Ó Siochrú, 'Extirpation and Annihilation in Cromwellian Ireland' in Ben Kiernan, *The Cambridge World History of Genocide*, vol. 2, *Genocide in the Indigenous, Early Modern, and Imperial Worlds, from c.1535 to World War One* (Cambridge, 2022)

Micheál Ó Siochrú and David Brown, 'The Down Survey and the Cromwellian Land Settlement' in Jane Ohlmeyer (ed.), *The Cambridge History of Ireland*, vol. 2. *Early Modern Ireland, 1550–1730* (Cambridge, 2018)

Jürgen Osterhammel, *Colonialism: A Theoretical Overview* (Munich, 1997)

Paddy O'Sullivan, 'The English East India Company at Dunaniel', *Bandon Historical Journal*, 4 (1988), pp. 3–14

Sarah E. Owens and Jane E. Mangan (eds.), *Women of the Iberian Atlantic* (Baton Rouge, Louisiana, 2012)

Patricia Palmer, *Language and Conquest in Early Modern Ireland: English Renaissance Literature and Elizabethan Imperial Expansion* (Cambridge, 2001)

Patricia Palmer, *The Severed Head and the Grafted Tongue: Literature, Translation and Violence in Early Modern Ireland* (Cambridge, 2014)

Jan Parmentier, 'The Irish Connection: The Irish Merchant Community in Ostend and Bruges during the late Seventeenth and Eighteenth Centuries', *Eighteenth-Century Ireland/Iris an dá chultúr*, 2005, 20 (2005), pp. 31–54

Michael Pawson and David Buisseret, *Port Royal, Jamaica* (Oxford, 1975)

Douglas M. Peers and Nandini Gooptu (eds.), *India and the British Empire* (Oxford, 2012)

Martine Pelletier, 'Telling Stories and Making Histories: Brian Friel and Field Day', *Irish University Review*, 24 (1994), pp. 186–97

Michael Perceval-Maxwell, *The Scottish Migration to Ulster in the Reign of James I* (London, 1973)

Michael Perceval-Maxwell, 'Ireland and the monarchy in the early Stuart multiple kingdom', *The Historical Journal*, 34 (1991), pp. 279–95

Elena Perekhvalskaya, 'Irish in the West Indies: Irish Influence on the Formation of English-based Creoles', *Studia Celto-Slavica*, 7 (2015)

Erin Peters, *Commemoration and Oblivion in Royalist Print Culture, 1658–1667* (London, 2017)

Erin Peters and Cynthia Richards (eds.), *Early Modern Trauma: Europe and the Atlantic World* (Lincoln, Nebraska, 2021)

Elodie Peyrol-Kleiber, *Les premiers Irlandais du Nouveau Monde: une migration atlantique (1618–1705)* (Rennes, 2016)

Elodie Peyrol-Kleiber, "Ffourty thousand to cut the Protestants throats": The Irish threat in the Chesapeake and the West Indies (1620–1700)' in Lauric Henneton and Louis Roper (eds.), *Fear and the Shaping of Early American Societies* (Leiden, 2016), pp. 160–81

Andrew Philips and J. C. Sharman, *Outsourcing Empire: How Company-States Made the Modern World* (Princeton, 2020)

Sheila Pim, 'The history of gardening in Ireland' in E. Charles Nelson and A. Brady (eds.), *Irish Gardening and Horticulture* (Dublin, 1979), pp. 45–69

Keith Pluymers, 'Taming the wilderness in sixteenth and seventeenth century Ireland and Virginia', *Environmental History* 16 (2011), pp. 610–32

Keith Pluymers, 'Cow Trials, Climate Causes of Violence', *Environmental History*, 25 (2020), pp. 287–309

Keith Pluymers, *No Wood, No Kingdom: Political Ecology in the English Atlantic* (Philadelphia, 2021)

Andrew Porter (ed.), *The Oxford History of the British Empire*, vol. 3. *The Nineteenth Century* (Oxford, 1999)

Simon J. Potter and Jonathan Saha, 'Global History, Imperial History and Connected Histories of Empire'. *Journal of Colonialism and Colonial History*, 16 (2015), retrieved 11 Jun. 2022 from doi:10.1353/cch.2015.0009

Orla Power, 'The "Quadripartite Concern" of St. Croix: An Irish Catholic Experiment in the Danish West Indies' in David T. Gleeson (ed.), *The Irish in the Atlantic World* (Columbia, South Carolina, 2010)

Orla Power, 'Friends, Foe, or Family? Catholic Creoles, French Huguenots, Scottish Dissenters: Aspects of the Irish Diaspora at St. Croix, Danish West Indies, 1760' in Niall Whelehan (ed.), *Transnational Perspectives on Modern Irish History* (New York, 2015)

Lydia M. Pulsipher and Conrad M. Goodwin, 'A sugar-boiling house at Galways: An Irish sugar plantation in Montserrat, West Indies', *Post-Medieval Archaeology*, 16 (1982), pp. 21–7

D. B. Quinn, 'Ireland and Sixteenth Century European Expansion' in T. D. Williams ed., *Historical Studies* (London, 1958)

D. B. Quinn, *Ireland and America: Their Early Associations, 1500–1640* (Liverpool, 1991)

Mark S. Quintanilla (ed.), *An Irishman's Life on the Caribbean Island of St Vincent, 1787–90: The Letter Book of Attorney General Michael Keane* (Dublin 2019)

Fernández Moya Rafael, 'The Irish Presence in the History and Place Names of Cuba', *Irish Migration Studies in Latin America*, 3 (2007), pp. 189–97 and pp. 272–7

Ronald Raminelli, 'The meaning of color and race in Portuguese America, 1640–1750' in *Oxford Research Encyclopaedia: Latin American History* (Oxford, 2020), pp. 1–21

Rory Rapple, 'Shakespeare, the Irish, and Military Culture' in Malcolm Smuts (ed.), *The Oxford Handbook of the Age of Shakespeare* (Oxford, 2016), pp. 103–20

Rory Rapple, '"Not Falstaff alone, but also Iago": Sir Ralph Lane's approach to officeholding in both Ireland and Virginia', *Journal of British Studies* (forthcoming, 2023)

Joan Redmond, 'Religion, civility and the "British" of Ireland in the 1641 Irish rebellion', *Irish Historical Studies* (2021), 45 (167), pp. 1–21

Cynthia Richard, 'Imperfect Enjoyments and Female Disappointments: Understanding Trauma in Aphra Behn's "The Disappointment" and *Oroonoko*' in Erin Peters and Cynthia Richards (eds.), *Early Modern Trauma: Europe and the Atlantic World* (Lincoln, Nebraska, 2021)

J. F. Richards, 'Fiscal states in Mughal and British India' in B. Yun-Casalilla and P. O'Brien (eds.), *The Rise of Fiscal States: A Global History, 1500–1914* (Cambridge, 2012)

Giorgio Riello, 'The Indian Apprenticeship: The trade of Indian textiles as the making of European cottons' in Giorgio Riello and Tirthankar Roy (eds.), *How India Clothed the World: The World of South Asian Textiles, 1500–1850* (Leiden, 2009)

Giorgio Riello, *Cotton: The Fabric that Made the Modern World* (Cambridge, 2013)

Nini Rodgers, 'Ireland and the Black Atlantic in the Eighteenth Century', *Irish Historical Studies*, 32 (2000), pp. 174–92

Nina Rodgers, 'The Irish and the Atlantic Slave Trade', *History Ireland* 15 (2007), pp. 17–23

Nini Rodgers, *Ireland, Slavery and Anti-Slavery, 1612–1685* (London, 2007)

Nini Rodgers, 'A Changing Presence: The Irish in the Caribbean in the seventeenth and eighteenth centuries' in Alison Donnell, Maria McGarrity, and Evelyn O'Callaghan (eds.), *Caribbean Irish Connections: Interdisciplinary Perspectives* (Kingston, Jamaica, 2015)

L. H. Roper, *Advancing Empire: English Interests and Overseas Expansion, 1613–1688* (Cambridge, 2017)

L. H. Roper, *The Torrid Zone: Caribbean Colonization and Cultural Interaction in the Long Seventeenth Century* (Columbia, South Carolina, 2018)

E. M. Rose, 'Viscounts in Virginia: A Proposal to Create American Noblemen (1619)', *Huntington Library Quarterly*, 83 (2020), pp. 184–95

Chaim M. Rosenberg, *Losing America, Conquering India: Lord Cornwallis and the Remaking of the British Empire* (Jefferson, North Carolina, 2017)

Richard J. Ross, 'Puritan Godly Discipline in Comparative Perspective: Legal Pluralism and the Sources of "Intensity"', *American Historical Review*, 113 (2008), pp. 975–1002

E. M. G. Routh, *Tangier: England's lost Atlantic outpost, 1661–1684* (1912)

Ulinka Rublack, *Dressing Up: Cultural Identity in Renaissance Europe* (Oxford, 2010)

Conrad Russell, *The Fall of the British Monarchies, 1637–1642* (Oxford, 1990)

Conrad Russell, *The Causes of the English Civil War* (Oxford 1990)

Colin Rynne and James Lyttleton (eds.), *Plantation Ireland: Settlement and Material Culture, c. 1550–c.1700* (Dublin, 2009)

Edward Said, *Orientalism* (London, 1978)

Edward Said, *Culture and Imperialism* (London, 1994)

Priya Satia, *Time's Monster: History, Conscience and Britain's Empire* (London, 2020)

H. M. Scott (ed.), *The European Nobilities in the Seventeenth and Eighteenth Centuries: Northern, Central and Eastern Europe*, 2 vols. (London, 1995)

William Robert Scott (ed.), *The Constitution and Finance of English, Scottish and Irish Joint-Stock Companies to 1720*, 3 vols. (Cambridge, 1910–12)

Patricia Seed, *Ceremonies of Possession in Europe's Conquest of the New World 1492–1640* (Cambridge, 1995)

Madeline Shanahan, *Manuscript Recipe Books as Archaeological Objects: Text and Food in the Early Modern World* (Lanham, Maryland, 2015)

Jenny Shaw, 'In the Name of the Mother: The Story of Susannah Mingo, a Woman of Color in the Early English Atlantic', *The William and Mary Quarterly*, 77 (2020), pp. 177–210

Jenny Shaw, *Everyday Life in the Early English Caribbean: Irish, Africans, and the Construction of Difference* (London, 2013)

Esther K. Sheldon, *Thomas Sheridan of Smock Alley* (Princeton, 1967)

Christopher Shepard, 'Cramming, instrumentality and the education of Irish imperial elites' in David Dickson, Justyna Pyz, and Christopher Shepard (eds.), *Irish Classrooms and British Empire: Imperial Contexts in the Origins of Modern Education* (Dublin, 2012)

Jill Sheppard, *The 'Redlegs' of Barbados, their Origins and History* (Millwood, New York, 1977)

Richard B. Sheridan, *Sugar and Slavery: An Economic History of the British West Indies, 1623–1775* (Kingston, 1974)

J. J. Silke, 'Primate Lombard and James I', *Irish Theological Quarterly*, 22 (1955)

J. J. Silke, 'Irish Scholarship and the Renaissance, 1580–1673', *Studies in the Renaissance*, 20 (1973), pp. 169–206

Michael Silvestri, *Ireland and India: Nationalism, Empire and Memory* (London, 2009)

Michael Silvestri, ' "The Sinn Fein of India": Irish Nationalism and the Policing of Revolutionary Terrorism in Bengal', *Journal of British Studies*, 39 (2000), pp. 478–85

Michael Silvestri, ' "An Irishman Is Specially Suited to Be a Policeman": Sir Charles Tegart & Revolutionary Terrorism in Bengal', *History Ireland*, 8 (2000), pp. 40–4

J. G. Simms, *The Williamite Confiscation in Ireland, 1690–1703* (London, 1956)

William Smyth, *Map-Making, Landscapes and Memory: A Geography of Colonial and Early Modern Ireland c.1530–1750* (Cork, 2006)

William Smyth, 'The Western Isle of Ireland and the eastern seaboard of America—England's first frontiers', *Irish Geography*, 11 (1978), pp. 1–23

Susan Migden Socolow, *The Women of Colonial Latin America* (2nd edition, Cambridge, 2015)

Kate Spanos, 'Locating Montserrat between the black and green', *Irish Migration Studies in Latin America*, 9 (2019), pp. 1–15

Scott Spurlock, 'Catholics in a Puritan Atlantic: The Liminality of Empire's Edge' in C. Gribben and S. Spurlock (eds.), *Puritans and Catholics in the Trans-Atlantic World 1600–1800* (Philadelphia, 2009)

Robert Louis Stein, *The French Sugar Business in the Eighteenth Century* (Baton Rouge, 1988)

T. Stein, 'Tangier in the Restoration Empire', *Historical Journal*, 54 (2011), pp. 985–1011

Philip J. Stern, 'British Asia and British Atlantic: Comparisons and Connections', *The William and Mary Quarterly*, 63 (2006), pp. 693–712

Philip J. Stern, ' "A Politie of Civill & Military Power": Political Thought and the Late Seventeenth-Century Foundations of the East India Company-State', *Journal of British Studies*, 47 (2008), pp. 253–83

Philip J. Stern, 'From the Fringes of History: Tracing the Roots of the English East India Company-State', in Sameetah Agha and Elizabeth Kolsky (eds.), *Fringes of Empire: People, Places, and Spaces in Colonial India* (New Delhi, 2009)

Philip J. Stern, *The Company-State: Corporate Sovereignty and the Early Modern Foundations of the British Empire in India* (Oxford, 2011)

Philip J. Stern, 'Corporate virtue: The languages of empire in early modern British Asia', *Renaissance Studies*, 26 (2012), pp. 510–30

Philip J. Stern, 'Company, state, and empire: governance and regulatory frameworks in Asia' in H. V. Bowen, Elizabeth Mancke, and John G. Reid (eds.), *Britain's Oceanic Empire: Atlantic and Indian Ocean Worlds, c.1550–1850* (Cambridge, 2012)

Jon Stobart, *Sugar and Spice: Grocers and Groceries in Provincial England, 1650–1830* (Oxford, 2013)

La Tourette Stockwell, *Dublin Theatre and Theatre Customs (1637–1820)* (Kingsport, Tennessee, 1937)

E. Stokes, *English Utilitarians and India* (Oxford, 1959)

Ann Laura Stoler, 'Colonial Archives and the Arts of Governance', *Archival Science*, 2 (2002), pp. 87–109

Ann Laura Stoler, 'Haunted by Empire: Domains of the Intimate and the Practices of Comparison' in Ann L. Stoler (ed.), *Haunted by Empire* (Durham, NC, 2006)

Ann Laura Stoler, *Along the Archival Grain: Epistemic Anxieties and Colonial Common Sense* (Princeton, 2008)

Ann Laura Stoler, *Imperial Debris: On Ruins and Ruination* (Durham, NC, 2013)

Ann Laura Stoler, *Duress: Imperial Durabilities in Our Times* (Durham, NC, 2016)

Sanjay Subrahmanyam, 'Connected Histories: Notes towards a Reconfiguration of Early Modern Eurasia', *Modern Asian Studies*, 31 *Special Issue: The Eurasian Context of the Early Modern History of Mainland South East Asia, 1400–1800* (1997), pp. 735–62

Sanjay Subrahmanyam, 'A Tale of Three Empires: Mughals, Ottomans, and Habsburgs in a Comparative Context', *Common Knowledge*, 12 (2006), pp. 66–92

David Sweetman, *The Medieval Castles in Ireland* (Cork, 1999)

Jane Stevenson and Peter Davidson (eds.), *Early Modern Women Poets: An Anthology* (Oxford, 2001)

Clodagh Tait, 'Writing the social and cultural history of Ireland, 1550–1660: wills as example and inspiration' in Sarah Covington, Vincent P. Carey, and Valerie McGowan-Doyle (eds.), *Early Modern Ireland: New Sources, Methods and Perspectives* (Abingdon, 2019), chapter 2

Clodagh Tait, 'From beer and shoes to sugar and slaves: Five Baptist Loobys in Cork and Antigua' in Terence Dooley, Mary Ann Lyons, and Salvador Ryan (eds.), *The Historian as Detective: Uncovering Irish Pasts. Essays in Honour of Raymond Gillespie* (Dublin, 2021), pp. 131–4

Clodagh Tait, 'Progress, challenges and opportunities in early modern gender history, c.1550–1720', *Irish Historical Studies*, 46 (2022), pp. 244–69

Shasi Tharoor, *Inglorious Empire: What the British Did to India* (London, 2016)

Keith Thomas, *In Pursuit of Civility: Manners and Civilization in Early Modern England* (New Haven, 2020)

Martin Thomas and Andrew S. Thompson (eds.), *The Oxford Handbook of The Ends of Empire* (Oxford, 2018)

Coll Thrush, *Indigenous London: Native Travelers at the Heart of Empire* (New Haven and London, 2016)

Christopher Tomlins, 'Legal Cartography of Colonization, the Legal Polyphony of Settlement: English Intrusions on the American Mainland in the Seventeenth Century', The Symposium: Colonialism, Culture, and the Law, 26 *Law & Soc. Inquiry* 315 (2001), pp. 315–65

Igor Pérez Tostado and Enrique García Hernán (eds.), *Irlanda y el Atlántico Ibérico. Movilidad, participación e intercambio cultural (1580–1823)/Ireland and the Iberian Atlantic: Mobility, Involvement and Cross-Cultural Exchange (1580–1823)* (Valencia, 2010)

Victor Treadwell, *Buckingham and Ireland, 1616–1628: A Study in Anglo-Irish Politics* (Dublin, 1998)

Thomas M. Truxes, *Irish-American Trade, 1660–1783* (Cambridge, 1988)

Thomas M. Truxes, 'London's Irish Merchant Community and North Atlantic Commerce in the Mid-Eighteenth Century' in David Dickson, Jan Parmentier, and Jane Ohlmeyer (eds.), *Irish and Scottish Mercantile Networks in Europe and Overseas in the Seventeenth and Eighteenth Centuries* (Ghent, 2007)

Sonia Tycko, 'The Legality of Prisoner of War Labour in England, 1648–1655', *Past and Present*, 246 (2020), pp. 35–68

Sonia Tycko, 'Bound and Filed: A Seventeenth-Century Service Indenture from a Scattered Archive', *Early American Studies: An Interdisciplinary Journal*, 19 (2021), pp. 166–90

Brian Walker, '1641, 1689, 1690 and All That: The Unionist Sense of History', *Irish Review*, 12 (1992), pp. 56–64

Peter Walmsley, 'Hans Sloane and the Melancholy Slave' in Erin Peters and Cynthia Richards (eds.), *Early Modern Trauma: Europe and the Atlantic World* (Lincoln, Nebraska, 2021)

Paul Walsh, *Will and Family of H. O'Neill, Earl of Tyrone* (Dublin, 1930)

James Walvin, *Fruits of Empire: Exotic Produce and British Taste, 1660–1800* (London, 1997)

D. Washbrook, 'Progress and Problems: South Asian Economic and Social story, c.1720–1860', *Modern Asian Studies*, 22 (1988), pp. 57–96

I. Bruce Watson, 'Fortifications and the "idea" of force in early English India Company relations with India' in Patrick Tuck (ed.), *The East India Company: 1600–1858. Vol. IV. Trade Finance and Power* (London, 1998)

Lorna Weatherall, *Consumer Behaviour and Material Culture in Britain 1660–1760* (London, 1996)

Niall Whelehan, 'Playing with Scales: Transnational History and Modern Ireland' in Niall Whelehan (ed.), *Transnational Perspectives on Modern Irish History* (New York, 2015)

Ian Whyte, *Migration and Society in Britain 1550–1830* (NY, 2000)

Jon E. Wilson, 'Early Colonial India beyond Empire', *The Historical Journal*, 50 (2007), pp. 951–70

Kathleen Wilson (ed.), *A New Imperial History: Culture, Identity and Modernity in Britain and the Empire 1660–1840* (Cambridge, 2004)

Kathleen Wilson, 'Rethinking the Colonial State: Family, Gender, and Governmentality in Eighteenth-Century British Frontiers', *American Historical Review*, 116 (2011), pp. 1295–322

Jenny Wormald for Scotland, 'The Creation of Britain: Multiple Kingdoms or Core and Colonies?', *Transactions of the Royal Historical Society*, sixth series, 2 (1992), pp. 175–94

Bartolomé Yun-Casalilla, *Iberian World Empires and the Globalization of Europe 1415–1668* (London, 2019)

Bartolomé Yun-Casalilla, Ilaria Berti, and Omar Svriz-Wucherer (eds.), *American Globalization, 1492–1850: Trans-Cultural Consumption in Spanish Latin America* (Abingdon, 2022)

UNPUBLISHED THESES

Lance A. Betros, 'A Glimpse of Empire: New York Governor Thomas Dongan and the Evolution of English Imperial Policy, 1683–1688' (Unpublished PhD thesis, Chapel Hill, 1988)

Alix Chartrand, 'The evolution of British Imperial perceptions in Ireland and India c.1650–1800' (Unpublished PhD thesis, Cambridge University, 2018)

Heidi J. Coburn, 'The built environment and material culture of Ireland in the 1641 Depositions, 1600–1653' (Unpublished PhD thesis, Cambridge, 2017)

John Cunningham, 'Transplantation to Connacht, 1641–1680: Theory and Practice' (Unpublished PhD thesis, NUI, Galway, 2009)

Leslie Herman, 'Building Narratives: Ireland and the "Colonial Period" in American Architectural History' (Unpublished PhD thesis, Columbia University, 2019)

Marie Sophie Hingst, 'One phenomenon, three perspectives: English colonial strategies in Ireland revisited, 1603–1680' (Unpublished PhD thesis, Trinity College Dublin, 2017)

Shona Helen Johnston, 'Papists in a Protestant World: The Catholic Anglo-Atlantic in the Seventeenth-Century' (Unpublished PhD thesis, Georgetown University, 2011)

Karst de Jong, 'The Irish in Jamaica during the long eighteenth century (1698–1836)' (Unpublished PhD thesis, Queens University Belfast, 2017)

Charlene McCoy, 'War and Revolution: County Fermanagh and its borders, c.1640–c.1666' (Unpublished PhD thesis, Trinity College Dublin, 2007)

Bethany Marsh, '"Distressed Protestants or Irish vagrants?" Charity and the organisation of relief to "Irish" refugees in England, 1641–1651' (Unpublished PhD thesis, Nottingham, 2019)

Hazel Maynard, 'Irish membership of the English inns of court, 1660–1699: lawyers, litigation and the legal profession' (Unpublished PhD thesis, University College Dublin, 2006)

Timothy Earl Miller, 'Gold for Secrets: The Hartlib Circle and The Early English Empire, 1630–1660' (Unpublished DPhil thesis, Oxford, 2020)

Alice O'Driscoll, 'Women, gender, and siege during the Wars of the Three Kingdoms, 1639–52' (Unpublished PhD thesis, Cambridge, 2021)

Luke Joseph Pecoraro, '"Mr. Gookin Out of Ireland, Wholly Upon his Owne Adventure": An Archaeological Study of Intercolonial and Transatlantic Connections in the Seventeenth Century' (Unpublished PhD thesis, Boston University, 2015)

Edward Owen Teggin, 'The East India Company Career of Sir Robert Cowan in Bombay and the Western Indian Ocean, c. 1719–35' (Unpublished PhD thesis, Trinity College Dublin, 2020)

Saumya Varghese, 'Urbanization and trade in Goa (1510–1660)' (Unpublished PhD thesis, Jawaharlal Nehru University, 2010)

Samantha Watson, 'To plant and improve: Justifying the consolidation of Tudor and Stuart imperial rule in Ireland, 1509 to 1625' (Unpublished PhD thesis, University of New South Wales, 2014)

Index

Note: Tables and figures are indicated by an italic "*t*", "*f*", and notes are indicated by "n." following the page number.

For the benefit of digital users, indexed terms that span two pages (e.g., 52–53) may, on occasion, appear on only one of those pages.